016.92   314811
Sab   Sable, Martin Howard
            A bio-bibliography of
         the Kennedy family

A Bio-Bibliography

of

The Kennedy Family

by

Martin H. Sable
*Associate Professor,
University of Wisconsin—Milwaukee*

The Scarecrow Press, Inc.

Metuchen, N.J.   1969

Copyright 1969, by Martin H. Sable

SBN 8108-0247-3

To The Memory of

MAURICE LEO CARROLL

1903-1957

Gentleman   Scholar   Friend

Table of Contents

	Page
Introduction	xi
Joseph P. Kennedy	
Biography...	15
Books by...	17
Articles by...	18
Books about...	19
Manuscript materials	19
Articles about...	20
Rose Elizabeth (Fitzgerald) Kennedy	
Biography...	24
Articles about...	26
The Joseph P. Kennedy Family	
Books about...	26
Articles about...	27
Joseph P. Kennedy, Jr.	
Biography...	30
Books about...	33
Memorials	33
Articles about...	33
Photographs	34
John Fitzgerald Kennedy	
Biography...	35
Books by...	42
Articles by...	51
Reviews of books by...	52
Presidential Campaign, 1960	
Books	57
Articles	58

John Fitzgerald Kennedy (Continued)

Religion	
Books	63
Articles	64
The Inauguration	
Books	68
Articles	69
Addresses and Official Messages	
Books...	70
Articles...	82
Public Papers	
Books	89
Domestic Affairs	
Books	90
Articles	94
International Affairs	
Books	118
Articles	129
The Death of President Kennedy	
Books	155
Articles	159
The Oswald Affair	
Books	176
Articles	177
Warren Report	
Books	179
Articles	181
Eulogies	
Books	184
Articles	186
Memorials	
Books	201
Articles	203
Memorabilia	
Books	206
Articles	207
Poetry in honor of President Kennedy	
Books	207
Articles	209
Fiction	210
Bibliography	
Books	210
Articles	210
Manuscript Materials	211
Biographies of President Kennedy	
Youth	
Books	214

Articles	214
Service in World War II	
Books	214
Articles	215
Adult Life & Career	
Books	215
Humor	
Books	218
Articles	218
Intellectual Life	
Books	219
Articles	220
Children's Books, about President Kennedy	221
Portraits, Photographs and Caricatures	
Books	223
Articles	225
Music	
Articles	225
Scores & Songs	226
Recordings	226
Documentary Phonograph Records	226
Motion Pictures and Filmstrips	228

Jacqueline Lee (Bouvier) Kennedy

Biography	231
Articles by...	233
Books about...	233
Articles about...	235
Photographs and Portraits	241
Motion Pictures	241

The Children of John F. Kennedy

Books	242
Articles	242

The John F. Kennedy Family

Books	244
Articles	244

Rose Marie Kennedy

Biography	246

Kathleen (Kennedy) Cavendish

Biography	247

Eunice (Kennedy) Shriver

Biography	249
Articles by...	251
Articles about...	251

Robert Sargent Shriver
    Biography   252
    Books by...   253
    Articles by...   254
    Books about...   256
    Articles about...   257

Patricia (Kennedy) Lawford
    Biography   259
    Articles about...   260

Robert Francis Kennedy
    Biography   261
    Books by...   265
    Reviews of books by...   266
    Speeches and Statements by...   267
    Articles by...   268
    Books about   274
    Articles about...   275
    Assassination of Robert F. Kennedy
        Books   287
        Articles   288
    Eulogies
        Articles   290
        Motion Pictures   290
        Memorials   290
    Photographs
        Books   291
        Motion Pictures   291

Ethel (Skakel) Kennedy
    Biography   292
    Articles about...   294

The Robert F. Kennedy Family
    Articles about...   294
    Photographs   295

Jean (Kennedy) Smith
    Biography   296

Stephen Edward Smith
    Biography   298
    Articles about...   300

Edward Moore Kennedy
    Biography   301

Books and Speeches by...	303
Articles by...	304
Addresses by...	304
Books about...	304
Articles about...	305
Photographs	308

Joan (Bennett) Kennedy
Biography	309
Articles about...	309

Edward M. Kennedy Family
Articles about	310
Photographs	310

Introduction

This Bio-Bibliography of the Kennedy Family contains brief biographies of the family of Joseph P. Kennedy and of the following Kennedy in-laws: Joan Bennett (Mrs. Edward M.) Kennedy; Jacqueline Bouvier (Mrs. John F.) Kennedy; Ethel Skakel (Mrs. Robert F.) Kennedy; Robert Sargent Shriver; and Stephen E. Smith.

The bibliographies given for the family members include writings in 37 languages, of which most are in English. In alphabetical order, the remaining 36 languages are as follows: Afrikaans, Arabic, Bengali, Burmese, Chinese, Czech, Danish, Dutch, French, German, Greek, Gujarati, Hebrew, Hindi, Hungarian, Icelandic, Indonesian, Italian, Japanese, Korean, Latvian, Malayalam, Marathi, Norwegian, Persian, Polish, Portuguese, Rumanian, Russian, Serbo-Croat, Spanish, Swedish, Tamil, Telugu, Turkish, and Vietnamese.

Almost all of the foreign-language entries refer to President John F. Kennedy; those that do not, deal with his brothers, the late Senator Robert F. Kennedy, and Senator Edward M. Kennedy.

Books by each biographee are listed first, followed by periodical articles written by him. These, in turn, are followed by books and periodical articles written about him. The amount of material, in some cases, requires further subdivision, so the subdivision of materials is given in detail in the Table of Contents. The term book is here used to include pamphlets, and government documents; and in order to aid in identification, the place of publication is given for foreign journals. Each bibliography entry is numbered; these run consecutively beginning with the eldest family member (Joseph P. Kennedy) to the youngest (Mrs. Joan Bennett Kennedy, wife of Senator Edward M. Kennedy).

Within each bibliographic division for each family member, items are arranged chronologically, from the oldest to the most recent, thereby offering a perspective in time.

Sections for the Kennedy in-laws directly follow those of their respective spouses; thus, for example, the section for Robert Sargent Shriver follows that of Eunice (Kennedy) Shriver. In the bibliographic section for each individual represented, books and articles by and about the respective family member are marked accordingly, as are specific topics, such as addresses, photographs, etc.

This reference source comprises practically all physical forms of material which convey information; books, pamphlets, government documents, conference proceedings, periodical articles, poetry, theses, photographs, motion pictures (including those produced for television), television scripts, film strips, music scores and songs, as well as both documentary and music phonograph records. To the extent that it lists other bibliographies, this work serves as a bibliography of bibliographies. To the extent that it includes biographical data on the Kennedy family members and in-laws, it serves as a biographical dictionary. The fact that it contains (in the sections allocated to President and Mrs. John F. Kennedy) poetry, speeches, fiction and humor, makes this work a literary source-book.

This book is intended for all who are interested in the personal and professional life of President John F. Kennedy. Students of American government and scholars in the field of international affairs at all levels, should be able to utilize this reference source, since it contains both advanced and popular materials, and students in junior and senior high school as well as college and graduate students will find materials useful to their research. Materials on the administration of President Kennedy have been divided according to their international and domestic political implications, and special topics, such as the President's intellectual life, his humor, poetry written about him, eulogies, memorabilia, etc., are included. Students and researchers should be aware that the John F. Kennedy Library at Harvard University houses personal effects, correspondence, and presidential papers, among other research materials. For specific information on holdings, those interested may write to John F. Kennedy Library, as well as to John F. Kennedy School of Government, Harvard University, Cambridge, Massachusetts 02138.

Those interested in the careers of Senators Robert F. Kennedy and Edward M. Kennedy will, likewise, be able to locate their books, pamphlets, government documents and periodical articles as well as the publications about them.

Of special historical interest are the items pertaining to the government service of the head of the family, Joseph P. Kennedy. Robert Sargent Shriver, first administrator of the Peace Corps and of the Office of Economic Opportunity, husband of Eunice (Kennedy) Shriver, is well represented by his own writings as well as books and articles about him.

The Kennedy family, in addition to its contributions in the field of American politics, has contributed to the economic life and intellectual history of the United States. The devotion of the family members to each other and to moral and religious principles, stands as a model for all American families.

In an age of general neglect of duty and responsibility, the members of the Kennedy family have presented to their fellow citizens a shining example of devotion to the welfare of their fellow citizens. History will record that one of their greatest achievements and contributions to their fellow citizens, especially significant in this day of irresponsibility and general irreverance to tried and true values of an earlier era, lies in the examples offered to us all, of constant striving to "fight for the right" in accordance with conscience. The traditional Kennedy interest in health, welfare, education and culture generally, have all made a deep impact on the thought of the American people. Such an influence is bound to be reflected in the nation's future social and cultural progress.

In paying homage to President Kennedy and his family through the medium of this book, I am also discharging an obligation to my old friend, Professor Maurice Leo Carroll, who was a Bostonian (as is this author), who passed away in 1957 at the age of 54. Those who were privileged to be acquainted with Leo Carroll were impressed by that rare combination of innate kindness and sophistication in the guise of a regular fellow. In recognition of his sage advice, kindnesses, and the pleasure of his company, I respectfully dedicate this book to the blessed memory of Maurice Leo Carroll.

There remain two gracious ladies to be thanked: my wife, Minna, who aided me in proofreading, but more importantly, understood the need for my prolonged absences from my family during the years I compiled the present work. Second, my mother, Mrs. Ida Sable of Chestnut Hill, Massachusetts, who is a long-time admirer of the qualities possessed by the Kennedy brothers, and the cohesiveness of the Kennedy family. It is my mother, therefore, quite possibly, who is indirectly responsible for the existence of this work.

Martin H. Sable

Joseph P. Kennedy

Joseph P. Kennedy was born on September 6, 1888, in Boston, Massachusetts, the son of Patrick J. and Mary (Hickey) Kennedy. Patrick J. Kennedy was a businessman with interests in city politics, and he eventually served in the Massachusetts Legislature. He also was an official of the City of Boston.

After attending Boston Latin School, Joseph Kennedy became a student at Harvard University, where he majored in economics, excelled in sports, and became a member of the Hasty Pudding Club and the Institute of 1770. While in preparatory school and college, he displayed his business acumen, earning considerable amounts of money through various of his own enterprises.

After graduating with an A.B. degree in 1912, Joseph Kennedy became a Massachusetts State bank examiner. He purchased a controlling interest in the Columbia Trust Company of Boston, and at the age of 25 became the youngest president of an American bank.

In 1914, at the age of 26, Joseph P. Kennedy married Rose Fitzgerald, a graduate of Manhattanville College of the Sacred Heart and an accomplished pianist and linguist. Rose Fitzgerald was the daughter of the popular mayor of Boston, John F. ("Honey") Fitzgerald.

From 1917 to 1919 Joseph Kennedy was Assistant General Manager of the Fore River Plant of the Bethlehem Steel Corporation, in Quincy, Massachusetts. Between 1919 and 1924 he was Manager of the investment banking firm of Hayden, Stone and Company, in Boston. It was during this period that he gained his knowledge of the stock market and made acquaintances in the financial world.

One of Mr. Kennedy's early investments was a group of motion picture theaters in the New England states, which he sold in 1926 in order to enter motion picture production. From 1926-1929 he served as President and Chairman of the Board of the Keith-Albee-Orpheum Theatres Corporation; then he relinquished this position to become Board Chairman of Pathé Exchange, Inc. In 1933 Joseph Kennedy, who had sold all of his stocks just prior to the 1929 stock-market crash, continued to build his fortune in finance.

During the 1930's the Kennedys maintained homes in Boston, Bronxville, New York, and Palm Beach, Florida.

Joseph P. Kennedy supported the candidacy of Franklin D. Roosevelt in the 1932 presidential campaign, and it is generally believed that he was the prime mover in obtaining the support of William Randolph Hearst for Roosevelt. In 1934 President Roosevelt appointed Mr. Kennedy to be first head of the newly-established Securities and Exchange Commission, a post in which he served well for over one year.

During the 1936 presidential campaign, Joseph P. Kennedy again backed President Roosevelt, writing a book entitled **I'm for Roosevelt.**

In 1937 Mr. Kennedy was appointed Chairman of the U.S. Maritime Commission, a new government agency established to assist in the building of a merchant marine. In only a little more than two months, Joseph P. Kennedy had realized plans for government subsidies to ocean carriers, among other achievements, thereby giving the U.S. Maritime Commission an auspicious beginning. In the same year President Roosevelt appointed him American Ambassador to the Court of St. James, and Mr. Kennedy served in this capacity from 1937 until November of 1940. A popular figure in London, he brought U.S.-British relations to a very high level of understanding and cordiality.

During the early 1940's Mr. Kennedy was appointed Chairman of the Special Massachusetts Commission to set up a Massachusetts Department of Commerce.

He founded the Joseph P. Kennedy, Jr. Foundation in 1945, in memory of his son who was lost while serving as a Navy pilot during World War II. The Foundation engages in medical research in the field of retardation, and currently maintains headquarters in Washington, D.C., where Mr. Kennedy's daughter, Eunice Kennedy Shriver, has administered its operations.

In 1947, and again in 1953, Joseph P. Kennedy was appointed a member of the U.S. Senate Committee on the Reorganization of the Executive Branch of the federal government.

Mr. Kennedy is a Grand Knight of the Order of Pius IX, and a Knight of the Equestrian Order of the Holy Sepulchre. He was awarded the Grand Cross of Leopold II of Belgium and received honorary doctorates from Notre Dame and Oglethorpe Universities, Colby College, the University of Dublin, and the British Universities of Manchester, Edinburgh, Bristol, Cambridge and Liverpool.

A well-known speaker and author of many articles on finance and international affairs, Joseph P. Kennedy's first published work was entitled The Story of the Films (Chicago, 1927, 377 pages). In 1950 he collaborated with James M. Landis on a book entitled The Surrender of King Leopold.

Books by Joseph P. Kennedy

1927

Kennedy, Joseph P., ed.
  The story of the films, as told by leaders of the industry to the students of the Graduate School of Business Administration, George F. Baker Foundation, Harvard University. Chicago, A.W. Shaw Co., 1927, 377p. 1

1934

Kennedy, Joseph P.
  Address of Hon. Joseph P. Kennedy, chairman of Securities and Exchange Commission, at National Press Club, July 25, 1934. Washington, G.P.O., 1934, 5p. 2

Kennedy, Joseph P.
  Address of Hon. Joseph P. Kennedy, chairman of Securities and Exchange Commission, at meeting of the Boston Chamber of Commerce, November 15, 1934. Washington, G.P.O., 1934, 10p. 3

1935

Kennedy, Joseph P.
  Address of Hon. Joseph P. Kennedy, chairman of Securities and Exchange Commission, at Union League Club of Chicago, Ill., February 8, 1935. Washington, G.P.O., 1935, 10p. 4

Kennedy, Joseph P.
  Address of Hon. Joseph P. Kennedy, chairman of Securities and Exchange Commission, before American Arbitration Association, New York City, March 19, 1935. Washington, G.P.O., 1935, 11p. 5

1936

Kennedy, Joseph P.
  I'm for Roosevelt. New York, Reynal & Hitchcock, 1936, 149p. 6
Reviewed in:
America 55, September 12, 1936, p. 549.

1950

Kennedy, Joseph P.
  The surrender of King Leopold, with an appendix containing the Keyes-Gort correspondence. By Joseph P. Kennedy & James M. Landis. New York, 1950, 61p.   7

Articles by Joseph P. Kennedy

1934

Kennedy, Joseph P.
  "The Regulation of Security Exchanges." Vital speeches 1, December 17, 1934, p. 187-191.   8

1936

Kennedy, Joseph P.
  "I'm for Roosevelt (Book Review)." America 55, September 12, 1936, p. 549.   9

Kennedy, Joseph P.
  "Why I'm for Roosevelt." Review of reviews 94, September 1936, p. 24-28.   10

1937

Kennedy, Joseph P.
  "Big Business, what now?" Saturday evening post 209, January 16, 1937, p. 10-11.   11

Kennedy, Joseph P.
  "New Blood in American Shipping." Vital speeches 3, June 15, 1937, p. 532-535.   12

1938

Kennedy, Joseph P.
  "Shipping; Strikes; Prices." Commonweal 27, March 4, 1938, p. 521.   13

Kennedy, Joseph P.
  "Would we Fight in Europe?" Vital speeches 4, April 1, 1938, p. 354-356.   14

Kennedy, Joseph P.
  "Kennedy's Speech: U.S. Denies Implication of a Retreat on Dictators." Newsweek 12, October 31, 1938, p. 10-11.   15

1939

Kennedy, Joseph P.
  "Ambassador to England" (abridged). Catholic digest 4, November 1939, p. 76-79.   16

1941

Kennedy, Joseph P.
  "My Views on our Foreign Policy." Vital speeches 7, February 1, 1941, p. 227-231.   17

1945

Kennedy, Joseph P.
  "The Dignity of American Citizenship." Vital speeches 12, November 15, 1945, p. 88-90.   18

1946

Kennedy, Joseph P.
  "The United States and the World." Life 20, March 18, 1946, p. 106-110.   19

1947

Kennedy, Joseph P.
  "Noonday Sun; on Future Economic-Foreign Policy of the U.S." Commonweal 45, March 28, 1947, p. 580-581.   20

1951

Kennedy, Joseph P.
"The Present Policy is Politically and Morally Bankrupt: Address, December 12, 1950."
<u>Vital speeches</u> 17, January 1, 1951, p. 170-173. 21

Books about Joseph P. Kennedy

1953

Kaufmann, W.W.
<u>Two American ambassadors</u> (In Craig, Gordon A., & Felix Gilbert, eds. <u>Diplomats, 1919-1939</u>. Princeton, Princeton University Press, 1953, p. 649-681). 22

1964

Whalen, Richard J.
<u>The founding father; the story of Joseph P. Kennedy</u>. New York, New American Library, 1964, 541p. 23

1965

Duncliffe, William J.
<u>The life and times of Joseph P. Kennedy</u>. New York, Macfadden-Bartell, 1965, 158p. 24

Manuscript Materials Concerning Joseph P. Kennedy

1957

Loening, Grover Cleveland, 1888- (MS 62-2702)
<u>Papers, 1900-42</u>. 22ft. (ca. 16,500 items)
In Library of Congress, Manuscript Division.
Businessman, aircraft engineer, and author. Correspondence, literary mss. (major works, articles, and speeches), clippings (some mounted in scrapbooks), photos, drawings, blueprints, and other printed matter, relating to aeronautical development, Richard E. Byrd's first Antarctic expedition, the Wright Co., and Loening's own aircraft company. Correspondents include...<u>Joseph P. Kennedy</u>...
Register published in 1959 by the Library of Congress. Also described in the Library's <u>Quarterly journal of current acquisitions</u>, v. 14, #3 (May 1957) p.123. Information on literary rights available in the Library.
Gift of Mr. Loening, 1956 & 1958. 25

1958

Land, Emory Scott, 1879- (MS 64-1573)
<u>Papers 1901-55</u>. 10 ft. (5,750 items)
In Library of Congress, Manuscript Division.
Naval officer and shipping administrator. Correspondence, diary notes, speeches, copies of orders, photos (many inscribed) scrapbooks, clippings, and other papers chiefly relating to Land's 48 years of Government service, particularly as chief of the U.S. Navy Bureau of Construction and Repair (1932-37), chairman of the U.S. Maritime Commission (1938-46), and chief administrator of the U.S. War Shipping Administration (1942-46). In-

cludes material relating to ship-building (1932-46), the need of ships during World War II, labor unions, use of the U.S. Army to control labor disorders, the strikes of 1941-42, Land's position as vice president and treasurer of the Daniel Guggenheim Fund for the Promotion of Aeronautics, Inc., his role as advisor for Charles A. Lindbergh (his cousin), on his tours (1927-28), and Land's testimony in the Lindbergh kidnapping case (1938). Correspondents include Joseph P. Kennedy...

Register published in 1958 by the Library.

Gift of Vice Admiral Land, 1956-58. 26

1961
Palmer, Paul, 1900-
(MS 62-3286)
Correspondence, 1929-60 (ca. 500 items)

In Yale University Library.

Journalist and editor. Palmer's professional correspondence with such prominent figures as...Joseph P. Kennedy ...Material is related to the library's Walter Lippman and Charles A. Lindbergh collections.

Catalogued individually in the library.

Information on literary rights available in the library.

Gift of Mr. Palmer, 1961. 27

Pollock, James Kerr, 1898-
(MS 65-487)
Papers, 1947-49. 8 ft.
In University of Michigan, Michigan Historical Collections.

Professor of political science at the University of Michigan. Correspondence and other papers dealing with Pollock's service with the Hoover Commission on reorganization of government. Correspondents include... Joseph P. Kennedy...

Gift of Mr. Pollock, 1961.
28

Articles about
Joseph P. Kennedy

1928
Kennedy, John B.
"Joe Kennedy has Never Liked any job he's Tackled: Interview." American magazine 105, May 1928, p. 32-33. 29

1934
"Appointment to Chairmanship of Stock Exchange Commission." New republic 79, July 11, 1934, p. 220-221. 30

"Wall Street's cop." Business week, July 14, 1934, p. 20. 31

"Stock Exchange Market Czar." Newsweek 4, August 4, 1934, p. 27-28. 32

1935
"Reform and Realism." Time 26, July 22, 1935, p. 41-43. 33

Flynn, John T.
"Other People's Money: Hail and Farewell to Mr.

Kennedy." New republic 84, October 9, 1935, p. 244. 34

1936
"Joseph P. Kennedy (Photograph)." Time 27, April 20, 1936, p. 73. 35

"Profitless Paramount." Time 28, July 27, 1936, p. 51-52. 36

1937
"Kennedy in." Time 29, March 22, 1937, p. 63-64. 37

"Kennedy Knocks his job: new Chairman of Maritime Commission Handicapped by Faulty 1936 law." Business week, April 10, 1937, p. 48. 38

"Mr. Fixit." Time 30, July 12, 1937, p. 16-17. 39

Mitchell, Jonathan
  "Sailor, Beware." New republic 92, August 11, 1937, p. 7-9. 40

"Mr. Kennedy, the Chairman." Fortune 16, September 1937, p. 56-59. 41

"Maritime Unions: a Caldron of Labor for Commissioner Kennedy to Stir." Fortune 16, September 1937, p. 123-128. 42

1938
"Kennedy vs. the CIO." The nation 146, February 26, 1938, p. 234. 43

"Kennedy Candor." Time 31, February 28, 1938, p. 17. 44

"Bitter bon Voyage from the National Maritime Union to Kennedy." Time 31, March 7, 1938, p. 13. 45

"Kennedy on Antagonisms." Time 32, October 31, 1938, p. 17. 46

"Kennedy and the Jews." The nation 147, November 26, 1938, p. 555. 47

1939
"London Legman." Time 34, September 18, 1939, p. 13-14. 48

1940
"Joseph P. Kennedy (Biography)." Current biography 1940, p. 450-453. 49

"Goodbye, Joe: Ambassador Kennedy Returns." Time 36, November 4, 1940, p. 19. 50

Binsse, H.L.
  "Repudiated Sense: Kennedy off the Record." Commonweal 33, November 22, 1940, p. 116. 51

Kirchwey, Freda
  "Watch Joe Kennedy! Appeasement Forces in the United States Begin to Coalesce." The nation 151, December 14, 1940, p. 593-594. 52

1941
"Mr. Kennedy Reports." Christian century 58, Jan-

uary 29, 1941, p. 142-143. 53

Laski, Harold J.
"British Democracy and Mr. Kennedy." Harper's magazine 182, April 1941, p. 464-470. 54

1945

"Joe Kennedy Buys Merchandise Mart." Time 46, July 30, 1945, p. 84. 55

"Joe Kennedy's Tour to Help Rejuvenate Massachusetts Business." Life 19, October 1, 1945, p. 38-39. 56

1947

"Noonday Sun." Commonweal 45, March 28, 1947, p. 580-581. 57

1960

"A Talk with the Silent Kennedy." U.S. news & world report 49, July 25, 1960, p. 63-65. 58

Deming, A.
"Kennedy Abroad." Newsweek 56, August 8, 1960, p. 23. 59

Lavine, Harold, & J. Stearn
"The Mystery of Joe Kennedy." Newsweek 56, September 12, 1960, p. 26-30. 60

Sidey, Hugh
"Joe Kennedy's Feelings About his son." Life 49, December 19, 1960, p. 32. 61

1961

"Dad's Gotten Sick." Time 78, December 29, 1961, p. 8-9. 62

Lader, Lawrence
"His Excellency, Joseph P. Kennedy, the United States Ambassador to the Court of St. James, Requests the Pleasure of Your---." Esquire 56, September 1961, p. 82-85. 63

1962

"The Amazing Story of Joseph Kennedy." U.S. news & world report 52, January 1, 1962, p. 47. 64

"Keep up your Courage." Newsweek 59, January 1, 1962, p. 10-11. 65

"Kennedy Horizon: Struggle Against Paralysis." Newsweek 59, May 14, 1962, p. 94. 66

1963

"How Kennedy's Father Made his Money." London, Time & tide, February 21-27, 1963, p. 10. 67

Whalen, Richard J.
"The Father of the President." Reader's digest 83, October 1963, p. 150-151. 68

Whalen, Richard J.
"How Joe Kennedy Made his Millions." Life 54, January 25, 1963, p. 59-60. 69

1964

de Bedts, R. F.
"First Chairmen of the Securities and Exchange Commission: Successful Ambassadors of the New Deal to Wall Street." American journal of

economics & sociology 23,
April 1964, p. 165-178.   70

    1965
Macleod, Jain
 "Joseph P. Kennedy." London, Spectator 7148, 1965,
p. 811.   71

"Dynast." London, The Times literary supplement 3305, July 1, 1965, p. 549-550.
    72
"Life With Father: The Fruitful Bough, Circulating Among Kennedy Friends and Relatives." Newsweek 66, November 1, 1965, p. 24.
    73

Rose Elizabeth (Fitzgerald) Kennedy

Born in Boston, Massachusetts on July 21, 1890, Rose Fitzgerald was the daughter of John F. ("Honey Fitz") Fitzgerald, a Congressman from Massachusetts and Mayor of Boston. She was graduated from the Dorchester High School at the age of fifteen with honors, and attended Manhattanville College of the Sacred Heart, subsequently spending one year in study at Blumental Academy, in Valls, Holland, where she took rapidly to languages and won a prize for piano performance.

Even in her teenage years, however, Rose Fitzgerald took to and naturally enjoyed the limelight offered a mayor's daughter. Trips to Latin America and Europe were also in order. Some time later she organized a group, the Ace of Clubs, to discuss domestic and international affairs.

In October of 1914, Rose Fitzgerald and Joseph P. Kennedy (Harvard, 1912) were married by Cardinal O'Connell of Boston. Rose was attended by her younger sister, Agnes. After a honeymoon to White Sulphur Springs, Virginia, the couple moved into their own home at 83 Beals Street, Brookline, a fashionable Boston suburb. In this house all of Rose Fitzgerald Kennedy's children (except for Joseph, Jr., the eldest) were born.

In the early 1930's, due to the press of Mr. Kennedy's business in New York City, the family moved to Bronxville, New York. The house was not as noisy during the school year, for Joseph Jr. and John were away at preparatory schools in Connecticut, while the girls attended the Sacred Heart convent school in Noroton, Connecticut. The Kennedys also maintained residences in Palm Beach, Florida, and in Hyannis Port, Massachusetts. Until the early 1930's Rose Kennedy bore the brunt of bringing up the family, due to the frequent business trips of her husband. After that time Joseph P. Kennedy took over the job of guiding his family to a great extent. Such events as Saturday trips into New York City from their Bronxville home were a weekly occurrence which all looked forward to eagerly.

Rose Elizabeth (Fitzgerald) Kennedy

On two occasions in the 1930's (prior to Mr. Kennedy's appointment as U.S. Ambassador to Great Britain), Mr. and Mrs. Kennedy took ocean voyages to Europe. In 1936 Rose Kennedy toured the Soviet Union with her daughter, Kathleen. Between 1937 and 1939, while the family resided in London, the Kennedy girls attended the Sacred Heart convent school in Roehampton, England. During vacations from Harvard, Joseph, Jr. and John F. Kennedy were assigned Embassy chores. Robert and Edward were attending private schools in London. The family returned to the United States in 1939, except for the Ambassador, who rejoined his family in 1940.

In 1946 Rose Kennedy and her daughters acted as hostesses and rang thousands of Boston doorbells, doing their utmost to assist John F. Kennedy in his successful efforts to win election as Congressman from Massachusetts.

Rose Kennedy has become an authority on the topic of child-rearing. After the election of John F. Kennedy, and during his presidential administration, his mother often lectured to civic and social groups in Massachusetts, telling how she kept a file on her children's innoculations and illnesses, height and weight, etc. The family atmosphere was also given considerable attention, and a family spirit of doing things together and of family loyalty was inculcated. Undoubtedly pride of parental accomplishment and of forebears were significant influences.

In her talks before groups Mrs. Kennedy, in discussing the upbringing of her children, would stress the fact that she attempted to interest them in cultural matters. Tabletalk, for example, centered on international affairs and current events generally. At the same time Mr. and Mrs. Kennedy encouraged their children's competitive spirit, urging them to win at physical contests. One of her most entertaining anecdotes concerned the card-file system which she kept on the health of each child, listing dates of injections, illnesses, treatments, etc. The Kennedy children never received allowances larger than those of other neighborhood children, and financial matters were never the topic of conversation in the Kennedy household. The well-known fact that each child received a one-million dollar gift on his twenty-first birthday was based on parental wishes for the financial independence of each.

On October 31, 1967 Mrs. Rose Kennedy appeared on the NBC Television Network in a special program dedicated to her son, John F. Kennedy. At the age of 77, she appeared very much younger than her age, was very well-groomed, spirited, and presented a profile of a cultured, educated lady, who stated that she felt privileged and honored to have given her country a president.

Articles about Mrs. Joseph P. Kennedy

1939
Sulzberger, Cyrus L.
"Mr. and Mrs. Joseph P. Kennedy." Ladies' home journal 56, February 1939, p. 23. 74

1961
Higgins, Marguerite
"Rose Fitzgerald Kennedy." McCall's 88, May 1961, p. 102-105. 75

1962
"First Lady's Substitute as Hostess: the President's Mother." U.S. news & world report 53, August 6, 1962, p. 16. 76

1967
"Rose Kennedy at 76." America 117, November 18, 1967, p. 595. 77

1968
Bergquist, Laura
"Visit with the Indomnitable Rose Kennedy." Look 32, November 26, 1968, p. 25-34. 78

Books about the Joseph P. Kennedy Family

1959
Dinneen, Joseph F.
The Kennedy family. Boston, Little, Brown, & Co., 1959, 238p. 79

1960
McCarthy, Joseph W.
The remarkable Kennedys. New York, Dial Press, 1960, 190p. 80

1961
Carr, William H. A.
Those fabulous Kennedy women. New York, Wisdom House, 1961, 157p. 81

Dan, Mariko
Ishoku no Kenedii ikka: ani no shikabane o koete. Tokyo, Shinoco Sha, 1961, 164p.
(The colorful Kennedy family; beyond the fallen brother.) 82

Lowe, Jacques
Portrait: the emergence of John F. Kennedy. New York, McGraw-Hill, 1961, 224p. 83

Tanzer, Lester, ed.
The Kennedy circle. Washington, Robert B. Luce, Inc., 1961, 315p. 84

1963
Cort, David
The case of the overexposed dynasty. (In his Social astonishments; essays. New York, Macmillan, 1963, p. 262-268). 85

1964

Friedman, Stanley P.
 The magnificent Kennedy women. Derby, Conn., Monarch Books, 1964, 157p.   86

Kennedy, Crawford H.
 The clan Kennedy. Beaver, Pa.? 1964, 802p.   87

Proctor, Kenneth M.
 The Kennedy brothers, a tribute to their greatness: Joseph P. Kennedy Jr., John Fitzgerald Kennedy, Robert Francis Kennedy, and Edward M. Kennedy. Manhattan Beach, Calif.? 1964, 32p.   88

1965

Hirsch, Phil & Edward Hymoff, eds.
 The Kennedy courage. New York, Pyramid Books, 1965, 128p.   89

Lawson, Don
 Famous American political families. New York, Abelard-Schuman, 1965, p. 205-236. 90

1967

Marvin, Susan
 The women around R.F.K. New York, Lancer Books, 1967, 158p.   91

1968

Associated Press
 Triumphs in tragedy: the story of the Kennedys. New York, 1968, 256p.   92

Articles about the Joseph P. Kennedy Family

1938

Cushman, W.
 "With the Kennedy Family in London Town." Ladies' home journal 55, October 1938, p. 30-31.   93

1939

Beatty, Jerome
 "Nine Kennedys and how They Grew." Reader's digest 34, April 1939, p. 83-85.   94

Hallinan, Hazel (Hunkins)
 "Nine Young U.S. Ambassadors." Parents' magazine 14, September 1939, p. 26-27.   95

1941

Beatty, Jerome
 "Cook for a King." American magazine 132, November 1941, p. 46-48.   96

1957

Martin, Helen (Hill)
 "The Amazing Kennedys." Saturday evening post 230, September 7, 1957, p. 19-21.   97

Dinneen, Joseph F.
 "Fabulous Boston Kennedys." Catholic digest 21, October 1957, p. 57-63.   98

1958

"Joe's Children with Their own." Life 44, April 21, 1958, p. 135.   99

1960

Hollis, Christopher
"Keeping up with the Kennedys." London, Spectator 6886, 1960, p. 871-873. 100

"Where Campaigning is a Family Affair." U.S. news & world report 48, March 14, 1960, p. 106-108. 101

"Pride of the Clan." Time 76, July 11, 1960, p. 19-23. 102

"Kennedy: a Family Political Machine." Look 24, July 19, 1960, p. 43-46. 103

"Here's Rest of the Kennedy Clan." U.S. news & world report 49, July 25, 1960, p. 60-62. 104

Maas, P.
"The Kennedy Women." Look 24, October 11, 1960, p. 93-102. 105

Schutzer, Paul
"Election Night Tension Inside Kennedy House." Life 49, November 21, 1960, p. 36-37. 106

1961

"Eltern und Geschwister des neuen US-Präsidenten: Die Familie Kennedy," by Joseph F. Dinneen, book review. Aschaffenburg, Germany, Katholischer digest 15, 1961, p. 193-196. ("Parents and Cousins of the New U.S. President: the Kennedy Family.") 107

Roddy, Jon
"The Irish Origins of a President." Look 25, March 14, 1961, p. 17-25. 108

"President as Godfather: the Radziwill Baptism." Tablet 215, June 10, 1961, p. 558. 109

Hennessey, Luella R.
"Bring up the Kennedys." Good housekeeping 153, August 1961, p. 52-57. 110

"Kennedy Living: Home of the Kennedy Clan." Time 78, September 1, 1961, p. 36-43. 111

1962

Studnitz, H.G. von
"Die Kennedys--eine Dynastie im Weissen Haus." Stuttgart, Christ und welt (15: 42), 1962, p. 32. ("The Kennedys: a Dynasty in the White House.") 112

Sclanders, Ian
"Look-alikes: the Attractive Kennedys and all America." Toronto, Maclean's magazine 75, April 7, 1962, p. 61. 113

Manchester, William
"John F. Kennedy, Portrait of a President." Holiday 31, June 1962, p. 64-65. 114

Coughlan, Robert
"Old Rivalries on a Changed Battlefield." Life 52, June 29, 1962, p. 62-63. 115

The Joseph P. Kennedy Family

Paye, Sister Mary P.
"The Kennedy Cult." The nation 195, August 11, 1962, p. 49-51.   116

"The Kennedy Family and the Press." London, Time & tide 43, August 16-23, 1962, p. 15-16.   117

"An American Genealogy." Time 80, September 28, 1962, p. 38-39.   118

Soloveytchik, G.
"Washington Today." London, Contemporary review 202, September 1962, p. 113-118.   119

1963

Sclanders, Ian
"The Kennedy Dynasty." Toronto, Maclean's magazine, January 5, 1963, p. 11-13, 42-44; January 26, 1963, p. 24-26; February 9, 1963, p. 24-25, 36; February 23, 1963, p. 20-21, 30-31; March 9, 1963, p. 27, 41-44; March 23, 1963, p. 26, 36.   120

Carter, Richard
"What Women Really Think of the Kennedys." Good housekeeping 156, June 1963, p. 73-75.   121

1964

Scanlon, J.
"This Year at Hyannis Port." Catholic digest 29, November 1964, p. 22-23.   122

1965

Walter, Frederica
"Die Kennedys Kämpfen um die Macht." Düsseldorf, Industriekurier (18: 100), 1965, p. 2.
("The Kennedys Struggle for Power.")   123

1966

Woodruff, D.
"The Kennedys; Review of Three Books." Tablet 220, February 19, 1966, p. 213-214.   124

1967

Fairlie, Henry
"Harvard: Power Base for the Kennedys? A Dean Gives Harvard's Side, by Don K. Price." U.S. news & world report 62, January 30, 1967, p. 37-40.   125

Vidal, Gore
"Holy Family." Esquire 67, April 1967, p. 99-103.   126

1968

Life Magazine
"The Kennedys." June 1968 (special edition), 95p.   127

Lurie, Diana
"Lord Harlech's Family Talks About the Kennedys." Ladies' home journal 85, June 1968, p. 57-59.   128

O'Neill, Paul
"Kennedys: They Draw the Lightning." Life 64, June 14, 1968, p. 75-84.   129

Joseph P. Kennedy, Jr.

The eldest of nine children born to Joseph P. Kennedy and Rose (Fitzgerald) Kennedy, Joseph P. Kennedy, Jr. arrived on July 25, 1915, while the Kennedys were vacationing at Nantasket, Massachusetts. It was said that Joseph, Jr. was in charge of the family while the elder Kennedy was away from home on extended business trips. He taught his brothers and sisters to ski, swim, skate and sail, and although he possessed a quick temper, they all adored him. In the book compiled by President John F. Kennedy to which all of the Kennedy family members contributed (As We Remember Joe, privately printed at the University Press, Cambridge, Massachusetts, 1945), Senator Edward M. ("Ted") Kennedy (then 13 years of age) recalled how his brother Joe tossed him into the water after he did not follow an order at once while they were out sailing. (Joe, of course, promptly pulled "Teddy" in after the soaking.)

Joseph Jr. prepared at Choate School, Wallingford, Connecticut, for Harvard, and won football honors at both institutions. He did not enter Harvard immediately upon graduation, but instead studied for one year at the London School of Economics under the famous Professor Harold Laski, who took quite a fancy to him, and invited him on a trip to Moscow. It was Laski who first predicted that Joseph, Jr. would eventually be President of the United States.

At Harvard Joe was popular, maintaining a wide circle of friends, and it was a foregone conclusion, based on his attractive personality, ambition and intelligence (he received his A.B. degree in Government cum laude), that he would aim for a career in politics.

From 1937 to 1940 while his father served as the United States Ambassador to Great Britain, Joseph, Jr. assisted him in Embassy chores. In addition, he managed to be in the European cities where significant events occurred: in Madrid, when General Franco took that city during the Spanish Civil War, and in Prague, when Czechoslovakia was ceded to Hitler at Munich by British Prime Minister Neville Chamberlain, with whom the Ambassador and his son were well acquainted.

Joseph P. Kennedy, Jr. was a delegate to the Democratic National Convention in 1940, and backed James A. Farley, a neutral in foreign affairs, opposing the program of President Franklin D. Roosevelt, who sought U.S. backing for the hard-pressed allies. In the same year he began his studies at the Harvard Law School, but in June of 1941, realizing that it was merely a matter of time until the United States would join England as a belligerent, he enlisted in the U.S. Naval Reserve as an aviation cadet, and was assigned to flight training at the Naval Air Stations in Squantum, Massachusetts, and Jacksonville, Florida. At Jacksonville Joseph, Jr. graduated first in his class, and was commissioned an ensign and naval aviator, in April of 1942. During most of that year he was assigned to the Transitional Squadron of the Atlantic Fleet, and after promotion to Lieutenant Junior Grade in January, 1943, was relocated to the San Juan, Puerto Rico, Naval Air Station, where he joined Patrol Bomber Squadron 203. Part of this Squadron was being detached to form Squadron VB-110, destined to fly Liberator bombers in an offensive action over the Bay of Biscay, aiming to destroy German submarines.

On September 20, 1943, Joe's crew of ten men left for their permanent base at Dunkeswell in Devonshire, England. Although Squadron VB-110 flew from two to four sorties daily, Joe did not encounter his first offensive action until November 9, 1943. Days passed into months, and by April of 1944, only one-half of the original complement of aircraft remained, the balance being lost in combat. During that month, Joe's commanding officer, in recommending Joe for promotion, said of him:

> A very capable officer, intelligent and forceful in character. In flying duties, Kennedy is outstanding. He is one of the most willing, enthusiastic and hard-working pilots in the Squadron, and will volunteer his time, energy and ideas freely to further the interests of the unit. In command of his plane, he has demonstrated unusual courage, judgment and leadership, and is respected and admired by officers and men for his airmanship.

Although he had earned a leave to return to the United States for reassignment in May of 1944, Joseph, Jr. requested his crew to remain with him in order to participate in the air action covering the invasion of Normandy, scheduled to begin on June 6, 1944. During the entire month of June and the early part of July, 1944, Joe and his Squadron took part in the action, Joe himself being credited with identifying (on June 8), five enemy vessels, which were later destroyed. He was promoted to Lieutenant Senior Grade on July 1. Prime Minister Churchill paid a compliment to Squadron VB-110 (and to squadrons engaged in similar activities) for the roles they played in the success of the Allied invasion.

The Germans, however, began at this time to rain V-1 robot bombs on England, and since anti-aircraft fire was ineffective, it was decided to send drone planes loaded with high explosives to crash into the rocket launching sites, and thus render them useless. Lieutenant Joseph Kennedy, Jr. volunteered for this work: he was to load the plane, guide it toward its target, and then bail out while the airplane was still flying over England. The drone plane would then be led by other planes toward the target on the continent.

Lieutenant Kennedy trained for the mission for several weeks during July and early August of 1944. On August 12, at 5:52 PM, Greenwich Mean Time, Joe and his co-pilot took off on what was to be their final mission. As their plane approached the English town of Beccles, it was ripped by two mighty explosions, and broke apart in mid-air. No trace of occupants remained following the accident. Despite detailed investigations, no definite cause for the mishap was ever established.

In his memory, a Navy destroyer, the Joseph P. Kennedy, Jr., was christened, and his younger brother, Robert F. Kennedy, served aboard it as a seaman during World War II. The Navy also awarded Lieutenant Kennedy the Navy Cross posthumously. The citation accompanying the Navy Cross read, in part:

> For extraordinary heroism and courage in aerial flight as Pilot of a United States Navy Liberator bomber on August 12, 1944...Well knowing the extreme dangers involved and totally unconcerned for his own safety, Lieutenant Kennedy

unhesitatingly volunteered to conduct an exceptionally hazardous and special operational mission. Intrepid and daring in his tactics, and with unwavering confidence in the vital importance of his task, he willingly risked his life in the supreme measure of service and by his great personal valor and fortitude in carrying out a perilous undertaking, sustained and enhanced the finest traditions of the United States Naval Service.

Tributes from far and wide deluged his sorrowing family. His memory, however, is far from forgotten, for in addition to the book dedicated to him by his family and published in 1945, his name and fame have been included in many recent works about the Kennedy family, and about President John F. Kennedy. He is also the subject of several recent books written for children.

Books about Joseph P. Kennedy, Jr.

1945
Kennedy, John F.
  As we remember Joe. Cambridge, Privately printed. University Press, 1945, 75p.   130

1966
Edmonds, I.G.
  Our heroes' heroes. New York, Criterion Books, 1966, p. 91-101. (Children's book)   131

1967
Sufrin, Mark
  Brave men: 12 portraits of courage. New York, The Platt & Munk Co., 1967, p. 1-29. (Children's book)   132

Memorials

1964
To learn to live (Motion picture). Trylon Films (1964). (Kennedy Child Study Center, New York City)   133

Articles about Joseph P. Kennedy, Jr.

1939
"Here They Come!" Atlantic monthly 164, October 1939, p. 545-546.   134

1951
Brooks, W.
  "Dream of a Guy Named Joe." Catholic digest 15, July 1951, p. 51-53. (Concerning Lt. Joseph P. Kennedy, Jr. Foundation)   135

1962
Land, R.
  "Clinic of Hope for Mentally Retarded Children." Apostle 40, February 1962,

p. 20-21. (Kennedy Child Study Center, New York City)   136

Morison, Samuel E.
"The Death of a Kennedy."
Look 26, February 27, 1962,
p. 105-106.   137

1964

Fink, L.
"Kennedy Child Study Center; Photo Essay." Today's family 39, January 1964, p. 36-43.   138

Cadden, V.
"John F. Kennedy's Tribute to his Older Brother." Redbook 122, February 1964, p. 46-47.   139

Fischer, G.
"The Kennedy Foundation." Catholic digest 28, October 1964, p. 54-57. (Concerning Kennedy Child Study Center, New York City).   140

Photographs

1940

"Joseph P. Kennedy, Jr. (photograph)." Time 35, April 8, 1940, p. 15.   141

John Fitzgerald Kennedy

John Fitzgerald Kennedy was born at 83 Beals Street, Brookline, Massachusetts, on May 29, 1917, to Joseph P. Kennedy and Rose (Fitzgerald) Kennedy, and was destined to become the thirty-fifth President of the United States. Undoubtedly he inherited some of his talent for politics from his forebears. His father was a United States Ambassador to Great Britain, and served his country as the head of federal agencies. John F. Kennedy's maternal grandfather, John F. ("Honey") Fitzgerald, was Mayor of Boston as well as a Congressman from Massachusetts, while his father's father served as an official of the City of Boston, and was a member of the Massachusetts Legislature.

The Kennedy family resided in Brookline until the early 1930's, when they moved to Bronxville, New York, but maintained residences in Massachusetts and Palm Beach, Florida. John attended Choate School in Wallingford, Connecticut, and in 1935 attended the London School of Economics, prior to entering Princeton University the same year. An attack of jaundice necessitated his leaving Princeton, and in the autumn of 1936 he entered Harvard University, from which he was graduated in 1940 with a Bachelor of Science degree (with honors) in political science.

In his senior year at Harvard John F. Kennedy presented a thesis (later published under the title, Why England Slept), based upon his first-hand view of European politics while serving as secretary to his father at the American Embassy in London during the years 1938-40. This experience was to be invaluable in his later career, for in addition to administrative experience gained, he became acquainted in his work and through travel with the leading political figures of the day, among them President and Mrs. Roosevelt, Winston Churchill, Neville Chamberlain, and others. Following graduation from Harvard, John studied business at Stanford University, subsequently traveling in Latin America.

The United States Army rejected John F. Kennedy when he attempted to enlist, but in 1941 after several months of special exercises (to improve a back injury sustained while playing college football), he entered the Navy as a Lieutenant Junior Grade. He was assigned to Naval Intelligence Headquarters in Washington, but shortly after Pearl Harbor he requested sea duty, and received training in the operation of torpedo boats. In the spring of 1943 he was sent to the South Pacific in command of a patrol torpedo boat.

On the night of August 2, 1943, in a counter-attack on the Japanese on New Georgia Island, two of his men were killed outright when his boat was cut in two by a Japanese destroyer. John F. Kennedy's heroic action in rallying and encouraging the survivors, towing a wounded man to shore after sustaining him above water during a five-hour swim, and his subsequent efforts to rejoin U.S. and allied forces displayed a dogged courage against overwhelming odds which was to stand in good stead and was to become his trademark. Malaria and recurrent back injuries required his hospitalization in the spring of 1944, and after an operation in early 1945, he was retired from the Navy. His heroism won the admiration of many, and was later the topic of many books, articles and a notable motion picture, PT-109.

During 1945 John F. Kennedy worked as a reporter for several newspapers, and he was assigned to cover the San Francisco Conference on the founding of the United Nations, as well as the Potsdam Conference. His career choice, however, was political life, and when the opportunity presented itself, he campaigned and won a seat in the U.S. House of Representatives from the Eleventh Massachusetts Congressional District, defeating nine opponents, and rolling up 42 percent of the vote. His tactics for victory, destined to win future election contests, included starting his campaign early, establishing his own organization, and assistance from family members who campaigned for him. John F. Kennedy toured his district, meeting as many voters as possible, speaking directly to the point on important issues. He repeated his earlier victory in 1948.

During his service in the House of Representatives, John F. Kennedy fought as a liberal in the Franklin D. Roosevelt tradition, for education and labor programs. He introduced bills for slum clearance and federally-funded housing programs. Although basically supporting President Truman, he showed his independent spirit through his stress on government cost-cutting and his denunciation of the State

John Fitzgerald Kennedy

Department's policies after the fall of Nationalist China in 1949. Following a trip through Western Europe in 1951, he stated that while the United States must maintain troops in Europe, the NATO nations should demonstrate their willingness to defend themselves by committing their own forces to NATO in significant numbers. After a world trip in late 1951, he became a supporter of Point Four foreign aid.

His predilection for foreign affairs was undoubtedly a factor in John F. Kennedy's decision to oppose Henry Cabot Lodge, incumbent Senator from Massachusetts, in the 1952 senatorial race in that state. It is of interest to note that Kennedy's paternal grandfather lost the same Senate seat to Senator Lodge's grandfather in 1916. Kennedy's campaign strategy proved its value, for in the Republican landslide year of 1952, John F. Kennedy won his Senate seat by 70,000 votes.

On September 12, 1953, John F. Kennedy and Jacqueline Lee Bouvier, a society reporter for a Washington, D.C. newspaper, were married in Newport, Rhode Island. They honeymooned in Acapulco, Mexico.

As a Senator from Massachusetts, John F. Kennedy served on the Select Committee on Labor-Management, and was instrumental in fashioning labor-reform bills, as well as supporting civil rights. During the year just prior to his election as President, he served on the Joint Economic Committee, and from 1957 to 1960 was a member of the Senate Foreign Relations Committee. John F. Kennedy fulfilled his campaign pledges to his constituents, yet was not sectional in his approach, taking into consideration, instead, the welfare of the nation as a whole. An example of this approach was his support of the St. Lawrence Seaway program and his backing of President Eisenhower's trade program special capabilities (granted to Eisenhower as President).

In foreign affairs John F. Kennedy was critical of the Eisenhower administration for failing to view and deal with the world situation realistically during the 1950's, especially as regards the newly developing nations. He fought to bolster national defense and missile research. Together with Senator Lister Hill of Alabama, Senator Kennedy sponsored a bill, passed in 1956, which created the National Library of Medicine.

At the Democratic National Convention in 1956, Senator Kennedy made the nominating speech in behalf of Adlai E. Stevenson for President. At the same Convention he almost obtained the vice-presidential nomination. In his 1958 senatorial campaign in Massachusetts, he was reelected by a tremendous plurality of 870,000 votes.

During the years 1954-55, John F. Kennedy's back ailments recurred, and he underwent surgery. During long recuperation he worked on a manuscript, based on the lives of courageous senators who risked their political careers because they refused to compromise their integrity. The resulting book he entitled Profiles in Courage, a work which won John F. Kennedy a Pulitzer Prize, and the Christopher Book Award, for the year 1956.

On November 27, 1957, a daughter, Caroline, was born to the Kennedys, and on November 25, 1960, John F. Kennedy, Jr., arrived.

On January 2, 1960, John F. Kennedy announced his candidacy for President. He won in primary elections throughout the nation because of his standard campaign techniques of beginning his campaign work early, his constant tours and direct confrontation with voters in many states, speaking to them frankly about problems which they and the nation faced, and in general, working around the clock. Despite his youth (43 years of age), and the fact that he was a Roman Catholic by religion (a qualification fatal to the candidacy of New York Governor Alfred E. Smith in 1928), John F. Kennedy was nominated for President on the first ballot at the Democratic National Convention at Los Angeles in July, 1960.

John F. Kennedy's campaign against the Republican nominee, Vice President Richard M. Nixon, pointed up his executive abilities and unique approaches to solving both domestic and international problems, and the comparison between the opponents was made manifest to viewers of their television debates. Mr. Kennedy offered logically-conceived, well-planned and practical solutions to the basic problems of international affairs, conservation and agriculture, education, civil rights, labor, business and social welfare. The election results gave him 300 votes of the electoral college to 219 for Vice President Nixon.

Those who witnessed the inauguration of President

John Fitzgerald Kennedy

John F. Kennedy on January 21, 1961 will remember a young man, hatless and coatless, standing in freezing temperatures, and delivering an address which, like Lincoln's address at Gettysburg, is a political as well as a literary classic. He called upon America's allies to assist underdeveloped nations in common cause with the United States (this statement subsequently led to the establishment of the Organization for Economic Cooperation and Development, headquartered in Paris). President Kennedy promised that the United States would support the United Nations, and requested the Communist nations to cooperate in a new search for peace. He sounded the keynote of the rising hopes of twentieth century man for an eventual victory over disease, poverty, tyranny and warfare. His final sentence in the Inaugural Address, "Ask not what your country can do for you, ask what you can do for your country," has become a national byword.

John F. Kennedy's presidential programs, including the establishment of the Peace Corps, foreign assistance world-wide under the aegis of the Agency for International Development (and especially to Latin America under the Alliance for Progress), his success in limiting the atmospheric testing of nuclear weapons (as a result of the signing of the nuclear test-ban treaty on August 5, 1963), and his efforts in strengthening Western Europe through economic cooperation under the Trade Expansion Act of 1962, all had their origins in pre-presidential planning.

President Kennedy's cabinet included his brother, Robert F. Kennedy as Attorney-General. Attorney-General Kennedy had assisted the President in all of his previous political campaigns and supplied valuable assistance in the Bay of Pigs and civil-rights matters which faced the President in 1961 and 1962. He also played an effective role in regard to the steel-price rollback during the spring of 1962.

Premier Khrushchev of the Soviet Union was the prime international opponent of President Kennedy, who told Khrushchev (at their Vienna meeting in 1961) that the United States would protect the rights of access to West Berlin because U.S. security was involved, in addition to the fact that the access rights were based on law. The climax to their confrontation came on October 29, 1962, when in a nationwide radio and television speech, President Kennedy informed the nation of the presence of Soviet missile bases in Cuba. He placed a quarantine around Cuba, under which ships of any nation approaching that island were searched for arms by United States naval vessels. As a result, Russian ships began to return to their home ports, and Premier Khrushchev agreed to dismantle the Cuban missile bases, which were subsequently returned to the Soviet Union. This event directly led to Premier Khrushchev's political demise, while President Kennedy received plaudits for preserving the peace.

Because so much effort was required on the international scene and in view of congressional lack of response during his administration, President Kennedy's forward-looking plans for domestic improvements were brought to fruition only after his death. These included greatly-increased aid to education, medical care for the aged, a tax reduction, laws to protect civil rights, the establishment of a new cabinet post for urban affairs, and increased federal housing assistance. President Kennedy also effected innovations which resulted in assisting missile and astronautical research, an area in which he had traditionally provided support. Subsequent to his death, Cape Canaveral, the space research center, was renamed Cape Kennedy, as were a host of libraries and other learned institutions throughout the world. Many model cities in Latin America, including housing projects erected under the terms of the Alliance for Progress, as well as boulevards in cities throughout the world were named for John F. Kennedy. Hundreds of monuments were erected world-wide in his honor. The National Cultural Center in Washington, D.C. was renamed the John F. Kennedy Center for the Performing Arts. The John F. Kennedy Memorial Library at Harvard University houses the Institute of Politics of the John F. Kennedy School of Government, established to train public servants. On May 29, 1969, the house in which he was born, on Beals Street, Brookline, Massachusetts, was dedicated as a national monument.

President John F. Kennedy was assassinated in Dallas, Texas on Friday, November 22, 1963. He visited the city as a locale for one of his frequent speeches, and ignored a warning to refrain from speaking there. The President's body lay in state until Monday, November 25, 1963, when he was given a military funeral (attended by most of the world's political leaders and reported on television) and buried in Arlington National Cemetery. Mrs. Kennedy lit the eternal torch which was placed over his grave. The official period of mourning in the United States was one month, while many Latin American nations had three days of mourning for the President.

Hans Habe, a German author, following a visit throughout the United States in the months following the assassination, summed up his thoughts in a book entitled The Wounded Land. For millions the loss seemed as personal as if one of their own family members had died. And it was indeed so, for John F. Kennedy had established a rapport with his countrymen of all ages, races, religions and classes. Youth identified with him because of his appearance and ease of manner. The elderly appreciated him in view of his efforts to secure medical care and other benefits for them. Minority groups hailed his efforts to achieve civil rights legislation. Labor applauded his efforts to assist workingmen through establishment of minimum wages. The business world appreciated his efforts to reduce taxes and understood his efforts to provide a sound economy at home, while increasing international trade. The "Kennedy Round" of GATT tariff agreements bears his name. Abroad he was respected as a brave opponent and as a champion of democracy, as well as a staunch ally whose candor, political acumen, breeding and style gained new prestige for the United States.

One of President Kennedy's most enduring contributions was his representation of the type of political leader needed by the United States. While in the past young, educated individuals have shunned political life, John F. Kennedy's example may perhaps serve as a model for such people to serve America in the future, not only in the civil service but in politics as well. President Kennedy himself often suggested political life as a worthwhile profession. In this sense he was not only a consummate practitioner but a teacher as well. A polished speaker and writer of periodical articles on political topics, he has also authored four first-class books: Why England Slept (first published in 1940, and republished in 1961); Profiles in Courage (1956); The Strategy of Peace, published in 1960, and To Turn the Tide, published in 1962. An intellectual and political leader, he served on the Board of Overseers of Harvard University from 1957 to 1963, and received over twenty-five honorary doctoral degrees from universities throughout the United States and abroad, as well as numerous awards and decorations.

It is interesting to note that of all of the thirty-four presidents who preceded him, John F. Kennedy was the only one who actually prepared for the position by majoring in political science and international relations at Harvard University. This fact may perhaps explain a part of his phenomenal success, but it cannot explain all. For book-learning can take one only so far. President Kennedy's political heritage, his pleasing personality, humor and courage, combined with a high degree of native intelligence and the basic qualities of common sense and extremely hard work seem to have been combined in him in the correct proportions.

There is a theory which holds that the Lord sends leaders to save the United States (as He sent leaders and prophets to save ancient Israel). Abraham Lincoln was such a leader, perhaps the only person then living who could have kept the Union whole. Franklin Delano Roosevelt saved the United States from anarchy and revolution through forceful control of political and economic factors, and saw the nation safely through World War II. (He must have made a powerful impression on the John F. Kennedy of the 1930's and early 1940's). President John F. Kennedy saved the United States from foreign aggression, while maintaining unity and fair play within. He fought for the rights and just needs of all people, throughout the United States and all over the world, never sparing of himself throughout his entire career to fight for the right. In this battle he was victorious, and he has earned the highest honor attainable on earth: a cherished memory in the hearts and minds of all mankind forever.

The Writings of John F. Kennedy

(See also: International Affairs in the Career of John F. Kennedy, as well as Humor and Intellectual Life. Following each of President Kennedy's books is a list of translations into foreign languages.)

Books by John F. Kennedy

1956
Kennedy, John F.
 Profiles in courage. New York, Harper, 1956, 266p.   142

1958
Kennedy, John F.
 Portraits of five senators in the Senate Reception Room. (In Baird, A.C., ed. Representative American speeches, 1957-1958. New York, Wilson, 1958, p. 83-95).   143

1959
Kennedy, John F.
 A nation of immigrants. New York, Anti-Defamation League of Bnai Brith, 1959, 40p.   144

Kennedy, John F.
 A nation of immigrants. Rev. & enl. ed. New York, Harper & Row, 1964, 111p. 145

Kennedy, John F.
En nasjon av nasjoner (A nation of immigrants, translated into Norwegian by Otto Minde). Oslo, Ansgar Forlag, 1965, 127p. 146

Kennedy, John F.
Ummah min al-muhājirīn (A nation of immigrants, translated into Arabic by Ahmad Hammūdah). Cairo, Mu'assassat Sijill al-'Arab, 1965, 125p. 147

1960
Kennedy, John F.
The strategy of peace. Edited by Allan Nevins. New York, Harper & Row, 1960, 233p. 148

Kennedy, John F.
Omez u-politika (The strategy of peace, translated into Hebrew by Daniel Sher). Tel Aviv, Massadah, 1960, 182p. 149

Kennedy, John F.
Strategia di pace (The strategy of peace, translated into Italian by Luciano Bianciardi). Milan, A. Mondadori, 1960, 282p. 150

Kennedy, John F.
Esterātezhi-ye solh (The strategy of peace, translated into Persian by 'Abdollāh Galledārī). Teheran, 1961, 298p. 151

Kennedy, John F.
Estrategia de la paz (The strategy of peace, translated into Spanish by José María Cañas). Barcelona, Plaza & Janés, 1961, 367p. 152

Kennedy, John F.
For å leve i fred (The strategy of peace, translated into Norwegian by Havar Skrede). Oslo, Nasjonalforlaget, 1961, 191p. 153

Kennedy, John F.
Heiwa no tame no senryaku; shinjidai no tankyu (The strategy of peace, translated into Japanese by Gunji Hosono & Hidejiro Kotani). Tokyo, Gaisei Gakkai, 1961, 449p. 154

Kennedy, John F.
Ke-hoach hòa bình (The strategy of peace, translated into Vietnamese by Lê-Hung-Tâm). Saigon, Ziên-Hong, 1961, 216p. 155

Kennedy, John F.
La stratégie de la paix (The strategy of peace, translated into French by Jean Bloch-Michel). Paris, Calmann-Levy, 1961, 229p. 156

Kennedy, John F.
Fredens strategi (The strategy of peace, translated into Swedish by Hans Dahlberg). Stockholm, Aldus/Bonnier, 1963, 189p. 157

Kennedy, John F.
Der Weg zum Frieden. Ed. by Allan Nevins (The strategy of peace, translated into German by Karl Mönch & Ulrich Kayser-Eichberg). Munich, Droemer/Knaur, 1964, 312p. 158

Kennedy, John F.
Ē stratēgikē tēs irēnēs (The strategy of peace, translated into Greek). Athens, Stratiotika Periodika, 1964, 160p. 159

Kennedy, John F.
Why go into politics (In Cannon, James M., ed. Politics U.S.A.: a practical guide to the winning of public office. Garden City, Doubleday, 1960, p. 59-69). 160

Kennedy, John F.
Why you should vote Democratic. Washington, Center for Information on America, 1960, 15p. 161

1961

Kennedy, John F.
Let us begin; the first hundred days of the Kennedy administration. Commentary by Martin Agronsky, and others. Edited by Richard L. Grossman. New York, Simon & Schuster, 1961, 144p. 162

Kennedy, John F.
Nyū furontia (President John F. Kennedy: his philosophy and his thinking, translated into Japanese by Shiho Sakanishi). Tokyo, Jiji Tsūshin -sha, 1961, 229p. 163

Kennedy, John F.
Profiles in courage; cardinal edition. New York, Pocket Books, 1961, 233p. 164

Kennedy, John F.
Profiles in courage. Inaugural edition. New York, Harper, 1961, 206p. 165

Kennedy, John F.
Profiles in courage; young readers edition, abridged. New York, Harper, 1961, 164p. 166

Kennedy, John F.
Profiles in courage, memorial edition. New York, Harper & Row, 1964, 287p. 167

Kennedy, John F.
Profiles in courage; young readers' memorial edition. New York, Harper & Row, 1964, 164p. 168

Kennedy, John F.
Fazilet mücadelesi (Profiles in courage, translated into Turkish by Arif H. Ozbilen). Istanbul, Doğan Kardeş Yayinlari A.Ş. Basimevi, 1958, 258p. 169

Kennedy, John F.
Gu'ong can dam tai nghi tru'ô'ng. (Profiles in courage, translated into Vietnamese). Saigon, Quáng-văn, 1958, 320p. 170

Kennedy, John F.
Dhairyasilanchi shabdachitren (Profiles in courage, translated into Marathi by P.V. Gadgil). Bombay, Vora & Co., 1959, 235p. 171

Kennedy, John F.
Dhairyasiloni virkathao (Profiles in courage, translated into Gujarati by Amritlal B. Yajnik). Bombay,

Vora & Co., 1959, 296p. 172

Kennedy, John F.
Dhiradeśabhimanikal (Profiles in courage, translated into Malayalam by P.J. Thomas). Kottayam, Deepika, 1959, 78p. 173

Kennedy, John F.
Sahas ke dhani (Profiles in courage, translated into Hindi by Narayan Datta). Bombay, Vora, 1959, 210p. 174

Kennedy, John F.
Suwar min al-shaja'ah (Profiles in courage, translated into Arabic by Abbās Hāfiz). Cairo, 1959? 175

Kennedy, John F.
Omets u-politikah (Profiles in courage, translated into Hebrew by Daniel Sher). Tel Aviv, Massadah, 1960, 182p. 176

Kennedy, John F.
Ritratti del coraggio (Profiles in courage, translated into Italian by H. Furst). Milan, Ediz. del "Borghese," 1960, 20p. 177

Kennedy, John F.
Yong'gamhan saramdeul (Profiles in courage, translated into Korean by Bag Heuiju). Seoul, Samjungdang, 1960, 317p. 178

Kennedy, John F.
Yong'gi inneun saramdeul (Profiles in courage, translated into Korean by Bag Jung-hi). Seoul, Hangugilbosa & Dong'ailbosa, 1960, 284p. 179

Kennedy, John F.
Gaung-saung hnint thart-ti (Profiles in courage, translated into Burmese by Theikpan Soe Hla). Rangoon, Shumawa, 1961, 200p. 180

Kennedy, John F.
Menn med mot (Profiles in courage, translated into Norwegian by Olav Haereid). Oslo, Ansgar Forlag, 1961, 231p. 181

Kennedy, John F.
Moed en karakter in de politiek. Beslissende momenten in het leven van Amerikaanse politici. (Profiles in courage, translated into Dutch by John Kooy). Amsterdam, Elsevier, 1961, 234p. 182

Kennedy, John F.
Sīmā-ye shojā'ān -e (Profiles in courage, translated into Persian by Khājeh Nūrī). Teheran, 1961, 240p. 183

Kennedy, John F.
Tang jên pu jang (Profiles in courage, translated into Chinese by Wang Yang Szǔ). Hongkong, World Today Press, 1961, 221p. 184

Kennedy, John F.
Hugprúdir menn (Profiles in courage, translated into Icelandic by Bárður Jakobsson). Reykjavík, Almenna Bokafelagio, 1962, 167p. 185

Kennedy, John F.
Simā-ye šojā'ān (Profiles in courage, translated into

Persian by Ebrāhim Xājenuri). Teheran, Pocket Books & Franklin, 1962, 240p.　186

Kennedy, John F.
Yûki aru hitobito (Profiles in courage, translated into Japanese by Muraji Shimojima). Tokyo, Nihon Gaisei Gakkai, 1962, 227p.　187

Kennedy, John F.
Cesaret ve fazilet mücadelesi (Profiles in courage, translated into Turkish by Nihal Yeğinobali). Istanbul, Ak Kitabevi, 1963, 143p.　188

Kennedy, John F.
Rasgos de valor (Profiles in courage, translated into Spanish by Francisco Bermeosolo). Barcelona, Plaza & Janés, 1963, 205p.　189

Kennedy, John F.
Le courage dans la politique; quelques grandes figures de l'histoire politique américaine (Profiles in courage, translated into French by Jean Rosenthal). Paris, Gonthier, 1964, 216p.　190

Kennedy, John F.
Maend af mod (Profiles in courage, translated into Danish by Harald Grut). Copenhagen, Samlerens Forlag, 1964, 203p.　191

Kennedy, John F.
Politica e coragem (Profiles in courage, translated into Portuguese by Reil R. da Silva). Bêlo Horizonte, Difusão Pan Americana do Livro, 1964, 238p.　192

Kennedy, John F.
Studier i mod (Profiles in courage, translated into Swedish by Sven Hallén). Stockholm, Aldus/Bonnier, 1964, 221p.　193

Kennedy, John F.
Zivilcourage (Profiles in courage, translated into German by Joseph Toch & Hans Lamm). With a foreword by Robert F. Kennedy. Munich, Hayne, 1964, 189p.　194

Kennedy, John F.
Su filosofía...sus ideas en sus discursos y escritos. Madrid, Casa Americana Madrid, 1961?, 44p.
(His philosophy...his ideas in his speeches and writings.)　195

Kennedy, John F.
Why England slept. New York, Funk & Wagnalls Co., 1961, 252p.　196

Kennedy, John F.
Men England sov (Why England slept, translated into Norwegian by C.J. Hambro). Oslo, Nasjonalforlaget, 1962, 205p.　197

Kennedy, John F.
Eikoku wa naze nemuttaka (Why England slept, translated into Japanese by Muraji Shimojima). Tokyo, Nihon Gaisei Gakkai, 1963, 257p.　198

Kennedy, John F.
Limādhā nāmat injiltirā

(Why England slept, translated into Arabic by Husayn al-Hūt). Cairo, al-Dār al-Qawmīyah, 1963, 125p. 199

Kennedy, John F.
Perché l'Inghilterra dormi (Why England slept, translated into Italian by Giuliana Cosco). Milan, Ediz. del Borghese, 1964, 240p. 200

Kennedy, John F.
Por qué dormía Inglaterra (Why England slept, translated into Spanish by Jesús Pardo). Barcelona, Plaza & Janés, 1965, 199p. 201

1962
Kennedy, John F.
Como piensa y actua el presidente Kennedy. México, Novaro-México, S.A., 1962, 347p.
(How President Kennedy thinks and acts.) 202

Kennedy, John F.
Due anni di presidenta, intervista all televisione, 17 novembre 1962 (Two years in the presidency, television interview, November 17, 1962). Rome, Ediz. U.S.I.S., 1962, 32p. 203

Kennedy, John F.
The quotable Mr. Kennedy. Edited by Gerald C. Gardner. New York, Abelard-Schuman, 1962, 65p. 204

Kennedy, John F.
Seika nyûmon (Politics, U.S.A.--a practical guide to the winning of public office, translated by Yasuhiro Nakasone & Tsuneo Watanabe). Tokyo, Kôbun-dô, 1962, 244p. 205

Kennedy, John F.
To turn the tide; a selection from his public statements from his election through the 1961 adjournment of Congress, setting forth the goals of his first legislative year. Edited by John W. Gardner. New York, Harper & Row, 1962, 235p. 206

Kennedy, John F.
La nueva frontera (To turn the tide, translated by Antonio Ribera). Barcelona, Plaza & Janés, 1963, 278p. 207

Kennedy, John F.
Le tournant; recueil de discours et messages, 9 janvier 1961-17 décembre 1962 (Translation into French, of To turn the tide: collection of speeches and messages, January 9, 1961-December 17, 1962). Paris, Calmann-Levy, 1963, 303p. 208

Kennedy, John F.
Li wan k'uang lan (To turn the tide, translated into Chinese by Li Ch'iu-shêng). Hong Kong, Chin Jih Shih Chien She, 1963, 196p. 209

Kennedy, John F.
Pravaher parivartan (To turn the tide, a selection from President Kennedy's public statements, translated into Bengali by Pasupati Chatterji). Calcutta, Parichay,

1963, 207p. 210

Kennedy, John F.
Sont salanir sont (To turn the tide, translated into Assamese by Ratna Oja). Calcutta, Sribhumi Pub. Co., 1963, 207p. 211

Kennedy, John F.
Dämme gegen die Flut; Reden und Erklärungen. Ed. by John W. Gardner (To turn the tide, translated into German by Karl Mönch). Frankfurt-am-Main, Fischer Bucherei, 1964, 188p. 212

Kennedy, John F.
Lat ultavaychi ahe (To turn the tide, translated into Marathi by Pandurang Vasudev Gadgil). Bombay, Vora & Co., 1965, 227p. 213

Kennedy, John F.
Visvanam vahen valava (To turn the tide, translated into Gujarati by Harin Sah). Bombay, Vora & Co., 1965, 251p. 214

Kennedy, John F.
Visva-santi ki or (To turn the tide, translated into Hindi by Mohini Rao). Delhi, Atmaram & Sons, 1965, 235p. 215

1963
Kennedy, John F.
Amerikanin aradiǧ, bariş... Istanbul, Yenilik Başimevi, 1963, 6p.
(Reconciliation among Americans). 216

Kennedy, John F.
A conversation with the President (In Baird, A.C., ed. Representative American speeches, 1962-1963. New York, Wilson, 1963, p. 145-172.) 217

Kennedy, John F.
Kennedy el hombre prometido, by Luis Humberto Delgado. Lima, Ariel Editores, 1963, 143p. (Translation of selections, from President Kennedy's writings, into Spanish.) 218

1964
Kennedy, John F.
An alternative to military service (In Madow, Pauline, ed. The Peace Corps. New York, Wilson, 1964, p. 17-20). 219

Kennedy, John F.
America the beautiful in the words of John F. Kennedy. Ed. by Robert L. Polley. Garden City, Doubleday, 1964, 97p. 220

Kennedy, John F.
The artist in America (In Colby, Vineta, ed. American culture in the sixties. New York, Wilson, 1964, p. 113-115). 221

Kennedy, John F.
The burden and the glory; the hopes and purposes of his second and third years in office, as revealed in his public statements and addresses. Ed. by Allan Nevins. New York, Harper & Row, 1964, 293p. 222

Kennedy, John F.
Bördan och äran (The burden and the glory, translated into Swedish by Sven Hallén). Stockholm, Aldus/Bonnier, 1964, 242p. 223

Kennedy, John F.
El deber y la gloria; testamento político de John F. Kennedy (The burden and the glory, translated into Spanish by Jaime Piñero). Barcelona, Bruguera, 1964, 350p. 224

Kennedy, John F.
Frihet og fred (The burden and the glory, translated into Norwegian by Olav Haereid). Oslo, Ansgar Forlag, 1964, 191p. 225

Kennedy, John F.
Glanz und Bürde...Botschaften und Reden, mit d. vollen Text aller öffentl. Ausserungen während seiner Deutschland-Reise, 1963. Ed. by Allan Nevins. Translated into German by Hans Lamm. Düsseldorf, Econ.-Verlag, 1964, 472p.
(The burden and the glory ...messages and speeches, with full text of all open pronouncements during his trip to Germany, 1963). 226

Kennedy, John F.
Il peso della gloria (The burden and the glory, translated into Italian by Mario Rivoire). Milan, Mondadori, 1964, 368p. 227

Kennedy, John F.
Le fardeau et la gloire (French translation of The burden and the glory, by Laurence Reynaud). Paris, Editions France-Empire, 1964, 380p. 228

Kennedy, John F.
Siyāsat al-ra'īs Kinidī min khuṭabuh (The burden and the glory, translated into Arabic by Aḥmad Ḥamzah). Cairo, Dar al-ma'rifah, 1964, 387p. 229

Kennedy, John F.
O pêso da glória (The burden and the glory, translated into Portuguese by Leônidas G. de Carvalho). São Paulo, Eds. Melhoramentos, 1965, 258p. 230

Kennedy, John F., et al
Creative America. Photographs by Magnum. Published for the National Cultural Center. New York, Ridge Press, 1964, 127p. 231

Kennedy, John F.
Every citizen holds office. Washington, National Education Association, Citizenship Committee, 1964, 20p. 232

Kennedy, John F.
The humor of JFK, compiled by Booton Herndon. Greenwich, Conn., Fawcett Publications, 1964, 127p. 233

Kennedy, John F.
John F. Kennedys sista resa (The torch is passed, translated into Swedish by Alf Sagnér). Malmö, Allhem, 1964, 95p. 234

Kennedy, John F.
 Kennedy no isan; kono wasureenu kotoba (The legacy of a president, translated into Japanese). Tokyo, Kodansha, 1964, 270p. 235

Kennedy, John F.
 Kennedy through Indian eyes. Ed. by Ram Singh & M.K. Haldar. Delhi, Vir Pub. House, 1964, 154p. 236

Kennedy, John F.
 The Kennedy wit. Edited by Bill Adler. New York, Citadel Press, 1964, 83p. 237

Kennedy, John F.
 Legacy of a president; the memorable words of John Fitzgerald Kennedy. Delhi, Indian Book Co., 1964? 108p. 238

Kennedy, John F.
 Naneun wae jeongchgaga doeeosna (A practical guide in the winning of public office, translated into Korean by Habdong Munhwasa Pyeonjibbu). Seoul, Habdon Munhwasa, 1964, 199p. 239

Kennedy, John F.
 On history. New York, American Heritage, 1964, 4p. 240

Kennedy, John F.
 The President's Advisory Council on the Arts (In Colby, Vineta, ed. American culture in the sixties. New York, Wilson, 1964, p. 106-109). 241

Kennedy, John F.
 The shining moments; the words and moods of John F. Kennedy. With the memorial tribute of Adlai E. Stevenson. Ed. by Gerald Gardner. Montreal, Pocket Books, 1964, unpaged. 242

Kennedy, John F.
 Vida e pensamento de Kennedy; uma antologia de textos precedida de uma nota biográfica de Vasco Pulido Valente e de um prefácio de Antonio Alçada Baptista. Lisbon, Morais, 1964, 323p. (The life and thought of Kennedy; an anthology of texts, preceded by a biographical note, by Vasco Pulido Valente and a preface by Antonio Alçada Baptista). 243

1965

Kennedy, John F.
 Memorable quotations. Compiled by Maxwell Meyersohn. New York, Crowell, 1965, 314p. 244

Kennedy, John F.
 More Kennedy wit. Edited by Bill Adler. New York, Citadel Press, 1965, 94p. 245

Kennedy, John F.
 The quotable Kennedy. Edited by Alex J. Goldman. New York, Citadel Press, 1965, 162p. 246

1966

Kennedy, John F.
 America the beautiful. Waukesha, Wis., Country Beautiful Foundation, Inc., 1966, 98p. 247

Kennedy, John F.
On education. Selected and edited by William T. O'Hara. New York, Teachers College Press, Teachers College, Columbia University, 1966, 305p. 248

1967
Kennedy, John F.
The complete Kennedy wit. Ed. by Bill Adler. 1st ed. New York, Citadel Press, 1967, 203p. 249

Kennedy, John F.
The wit of President Kennedy (In Three faces of wit. London, L. Frewin, 1967, 304p.). 250

Kennedy, John F.
Words to remember, by John F. Kennedy. With a foreword by Robert F. Kennedy. Color illus. by Frank V. Szasz. Kansas City, Mo., Hallmark Editions, 1967, 59p. 251

Articles by John F. Kennedy

1946
Kennedy, John F.
"A Promise Kept." Time 48, July 1, 1946, p. 23. 252

1949
Kennedy, John F.
"The Need for Revision of Policy on Airline Competition and Mail Subsidy." Congressional digest 28, January 1949, p. 28. 253

1951
Kennedy, John F.
"How Should Cadets be Picked?" New York times magazine, August 19, 1951, p. 16. 254

1952
Kennedy, John F.
"The Case for Home Rule for Washington." Congressional digest 31, December 1952, p. 304. 255

1953
Kennedy, John F.
"What's Wrong with Social Security." American magazine 156, October 1953, p. 19. 256

Kennedy, John F.
"What's the Matter with New England?" New York times magazine, November 8, 1953, p. 12. 257

1954
Kennedy, John F.
"New England and the South." Atlantic monthly 193, January 1954, p. 32-36. 258

Kennedy, John F.
"Social Security: Constructive if not Bold." New republic 130, February 8, 1954, p. 14-15. 259

1955
Kennedy, John F.
"A Great day in American History." Collier's 136, November 25, 1955, p. 40-42. 260

Kennedy, John F.
"Ross of Kansas." Harper's magazine 211, December 1955, p. 40-44. 261

Kennedy, John F.
"The Challenge of Political Courage." New York times magazine, December 18, 1955, p. 13. 262

1956

Kennedy, John F.
"Courage and Congress." Ave Maria 83, January 7, 1956, p. 5. 263

Kennedy, John F.
"To Keep the Lobbyist Within Bounds." New York times magazine, February 19, 1956, p. 11. 264

Kennedy, John F.
"Take the Academies out of Politics." Saturday evening post 228, June 2, 1956, p. 36-37. 265

1957

Kennedy, John F.
"The Search for the Five Greatest Senators." New York times magazine, April 14, 1957, p. 14-16. 266

Kennedy, John F.
"The Education of an American Politician: Excerpt from an Address." National parent-teacher 51, May 1957, p. 10-12. 267

Kennedy, John F.
"The Profession of Politics: Address, June 3, 1957." Vital speeches 23, August 15, 1957, p. 657-659. 268

1958

Kennedy, John F.
"The Fate of the Nation." NEA journal 47, January 1958, p. 10-11. 269

Kennedy, John F.
"Three Women of Courage." McCall's 85, January 1958, p. 36-37. 270

Kennedy, John F.
"The Spirit of one Man's Independence." Reader's digest 73, July 1958, p. 104-106. 271

Kennedy, John F.
"Shameful State Governments Hold Back Cities' Progress." Alabama municipal journal 16, August 1958, p. 5-7. 272

Kennedy, John F.
"When the Executive Fails to Lead." The reporter 19, September 18, 1958, p. 14-17. 273

1959

Kennedy, John F.
"Labor Racketeers and Political Pressure." Look 23, May 12, 1959, p. 17-21. 274

Reviews of Books
Written by
John F. Kennedy

1956

Kennedy, John F.
Profiles in courage. New

York, Harper & Row, 1956, 266p.
Reviewed in:
America 94, February 11, 1956, p. 538.
Best sellers 15, February 15, 1956, p. 351.
Books on trial 14, March 1956, p. 296.
Catholic historical review 43, October 1957, p. 351.
Catholic library world 27, March 1956, p. 289.
Commonweal 63, March 30, 1956, p. 668.
Večernji Sarajevski list (Sarajevo, Yugoslavia) 19, December 12, 1963, p. 288-304.

1960
Kennedy, John F.
The strategy of peace. Ed. by Allan Nevins. New York, Harper & Row, 1960, 233p.
Reviewed in:
ALA booklist & subscription books bulletin 56, May 1, 1960, p. 533.
Bookmark 19, July 1960, p. 257.
Bulletin 28, Virginia Kirkus Service, February 1, 1960, p. 125.
Critic 19, September 1960, p. 22.
Foro internacional (Mexico City, Colegio de Mexico, I: 4), April-June 1961, p. 626-629.
Foreign affairs 39, October 1960, p. 148.
Library journal 85, March 15, 1960, p. 1129.
Saturday review 43, May 28, 1960, p. 19.
Spectator (London), September 2, 1960, p. 347.
Times literary supplement (London), August 19, 1960, p. 523.
Wisconsin library bulletin 56, May 1960, p. 162.

1961
Kennedy, John F.
Profiles in courage (abridged young readers' edition). New York, Harper & Row, 1961, 164p.
Reviewed in:
Best sellers 21, April 15, 1961, p. 45.
Bulletin, Virginia Kirkus Service, March 1, 1961, p. 218.
Christian Science monitor, May 11, 1961, p. 4-B.
Commonweal 74, May 26, 1961, p. 237.
Horn book 37, June 1961, p. 277.
Library journal 86, June 15, 1961, p. 2357.
New York times book review, March 26, 1961, p. 36.
Saturday review 44, May 13, 1961, p. 52.
Wisconsin library bulletin 57, July 1961, p. 252.

Kennedy, John F.
Why England slept. New York, Funk & Wagnalls Co., 1961, 252p. (Originally published in 1940 by W. Funk & Co., 252p.)
Reviewed in:
America 63, August 31, 1940, p. 581.
ALA booklist & subscription books bulletin 37, October 1, 1940, p. 33.
Bookmark, November 1940,

p. 13.
Catholic world 152, October 1940, p. 126.
Christian Science monitor, August 31, 1940, p. 10.
The economist (London), May 5, 1962, p. 444.
The new leader, December 11, 1961, p. 10.
New republic 103, September 16, 1940, p. 393.
New York times, August 11, 1940, p. 3.
New Yorker 16, August 10, 1940, p. 62.
New York herald tribune, November 26, 1961, p. 11.
Newsweek, October 23, 1961, p. 107.
New statesman (London), June 22, 1962, p. 910.
Punch (London), May 9, 1962, p. 735.
Saturday review of literature 22, September 7, 1940, p. 20.
Saturday review, January 13, 1962, p. 56.
Thought 15, December 1940, p. 692-693.
Time 36, August 12, 1940, p. 64. 278

1962
Kennedy, John F.
To turn the tide; a selection from President Kennedy's public statements from his election through the 1961 adjournment of Congress, setting forth the goals of his first legislative year. Ed. by John W. Gardner. New York, Harper & Row, 1962, 235p.
Reviewed in:
ALA booklist & subscription books bulletin 58, March 1, 1962, p. 434.
Ave Maria 95, March 17, 1962, p. 26.
Bookmark 21, February 1962, p. 128.
Bulletin 29, Virginia Kirkus Service, December 1, 1961, p. 1068.
Library journal 87, January 15, 1962, p. 227.
New statesman (London) 63, June 22, 1962, p. 910.
New York times book review, January 14, 1962, p. 3.
Times literary supplement (London), May 4, 1962, p. 295. 279

1964
Kennedy, John F.
America, the beautiful... by the editors of Country Beautiful magazine.... Elm Grove, Wisconsin, Country Beautiful Foundation, Inc., for sale by Doubleday, Inc., Garden City, N.Y. 1964, 98p.
Reviewed in:
Book week, May 3, 1964, p. 3.
Library journal 89, May 15, 1964, p. 2077. 280

Kennedy, John F.
The burden and the glory; the hopes and purposes of President Kennedy's second and third years in office as revealed in his public statements and addresses. Ed. by Allan Nevins. New York, Harper & Row, 1964, 293p.
Reviewed in:
Best sellers 24, June 1, 1964, p. 95.
Book week, May 31, 1964,

p. 1.
Christian Science monitor, June 11, 1964, p. 9.
Critic 23, August 1964, p. 71.
The economist (London), 213, October 3, 1964, p. 56.
Library journal 89, April 1, 1964, p. 1615.
Saturday review 47, June 27, 1964, p. 24.
Times literary supplement (London), September 10, 1964, p. 835.   281

Kennedy, John F., et al
Creative America. Photographs by Magnum. Published for the National Cultural Center. New York, Ridge Press, 1964, 127p.
Reviewed in:
Book week, February 2, 1964, p. 1.
Library journal 89, March 15, 1964, p. 1230.
Kenyon review 27, Spring 1965, p. 359.   282

Kennedy, John F.
A nation of immigrants.
New York, Harper & Row, 1964, 111p.
Reviewed in:
Best sellers 24, November 1, 1964, p. 306.
Book week, November 22, 1964, p. 4.
Catholic library world 36, January 1965, p. 335.
Choice 1, February 1965, p. 591.
The economist (London), 213, November 28, 1964, p. 982.
Hadassah magazine 46, December 1964, p. 13.
Jewish teacher 33, February 1965, p. 27.

Library journal 89, October 15, 1964, p. 3969.
National Jewish monthly 79, December 1964, p. 20.
Newsweek 64, October 12, 1964, p. 124.
Saturday review 47, October 31, 1964, p. 51.   283

Kennedy, John F.
Profiles in courage. New York, Watts, 1964, 319p.
Reviewed in:
ALA booklist & subscription books bulletin 61, July 15, 1965, p. 1058.
Books & bookmen 10, July 1965, p. 47.
Best sellers 23, March 1, 1964, p. 420.   284

Kennedy, John F.
Public papers of the Presidents of the United States, containing the public messages, speeches, and statements of the President, January 1 to November 22, 1963. Washington, G.P.O., 1964, 1007p.
Reviewed in:
American historical review 70, January 1965, p. 592.
ALA booklist & subscription books bulletin 61, February 1, 1965, p. 530.
Catholic historical review 108, January 1964, p. 596.
Journal of southern history 314, February 1965, p. 127.
Library journal, August 1964, p. 3021.
Special libraries 56, January 1965, p. 67.   285

1965

Kennedy, John F.
The faith of JFK. Ed. by T.S. Settel. New York, Dutton, 1965, 127p.
Reviewed in:
Bulletin 33, Virginia Kirkus Service, August 1, 1965, p. 799.
Christian century 82, September 29, 1965, p. 1200.
Library journal 90, October 15, 1965, p. 4349.   286

Kennedy, John F.
The first book edition of John F. Kennedy's inaugural address. New York, Watts, 1965, 39p.
Reviewed in:
Library journal 89, November 15, 1964, p. 4641.
New York times book review, October 18, 1964, p. 30.
Saturday review 47, November 7, 1964, p. 54.   287

John Fitzgerald Kennedy... as we remember him. Ed. & produced under direction of Goddard Lieberson... New York, Atheneum, 1965, 241p.
Reviewed in:
Harper's magazine 231, December 1965, p. 137.
Best sellers 25, November 15, 1965, p. 334.
Book week, December 12, 1965, p. 6.
Library journal 90, November 15, 1965, p. 4968.
New York times book review, November 7, 1965, p. 91.   288

Kennedy, John F.
The Kennedy wit. Ed. by Bill Adler. New York, Citadel Press, 1965, 83p.
Reviewed in:
The economist (London) 213, November 28, 1964, p. 982.
Library journal 89, October 1, 1964, p. 3751.
New York review of books 453, January 28, 1965, p. 1.
Spectator (London), January 22, 1965, p. 108.
Tablet (London), December 26, 1964, p. 1467.   289

Kennedy, John F.
The wisdom of JFK. Ed. by T.S. Settel. 1st ed. New York, Dutton, 1965, 128p.
Reviewed in:
ALA booklist & subscription books bulletin 61, April 15, 1965, p. 768.
Christian century 82, March 31, 1965, p. 400.
Library journal 90, March 15, 1965, p. 1335.   290

1966

Kennedy, John F.
John F. Kennedy on education. Ed. by William T. O'Hara. New York, Teachers College Press, Columbia University, 1966, 305p.
Reviewed in:
Choice 3, December 1966, p. 934.
Harvard educational review 36, Summer 1966, p. 374.
Instructor 76, January 1967, p. 11.
Journal of American history 53, September 1966, p. 421.
Journal of higher education 38, January 1967, p. 57.

Library journal 91, May 1,
1966, p. 2330.
Social studies 58, October
1967, p. 219. 291

Kennedy, John F.
Kennedy and the press, the
news conferences. Ed. & annotated by Harold W. Chase
& Allen H. Lerman. New
York, Crowell, 1966, 555p.
Reviewed in:
ALA booklist & subscription
books bulletin 61, May 15,
1965, p. 899.
Bulletin 33, Virginia Kirkus
Service, April 1, 1965,
p. 406.
Choice 2, July 1965, p. 335.
Journal of American history
52, December 1965, p. 675.
Library journal 90, May 15,
1965, p. 2277. 292

Kennedy, John F.
Memorable quotations of
John F. Kennedy. Comp. by
Maxwell Meyersohn. New York,
Crowell, 1966, 314p.
Reviewed in:
ALA booklist & subscription
books bulletin, July 1965,
p. 47.
Catholic library world 37,
December 1965, p. 263.
Choice 2, February 1966,
p. 849.
Library journal 90, October
15, 1965, p. 4350. 293

Presidential Campaign: 1960
Books

1959
Sevareid, Eric, ed.
Candidates 1960: behind the
headlines in the presidential
race. New York, Basic Books,
1959, 369p. 294

1960
Gantman, Vladimir I.
SShA: vneshniaia politika i
vybory 1960 goda. Moscow,
Izd-vo In-ta Mezhdunarodnykh
Otnoshenii, 1960, 79p.
(USA: Internal politics and
elections, 1960.) 295

Kennedy, John F.
The great debates, numbers 1-4; John F. Kennedy
vs. Richard M. Nixon, September 26, 1960-October 21,
1960. [n.p.] 1960? 156p. 296

Kennedy, John F.
Speeches delivered during
the 1960 presidential campaign. Washington, Democratic National Committee,
1960- 297

Martin, Ralph G. & Ed Plaut
Front runner, dark horse.
New York, Doubleday, 1960,
473p. 298

Schlesinger, Arthur M.
Kennedy or Nixon: does it
make any difference? New
York, Macmillan, 1960,
51p. 299

1961
David, Paul T., et al, eds.
The presidential election
and transition, 1960-1961.
Washington, Brookings Institution, 1961, 353p. 300

Kennedy, John F.
The joint appearances of

Senator John F. Kennedy and Vice President Richard M. Nixon and other 1960 presidential campaign presentations. Washington, U.S. Senate Committee on Commerce (Freedom of communications, 3), 1961, 699p. 301

Michener, James A.
Report of the county chairman. New York, Random House, 1961, 310p. 302

U.S. 87th Congress. Senate. Report 994 (part 3) Freedom of communications. Final report of Committee on Commerce prepared by its Subcommittee on Communications pursuant to S. Res. 305, 86th Congress: pt. 3, Joint appearances of Senator John F. Kennedy and Vice President Richard M. Nixon and other 1960 campaign presentations; December 11, 1961. Title on cover is: Joint appearances of Senator John F. Kennedy and Vice President Richard M. Nixon, presidential campaign of 1960. (Item 1008-A). Washington, 1961, 699p. 303

White, Theodore M.
The making of the president, 1960. New York, Atheneum Pub., 1961, 400p. 304

1962
Katz, E., & J.J. Feldman
The debates in the light of research: a survey of surveys (In Kraus, Sidney, ed. The great debates: background, perspective, effects. Bloomington, Indiana University Press, 1962, p. 173-223). 305

Kraus, Sidney, ed.
The great debates: background, perspective, effects. Bloomington, Indiana University Press, 1962, 439p. 306

Rutgers, the State University, New Brunswick, N.J. Eagleton Institute of Politics
Inside politics: the national conventions, 1960. Ed. by Paul Tillet. Dobbs Ferry, Oceana Pubs., 1962, 281p. 307

Seltz, H.A. & R.D. Yoakam
Production diary of the debates (In Kraus, Sidney, ed. The great debates: background, perspectives, effects. Bloomington, Indiana University Press, 1962, p. 73-126). 308

1964
Christopherson, Edmund
Westward I go free; the story of JFK in Montana. Missoula, Earthquake Press, 1964, 88p. 309

1965
Hechler, Kenneth W.
West Virginia memories of President Kennedy. Baltimore, 1965, 37p. 310

Articles

1958
Cort, J.O.
"Kennedy for President?" Sign 38, August 1958, p.

John Fitzgerald Kennedy

26-29. 311

Phillips, Cabell
"How to be a Presidential Candidate." New York times magazine, July 13, 1958, p. 11. 312

1959

Rovere, Richard H.
"Kennedy's Last Chance to be President." Esquire (LI: 4), April 1959, p. 63. 313

Collins, Frederic W.
"Timber (Presidential)." The nation 188, April 4, 1959, p. 291-293. 314

McNutt, James
"Presidential Prospects." Manila, Saturday times magazine (14: 40), May 17, 1959, p. 42-46; (14: 41) May 24, 1959, p. 42-45. 315

Coffin, Tristram
"John Kennedy: Young man in a Hurry." Progressive 23, December 1959, p. 10-18. 316

Cater, Douglass
"The Cool eye of John F. Kennedy." The reporter 21, December 10, 1959, p. 27-32. 317

"The Next President? 1. John F. Kennedy." London, The economist, December 12, 1959, p. 1067-1068. 318

1960

Balough, Thomas
"The Lessons of Kennedy's Campaign." London, New statesman & nation (60: 1543), 1960, p. 510-511. 319

Deuerlein, E.
"John Fitzgerald Kennedy: Porträt eines Präsidentschaftskandidaten." Cologne, Die politische meinung (48: 5), 1960, p. 51-58.
("John Fitzgerald Kennedy: Portrait of a Presidential Candidate.") 320

Joesten, Joachim
"Mr. Kennedy Will ins Weisse Haus." Wiesbaden, Das neue journal (9: 13), 1960, p. 14-16.
("Mr. Kennedy Wants the White House.") 321

Lachelier, B.B.G.
"Un Candidat Démocrate à la Présidence, le Sénateur Kennedy." Paris, Revue des deux mondes 2, 1960, p. 225-234.
("A Democratic Candidate for the Presidency, Senator Kennedy.") 322

Remus, Bernhard
"John Kennedy Bleibt Heisser Favorit." Zürich, Weltwoche (28: 1382), 1960, p. 9.
("John Kennedy Remains a Heavy Favorite.") 323

Sommer, Theo
"John F. Kennedy auf dem Marsch zum Weissen Haus." Hamburg, Die zeit (15: 30), 1960, p. 3.
("John F. Kennedy on the March to the White House.") 324

Hessler, William H.
"How Kennedy Took Ohio." The reporter 22, March 3, 1960, p. 21-22.   325

Davis, T.N.
"Cabots and Kennedys." America 102, March 5, 1960, p. 675-677.   326

"Kennedy and Humphrey Answer Five Key Questions." New leader 43, March 28, 1960, p. 3-7.   327

Fischer, John
"Editor's Easy Chair: Hard Questions for Senator Kennedy." Harper's magazine 220, April 1960, p. 16, 21-23.   328

"Presidential Candidates on Federal Aid." Phi Delta Kappan 41, April 1960, p. 13-14.   329

Alsop, Stewart
"Battle of Wisconsin: Kennedy vs. Humphrey." Saturday evening post 232, April 2, 1960, p. 19-21.   330

Abogadie, Benjamin A.
"I met Senator Jack Kennedy." Manila, Philippines free press (53: 18), April 30, 1960, p. 16.   331

"Kennedy's Biography, Voting Record, Stands on Issues." Congressional quarterly weekly report 18, May 13, 1960, p. 843-851.   332

"John Kennedy: Who he is and What he Stands for." U.S. news & world report 48, May 30, 1960, p. 75-78.   333

"Caresses and Brass Knuckles: Nixon vs. Kennedy." Time 75, June 27, 1960, p. 15-17.   334

Cooke, Alistair
"Senator John Kennedy: Bostonian Phlegm." Manchester, Manchester guardian, July 8, 1960, p. 8.   335

"Johnson, Kennedy, Symington Votes Compared." Congressional quarterly weekly report 18, July 8, 1960, p. 1195-1196.   336

Cooke, Alistair
"Has Mr. Kennedy the Gift of Leadership? Reflections on the U.S. Democratic Convention." London, Listener, July 21, 1960, p. 96-97.   337

"Kennedy: his Probable Course as Nominee and President." Congressional quarterly weekly report 18, July 22, 1960, p. 1303-1304.   338

Margolis, H.
"Democratic Convention: Kennedy's Brain Trust and his Plans for a new New Deal." Science 132, July 22, 1960, p. 209-211.   339

"This is Where Kennedy Stands: Position on Major Issues." U.S. news & world report 49, July 25, 1960, p. 65.   340

"America's next President?" Manila, This week (15: 31), July 31, 1960, p. 44-45. 341

Craig, G. M.
"Luck of the Irish: New Style." Toronto, Canadian forum 40, August 1960, p. 103-104. 342

Cater, Douglass
"The Tide in the Affairs of John F. Kennedy." The reporter 23, August 4, 1960, p. 16-18. 343

Novak, Robert D.
"Kennedy's Braintrust: More Professors Enlist, but they Play Limited Policy-Making Role." Wall Street journal 156, August 4, 1960, p. 1. 344

"John F. Kennedy: Democratic Challenger is a Catholic Intellectual." Manila, Sunday times magazine (16: 1), August 14, 1960, p. 29-31. 345

Meyer, Karl E.
"The Men Around Kennedy." Progressive 24, September 1960, p. 18-20. 346

"The Next President." London, The economist 196, September 17, 1960, p. 1078-1079. 347

Burns, James MacG.
"Kennedy's Liberalism." Progressive 24, October 1960, p. 18-21. 348

"Here's Where the Candidates Stand." Farm journal 84, October 1960, p. 36-37. 349

Kennedy, John F.
"Special Statement Prepared for the NEA Journal." NEA journal 49, October 1960, p. 10. 350

Kerr, H. P.
"John F. Kennedy." Quarterly journal of speech 46, October 1960, p. 241-242. 351

Osborne, John
"Economics of the Candidates." Fortune 62, October 1960, p. 136-141. 352

West, A. P.
"Mr. Kennedy woos the Peasants." Toronto, Saturday night 75, October 1, 1960, p. 31-32. 353

Fisher, J.
"How to be a President." Toronto, Financial post 54, October 8, 1960, p. 6. 354

Johnson, Gerald W.
"In Search of Identity: First TV Debate." New republic 143, October 10, 1960, p. 20. 355

"Presidential Candidates' Voting Records Compared." Social legislation information service, October 10, 1960, p. 449-454. 356

"Complete Text of October 7 (1960) Nixon-Kennedy Debate." Congressional quarterly weekly report 18, October 14, 1960, p. 1715-1721. 357

"Complete Text of October 13, 1960 Kennedy-Nixon Radio-TV Debate." Congressional quarterly weekly report 18, October 21, 1960, p. 1753-1759. 358

"Farm Problems Examined, Candidates' Stands Explained." Congressional quarterly weekly report 18, October 21, 1960, p. 1739-1746. 359

"What is the Kennedy Solution for Strikes?" Saturday evening post 233, October 22, 1960, p. 10. 360

"Complete Text of October 21, 1960 Nixon-Kennedy TV-Radio Debate." Congressional quarterly weekly report 18, October 28, 1960, p. 1795-1801. 361

Gatbonton, Juan T.
"Nixon vs. Kennedy." Manila, Saturday times magazine (16: 12), October 30, 1960, p. 10-11. 362

"Etats-Unis." Montreal, Relations 239, November 1960, p. 298-299.
("United States.") 363

Mailer, Norman
"Superman Comes to the Supermart." Esquire (LIV: 5), November 1960, p. 119. 364

Pacis, Vicente A.
"Our Stakes in the American Elections." Manila, Weekly graphic (27: 20), November 2, 1960, p. 18-19. 365

Pacis, Vicente A.
"We and the American Presidential Elections." Manila, Weekly graphic (27: 19), November 2, 1960, p. 6-7, 29. 366

"Debating the Great Issue: Symposium." The nation 191, November 5, 1960, p. 342-347. 367

"Democratic Victory." Business week, November 12, 1960, p. 25-34. 368

Margolis, H.
"John Kennedy's New Frontier: the Margin was Narrow but the Responsibility is Clear." Science 132, November 18, 1960, p. 1472-1473. 369

"The American Election (Editorial)." Manila, American Chamber of Commerce of the Philippines journal (36: 12), December 1960, p. 587-588. 370

Harding, H. F.
"John F. Kennedy, Campaigner." Quarterly journal of speech 46, December 1960, p. 362-364. 371

1961

"220 Kennedy Campaign Policy Declarations Listed." Congressional quarterly weekly report 19, January 13, 1961, p. 132-142. 372

Ty, Leon O.
"Before he Became President." Manila, Philippines free press (54: 3), January

21, 1961, p. 32, 57.   373

Roucek, Joseph S.
"The Vote of the American Minorities in President Kennedy's 1960 Election." Pavia, Politico (26: 1), March 1961, p. 33-42.   374

Barrow, Lionel C.
"Factors Related to Attention to the First Kennedy-Nixon Debate." Journal of broadcasting (5: 3), Summer 1961, p. 229-238.   375

1962
Katz, Elihu & Jacob J. Feldman
"The Kennedy-Nixon Debates: a Survey of Surveys." Studies in public communication 4, Autumn 1962, p. 127-163.   376

1963
Mullen, James J.
"Newspaper Advertising in the Kennedy-Nixon Campaign." Journalism quarterly (40: 1), Winter 1963, p. 3-11.   377

Powell, James G.
"An Analytical and Campaign Study of the Persuasion of Kennedy and Nixon in the 1960 Campaign." Dissertation abstracts (24: 6), December 1963, p. 2620-2621.   378

Rider, John R.
"The Charleston Study: The Television Debate of the Nixon-Kennedy Debates." Dissertation abstracts (24: 6), December 1963, p. 2621.   379

1964
David, Fernando S.
"Boston: the Week Kennedy was Elected President." Manila, Philippines free press (57: 44), October 31, 1964, p. 30, 32, 34, 63.380

1965
Gray, Charles H.
"A Scale Analysis of the Voting Records of Senators Kennedy, Johnson and Goldwater, 1957-1960." American political science review 59, September 1965, p. 615-621.   381

1966
Polisky, Jerome B.
"The Kennedy-Nixon Debates: a Study in Political Persuasion." Dissertation abstracts (26: 9), March 1966, p. 5598.   382

Sherman, Roger N.
"An Objective Analysis of Language Choice in the First Nixon-Kennedy Debate." Dissertation abstracts (27: 2), August 1966, p. 549A.   383

Religion
Books

1965
Kennedy, John F.
The faith of JFK. Edited by T.S. Settel. New York, Dutton, 1965, 127p.   384

Kennedy, John F.
Quotations from the Scriptures. New York, Catholic Family Library, 1965, unpaged. (Excerpts from Presi-

dent Kennedy's public speeches which contain quotations from the Bible. Includes the eulogy delivered by Bishop P. M. Hannan at the President's funeral.) 385

Kennedy, John F.
Religious views of President John F. Kennedy in his own words. Comp. by Nicholas A. Schneider. St. Louis, Herder, 1965, 125p. 386

1967

Fuchs, Lawrence H.
John F. Kennedy and American Catholicism. Des Moines, Meredith, 1967, 271p. 387

Nielsen, Svend A.
John F. Kennedys livssyn. Copenhagen, Samleren, 1967, 111p.
(The religion of John F. Kennedy.) 388

Articles

1958

Fuchs, Lawrence H.
"A Catholic as President?" America 99, September 13, 1958, p. 620-623. 389

1959

"Katholiken: Kirche über Kennedy." Hamburg, Der spiegel (13: 52), 1959, p. 63-64.
("Catholics: the Church Above Kennedy.") 390

"Catholics, Protestants, '60." Newsweek 53, June 1, 1959, p. 25-28. 391

"Kennedy, Katholik im Weissen Haus?" Hamburg, Der spiegel (13: 10), 1959, p. 55-58.
("Kennedy, a Catholic in the White House?") 392

Knebel, Fletcher
"Democratic Forecast: a Catholic in 1960." Look 23, March 3, 1959, p. 13-17. 393

"A Catholic for President?" Commonweal 69, March 6, 1959, p. 587-588. 394

"On Questioning Catholic Candidates." America 100, March 7, 1959, p. 651. 395

Johnson, Gerald W.
"Religious Issue." New republic 140, March 9, 1959, p. 10. 396

"Catholic Editors Comment on Senator Kennedy's Church and State Position." Catholic messenger 77, March 12, 1959, p. 1. 397

"Third Degree for Catholics." America 100, March 14, 1959, p. 675. 398

"Aftermath of the Kennedy Statement: Church and State." Commonweal 69, March 20, 1959, p. 635-636. 399

Cogley, J.
"Catholic for President?" Commonweal 69, March 27, 1959, p. 667. 400

Sheerin, J.B.
"Senator Kennedy Vetoes aid to Catholic Education." Catholic world 189, April 1959, p. 4-7. 401

"Catholic Candidates Discussed." America 101, April 4, 1959, p. 30. 402

Bridge, John F.
"Kennedy and Catholicism." Wall Street journal 154, July 30, 1959, p. 6. 403

"Will the Religious Issue Stop Kennedy in '60?" U.S. news & world report 47, September 7, 1959, p. 42-43. 404

Cooke, Alistair
"A Catholic as U.S. President?" London, Listener, December 10, 1959, p. 1021-1022. 405

Poling, Daniel A.
"Interfaith Chapel: Dr. Poling, Senator Kennedy and an Invitation Declined, with Senator Kennedy's Side of the Episode." U.S. news & world report 47, December 21, 1959, p. 64-65. 406

Clark, Albert
"The Catholic Issue: it Balks Kennedy's Drive for top Spot, but Second Place is Mandatory." Wall Street journal 154, December 29, 1959, p. 41-42. 407

1960
Dietz, T.
"Ein Rom-Katholik im Weissen Haus." Bonn, Alt-Katholischekirchenzeitung (new series), 1960, p. 76-77.
("A Roman Catholic in the White House.") 408

Kyle, K.
"Religion and the not-so-new Nixon." London, Time & tide (41: 45), 1960, p. 1321-1322. 409

Renshaw, P.
"The Religious Spectre." London, Time & tide (41: 40), 1960, p. 1147-1148. 410

Schubert, John
"Der Katholik Kennedy." Zürich, Orientierung 24, 1960, p. 163-164.
("The Catholic Kennedy.") 411

"Church and State." New republic 142, January 25, 1960, p. 3-5. 412

"Senator Kennedy and the Chapel." Commonweal 71, January 29, 1960, p. 479-480. 413

Sheerin, John B.
"How Fair are Kennedy's Critics?" Catholic world 190, March 1960, p. 333-336. 414

"Question of Bigotry." New republic 142, April 25, 1960, p. 5. 415

Kennedy, John F.
"I am not the Catholic Candidate for President: Address, April 21, 1960." U.S. news & world report 48, May 2, 1960, p. 90-92. 416

Hoyt, R. & J. Cogley
"An Exchange of Views."
Commonweal 72, June 10,
1960, p. 280-281. 417

"Religion and the Elections."
Commonweal 72, July 22,
1960, p. 365. 418

"Test of Religion." Time 76,
September 26, 1960, p. 21-
22. 419

"Both Sides of the Catholic Issue..." U.S. news & world report 49, September 26, 1960, p. 74-78. 420

Kennedy, John F.
"Statement on Separation of Church and State." Catholic messenger 78, September 29, 1960, p. 3. 421

Duff, E. & L. d'Apollonia
"La Grande Crainte." Montreal, Relations 238, October 1960, p. 254-256.
("The Great Fear.") 422

Duff, Edward
"Church and State in the American Environment." Manila, Philippine studies (8:4), October 1960, p. 717-743. 423

Fuchs, Lawrence H.
"The Religious Vote: Fact or Fiction?" Catholic world 192, October 1960, p. 9-14. 424

Turnbull, John W.
"The Clergy Faces Mr. Kennedy." The reporter 23, October 13, 1960, p. 32-34. 425

Kirwan, M.J.
"Vote for Kennedy: Debate."
Ave Maria 92, October 22,
1960, p. 6. 426

Sterling, Claire
"The Vatican and Kennedy."
The reporter 23, October 27,
1960, p. 26-27. 427

Hoyt, Robert G.
"Opinion Worth Noting."
America 104, November 5,
1960, p. 171-175. 428

"The Pope to Mr. Kennedy: text of the Telegram of Congratulation." Tablet
214, November 19, 1960,
p. 1076. 429

Hoyt, Robert G.
"Kennedy, Catholicism and the Presidency." Jubilee 8,
December 1960, p. 13-15. 430

"Privacy and Presidents; in Church?" America 104,
December 10, 1960, p. 366. 431

Folliard, E.T.
"President at Mass; Reply."
America 104, December 31,
1960, p. 413. 432

1961

"Präsident Kennedy und die Katholische Kirche." Basel, Kirchenblatt für die reformierte Schweiz 117,
1961, p. 154-155.
("President Kennedy and the Catholic Church.") 433

Heller, Ernst
"Kennedy, Präsident Kath-

olik." Vienna, Der grosse entschluss 16, February 1961, p. 218-221.
("Kennedy, Catholic President.") 434

LaFarge, J.
"Open Letter to President Kennedy on Religious Belief and Personal Religion." America 104, February 18, 1961, p. 670-671. 435

"Mr. Kennedy and the Cardinals." Tablet 215, March 11, 1961, p. 218-219. 436

"Bishops vs. Kennedy." America 105, May 20, 1961, p. 309. 437

1962

Scholl, Klaus
"Präsident Kennedy als Katholik." Cologne, Begegnung 17, 1962, p. 67-68.
("President Kennedy as a Catholic.") 438

"Church and President: Kennedy's First Year." America 106, January 13, 1962, p. 461-462. 439

"Church and President." Time 79, January 19, 1962, p. 58. 440

"The Church and Mr. Kennedy: Catholic and non-Catholic Evaluations." Commonweal 75, February 9, 1962, p. 503-504. 441

"Church and President: Replies." America 106, March 3, 1962, p. 718-719. 442

Baldwin, D.
"How Protestants View Kennedy now." Information 76, April 1962, p. 2-7. 443

Riemer, George
"Kennedy's Priests." Good housekeeping 155, July 1962, p. 49-51. 444

Sigel, R.S.
"Race and Religion as Factors in the Kennedy Victory in Detroit, 1960." Journal of Negro education 31, Fall 1962, p. 436-447. 445

Riemer, G.
"President at Mass in Middleburg." Catholic digest 26, October 1962, p. 16-22. 446

1963

"American in Rome: Why was the Visit to Pope Paul Unofficial?" America 109, July 13, 1963, p. 32. 447

"Pope John's Influence?" Sign 43, August 1963, p. 33-34. 448

"The President and the Priest: Father LaFarge." Interracial review 36, December 1963, p. 230-231. 449

1964

Bauman, A.
"Kennedy the Catholic." St. Joseph magazine 65, January 1964, p. 2. 450

Cogley, J.
"Kennedy the Catholic." Commonweal 79, January 10, 1964, p. 422-424. 451

Blake, E.
"Kennedy and his Church."
Catholic mind 62, March 1964,
p. 40-41.   452

Fleming, T.
"Kennedy the Catholic."
U.S. Catholic 30, August 1964,
p. 53-54.   453

"Does Kennedy Prove Catholic
School Failure?" Catholic
messenger 82, October 29,
1964, p. 8.   454

Joyce, J.
"Would Catholic Education
Have Spoiled JFK?" Critic 23,
October-November 1964, p.
21-23.   455

Wagner, J.
"Unwarranted Criticism: Fr.
J. Joyce on Catholic Schools
and J.F. Kennedy." Catholic
educator 35, November 1964,
p. 226-227.   456

1965
"The World and God and JFK"
(condensed from Religious
news service, August, 1964).
Catholic digest 29, January
1965, p. 21-23.   457

Smith, W.D.
"Alfred E. Smith and John
F. Kennedy: the Religious Is-
sue During the Presidential
Camgaigns of 1928 and 1960."
Dissertation abstracts (25:9),
March 1965, p. 5449.   458

1967
Fuchs, Lawrence H.
"John F. Kennedy and American Catholicism (Review by
James O'Gara)." Commentary
44, November 1967, p. 105-
108.   459

Inauguration
Books

1961
Frost, Robert
Dedication and the Gift out-
right, by Robert Frost. The
inaugural address of John
Fitzgerald Kennedy, Washing-
ton, D.C., January the twen-
tieth, 1961. New York,
Printed for the friends of
the Spiral Press, 1961, 19p.
                                                 460
U.S. President
The inaugural addresses of
the American Presidents,
from Washington to Kennedy.
Annotated by Davis Newton
Lott. New York, Holt, Rine-
hart & Winston, 1961, 299p.
                                                 461
Washington, D.C. Inaugural
Committee, 1961
The inauguration of John
Fitzgerald Kennedy and Lyn-
don Baines Johnson, January
20, 1961. Edward H. Foley,
chairman. Samuel C. Bright-
man, director of publicity.
John P. Anderson, editor.
Washington, 1962? unpaged.
                                                 462
Washington, D.C. Inaugural
Committee, 1961
Official program, inaugural
ceremonies of John F. Ken-
nedy, thirty-fifth President of
the United States and Lyndon
B. Johnson, thirty-seventh
Vice President of the United
States. Washington, D.C.,

January 20, 1961. Washington, 1961, 63p. 463

1964

U.S. General Services Administration. National Archives & Records Service Preliminary inventory (162) of records of 1961 inaugural committee (record group 274); compiled by Marion M. Johnson. National Archives publication 65-5. Washington, 1964, 18p. 464

Articles

1961

"Der Wortlaut der Rede des neuen Amerikanischen Präsidenten zu seiner Amtseinführung am 20. Januar 1961." Dortmund, Junge kirche 22, 1961, p. 112-114. ("Inaugural Address of the new U.S. President, January 20, 1961.") 465

Lewis, J. & T. Goth
"Black Tie and Shovel." Variety 221, January 25, 1961, p. 2. 466

"Texts of Three Songs Written for Ball: One for Mrs. Kennedy, One for Mrs. Johnson, and One for the New Frontier." New York times, January 12, 1961, p. 19, columns 1, 2. 467

"Let us Begin: Reflections on the Inaugural Address." New republic 144, January 30, 1961, p. 3-4. 468

"Inauguration: 1961." Commonweal 73, February 3, 1961, p. 471-472. 469

"Will you Join (in Answering the Inaugural Call?)" Ave Maria 93, February 4, 1961, p. 16. 470

Kennedy, John F.
"Inaugural Address of John Fitzgerald Kennedy: Delivered at the Capitol, Washington, D.C., January 20, 1961." Dept. of State bulletin 44, February 6, 1961, p. 175-176. 471

"The Eisenhower Farewell and the Kennedy Inaugural Addresses (Editorial)." Manila, American Chamber of Commerce of the Philippines journal (37: 2), February 1961, p. 53-54. 472

"A Great Inaugural." America 104, February 4, 1961, p. 586. 473

Schnell, Betty
"I saw the Kennedy Inauguration." Manila, Weekly graphic (27: 35), February 22, 1961, p. 10-11, 24. 474

Sicat, A.C.
"JFK's Inaugural Address and its Bearing on Social Work." Manila, Social work (6: 2), February 1961, p. 524. 475

Twomey, L.J.
"A Struggle Against the Common Enemies of Man: Kennedy's Inaugural Address, Pius XII, and Internationalism." Queen's work 53, April 1961, p. 8-9. 476

Wolfarth, D. L.
"John F. Kennedy in the Tradition of Inaugural Speeches." Quarterly journal of speech 47, April 1961, p. 124-132. 477

1964
Kennedy, John F.
"The Inaugural Address: English Text and Latin Translation." Classical folia 18, 1964, p. 46-53. 478

Addresses
and Official Messages
of John F. Kennedy

(See also International Affairs in the Career of John F. Kennedy, and Public Papers)

Note: Transcripts of President Kennedy's press conferences may be found in the weekly issues of Congressional Quarterly Weekly Report, 1961-64.

Books

1947
Kennedy, John F.
Supplemental minority report (In U.S. Congress. House. Committee on Education and Labor. Labor-management relations act, 1947... report to accompany H.R. 3020. Washington, G.P.O., 1947, p. 113-115).
(80th Congress, first session. House Report 245.) 479

1953
Kennedy, John F.
The economic problems of New England; a program for Congressional action. Remarks in the Senate of the United States. Washington, G.P.O., 1953, 96p.
(At head of Title: Congressional record. Proceedings and debates of the 83d Congress, first session. Includes texts of speeches delivered May 18, 20, 25, 1953.) 480

1956
Kennedy, John F.
Address of Senator John F. Kennedy. The National book award, New York City, February 7, 1956. New York? 1956, 9p. 481

1957
Kennedy, John F.
The outlook for labor and social legislation. Washington, American Federation of Labor & Congress of Industrial Organizations, Industrial Union Dept., 1957, 14p. 482

1958
Kennedy, John F.
Meet the press: guest, the Honorable John F. Kennedy, United States Senator. Washington, Merkle Press, 1958, 9p. 483

1959
Kennedy, John F.
The Kennedy-Ives Bill (In Baird, A.C., ed. Representative American speeches, 1958-1959. New York, Wilson, 1959, p. 79-83). 484

1960

Kennedy, John F.
Meet the press: guest, Senator John F. Kennedy, Democrat, Massachusetts. Washington, Merkle Press, 1960, 11p. 485

Kennedy, John F.
Meet the press: guests, Senator John F. Kennedy, Democrat of Massachusetts; Senator Lyndon B. Johnson, Democrat of Texas; Senator Stuart Symington, Democrat of Missouri. Washington, Merkle Press, 1960, 35p. 486

Kennedy, John F.
The role of the President (In Baird, A.C., ed. Representative American speeches: 1959-1960. New York, Wilson, 1960, p. 123-130). 487

1961

Kennedy, John F.
Address of President-elect of the United States John F. Kennedy, delivered to a joint convention of the two Houses of the General Court of Massachusetts, January 9, 1961. Boston, Wright & Potter Print. Co., 1961, 5p.
(Massachusetts, General Court, 1961. House of Representatives document 2660.) 488

Kennedy, John F.
An address by John F. Kennedy, delivered before the Massachusetts Legislature, January 9, 1961...Stamford, Conn., The Overbrook Press, 1961, 2p. 489

Kennedy, John F.
Il discorso d'insediamento del president John F. Kennedy. Testo inglese e italiano. Washington, 20 gennaio, 1961 (The inaugural address of President John F. Kennedy. English and Italian texts. Washington, January 20, 1961). Rome, U.S.I.S. (Tip. Apollon), 1961, 21p. 490

Kennedy, John F.
Il messaggio di Kennedy sullo stato dell'Unione. Washington 30 gennaio 1961 (Italian translation of Kennedy's State of the Union Message, January 30, 1961). Rome, U.S.I.S. (Tip. Apollon), 1961, 21p. 491

Kennedy, John F.
The inaugural address of John Fitzgerald Kennedy, President of the United States, delivered at the Capitol, Washington, January 20, 1961. Worcester, Achille J. St. Onge, 1961, 30p. 492

Kennedy, John F.
The new frontier (In Baird, A.C., ed. Representative American speeches, 1960-1961. New York, Wilson, 1961, p. 7-14). 493

Kennedy, John F.
Nyû furontia. 3v. Tokyo, Jiji Tsûshin Sha, 1961?-1963.
(New frontiers. Translations into Japanese of messages and addresses). 494

Kennedy, John F.
Política económica de Norteamérica. Madrid, Oficina de Coordinación y Programación Económica, 1961, 214p.
(Translation of State of the Union message, January 1961). 495

Kennedy, John F.
President John F. Kennedy (In Handlin, Oscar, ed. American principles and issues: the national purpose. New York, Holt, Rinehart & Winston, 1961, p. 3-8). 496

Kennedy, John F.
President Kennedy speaks. Washington, U.S. Information Service, 1961? 130p. 497

Kennedy, John F.
Statement by the Honorable John F. Kennedy, President of the United States. (In National Industrial Conference Board. Government-Industry Conference, 1961. New York, 1961, p. 31-35). 498

U.S. 87th Congress. House of Representatives
State of the Union, address of President of United States delivered before joint session of Senate and House of Representatives, January 30, 1961. Item 996. Washington, 1961, 11p. (Document 73). 499

U.S. 87th Congress. House of Representatives
Urgent national needs, address of President of United States delivered before joint session of Senate and House of Representatives relative to urgent national needs, May 25, 1961. Item 996. Washington, 1961, 14p. (Document 174). 500

U.S. President, 1961- (Kennedy)
American agriculture; message relative to American agriculture. Washington, G.P.O., 1961, 10p.
(87th Congress, first session. House of Representatives document 109). 501

U.S. President, 1961- (Kennedy)
American education. Message...Washington, G.P.O., 1961, 6p.
(87th Congress, first session. House of Representatives document 92). 502

U.S. President, 1961- (Kennedy)
Budget and fiscal policy; message relative to budget and fiscal policy. Washington, G.P.O., 1961, 10p.
(87th Congress, first session. House of Representatives document 120). 503

U.S. President, 1961- (Kennedy)
Ethical conduct in the Government; message... Washington, G.P.O., 1961, 10p.
(87th Congress, first session. House of Representatives document 145). 504

U.S. President, 1961- (Kennedy)
Federal pay-as-you-go

highway program. Message relative to our Federal pay-as-you-go highway program. Washington, G.P.O., 1961, 9p.
(87th Congress, first session. House of Representatives document 96). 505

U.S. President, 1961- (Kennedy)
Health program. Message transmitting recommendations relating to a health program. Washington, G.P.O., 1961, 7p.
(87th Congress, first session. House of Representatives document 85). 506

U.S. President, 1961- (Kennedy)
Inaugural address. Discurso inaugural. Washington, Servicio de Información de los Estados Unidos, 1961, 9p. 507

U.S. President, 1961- (Kennedy)
The inaugural address of John Fitzgerald Kennedy, President of the United States, delivered at the Capitol, Washington, January 20, 1961. Haarlem, Holland, Joh. Enschede en Zonen, 1961, 30p. 508

U.S. President, 1961- (Kennedy)
Inaugural address of John Fitzgerald Kennedy, Thirty-fifth President of the United States of America, Washington, D.C., Inauguration Day: 20 January 1961. Los Angeles? 1961? 13p.
(Printed by students of "The Art of the Book" at the Press of the Department of Fine Arts, University of Southern California). 509

U.S. President, 1961- (Kennedy)
...Increases in limitations on administrative expenses for the Federal Home Loan Land Bank Board; communication from the President of the United States, transmitting amendments to the budget for the fiscal year 1962 involving increases in limitations on administrative expenses in the amount of $245,000 for the Federal Home Loan Bank Board... Washington, G.P.O., 1961, 2p.
(87th Congress, first session. House of Representatives document 168). 510

U.S. President, 1961- (Kennedy)
Natural resources. Message relative to our natural resources. Washington, G.P.O., 1961, 9p.
(87th Congress, first session. House of Representatives document 94). 511

U.S. President, 1961- (Kennedy)
Our Federal tax system. Message relative to our Federal tax system. Washington, G.P.O., 1961, 15p.
(87th Congress, first session. House of Representatives document 140). 512

U.S. President, 1961- (Ken-

nedy)
Our nation's housing. Message relative to our nation's housing. Washington, G.P.O., 1961. 9p.
(87th Congress, first session. House of Representatives document 102). 513

U.S. President, 1961- (Kennedy)
President's tax message along with principal statement, detailed explanation, and supporting exhibits and documents, submitted by Secretary of the Treasury Douglas Dillon, in connection with the President's recommendations contained in his message on taxation at hearings conducted by Committee on Ways and Means, House of Representatives, May 3, 1961. Washington, G.P.O., 1961, 295p. 514

U.S. President, 1961- (Kennedy)
Program to restore momentum to the American economy. Message relative to proposing a program to restore momentum to the American economy. Washington, G.P.O., 1961, 14p.
(87th Congress, 1st session. House of Representatives document 81). 515

U.S. President, 1961- (Kennedy)
Recommendations relating to our defense budget: message ...Washington, G.P.O., 1961, 14p.
(87th Congress, first session. House of Representatives document 123). 516

U.S. President, 1961- (Kennedy)
Regulatory agencies of our Government; message relative to the regulatory agencies of our Government. Washington, G.P.O., 1961, 10p.
(87th Congress, first session. House of Representatives document 135). 517

U.S. President, 1961- (Kennedy)
...Reorganization plan no. 1 of 1961. Message from the President of the United States, transmitting Reorganization plan no. 1 of 1961, prepared in accordance with the Reorganization Act of 1949 as amended, and providing for reorganization in the Securities and Exchange Commission...Washington, G.P.O., 1961, 3p.
(87th Congress, first session. House of Representatives document 146). 518

U.S. President, 1961- (Kennedy)
...Reorganization plan no. 2 of 1961; message from the President of the United States transmitting Reorganization plan no. 2 of 1961, prepared in accordance with the Reorganization Act of 1949, as amended, and providing for reorganization in the Federal Communications Commission ...Washington, G.P.O., 1961, 3p.
(87th Congress, first ses-

John Fitzgerald Kennedy

sion. House of Representatives document 147). 519

U.S. President, 1961- (Kennedy)
...Reorganization plan no. 3 of 1961; message from the President of the United States, transmitting Reorganization plan no. 3 of 1961, prepared in accordance with the Reorganization in the Civil Aeronautics Board...Washington, G.P.O., 1961, 3p.
(87th Congress, first session. House of Representatives document 152). 520

U.S. President, 1961- (Kennedy)
...Reorganization plan no. 4 of 1961; message from the President of the United States, transmitting Reorganization plan no. 4 of 1961, prepared in accordance with the Reorganization Act of 1949, as amended, and providing for reorganization in the Federal Trade Commission...Washington, 1961, 3p.
(87th Congress, first session. House of Representatives document 159). 521

U.S. President, 1961- (Kennedy)
...Reorganization plan no. 5 of 1961; message from the President of the United States, transmitting reorganization plan no. 5 of 1961, prepared in accordance with the Reorganization Act of 1949, as amended, and providing for reorganization in the National Labor Relations Board... Washington, G.P.O., 1961, 3p.
(87th Congress, first session. House of Representatives document 172). 522

U.S. President, 1961- (Kennedy)
...Reorganization plan no. 7 of 1961. Message from the President of the United States transmitting Reorganization plan no. 7 of 1961, prepared in accordance with the Reorganization Act of 1949, as amended, and providing for the reorganization of maritime functions...Washington, G.P.O., 1961, 6p.
(87th Congress, first session. House of Representatives document 187). 523

U.S. President, 1961- (Kennedy)
Special feed grain program for 1961. Communication transmitting a draft of a proposed bill entitled "A Bill to provide a special program for feed grains for 1961." Washington, G.P.O., 1961, 5p.
(87th Congress, first session. Senate document 12). 524

U.S. President, 1961- (Kennedy)
Special message on regulatory agencies. Washington, 1961, 10p. 525

U.S. President, 1961- (Kennedy)
Urgent national needs; address of the President of the United States delivered be-

fore a joint session of the Senate and the House of Representatives relative to urgent national needs. Washington, G.P.O., 1961, 14p. (87th Congress, first session. House of Representatives document 174). 526

U.S. President, 1961- (Kennedy)
Urgent national needs; a special message to Congress by President Kennedy, May 25, 1961. Publication 7204. Washington, Dept. of State, 1961, 37p. 527

U.S. President, 1961-1963 (Kennedy)
Executive communication transmitting draft legislation to provide for aid to social and economic development under an act for international development and to provide for military assistance under an International peace and security act. Washington, G.P.O., 1961, 5p. 528

1962
Kennedy, John F.
Uchû kaihatsu (United States aeronautics and space activities, translated into Japanese by Hideo Sekino). Tokyo, Jiji Tsûshin-sha, 1962, 226p. 529

U.S. 87th Congress. House of Representatives
State of the Union, address by President of United States delivered before joint session of Senate and House of Representatives, January 11, 1962. (Item 996). Washington, 1962, 13p. (Document 251). 530

U.S. President, 1961- (Kennedy)
Agriculture program; message relative to an agriculture program. Washington, G.P.O., 1962, 10p. (87th Congress, 2d session. House of Representatives document 323). 531

U.S. President, 1961- (Kennedy)
Consumers' protection and interest program: message. Washington, G.P.O., 1962, 10p. (87th Congress, 2d session. House of Representatives document 364). 532

U.S. President, 1961- (Kennedy)
Educational program. Message relative to an educational program. Washington, G.P.O., 1962, 10p. (87th Congress, 2d session. House of Representatives document 330). 533

U.S. President, 1961- (Kennedy)
Health program; message. Washington, G.P.O., 1962, 11p. (87th Congress, 2d session. House of Representatives document 347). 534

U.S. President, 1961- (Kennedy)
Our conservation program. Message relative to our conservation program. Washington, G.P.O., 1962, 10p.

(87th Congress, 2d session, 1962. House of Representatives document 348). 535

U.S. President, 1961-1963 (Kennedy)
President Kennedy's message on conservation to the Congress of the United States, March 1, 1962. Washington, Dept. of the Interior, 1962, 18p. 536

U.S. President, 1961-1963 (Kennedy)
Preventing conflicts of interest on the part of advisers and consultants to the Government; the President's memorandum of February 9, 1962. Washington, G.P.O., 1962, 14p. 537

U.S. President, 1961-1963 (Kennedy)
Public assistance and welfare program: message. Washington, G.P.O., 1962, 7p.
(87th Congress, 2d session. House of Representatives document 325). 538

U.S. President, 1961-1963 (Kennedy)
Reorganization plan no. 1 of 1962. Message transmitting Reorganization plan no. 1 of 1962, which would create a Department of Urban Affairs and Housing, and the appointment by the President of a Secretary of Urban Affairs. Washington, 1962, 6p.
(87th Congress, 2d session. House of Representatives document 320). 539

U.S. President, 1961-1963 (Kennedy)
Reorganization plan no. 2 of 1962. Message transmitting Reorganization plan no. 2 of 1962, providing for certain reorganizations in the field of science and technology. Washington, G.P.O., 1962, 7p.
(87th Congress, 2d session. House of Representatives document 372). 540

U.S. President, 1961-1963 (Kennedy)
Salary increases for Federal service employees. Message relative to salary increases for Federal service employees. February 20, 1962. Washington, G.P.O., 1962, 7p.
(87th Congress, 2d session. House of Representatives document 344). 541

U.S. President, 1961-1963 (Kennedy)
The transportation system of our nation. Message relative to the transportation system of our nation. Washington, G.P.O., 1962, 17p.
(87th Congress, 2d session. House of Representatives document 384). 542

U.S. President, 1961-1963 (Kennedy)
President Kennedy's message on conservation to the Congress of the United States. Washington, U.S. Dept. of the Interior; for sale by the Superintendent of Documents, G.P.O., 1962, 18p. 543

1963
Kennedy, John F.
The Amherst address delivered by President Kennedy, October 26, 1963. New York? 1963, 19p.
(Designed and printed by the Typography Workshop of the Cooper Union Art School in the fall of 1963 at the Ram Press.) 544

Kennedy, John F.
Neither the fanatics nor the faint-hearted; the tour leading to the President's death and the two speeches he could not give. Ed. by John H. Jenkins. Austin, Pemberton Press, 1963, 15p. 545

Kennedy, John F.
President John F. Kennedy's tale ved American University, Washington, D.C. (Translation of President John F. Kennedy's address at American University, Washington, D.C., June 1963). Oslo, U.S. Information Service 1963, 10p. 546

Kennedy, John F.
Remarks; celebration of 30th anniversary of TVA, Muscle Shoals, May 18, 1963. Knoxville, Tennessee Valley Authority, 1963, 8p. 547

U.S. 88th Congress. House of Representatives
State of the Union, address of President of United States delivered before joint session of Senate and House of Representatives, January 14, 1963. (Item 996). Washington, 1963, 11p. (Document 1). 548

U.S. President
State of the Union; highlights of American history, momentous events and policies in the political, social, and military life of the Nation as revealed in the State-of-the-Union and war messages of the Presidents: George Washington to John F. Kennedy. Selected & edited by Edward Boykin. New York, Funk & Wagnalls Co., 1963, 501p. 549

U.S. President, 1961-1963 (Kennedy)
Agricultural program; message transmitting recommendations relative to an agricultural program. Washington, G.P.O., 1963, 8p.
(88th Congress, first session. House of Representatives document 55). 550

U.S. President, 1961-1963 (Kennedy)
Civil rights; message. Washington, G.P.O., 1963, 11p.
(88th Congress, first session. House of Representatives document 75). 551

U.S. President, 1961-1963 (Kennedy)
Civil rights. Message relative to civil rights, and a draft of a bill to enforce the constitutional right to vote, to confer jurisdiction upon the District Courts of the United States to provide injunctive relief against discrimination in public accomodations, to authorize the At-

John Fitzgerald Kennedy

torney-General to institute suits to protect constitutional rights in education, to establish a community relations service, to extend for four years the Commission on Civil Rights, to prevent discrimination in Federally assisted programs, to establish a Commission on Equal Employment Opportunity and for other purposes. Washington, 1963, 24p. 552

U.S. President, 1961-1963 (Kennedy)
Elderly citizens of our Nation; message...Washington, G.P.O., 1963, 16p.
(88th Congress, first session. House of Representatives document 72). 553

U.S. President, 1961-1963 (Kennedy)
Health program; message... Washington, G.P.O., 1963, 11p.
(88th Congress, first session. House of Representatives document 60). 554

U.S. President, 1961-1963 (Kennedy)
Manpower report of the President and a Report on manpower requirements, resources, utilization, and training, by the U.S. Dept. of Labor. Transmitted to the Congress March 1963. Washington, for sale by the Superintendent of Documents, G.P.O., 1963, 204p. 555

U.S. President, 1961-1963 (Kennedy)
Mental illness and mental retardation; message...Washington, G.P.O., 1963, 14p.
(88th Congress, first session. House of Representatives document 58). 556

U.S. President, 1961-1963 (Kennedy)
Our nation's youth; message...Washington, G.P.O., 1963, 10p.
(88th Congress, first session. House of Representatives document 66). 557

U.S. President, 1961-1963 (Kennedy)
President's 1963 tax message along with principal statement, technical explanation, and supporting exhibits and documents, submitted by Secretary of the Treasury Douglas Dillon, in connection with the President's recommendations contained in his 1963 message on taxation at hearings conducted by Committee on Ways and Means, House of Representatives. Washington, for sale by the Superintendent of Documents, G.P.O., 1963, 527p. 558

U.S. President, 1961-1963 (Kennedy)
Program for education. Message relative to a proposed program for education, and a draft of a bill to strengthen and improve educational quality and educational opportunities in the Nation. Washington, G.P.O., 1963, 68p.
(88th Congress, first session. House of Representa-

tives document 54). 559

U.S. President, 1961-1963 (Kennedy)
Railroad-labor dispute; message...Washington, G.P.O., 1963, 32p.
(88th Congress, first session. House of Representatives document 142). 560

U.S. President, 1961-1963 (Kennedy)
Revision of our tax structure; message transmitting recommendations relative to a revision of our tax structure. Washington, G.P.O., 1963, 24p.
(88th Congress, first session. House of Representatives document 43). 561

U.S. President, 1961-1963 (Kennedy)
John Fitzgerald Kennedy's Thanksgiving proclamation for 1963. Washington, G.P.O., 1964, 4p.
(88th Congress, 2d session. House document 186). 562

U.S. President, 1961-1963 (Kennedy)
President's special message on balance of payments, along with H.R. 8000, and description and technical explanation of H.R. 8000, the "Interest equalization tax act of 1963." Prepared and submitted by the Department of the Treasury to the Committee on Ways and Means, House of Representatives. Washington, G.P.O., 1963, 56p. 563

U.S. President, 1961-1963 (Kennedy)
Preventing conflicts of interest on the part of special Government employees; the President's memorandum of May 2, 1963. Washington, G.P.O., 1963, 19p. 564

1964

Kennedy, John F.
Kennedy daitôryô enzetsushû (Major speeches, translated into Japanese by Kuroda Kazuo). Tokyo, Hara Shobô, 1964, 231p. 565

Kennedy, John F.
Moral crisis; the case for civil rights, as stated by John F. Kennedy, and others. Minneapolis, Gilbert Pub. Co., 1964, 185p. 566

Kennedy, John F.
The place of the artist in society. Spoken at the dedication of the Robert Frost Library, Amherst College, Mass. New York? 1964? 11p.
(Issued as holiday greetings, December 1964, by Ann and Joseph Blumenthal). 567

Kennedy, John F.
President Kennedy speaks. Eine ausw. aus seinem Reden. Mit Einf. und Anm. von Hildegard Gauger und Hermann Metzger. Tübingen, Niemeyer, 1964, 64p.
(President Kennedy speaks. A selection of his speeches, with introduction and notes by Hildegard Gauger and Hermann Metzger). 568

Kennedy, John F.
Statements, July-November, 1963. Washington, U.S. Information Service, 1964, 165p.
569

Kennedy, John F.
Taler og kortere officielle ytringer (Statements and official messages, translated into Danish by Inger Kofod-Hansen). Copenhagen, Berlingske Forlag, 1964, 184p.
570

U.S. 88th Congress. House of Representatives
Inaugural address of John Fitzgerald Kennedy, President of United States, Washington, D.C., January 20, 1961 (poster suitable for framing). Washington, for sale by Superintendent of Documents, 1964. (Document 190).
571

U.S. House of Representatives
John Fitzgerald Kennedy's Thanksgiving proclamation for 1963; January 29, 1964. Washington, House Document Room, 1964, 4p. (Document 186). 572

U.S. President, 1961-1963 (Kennedy)
The first book edition of John F. Kennedy's inaugural address. Proclamation by Lyndon B. Johnson. Illustrated by Leonard Everett Fisher. New York, F. Watts, 1964, 39p.
573

U.S. President, 1961-1963 (Kennedy)
The unspoken speech of John F. Kennedy at Dallas, November 22, 1963. [n.p.] Privately printed for Stanley Marcus, 1964, 12p.

(Colophon: Carl Hertzog, El Paso, Texas).
574

1965
Kennedy, John F.
Inaugural address, January 20, 1961 (In The chief executive, inaugural addresses of the presidents of the United States from George Washington to Lyndon B. Johnson... New York, Crown Pub., 1965, p. 301-306).
575

Kennedy, John F.
Kennedy and the press: news conferences. Edited & annotated by Harold W. Chase & Allen H. Lerman. New York, Crowell, 1965, 555p.
576

U.S. President, 1961-1963 (Kennedy)
The inaugural address, by John F. Kennedy, January 20, 1961. Washington, Colortone Press, 1965? unpaged.
577

U.S. President, 1961-1963 (Kennedy)
Inaugural address of John Fitzgerald Kennedy, 35th President of the United States, delivered at the Capitol, Washington, January 20, 1961. Los Angeles, 1965, 47p.
(Handset, printed and bound by Bela Blau, Los Angeles, California, January 20, 1965).
578

Articles

1953

Kennedy, John F.
"Floor Beneath Wages is Gone." New republic 128, July 20, 1953, p. 14-15. 579

1957

Kennedy, John F.
"The Intellectual and the Politician." (Speech Delivered at Commencement Exercises, Harvard University, June 14, 1956.) In Representative American speeches 1956-1957, New York, Wilson, 1957, p. 165-172. 580

Costelloe, M.J.
"Interview with Senator Kennedy of Massachusetts." Queen's work 49, May 1957, p. 16-17. 581

Kennedy, John F.
"Citadel, the Story of the U.S. Senate, by William S. White (Book Review)." Vanderbilt law review 10, June 1957, p. 874. 582

Kennedy, John F.
"Congressional Lobbies: a Chronic Problem Reexamined." Georgetown law journal 45, Summer 1957, p. 535-567. 583

1958

Kennedy, John F.
"Union Racketeering: the Responsibility of the Bar." American Bar Association journal 44, May 1958, p. 437. 584

Kennedy, John F.
"When the Executive Fails to Lead." The reporter 19, September 18, 1958, p. 14-17. 585

1959

Kennedy, John F.
"What's Happening to our Cities?" Voice of St. Jude 24, February 1959, p. 6-8. 586

Kennedy, John F.
"Labor's Goal for America's Future." Labor leader 22, August 1959, p. 1. 587

Kennedy, John F.
"Ethical Practices and the Bar." Work 17, December 1959, p. 10. 588

1960

Kennedy, John F.
"Presidential Race will Test a Very Great Unspoken Issue." Alabama municipal journal 17, January 1960, p. 5-7. 589

Kennedy, John F.
"Let's get rid of College Loyalty Oaths." Coronet 47, April 1960, p. 88-94. 590

Kennedy, John F.
"The Challenge of Education." Wisconsin journal of education 93, October 1960, p. 7. 591

Kennedy, John F.
"Special Report to Businessmen. Business Policies in the Next Administration, by Richard M. Nixon." Executive 5, October 1960,

p. 3-8. 592

"An Interview with John Kennedy." Bulletin of the atomic scientists 16, November 1960, p. 346-347. 593

"The New Frontier, an Exclusive Interview with Senator John F. Kennedy." Catholic world 192, November 1960, p. 80-86. 594

1961
"Message du Président Kennedy sur les Problèmes Agricoles." Paris, Problèmes économiques 697, 1961, p. 23-24.
("President Kennedy's Message on Agricultural Problems.") 595

Kennedy, John F.
"Address Before the National Press Club, Washington, D.C., January 14, 1960." Progressive 25, January 1961, p. 14-16. 596

Kennedy, John F.
"How Does the President Feel About Counties?" County officer 26, January 1961, p. 6-8. 597

Kennedy, John F.
"President-elect Kennedy Talks About our Children." Parents' magazine 36, January 1961, p. 35. 598

Kennedy, John F.
"John F. Kennedy on Libraries: Letter to Minneapolis Public Library." Wilson library bulletin 35, January 1961, p. 338. 599

Kennedy, John F.
"Television and Politics." Manila, Mirror, January 21, 1961, p. 12. 600

Kennedy, John F.
"How Soft are the Americans?" Manila, Mirror, January 28, 1961, p. 14-15. 601

Kennedy, John F.
"America's new Frontier." Manila, Mirror, February 11, 1961, p. 6-7. 602

Kennedy, John F.
"Text of President's February 13, 1961 Speech to Business Leaders." Congressional quarterly weekly report 19, February 17, 1961, p. 291-292. 603

Kennedy, John F.
"Political Philosophy and Economic Policy." Manila, Mirror, February 25, 1961, p. 18-19. 604

"Words from the White House." Commonweal 73, March 10, 1961, p. 600-601. 605

Kennedy, John F.
"Text of Kennedy's Address Before the American Society of Newspaper Editors, Washington, D.C., April 20, 1961." Wall Street journal 157, April 21, 1961, p. 14. 606

Kennedy, John F.
"President Calls for 'Self-

Restraint' in News Coverage." Congressional quarterly weekly report 19, May 5, 1961, p. 776-777. 607

Kennedy, John F.
"JFK on the First 100 Days." Newsweek 57, May 8, 1961, p. 23-24. 608

Kennedy, John F.
"The President's Message on Education to the Congress of the United States, February 20, 1961." Current history 40, June 1961, p. 364-367. 609

Kennedy, John F.
"What my Illness Taught me." Catholic digest 25, July 1961, p. 17-19. 610

Kennedy, John F.
"We Need Your Help: Remarks at Meeting of National Academy of Sciences, April 1961." Bulletin of the atomic scientists 17, October 1961, p. 344. 611

Kennedy, John F.
"The Public Responsibility of Educated men: October 12, 1961." Dept. of State bulletin 45, October 30, 1961, p. 699-701. 612

1962
Kennedy, John F.
"Public Assistance and Welfare Program: Message, February 1, 1962." Wall Street journal 159, February 2, 1962, p. 10. 613

Kennedy, John F.
"The Next 25 Years: 'I Possess Many Hopes'." Manila, Sunday times magazine (17: 26), February 11, 1962, p. 18-23. 614

Kennedy, John F.
"The President's Plan for Expanding Recreation Areas ...March 1, 1962." Recreation 55, April 1962, p. 181-183. 615

Kennedy, John F.
"Essential Nourishment (Statement on National Library Week)." Publishers weekly 181, April 16, 1962, p. 76. 616

Kennedy, John F.
"The Role of the University in the Building of a Flexible World Order: Address, March 23, 1962." Dept. of State bulletin 46, April 16, 1962, p. 615-618. 617

Kennedy, John F.
"President Kennedy Proposes More Federal Services for Consumers: Excerpt from Message, March 15, 1962." Consumer bulletin 45, May 1962, p. 33. 618

Kennedy, John F.
"Text of Kennedy's Speech at Auto Workers' Union Convention." Wall Street journal 159, May 9, 1962, p. 20. 619

Kennedy, John F.
"What Happened when Kennedy met with Businessmen ...May 21, 1962." U.S. news & world report 52, June 4, 1962, p. 100-102.620

Kennedy, John F.
"Transcript of the President's Economic Address at Yale." Congressional quarterly weekly report 20, June 15, 1962, p. 1039-1042. 621

Kennedy, John F.
"Transcript of the President's Independence Day Address, July 4, 1962." Congressional quarterly weekly report 20, July 13, 1962, p. 1189-1190. 622

Kennedy, John F.
"Myth and Reality in our National Economy: June 11, 1962." Vital speeches 28, July 15, 1962, p. 578-581. 623

Kennedy, John F.
"Vigor we Need." Sports illustrated 17, July 16, 1962, p. 12-14. 624

Kennedy, John F.
"The Strength and Style of our Navy Tradition." Life 53, August 10, 1962, p. 79, 83-84. 625

Kennedy, John F.
"Why There Will be no tax cut now." U.S. news & world report 53, August 27, 1962, p. 74-78. 626

"Text of President Kennedy's Conference with Business Editors." Congressional quarterly weekly report 20, October 5, 1962, p. 1814-1817. 627

"Not Lost Forever: the President's Pulaski Day Speech." America 107, October 27, 1962, p. 943. 628

"Complete Text of President's Mid-term Review on Radio-TV: December 17, 1962 of his First two Years in Office..." Congressional quarterly weekly report 20, December 21, 1962, p. 2277-2284. 629

1963

Kennedy, John F.
"Gravest U.S. Problem Rising Unemployment: Digest of State of the Union Message." Toronto, Monetary times annual, 1963, p. 16. 630

"Präsident Kennedy in Berlin." Bonn, Bulletin des Presse- und Informationsamtes der Bundes-regierung 110, 1963, p. 981-990.
("President Kennedy in Berlin.") 631

Kennedy, John F.
"Special Tax Message to Congress." Amsterdam, Bulletin for international fiscal documentation 17, January-February 1963, p. 1. 632

Kennedy, John F.
"Text of the President's Economic Report to Congress, January 21, 1963." Congressional quarterly weekly report 21, January 25, 1963, p. 98-104. 633

Kennedy, John F.
"The Private Letters of John F. Kennedy. Edited by

R.G. Deindorfer. " Good Housekeeping 156, February 1963, p. 74-75. 634

Kennedy, John F.
"Exactly how Kennedy Would cut and Raise Taxes: Summary of Message to Congress, January 24, 1963." U.S. news & world report 54, February 4, 1963, p. 46-53. 635

Kennedy, John F.
"For a Community-Centered MH Program." Quezon City, Focus on mental health (12: 2), March-April 1963, p. 4-6. 636

Kennedy, John F.
"Transcript of the President's February 25, 1963 Address to the Bankers Association." Congressional quarterly weekly report 21, March 1, 1963, p. 282-286. 637

Kennedy, John F.
"Text of President Kennedy's March 13, 1963 Speech to Advertising Council." Congressional quarterly weekly report 21, March 15, 1963, p. 337-339. 638

Kennedy, John F.
"President's March 23, 1963 Chicago Speech on Unemployment." Congressional quarterly weekly report 21, March 29, 1963, p. 460-462. 639

Kennedy, John F.
"President Cites Importance of Home Improvement Programs." American home 66, April 1963, p. 85. 640

Kennedy, John F.
"Transcript of President's Speech to Newspaper Editors." Congressional quarterly weekly report 21, April 26, 1963, p. 668-672. 641

Kennedy, John F.
"Transcript of President Kennedy's Economic Speech before CED." Congressional quarterly weekly report 21, May 17, 1963, p. 779-782. 642

Kennedy, John F.
"Special Message on our Nation's Youth." American journal of Catholic youth work 4, Summer 1963, p. 3-5. 643

Kennedy, John F.
"Message from the President of the United States Relative to Mental Illness and Mental Retardation." American psychologist (18: 6), June 1963, p. 280-289. 644

Kennedy, John F.
"President Kennedy's Address to Mayors on Race Relations: Remarks of the President, June 9, 1963, at U.S. Conference of Mayors, Honolulu, Hawaii." Congressional quarterly weekly report 21, June 14, 1963, p. 974-976. 645

Kennedy, John F.
"President Kennedy's Radio-TV Address on Civil Rights." Congressional quarterly weekly report 21, June 14, 1963, p. 970-971. 646

Kennedy, John F.
"Supersonic Transport." Congressional quarterly weekly report 21, June 21, 1963, p. 1035. 647

Kennedy, John F.
"Race Problem: the Solution as the President sees it: Address, June 11, 1963." Vital speeches 29, July 1, 1963, p. 546-547. 648

Kennedy, John F.
"New Social Order: Address, June 25, 1963." Vital speeches 29, July 15, 1963, p. 578-581. 649

"Text of President Kennedy's August 1, 1963 Press Conference." Congressional quarterly weekly report 21, August 9, 1963, p. 1412-1415. 650

"Transcript of President Kennedy's August 20, 1963 Press Conference." Congressional quarterly weekly report 21, August 23, 1963, p. 1485-1488. 651

Kennedy, John F.
"What Business can do for America." Nation's business 51, September 1963, p. 29-31. 652

"Transcript of President Kennedy's September 2, 1963 TV Interview by Newscaster Walter Cronkite." Congressional quarterly weekly report 21, September 6, 1963, p. 1547-1548. 653

Kennedy, John F.
"Transcript of President Kennedy's September 18, 1963 Tax Address." Congressional quarterly weekly report 21, September 20, 1963, p. 1666-1669. 654

"Transcript of President Kennedy's September 12, 1963 Press Conference." Congressional quarterly weekly report 21, September 20, 1963, p. 1661-1664. 655

Kennedy, John F.
"Prosperity Insurance: Address, September 18, 1963." Vital speeches 29, October 1, 1963, p. 738-740. 656

"Text of President Kennedy's October 9, 1963 Press Conference." Congressional quarterly weekly report 21, October 11, 1963, p. 1777-1781. 657

"Text of President Kennedy's October 31, 1963 Press Conference." Congressional quarterly weekly report 21, November 8, 1963, p. 1921-1924. 658

Kennedy, John F.
"Time the U.S. Caught up: Excerpt from Address to the National Council of Senior Citizens, June 13, 1963." New republic 149, November 9, 1963, p. 35. 659

Kennedy, John F.
"Address by President Ken-

nedy, November 18, 1963, to
the Florida State Chamber of
Commerce, Tampa, Florida."
Congressional quarterly weekly
report 21, November 22, 1963,
p. 2055-2058. 660

"Text of President Kennedy's
November 14, 1963 Press
Conference." Congressional
quarterly weekly report 21,
November 22, 1963, p.
2047-2050. 661

Kennedy, John F.
"Last Speeches of the Late
President Kennedy." Congressional quarterly weekly report
21, November 29, 1963, p.
2091-2096. 662

"Some Events and Extracts
from Speeches During the
Three-Year Presidency of
John F. Kennedy." London,
Illustrated London news 243,
November 30, 1963, p. 896-897. 663

"In Last Speech to Labor...
Kennedy Appeals for job
Growth to Promote Freedom." The American federationist 70, December
1963, p. 8-9. 664

Kennedy, John F.
"Filmed Statement in Observance of Bill of Rights Day."
New York times, November
13, 1963, p. 35, column 1.
665

Kennedy, John F.
"President Kennedy's Messages to ZOA Annual Conventions: 1961, 1962, and 1963:
Excerpts." American Zionist
54, December 1963, p. 3.
666

Kennedy, John F.
"Goal of the United States:
Text of Speech to Have Been
Delivered Before the Dallas
Citizens Council, Dallas,
Texas, November 22, 1963."
Vital speeches 30, December
1, 1963, p. 105-107. 667

Kennedy, John F.
"Words of John Fitzgerald
Kennedy: a man Does What
he Must: Quotations from Addresses." Newsweek 62, December 2, 1963, p. 46-47.
668

Kennedy, John F.
"Ideas, Attitudes, Purposes: Gleanings from Writings and Speeches." Saturday
review 46, December 7,
1963, p. 26. 669

1964
Kennedy, John F.
"We Expect Something of
You." American journal of
Catholic youth work 5, Winter 1964, p. 3. 670

Kennedy, John F.
"Forests are Monuments to
Eternity." Land and life 22,
January 1964, p. 5. 671

Kennedy, John F.
"Jewish National Fund"
(excerpt from address). Land
and life 22, January 1964,
p. 3. 672

Kennedy, John F.
"'Except the Lord Keep
the City' (Closing Paragraphs

of Address That was to Have Been Given in Dallas)." Catholic digest 28, February 1964, p. 50. 673

Kennedy, John F.
'On History." American heritage 15, February 1964, p. 2-4. 674

Kennedy, John F.
"Poetry and Power." Atlantic 213, February 1964, p. 53-54. 675

Kennedy, John F.
'Our Commitment to Future Generations." Country beautiful 3, February-March 1964, p. 12-14. 676

Kennedy, John F.
"Late President's Last Reflections on the Arts: Excerpt from Creative America." Saturday review 47, March 28, 1964, p. 16-17. 677

Costelloe, M.
"Interview with Senator Kennedy" (reprint from May 1957 issue). Queen's work 56, May 1964, p. 10-11. 678

1965
"Edilizia d'Abitazione e Sviluppo delle Comunitá: Discorso al Congresso, 9 Marzo 1961 (Excerpt)." Milan, Casabella 294-295, December 1964-January 1965, p. 13.
("Housing Improvement and Community Development: Message to Congress, March 9, 1961: Excerpt)." 679

Schrenk, M.
"John F. Kennedys Botschaft für die Geisteskranken." Wiesbaden, Zeitschrift für sozialreform (11: 7), 1965, p. 381-384.
("John F. Kennedy's Message on the Mentally Ill.") 680

Kennedy, John F.
'Dreamer Wide Awake; Letter." American heritage 16, October 1965, p. 77-81. 681

1966
Kennedy, John F.
"Conversation With President Kennedy. Edited by Stuart Alsop." Saturday evening post 239, January 1, 1966, p. 9. 682

Public Papers
Books

1962
U.S. General Services Administration. Federal Register Office
Public papers of Presidents of United States: John F. Kennedy, 1961, containing public messages, speeches and statements of President, January 20-December 31, 1961. (Item 574-A. GS 4.113: 961).
Washington, 1962, 908p. 683

U.S. President, 1961-1963 (Kennedy)
John F. Kennedy. Containing the public messages, speeches, and statements of the President. 3v. Washington, G.P.O., 1962-64. 684

1963
Kennedy, John F.
Nyū furonchia (Addresses and messages). 2v. Tokyo, Jiji Tsūshin-sha, 1963. 685

U.S. General Services Administration. Federal Register Office
Public papers of Presidents of United States: John F. Kennedy, 1962, containing public messages, speeches and statements of President, January 1-December 31, 1962. (Item 574-A. GS 4.113: 962). Washington, 1963, 1019p. 686

1964
U.S. General Services Administration. Federal Register Office
Public papers of Presidents of United States: John F. Kennedy, 1963, containing public messages, speeches, and statements of the President, January 1 to November 22, 1963. (Item 574-A. GS 4.113: 963). Washington, 1964, 1007p. 687

U.S. Senate
John Fitzgerald Kennedy, compilation of statements and speeches made during his service in Senate and House of Representatives, pursuant to S. Res. 294, 88th Congress (compiled and edited by Doris Whitney). Legislative Reference Service, Library of Congress; Feb. 4, 1964. From Congressional Record, 80th-86th Congress, 1947-60. Washington, for sale by Superintendent of Documents, 1964, 1143p. (Document 79). 688

Domestic Affairs in the Career of John F. Kennedy
Books

1960
Chatelain, Nicolas
Le Président Kennedy; la nouvelle vague à la Maison Blanche. Paris, Plon, 1960, 114p.
(President Kennedy: the new wave in the White House.) 689

Landis, James M.
Report on regulatory agencies to the President-elect, submitted by the chairman of the Subcommittee on Administrative Practice and Procedure to the Committee on the Judiciary of the United States Senate. Washington, G.P.O., 1960, 87p.
(86th Congress, 2d session. Committee print). 690

1961
Crown, James T. & George P. Penty
Kennedy in power. New York, Ballantine Books, 1961, 192p. 691

Joesten, Joachim
Präsident John Fitzgerald Kennedy und seine Regierung. Bad Godesburg, U.S. Information Service, 1961, 48p.
(President John Fitzgerald Kennedy and his administration.) 692

Kluckhohn, Frank L.
America: listen! An honest report to the nation which reveals that the threat to our survival is greater than Americans have been permitted to realize. Derby, Conn., Monarch Books, 1961, 155p. 693

New frontiers of the Kennedy administration; the texts of the Task Force reports prepared for the President. Ed. by M.B. Schanpper. Washington, Public Affairs Press, 1961, 170p. 694

Opotowsky, Stan
The Kennedy government. New York, Dutton, 1961, 208p. 695

1962
Adler, Bill, comp.
Kids' letters to President Kennedy. New York, Morrow, 1962, 160p. 696

Brissaud, André
Les américains de Kennedy. Paris, Eds. de la Table Ronde, 1962, 292p.
(Kennedy's Americans.) 697

Fuller, Helen
Year of trial; Kennedy's crucial decisions. New York, Harcourt, Brace & World, Inc., 1962, 307p. 698

Harris, Seymour E.
The economics of the political parties, with special attention to Presidents Eisenhower and Kennedy. New York, Macmillan, 1962, 382p. 699

Schlamm, William S.
Die jungen Herren der alten Erde; vom neuen Stil der Macht. Stuttgart, Seewald, 1962, 302p.
(The young men of the old earth; about the new style of power.) 700

1963
Goodman, P.
The devolution of democracy (In Gold, Herbert, ed. First person singular: essays for the sixties. New York, Dial Press, 1963, p. 101-126). 701

Kluckhohn, Frank L.
America: listen! An up-to-the-minute report on the chaos in today's Washington. The fumblings of the Kennedy administration. The search for power. The image building. The wielding of influence on business and the press. Completely updated new enlarged edition. Derby, Conn., Monarch Books, 1963, 315p. 702

Molènes, Charles M. de
La carrière du Président Kennedy et la vie politique américaine; contribution à l'étude du personnel gouvernemental et des courants d'opinion dans les Etats-Unis d'aujourd'hui. Paris, Cujas, 1963, 596p.
(The career of President Kennedy and American political life: a contribution to the study of government personnel and currents of opinion in the United States to-

day.) 703

Od Roosevelta ke Kennedy mu.
Prehl. polit. Vývoje USA v letech 1945-1963. 1st ed. Prague, NPL, 1963, 110p.
(From Roosevelt to Kennedy: a survey of the political evolution of the United States, 1945-1963.) 704

Rabinowitch, Eugene I.
Hail and farewell (In his The dawn of a new age; reflections on science and human affairs. Chicago, University of Chicago Press, 1963, p. 171-179). 705

Reifenberg, Jan
Notiert in Washington, 1955-1963. Von Eisenhower zu Kennedy. Stuttgart, Steingrüben Verlag, 1963, 342p.
(Noted in Washington, 1955-1963: from Eisenhower to Kennedy.) 706

Stuart, Roger W.
The thought brigade: America's influential ghosts in government. New York, Obolensky, 1963, 235p. 707

1964
Bishop, James A.
A day in the life of President Kennedy. New York, Random House, 1964, 108p. 708

Cleveland, Harlan
Great power and great diversity; the perceptions and policies of President Kennedy. Washington, Office of Media Services, Bureau of Public Affairs, Dept. of State, 1964, 12p. (Dept. of State publication 7651). 709

Dahlberg, Hans
Den nya horisonten: John F. Kennedys politiska program. Stockholm, Aldus/Bonnier, 1964, 192p.
(The New Frontier: John F. Kennedy's political program.) 710

Gershenson, Alvin H.
Kennedy and big business. Beverly Hills, Book Co. of America, 1964, 256p. 711

Golden, Harry L.
Mr. Kennedy and the Negroes. Cleveland, World Pub. Co., 1964, 319p. 712

Harris, Seymour E.
Economics of the Kennedy years and a look ahead. New York, Harper, 1964, 273p. 713

Lane, Thomas A.
The leadership of President Kennedy. Caldwell, Idaho, Caxton Printers, 1964, 114p. 714

Lehde, Norman B., ed.
When President Kennedy visited Pike County. Milford, Pa., Pike County Chamber of Commerce, 1964? 70p. 715

Mailer, Norman
The presidential papers. New York, Putnam's, 1964, 310p. 716

Rowen, Hobart
The free enterprisers: Kennedy, Johnson and the business establishment. New

York, Putnam's, 1964, 319p. 717

U.S. Senate
Summary of 3-year Kennedy record and digest of major accomplishments of 87th Congress and 88th Congress, 1st session, January 3, 1961-December 30, 1963 together with statement by Mike Mansfield, Senate Majority Leader; December 13, 1963. Washington, Senate Document Room, 1964, 303p. (Document 53). 718

Warren, Sidney
John Fitzgerald Kennedy: unfinished achievement (In his The president as world leader. Philadelphia, Lippincott, 1964, p. 417-430). 719

Westin, Alan F., ed.
The centers of power; 3 cases in American national government. Contributors: Louis W. Koenig, Hugh Douglas Price, and Alan F. Westin. New York, Harcourt, Brace & World, 1964, 160p. 720

1965

Adams, James T. & Jacob E. Cooke
The Kennedy years (The march of democracy, a history of the United States, v. 7). New York, Scribner's, 1965, 168p. 721

Adler, Bill, ed.
John F. Kennedy and the young people of America. New York, McKay, 1965, 146p. 722

Comstock, Jim F.
Pa and Ma and Mister Kennedy. Richwood, W. Va., Appalachian Press, 1965, 128p. 723

Mythology vs. economic knowledge (In Okun, A.M., ed. The battle against unemployment. New York, Norton, 1965, p. 1-5). 724

Roche, John P.
The breakthrough to modernity: the Kennedy legacy and public opinion (In Morgenthau, Hans J., ed. The crossroad papers: a look into the American future. New York, Norton, 1965, p. 258-275). 725

Schlesinger, Arthur M.
A thousand days: John F. Kennedy in the White House. Boston, Houghton, Mifflin, 1965, 1,087p. 726

U.S. 89th Congress (Public Law 274)
S.J. Res. 106, joint resolution to allow showing in United States, Information Agency film John F. Kennedy, years of lightning, day of drums. Approved October 20, 1965. Washington, 1965, 1p. 727

1966

Aragón, Leopoldo
Washington por dentro; la era de Kennedy. Lima, F. Moncloa, 1966, 270p.
(Inside Washington; the Kennedy era.) 728

Di Salle, Michael V.
Second choice. New York, Hawthorn Books, 1966, p.

196-230. 729

Donald, Aida (DiPace), ed.
John F. Kennedy and the new frontier. New York, Hill & Wang, 1966, 264p. 730

Gómez Pérez, Fernando
Boston-Dallas: biografía de John F. Kennedy. Medellín, Eds. Carpel-Antorcha, 1966, 183p.
(Boston-Dallas: biography of John F. Kennedy.) 731

Hanson, Galen A.
A summons for all seasons; an interpretive study of President John F. Kennedy's commencement address at American University, June 10, 1963. Detroit, Harlo, 1966, 64p. 732

Hargrove, Erwin C.
Presidential leadership. New York, Macmillan, 1966, p. 146-151. 733

1967
Galindo Herrero, Santiago
Kennedy y las communicaciones sociales; un trabajo en equipo. Madrid, E70, 1967, 178p.
(Kennedy and social communications; a team effort.) 734

Ions, Edmund S.
The politics of John F. Kennedy. New York, Barnes & Noble, 1967, 228p. 735

Lawrence, Lincoln (pseud.)
Were we controlled? New York, University Books, 1967, 173p. 736

1968
Gromyko, Anatoly
1036 dnei Presidenta Kennedi. Moscow, Izdatel'stvo "Politizdat," 1968, 280p.
(The 1,036 days of President Kennedy.) 737

Wicker, Tom
JFK and LBJ: a study of the influence of personality on politics. New York, Morrow, William & Co., 1968, 286p. 738

Articles

1946
"A Kennedy runs for Congress: the Boston-bred Scion of a Former Ambassador is a Fighting-Irish Conservative." Look 10, June 11, 1946, p. 32, 34-36. 739

1952
"We Agree, Mr. Kennedy." Life 33, August 25, 1952, p. 22. 740

"Lodge's Fight." Newsweek 40, September 1, 1952, p. 19-20. 741

Michelson, Edward J.
"Lodge Dislodged?" The nation 175, October 4, 1952, p. 297-298. 742

Mallan, John P.
"Massachusetts: Liberal and Corrupt." New republic 127, October 13, 1952, p. 10-12. 743

Phillips, Cabell
"The Case History of a Senate Race." New York times magazine, October 26, 1952, p. 10-11. 744

1953
Healy, Philip F.
"The Senate's gay Young Bachelor." Saturday evening post 225, June 13, 1953, p. 26-27. 745

O'Grady, R.
"Massachusetts' Senator Jack." Extension 48, October 1953, p. 13. 746

"Senator Attacks." Newsweek 42, December 21, 1953, p. 69-70..
(Concerning struggle to retain industry in New England.) 747

1954
McConaughy, James L.
"Boy." Life 36, April 19, 1954, p. 114-115. 748

1956
"For Vice President: Democrats with a Chance." Newsweek 47, June 18, 1956, p. 46. 749

Malcolm, Donald F.
"The man who Wants Second Place." New republic 135, July 30, 1956, p. 13-14. 750

"Possible Vice Presidential Nominee's Record: on Senator John F. Kennedy." Congressional quarterly weekly report 14, August 3, 1956, p. 944-947. 751

"Senator Kennedy and the Convention." America 95, September 1, 1956, p. 497. 752

"Kennedy and the South." America 95, September 15, 1956, p. 552. 753

1957
Turner, Russell
"Senator Kennedy, the Perfect Politician." American mercury 84, March 1957, p. 33-40. 754

"Democrat says Party must lead or get left." Life 42, March 11, 1957, p. 164-166. 755

Harris, Eleanor
"The Senator is in a Hurry." McCall's 84, August 1957, p. 44-45. 756

"Most-talked-about Candidate for 1960." U.S. news & world report 43, November 8, 1957, p. 62-64. 757

"The Senator's Conscience." Ave Maria 86, November 16, 1957, p. 4. 758

1958
Roosevelt, Eleanor
"On my own." Saturday evening post 230, March 8, 1958, p. 32-33. 759

Hines, G. F.
"Personalities--U.S.A." Magnificat 101, June 1958, p. 27-28. 760

Wyden, Peter & S. Shaffer
"This is John Fitzgerald Kennedy." Newsweek 51, June 23, 1958, p. 29-30.   761

Kuenster, John
"Whither John F. Kennedy?" Voice of St. Jude 24, July 1958, p. 28-29.   762

Van Camp, John
"What Happened to the Labor Reform Bill." The reporter 19, October 2, 1958, p. 24-28.   763

"Extensive Travel Behind Kennedy Nomination Drive." Congressional quarterly weekly report 16, December 19, 1958, p. 1533-1534.   764

1959
"Senator Kennedy and his Critics: 7 Comments on the Look Article." Commonweal 69, March 20, 1959, p. 645-648.   765

Hanley, J.C.
"Senator Kennedy Faces the Nation." Today 14, April 1959, p. 27-28.   766

Huttlinger, J. & C. Cronan
"Report from the Capital." Jubilee 7, May 1959, p. 2-4.   767

Sheerin, John B.
"Did Kennedy Downgrade Conscience?" Catholic world 189, June 1959, p. 182-184.   768

1960
Araneta-Villasor, Milagros
"I had a Chat with Kennedy." Manila, Weekly graphic (27: 23), November 30, 1960, p. 18-19.   769

"The Best News of 1960." London, Time & tide 41, 1960, p. 1351-1352.   770

Dürrenmatt, Peter
"Die Wahl des Präsidenten der Vereinigten Staaten. Die Wahl und ihre Auswirkungen." Zürich, Reformatio 9, 1960, p. 648-651.
("The Election of the President of the United States of America. The Election and its Consequences.")   771

Kyle, K.
"The Man with 300 Jobs to Fill." London, Time & tide (41: 50), 1960, p. 1528-1532.   772

"Mr. Kennedy Inherits a Recession." London, Banker's insurance 190, 1960, p. 392-395.   773

Radenkovic, G.
"Kenedi, 'sin Nove Epohe'." Novi Sad, Jugoslavia, Letopis matice srpske 386, 1960, p. 503-506.
("Kennedy, son of a new Era.")   774

Silesius, pseud.
"John Fitzgerald Kennedy: 35. Präsident der USA." Recklinghausen, Der Schlesier (12: 46), 1960, p. 1-2.
("John Fitzgerald Kennedy: 35th President of the USA.")   775

Steinitz, Hans
"Tatendurst, Dynamit, In-

itiative." Bad Reichenhall, Europa (12: 11), 1960, p. 6-8. ("Strenuous Activity, Dynamite, Initiative.") 776

Strasser, Rudolf
"John F. Kennedy: eine neue Phase der US-Geschichte?" Vienna, Osterreichische monatshefte (16: 12), 1960, p. 5-7. ("John F. Kennedy: a new Phase of U.S. History?") 777

"USA-Kennedy: Gefährdeter Sieg." Hamburg, Der spiegel 14, 1960, p. 64-66. ("USA-Kennedy: Imperiled Victory.") 778

"Zweiter Roosevelt?" Hamburg, Der spiegel (14: 48), 1960, p. 66-70. ("A Second Roosevelt?") 779

Alsop, Joseph
"A Great Political Talent." Manchester, Manchester guardian, November 14, 1960, p. 16. 780

Kennedy, John F.
"Kennedy Announces First Appointments, Discusses Election: November 10 Press Conference held by President-designate Kennedy at the Hyannis Port, Massachusetts Armory." Congressional quarterly weekly report 18, November 18, 1960, p. 1909-1913. 781

"Kennedy Gets Into Action Fast." Business week, November 19, 1960, p. 39-41. 782

Lerner, Daniel
"Europe's Image of Kennedy: Europeans Imbue the new U.S. President with Their own Hopes, Desires and Aspirations." New leader 43, December 5, 1960, p. 3-6. 783

Rovere, Richard H.
"Letter from Washington." New Yorker 36, November 19, 1960, p. 203-210. 784

"U.S. Election Means Smiles and Frowns in Canada." Toronto, Financial post 54, November 19, 1960, p. 3. 785

"The American Presidency." Tablet 214, November 19, 1960, p. 1059-1060. 786

Pacis, Vicente A.
"The Kennedy Victory and the Philippines." Manila, Weekly graphic (27: 22), November 23, 1960, p. 6-7, 19. 787

Leon, Bernardo de
"Kennedy and the new Leadership." Manila, Mirror, November 26, 1960, p. 6-7. 788

Burns, James MacG.
"Size-up of Kennedy: Interview." U.S. news & world report 49, November 28, 1960, p. 72-76. 789

Folliard, E.T.
"How Kennedy Views Nation's Mood." Nation's business 48, December 1960, p. 27-28. 790

Mencias, Benito
"A Good Look at Kennedy." Quezon City, Philippine educator (15: 7), December 1960, p. 412-414.   791

Gebhart, G.
"No Inflation in the Offing: Careful Appraisal of What we can Expect From Mr. Kennedy." Magazine of Wall Street 107, December 3, 1960, p. 272-274.   792

Gatbonton, Juan T.
"Victory for Kennedy." Manila, Saturday times magazine (16: 17), December 4, 1960, p. 18-21.   793

Warner, R.
"Picture-Conscious President: How Kennedy's Court Photographer Helped win the Election." Editor & publisher 93, December 10, 1960, p. 10-11.   794

Kennedy, John F.
"Kennedy Announces Rusk, Stevenson, Bowles Appointments; partial Transcript of a December 12 Joint News Conference at Palm Beach, Florida by President-designate John F. Kennedy and Dean Rusk, his Appointee as Secretary of State." Congressional quarterly weekly report 18, December 16, 1960, p. 1973-1974.
795

"The President and his Cabinet." Commonweal 73, December 23, 1960, p. 328-329.   796

1961
Landscheidt, Theodor
"Der Wahlsieg des Präsidentschaftskandidaten John Fitzgerald Kennedy." Aalen/Würtemburg, Kosmobiologie 28, 1961, p. 5-7.
("The Election Victory of Presidential Candidate John Fitzgerald Kennedy.")   797

Bendiner, Robert
"Liberals and Lawmakers." London, New statesman & nation (61: 1559), 1961, p. 130-132.   798

Berger, Kurt M.
"Präsident Kennedy." Bad Godesburg, Gemeinschaft und politik 9, 1961, p. 18-21.
("President Kennedy.") 799

Brogan, Denis W.
"The New Frontier." London, Spectator 6927, 1961, p. 433-434.   800

Chatelain, Nicolas
"Un Mandat Ambigu." Paris, Revue de Paris (68: 2), 1961, p. 88-98.
("An Ambiguous Mandate.")
801
Converse, P.E., et al
"John Fitzgerald: Stability and Change in 1960; a Reinstating Election." American political science review 55, 1961, p. 269-281.   802

Eckstein, Günther
"Was ist von Kennedy zu Erwarten?" Cologne, Gewerkschaftliche monatshefte 12, 1961, p. 67-69.
("What can we Expect from

Kennedy?") 803

Gresham, M.
"Wall Street Likes Kennedy."
London, Time & tide (42: 5),
1961, p. 173. 804

"Kenedi na Kormilu Sjedinjenih
Americkih Drzava." Sara-
jevo, Pregled (13: 1), 1961,
p. 187-190.
("Kennedy in Control in the
United States.") 805

"Kennedy, John Fitzgerald."
Current biography, 1961,
p. 241-244. 806

Kyle, K.
"President Kennedy and his
First Congress." London,
Time & tide (42: 4), 1961, p.
124. 807

"Les Conseillers Economiques
du Président Kennedy."
Paris, Problèmes économ-
iques 722, 1961, p. 8-14.
("The Economic Advisers of
President Kennedy.") 808

Martin, Kingsley
"The Kennedy Dilemma."
London, New statesman & nation (62: 1602), 1961, p. 776-
778. 809

Mathoit, André
"La Présidence des Etats-
Unis en 1961." Paris, Revue
française de science politique
(11: 4), 1961, p. 862-905.
("The U.S. Presidency in
1961.") 810

Oppen, Beate R. von
"Kennedy wird nicht Golf
Spielen: Politischer Brief
aus Washington." Freibourg-
im-Breisgau, Wort und wahrheit 16, 1961, p. 63-66.
("Kennedy Won't Play Golf:
Political Letter from Washington.") 811

Osthold, Paul
"Kennedy bei der Arbeit."
Düsseldorf, Der arbeitgeber
13, 1961, p. 191-192.
("Kennedy at Work.") 812

Osthold, Paul
"Roosevelt Redivivus?
Kennedy." Düsseldorf, Der
arbeitgeber 13, 1961, p. 93-
95.
("Roosevelt Revival? Ken-
nedy.") 813

Peeters, Paul L.
"Les Cent Jours de Mr.
Kennedy." Paris, Economie
contemporaine (19: 166),
1961, p. 6-10.
("Mr. Kennedy's 100
Days.") 814

"Präsidentschaft: An Krück-
en." Hamburg, Der spiegel
(15: 26), 1961, p. 43-44.
("The Presidency: on
Crutches.") 815

"Programme Agricole du
Président Kennedy." Paris,
Problèmes économiques
679, 1961, p. 16-17.
("President Kennedy's Farm
Program.") 816

Ruff, G.H.
"Les Huit Premiers Mois
du Président Kennedy."
Paris, La table ronde 165,

1961, p. 89-98.
("President Kennedy's First Eight Months.") 817

Steinitz, Hans
"Der neue Mann Gewinnt Profil." Bad Reichenhall, Europa (12: 3), 1961, p. 2-4.
("The New Man Wins a Profile.") 818

"Weisses Haus: Kein Platz für Amateure." Hamburg, Der spiegel (15: 6), 1961, p. 52-54.
("The White House: no Place for Amateurs.") 819

Wilde, R. de
"Mann kann Kennedys Unerfahrenheit in Agrarsachen Fürchten--nicht aber Seine Untätigkeit." Munich, Agriforum (466: 1), 1961, p. 54-55.
("One can Fear Kennedy's Inexperience in Agricultural Matters, but not his Inaction.") 820

"Zweihundert Tage Kennedy." Cologne, Dokumente 17, 1961, p. 247-252.
("Kennedy's Two Hundred Days.") 821

Leuchtenberg, William E.
"John Fitzgerald Kennedy." Bologna, American review 1, Winter 1961, p. 12-27. 822

Booker, Simeon
"What Negroes can Expect from Kennedy." Ebony 16, January 1961, p. 33-36. 823

Duggan, M.
"World Trends in 1961: Kennedy and the Year Ahead." Queen's work 53, January 1961, p. 3-5. 824

Folliard, E.T.
"Business's Place in Kennedy Plans." Nation's business 49, January 1961, p. 23-24. 825

Hanley, J.C.
"The Great Change-over." Today 15, January 1961, p. 27-28. 826

Healy, Philip F.
"The Kennedy I Know." Sign 40, January 1961, p. 24-26. 827

Lauzon, A.
"Kennedy 'Sauveur de la Tribu'?" Montreal, Cité libre 11, January 1961, p. 10-11.
("Kennedy: Savior of the Nation?") 828

"Man of the Year." View 25, January 1961, p. 5-8. 829

Sanchez Sarto, Manuel
"John F. Kennedy, el Presidente Para una Era Nueva." Mexico City, Cuadernos Americanos (114: 1), January-February 1961, p. 28-48.
("John F. Kennedy, President for a new era.") 830

White, William S.
"High Style in White House Politics." Harper's magazine 222, January 1961, p. 94. 831

Gatbonton, Juan T.
"The Kennedy Team Takes Over." Manila, Saturday times magazine (16: 24), January 2, 1961, p. 18-20. 832

"Kennedy and the Government Power Bloc." Public utilities fortnightly 67, January 5, 1961, p. 36-39. 833

Cooke, Alistair
"The end of a Honeymoon: Coming to Power of Mr. Kennedy." London, Listener 65, January 19, 1961, p. 119-120. 834

Mills, Bert
"President Kennedy: 'Lobbying for the Consumer'." Sales management 86, January 20, 1961, p. 33-37. 835

"Mr. Kennedy Today: the Change in him." Newsweek 57, January 23, 1961, p. 16-20. 836

"The President's Official Family." Manila, Weekly graphic (27: 31), January 25, 1961, p. 58, 60-62, 64. 837

Romulo, Carlos P.
"Why Filipinos Believe in John F. Kennedy." Manila, Weekly graphic (27: 3), January 25, 1961, p. 4-5. 838

"The new Frontier: the United States." Manila, Philippines free press (54: 4), January 28, 1961, p. 3, 71. 839

Pace, Eric D.
"Youth and the 'Kennedy Effect'." New leader 44, January 30, 1961, p. 5-6. 840

Barcella, Ernest
"New Man in the White House..." Today's health 39, February 1961, p. 22-27.
(Concerning the President's health). 841

Delgado, F.
"Nuevo Presidente en Estados Unidos." Madrid, Razón y fé 163, February 1961, p. 131-138.
("New President in the United States.") 842

Kennedy, John F.
"Will Kennedy Walk in Teddy's Path? New President's Statements Indicate he'll Fight to Preserve America's Natural Resources." Parks & recreation 44, February 1961, p. 84-85. 843

"The new President of the United States." Manila, Home, school & community (8: 4), February 1961, p. 6-7. 844

Rovere, Richard H.
"Letter from Washington: Crowded Week for the President." New Yorker 36, February 4, 1961, p. 108-112. 845

"Těžké Neduhy Amerického Zdravotnictvi." Prague, Rudé právo, February 10, 1961, p. 4.
("The Great Defects of U.S. Medical Care.") 846

Schnell, Betty
"Kennedy goes to the White House." Manila, Weekly graphic (27: 34), February 15, 1961, p. 6-7. 847

Ascoli, Max
"The Cool Precision of J.F.K." The reporter 24, February 16, 1961, p. 22. 848

Blackmoore, Colette
"How Russia sees Kennedy: in the Soviet Press." New leader 44, February 27, 1961, p. 15-16. 849

Bilainkin, George
"President Kennedy: 1940 and 1961." London, Contemporary review 199, March 1961, p. 113-119, 141. 850

Craig, G.M.
"Kennedy's First Weeks." Toronto, Canadian forum 40, March 1961, p. 266, 268. 851

Rulli, G.
"Principi di Diritto Naturale nel Programma di J.F. Kennedy." Rome, Civiltá cattólica (112: 1), March 1961, p. 500-505.
("Principles of Natural Law in the Program of John F. Kennedy.") 852

Hoyos, Rubén J. de
"John Fitzgerald Kennedy, President." Buenos Aires, Estudios (49: 522), March-April 1961, p. 105-109. 853

McGrory, Mary
"The President in Person." Progressive 25, March 1961, p. 16-17. 854

"Philosophy of Leadership: Courage, Judgment, Integrity, Dedication." Columbia 41, March 1961, p. 4. 855

"How Kennedy Works: Exclusive Story of the President in Action." U.S. news & world report 50, March 6, 1961, p. 40-49. 856

Kennedy, John F.
"How JFK Looks at Business (Digest of Address)." Toronto, Financial post 55, March 11, 1961, p. 6. 857

Whelan, C.M.
"Only Higher Education, Mr. President? The Mistaken Clarity of Constitutional Grounds." America 104, March 11, 1961, p. 758-760. 858

"The Kennedy Style." London, The economist 198, March 18, 1961, p. 1044-1045. 859

McNaught, K.
"On Understanding Mr. Kennedy." Toronto, Saturday night 76, March 18, 1961, p. 13-15. 860

"V Rozpočtu USA se Počítá s Deficitem." Prague, Rudé právo, March 25, 1961, p. 6.
("In the U.S. Budget a Deficit is Expected.") 861

"This Aid-to-Education Fuss." Ave Maria 93, March 25,

1961, p. 16. 862

Gass, Oscar
"Political Economy and the new Administration." Commentary 31, April 1961, p. 277-287. 863

White, William S.
"Kennedy's Seven Rules for Handling the Press." Harper's magazine 222, April 1961, p. 92-97. 864

Kennedy, John F.
"Message to National Committee for Labor Israel Passover Fete, New York City." New York times, April 3, 1961, p. 25, column 1. 865

Burns, James MacG.
"John Kennedy and his Spectators." New republic 144, April 3, 1961, p. 7. 866

Speaight, R.
"New Look in Washington: a Visitor's Impressions." Tablet 215, April 8, 1961, p. 324-325. 867

Carvel, Robert
"Mr. Gaitskell on Mr. Kennedy." Manila, Saturday times magazine (16: 35), April 9, 1961, p. 38-39. 868

Cogley, J.
"The Presidential Image." New republic 144, April 10, 1961, p. 29-31. 869

Novak, Robert D.
"Reports from home: Congress says Kennedy is Rising in Popularity, but his Program Isn't." Wall Street journal 157, April 12, 1961, p. 1. 870

Moley, Raymond
"FDR-JFK: a Brain Truster Compares 2 Presidents, 2 Programs." Newsweek 57, April 17, 1961, p. 32-34. 871

Knebel, Fletcher
"Kennedy and his Pals." Look 25, April 25, 1961, p. 117-118. 872

Green, Joseph
"The Public Image of President Kennedy." Catholic world 193, May 1961, p. 106-112. 873

Roberts, Edwin A.
"Conservative Kennedy? Midwesterners Believe his 'Liberalism' is Mostly Show." Wall Street journal 157, May 1, 1961, p. 10. 874

Sutherland, J.P.
"How Kennedy Differs from Ike." U.S. news & world report 50, May 1, 1961, p. 68-70. 875

Fogarty, M.P.
"J.F.K.: a British View; anti-Organization Man." Commonweal 74, May 5, 1961, p. 147-148. 876

"How do ad men Rate JFK Regime so far?" Printer's ink 275, May 19, 1961, p. 11-12. 877

Knebel, Fletcher
"Kennedy's Decisions: How he Reaches them." Look 25,

June 20, 1961, p. 27-29. 878

McGrory, Mary
"Learning Process in the White House." America 105, July 1, 1961, p. 480. 879

Travell, Janet (Graeme)
"Latest on Kennedy's Health: Excerpts from News Conference, June 22, 1961." U.S. news & world report 51, July 3, 1961, p. 32-33. 880

Borje, Consorcio
"New Declaration of Freecom." Manila, Weekly graphic (28: 2), July 5, 1961, p. 10-11, 44. 881

Tingson, Gregorio
"My Impressions of President John F. Kennedy." Manila, Philippines free press (54: 30), July 29, 1961, p. 9. 882

Pellerin, J.
"Lettre Ouverte à M. Kennedy." Montreal, Cité libre 12, August-September 1961, p. 19-20.
("Open Letter to Mr. Kennedy.") 883

Burke, V. & F. Eleazar
"How Kennedy gets what he Wants." Nation's business 49, September 1961, p. 96-102. 884

Hutchison, Earl R.
"Kennedy and the Press: the First Six Months." Journalism quarterly (38: 4), Autumn 1961, p. 453-459. 885

"News vs. Security: Excerpts from a Debate Between the President and the Press..." Columbia journalism review, Fall 1961, p. 45-47. 886

"A President's Privacy." America 106, October 21, 1961, p. 66-67. 887

"Kennedy Support: Congress Backs President on 82 percent of 1961 Tests." Congressional quarterly weekly report 19, November 10, 1961, p. 1828-1839. 888

Forbes, M.S.
"Kennedy; so far so Good." Forbes 88, November 15, 1961, p. 11-12. 889

Folliard, E.T.
"JFK Turns the Other Cheek: Forbearance Toward Eisenhower's Criticism." America 106, November 18, 1961, p. 238. 890

Alberse, J.D.
"Please be Lonelier, Mr. President." Friar 16, December 1961, p. 7-11. 891

Burns, James MacG.
"New Size-up of the President: Interview." U.S. news & world report 51, December 4, 1961, p. 44-46. 892

Folliard, E.T.
"Seeds of Doubt and Hate: Kennedy's Attack on Extremists." America 106, December 9, 1961, p. 357. 893

"Harvard, 6; Irish, 6; Irish Background and Anglo-American Education."

America 106, December 9, 1961, p. 358. 894

Duke, Paul
"Kennedy 'Cult': in a Tennessee Town, the President's Stock Climbs High." Wall Street journal 158, December 11, 1961, p. 12. 895

Halle, Louis J.
"Proper Washingtonian." New republic 145, December 11, 1961, p. 9-10. 896

Leon, Bernardo de
"One Year on the new Frontier." Manila, Sunday times magazine (17: 19), December 17, 1961, p. 3-4. 897

"The Columnists JFK Reads Every Morning." Newsweek 58, December 18, 1961, p. 65-67. 898

1962
"L'Administration Kennedy et les Problèmes Economiques." Paris, Problèmes économiques 778, 1962, p. 9-13.
("The Kennedy Administration and Economic Problems.") 899

Chatelain, Nicolas
"L'Equipe Kennedy Fait ses Preuves." Paris, Revue de Paris (69: 12), 1962, p. 14-23.
("The Kennedy Team is put to the Test.") 900

Chatelain, Nicolas
"Nouveau Style à la Maison Blanche." Paris, Revue de Paris (69: 8), 1962, p. 28-38.
("New Style at the White House.") 901

"J.F. Kennedy Comprend-il la Necessité de l'Entreprise Libre?" Paris, Economie (18: 822), 1962, p. 3.
("Does J.F. Kennedy Understand the Needs of Free Enterprise?") 902

"Kennedy's Politics: How to make the Republicans Look Nasty, the GOP Searching for a Response." Science (135: 3502), 1962, p. 414-415. 903

"Le Libéralisme de M. Kennedy Face au Congrès." Paris, Economie (18: 806), 1962, p. 4.
("Mr. Kennedy's Liberalism vis-à-vis Congress.") 904

Meyer, Karl E.
"Bicameral Blues." London, New statesman & nation (63: 1612), 1962, p. 153-154. 905

Meyer, Karl E.
"The Second Year." London, New statesman & nation (63: 1611), 1962, p. 108-109. 906

Meyer, Karl E.
"The Trouble with Kennedy." London, New statesman & nation (64: 1637), 1962, p. 105-106. 907

Mühlen, Norbert
"Kennedy Populärer als Ike." Zürich, Weltwoche (30: 1471), 1962, p. 11.
("Kennedy more Popular

than Ike.") 908

Pächter, Heinz
"Wie Kennedy Regiert."
Cologne, Die politische meinung (75: 7), 1962, p. 72-77.
("How Kennedy Governs.") 909

"President Kennedy Tightens the Rein." London, Times review of industry (16: 185), 1962, p. 172. 910

Rauschning, H.
"Das Erste Jahr John F. Kennedys." Cologne, Blätter für deutsche und internationale politik (7: 2), 1962, p. 106.
("John F. Kennedy's First Year.") 911

Schoenthal, Klaus
"Präsident Kennedys Regierungsform." Stuttgart, Aussenpolitik 13, 1962, p. 246-252.
("President Kennedy's Method of Governing.") 912

"The USA Under Kennedy." London, Political quarterly (33: 2), 1962, p. 109-113. 913

"USA-Stahlpreise: Arrogante Ideen." Hamburg, Der spiegel (16: 17), 1962, p. 48-50.
("U.S. Steel Prices: Arrogant Ideas.") 914

"Wall Streetul şi Presedintele Kennedy." Bucharest, Timpuri, July 31, 1962, p. 5-8.
("Wall Street and President Kennedy.") 915

Craig, G.M.
"Kennedy's First Year."
Toronto, International journal 17, Winter 1961-62, p. 7-16. 916

Kilpatrick, Carroll
"The Kennedy Style and Congress." Virginia quarterly review 39, Winter 1962, p. 1-11. 917

"Monogram on this man's Shirt is J.F.K.: Fashion Report." Esquire 57, January 1962, p. 35-40. 918

Morgenthau, Hans J.
"The Trouble with Kennedy." Commentary 33, January 1962, p. 51-55. 919

Burns, James MacG.
"Kennedy's First Year." The nation 194, January 6, 1962, p. 14-15. 920

"Shaping new Policy Line: President Feels First Year has Taught him Much." Business week, January 6, 1962, p. 15-16. 921

Burns, James MacG.
"Four Kennedys of the First Year." New York times magazine, January 14, 1962, p. 9. 922

Haines, A.B.
"Champion of the New Frontier." Torch 46, February 1962, p. 4-7. 923

White, William S.
"The Kennedy era: Stage 2, the Coming Battle with

Congress." Harper's magazine 224, February 1962, p. 96-97. 924

West, A. P.
"State of the Union: Great Days Ahead." Toronto, Saturday night 77, February 3, 1962, p. 28-29. 925

Leon, Bernardo de
"Kennedy's First Year." Manila, Sunday times magazine (17: 27), February 11, 1962, p. 18-23. 926

"Kennedy's Strategy for Winning Elections, How it Works." U.S. news & world report 52, February 12, 1962, p. 74-76. 927

Roberts, David
"Washington and Kennedy." Manila, Sunday times magazine (17: 28), February 18, 1962, p. 6-9. 928

Meyer, Karl E.
"JFK's Pressmanship." London, New statesman 63, February 23, 1962, p. 253. 929

"Leader Must Lead: Kennedy's View of Presidency." Business week, March 17, 1962, p. 25-27. 930

Robson, W.A. & T.E.M. McKitterick, eds.
"The USA Under Kennedy." London, Political quarterly (33: 2), April-June 1962, p. 109-217. 931

Vile, Maurice J.C.
"The Formation and Execution of Policy in the United States." London, Political quarterly 33, April-June 1962, p. 162-171. 932

Crossman, R.H.S.
"How Kennedy won." London, New statesman 63, April 6, 1962, p. 491-492. 933

"The Kennedy Image: How it's Built." U.S. news & world report 52, April 9, 1962, p. 56-59. 934

Bingham, Worth & Ward S. Just
"The President and the Press." The reporter 26, April 12, 1962, p. 18-23. 935

Wicker, Tom
"Total Political Animal." New York times magazine, April 15, 1962, p. 26. 936

"Steel Sequel: Business, Labor Like to shy from Challenge to President's Policies." Wall Street journal 159, April 16, 1962, p. 1. 937

"Why are Some Liberals Cool to the Kennedy Administration?" Newsweek 59, April 16, 1962, p. 29-31. 938

Cooke, Alistair
"The 'Cold Fury' of President Kennedy." London, Listener 67, April 19, 1962, p. 671-672. 939

Lomax, Louis E.
"Kennedys Move in on Dixie." Harper's magazine 224, May 1962, p. 27-33. 940

Brogan, Denis W.
"De verenigde Staten onder het Presidentschap van John F. Kennedy." The Hague, Internationale spectator (16: 9), May 8, 1962, p. 211-225. ("The United States under the Presidency of John F. Kennedy.") 941

Cater, Douglass
"What's Happening to the Democratic Party?" The reporter 26, May 10, 1962, p. 23-26. 942

Varga, Eugene
"President Kennedy and the Steel Barons." Moscow, New times 20, May 16, 1962, p. 10-13. 943

Kempton, Murray
"Kennedy Regnat." London, Spectator, May 25, 1962, p. 674-676. 944

Kempton, Murray
"The Invulnerable President." London, Spectator, June 22, 1962, p. 813-814. 945

Bagdikian, Ben H.
"Television-'the President's Medium'?" Columbia journalism review 1, Summer 1962, p. 34-38. 946

Lewis, T.
"Congress vs. Kennedy." The nation 195, July 14, 1962, p. 4-6. 947

Sclanders, Ian
"When Flattery didn't Work on Congress, Kennedy Reached for a big Stick: Public Opinion." Toronto, Maclean's magazine 75, July 14, 1962, p. 2-3. 948

Hyman, Sidney
"Kennedy in '64: the Historic odds." New York times magazine, July 15, 1962, p. 9. 949

"JFK and his Critics." Newsweek 60, July 16, 1962, p. 15-19. 950

"Power of the Kennedy Brothers: a Comparison with Other First Families." U.S. news & world report 53, July 16, 1962, p. 56-59. 951

Cooke, Alistair
"South Holding Kennedy to Ransom: Only 20 of 285 Laws Passed." Manchester, Manchester guardian, July 19, 1962, p. 9. 952

"Mr. Kennedy, the man Behind the Smile." London, Time & tide 43, July 19-26, 1962, p. 6-7. 953

Knebel, Fletcher
"Kennedy vs. the Press." Look 26, August 28, 1962, p. 17-21. 954

"Business Against Kennedy; a one-sided Hostility." London, Round table, September 1962, p. 355-360. 955

Gregg, R.W.
"The new Frontier: Myth and Reality." Wellington, Political science 14, Septem-

ber, 1962, p. 58-65. 956

Mansfield, Mike
"Why Kennedy's Program is in Trouble with Congress: Interview." U.S. news & world report 53, September 17, 1962, p. 62-69. 957

Ecroyd, D.H.
"Recording the President." Quarterly journal of speech 48, October 1962, p. 336-340. 958

Hanley, J.C.
"Blisters and Blessings: the President's Summer." Today 18, October 1962, p. 24-25. 959

Roche, John P.
"The Limits of Kennedy's Liberalism." New leader 45, October 1, 1962, p. 8-11. 960

Rudin, Stanislav
"Jakým Nebezpecim Muze být President." Prague Ceskoslovensky voják (11: 9), October 1, 1962, p. 4-5.
("In What Danger the President Must Live.") 961

McGeachy, J.B.
"Historical odds are Against JFK in American mid-term Elections." Toronto, Financial post 56, October 13, 1962, p. 7. 962

"May the Press Gossip About the President?" Quezon City, Weekly graphic (29: 18), October 24, 1962, p. 10-11. 963

Mann, Roderick
"Why Kennedy has Turned Cool on Sinatra's Clan." Manila, Mirror, October 27, 1962, p. 14-15. 964

Percy, Charles H. & Chester Bowles
"Promises and Preformance: Two Views of the Kennedy Record." U.S. news & world report 53, October 29, 1962, p. 112-118. 965

Kraft, Joseph
"Kennedy's Working Staff." Harper's magazine 225, December 1962, p. 29-36. 966

"Friends of the First Family Rally Round; Minow, Salinger Queer use of Meader Promos." Broadcasting 63, December 17, 1962, p. 74-75. 967

"God Speed you, Merry Gentlemen (President Kennedy's Young Men): Bolt from the President." London, The economist 205, December 22, 1962, p. 1201-1202. 968

Martire, D.
"What we Have Learned About President Kennedy's Thinking for 1963." Magazine of Wall Street, December 29, 1962, p. 360-362. 969

1963

"L'Administration Kennedy et l'Economie Américaine." Paris, Revue économique 14, 1963, p. 537-554.
("The Kennedy Administration and the U.S. Economy.") 970

Augstein, Rudolf
"Der Präsident der Stärke und des Friedens." Hamburg, Der spiegel (17: 49), 1963, p. 22-23.
("The Strong and Happy President.") 971

Berger, Kurt M.
"Das Ende einer 'Führungsmacht'." Heidelberg, Zeitschrift für geopolitik (34: 11-12), 1963, p. 339-342.
("The End of a Power of Leadership.") 972

Birrenbach, K.
"Kennedy und Johnson." Cologne, Die politische meinung (90: 8), 1963, p. 3.
("Kennedy and Johnson.") 973

Boussard, Léon
"Kennedy à mi-Course." Paris, Revue de deux mondes 1, 1963, p. 20-30.
("Kennedy at mid-Course.") 974

Daniel, W.G.
"President's Message on Civil Rights and the Progress of the American Negro." Journal of Negro education 32, Spring 1963, p. 99-106. 975

"Die Seltsame Wandlung des John F. Kennedy. Peter Brugge im Gefolge des US-Präsidenten." Hamburg, Der spiegel (17: 27), 1963, p. 18-22.
("The Strange Transformation of John F. Kennedy. Peter Brugge with the Entourage of the U.S. President.") 976

"John F. Kennedy als Mensch und Staatsmann." Bonn, Internationale politik (14: 328), 1963, p. 4-5.
("John F. Kennedy as Man and Statesman.") 977

"Kennedys 'State of the Union' Botschaft." Munich, Wehrkunde 12, 1963, p. 103-104.
("Kennedy's 'State of the Union' Message.") 978

Kessel, J.H.
"Mr. Kennedy and the Manufacture of News." London, Parliamentary affairs 16, 1963, p. 293-302. 979

Kilpatrick, Carroll
"The Kennedy Style and Congress." Virginia quarterly review (39: 1), 1963, p. 1-11. 980

Krag, J.O.
"John F. Kennedy." Copenhagen, Gutenberghus, 1963, p. 58-59. 981

"Le Message Agricole du Président Kennedy au Congrès." Paria, Problèmes économiques 806, 1963, p. 19-20.
("President Kennedy's Message to Congress on Agriculture.") 982

Meyer, Karl E.
"Kennedy in mid-Passage." London, Illustrated London news (65: 1685), 1963, p. 961-962. 983

Röpke, Wilhelm
"Die Nationalökonomie des 'New Frontier.'" Allgemeine

Deutung der Regierung Kennedy." Düsseldorf, Ordo 14, 1963, p. 79-107.
("The Domestic Economics of the 'New Frontier.' The General Significance of the Kennedy Administration.") 984

Schoeck, H.
"Geist und Macht im Weissen Haus. Kennedys Intellektuelles Berater-Team." Cologne, Die politische meinung (82: 8), 1963, p. 60-67.
("Intelligence and Strength in the White House. Kennedy's Team of Intellectual Advisors.") 985

Speel, Charles J.
"Theological Concepts of Magistracy: a Study of Constantius, Henry VIII and John F. Kennedy." Church history (32: 2), 1963, p. 130-149. 986

Sottile, Antoine
"Le Président John Kennedy." Paris, Revue de droit international des sciences diplomatiques et politiques (41: 4), 1963, p. 289-291.
("President John Kennedy.") 987

Thonnessen, W.
"Kennedy Plant Steuersenkung." Frankfurt am Main, Der gewerkschafter (11: 11), 1963, p. 419.
("Kennedy's Tax Reduction for Industry.") 988

Ulloa, Alberto
"El Presidente Kennedy." Lima, Revista peruana de derecho internacional (23: 63), 1963, p. 3-17.

("President Kennedy.") 989

von Brentano, Heinrich
"Kennedy hat Geschichte Gemacht." Cologne, Rheinischer merkur (18: 48), 1963, p. 1-2.
("Kennedy has Made History.") 990

Fine, B.
"President's Column." Pioneer woman 39, January 1963, p. 3-4. 991

Lippman, Walter
"Kennedy at Mid-term." Newsweek 61, January 21, 1963, p. 24-26. 992

"New Help for Kennedy in Senate." U.S. news & world report 54, January 21, 1963, p. 34-37. 993

Blough, Roger M.
"My Side of the Steel Price Story, as told to Eleanor Harris." Look 27, January 29, 1963, p. 19-23. 994

Smith, Merriman
"Midterm Tone; Softer at Home, Tougher Abroad." Nation's business 51, February 1963, p. 23-24. 995

Lewis, T.
"Kennedy, Profile of a Technician." The nation 196, February 2, 1963, p. 81, 92-94. 996

Townshend, William
"Is he the Richest-ever US President?" Manila, Mirror, February 2, 1963,

Rossant, M.J.
"The Economic Education of John F. Kennedy." The reporter 28, February 14, 1963, p. 22-25. 998

"President Kennedy's Father Forced him into Politics." London, Time & tide, February 28-March 6, 1963, p. 12. 999

Steamer, Robert J.
"Presidential Stimulus and School Desegregation." Phylon 24, Spring 1963, p. 20-33. 1000

Krock, Arthur
"Mr. Kennedy's Management of the News." Fortune 67, March 1963, p. 82, 199, 201-202. 1001

Shannon, William V.
"Taxes, Politics and the President." Progressive 27, March 1963, p. 10-13. 1002

Cogley, J.
"New Breed of Cat: Kennedy's Political Pragmatism Reflected in the Life of the Nation." Commonweal 77, March 8, 1963, p. 609-611. 1003

"Why Congress Doesn't Give JFK What he Wants, Answers by Leading Congressmen." U.S. news & world report 54, March 18, 1963, p. 38-42. 1004

Rovere, Richard H.
"Letter from Washington: Managed News." New Yorker 39, March 30, 1963, p. 164-169. 1005

Smith, Merriman
"Cracks in Image Mirror Irritate Kennedy Fans." Nation's business 51, April 1963, p. 23-24. 1006

Cooke, Alistair
"The Invisible Rulers." London, Listener 69, April 4, 1963, p. 579-580. 1007

Blumenthal, Fred
"A Working Weekend with President Kennedy." Manila, Mirror, April 6, 1963, p. 26-27. 1008

Marder, G.J.
"The Haunted President." Manila, Philippines herald magazine, April 27, 1963, p. 14-15. 1009

"Kennedy as Target. Kennedy and the Liberals, by Seymour E. Harris." New republic 148, June 1, 1963, p. 3-5, 15-16. 1010

"An end and a Beginning: Concerning President's TV-radio Speech on the American Dilemma of Race." Newsweek 61, June 24, 1963, p. 29-34. 1011

Lopez Felix, Francisco
"La Era Kennedy." Mexico City, Istmo, revista del Centro de América 27, July-August 1963, p. 35-39. ("The Kennedy Era.") 1012

"The man to see on Business

Issues: as a six-year Confidant of Kennedy, Myer Feldman has more Influence with the President." Business week, July 13, 1963, p. 50, 52, 55.   1013

McNaught, K.
"Kennedy Steps into Lincoln's Shoes." Toronto, Saturday night 78, August 1963, p. 13-15.   1014

"Kennedy's Strategy for the '64 Election." U.S. news & world report 55, August 19, 1963, p. 34-36.   1015

Greer, Herb
"The new American." London, Views 3, Autumn-Winter 1963, p. 141-144.   1016

"Towards a Second Term: Mr. Kennedy's Record and Prospects." London, The round table 53, September 1963, p. 353-357.   1017

"Migrant Altarpiece: Portrait of Angel Posed for by President Kennedy." Priest 19, October 1963, p. 781-782.   1018

Wechsler, James A.
"Victor Lasky's Loaded dice (Review of the book Entitled J.F.K.: the Man and the Myth, by Victor Lasky." Progressive 27, November 1963, p. 24-27.   1019

"Is JFK Weaker Politically?" U.S. news & world report 55, November 18, 1963, p. 43-46.   1020

Patten, Thomas H.
"The Industrial Integration of the Negro." Phylon (24: 4), Winter 1963, p. 334-352.   1021

"The man who was Forced into Politics." London, Time & tide, November 28-December 4, 1963, p. 9-10.   1022

Adams, David K.
"Roosevelt and Kennedy." Manchester, Bulletin of the British Association for American studies 7, December 1963, p. 29-39.   1023

Neustadt, Richard E.
"Approaches to Staffing the Presidency: Notes on FDR and JFK." American political science review (57: 4), December 1963, p. 855-862.   1024

"Late President, Successor saw Development of Space Program." Aviation week 79, December 2, 1963, p. 30-31.   1025

Morgenthau, Hans J.
"The Kennedy Legacy: Significance in History. A Tentative Assessment, by Reinhold Niebuhr. The Elusive JFK, by George E. Herman. An End and a Beginning, by Karl E. Meyer." New leader 46, December 9, 1963, p. 4-13.   1026

"Style and Anti-style." London, The Times literary supplement 3226, December 26, 1963, p. 1065.   1027

1964

Adam, R.
"Das Innerpolitische Fazit der Regierung Kennedys." Wiesbaden, Zeitschrift für sozialreform (10: 3), 1964, p. 129-139.
("On the Domestic Political Achievements of the Kennedy Administration.") 1028

Birnbaum, Norman
"Die Regierungszeit Kennedys: Ära oder Episode?" Frankfurt am Main, Frankfurter hefte (19: 10), 1964, p. 681-690.
("The Period of the Kennedy Administration: Era or Episode?") 1029

Carleton, William C.
"Kennedy in History: an Early Appraisal." Antioch review (24: 3), 1964, p. 277-299. 1030

Krippendorff, Ekkehart
"John F. Kennedy--Rückblick nach einem Jahr." Berlin, Zeitschrift für politik (11: 4), 1964, p. 309-322.
("John F. Kennedy--a Glance Backward after one Year.") 1031

Lübke, Heinrich
"John F. Kennedy: unser Vorbild." Bonn, Bulletin der Presse- und Informationsamtes der Bundesregierung 175, 1964, p. 1617-1618.
("John F. Kennedy: our Model.") 1032

Pechel, Peter
"Die Ära Kennedy." Baden-Baden, Deutsche rundschau (90: 3), 1964, p. 9.

("The Kennedy Era.") 1033

McMahan, Ian
"The Kennedy Myth." New politics 3, Winter 1964, p. 40-48. 1034

Kaplan, H.
"The Kennedy Years." Toronto, Canadian forum 43, January 1964, p. 221-222. 1035

Max, Alfred
"The Four Strong Men: an Assessment, Based on Conversations with Statesmen in Various Countries of the Aims Underlying the Policies of the Late President Kennedy, Khrushchev, de Gaulle and Mao Tse-tung." Paris, Réalités, English edition, January 1964, p. 19-23. 1036

"What was Kennedy's Greatest Accomplishment? (Six Replies to a Question from Americas Asked on November 27, 1963)." Americas (16: 1), January 1964, p. 2-3.
(Answers by Richard L. Coe, Richard N. Goodwin, Teodoro Moscoso, Norman Podhoretz, Arthur Schlesinger, Jr., and Arturo Morales Carrion.) 1037

"The World Figure Most Admired in Asia." Hong Kong, Asia magazine (4: 3), January 19, 1964, p. 3. 1038

Grodin, Joseph
"The Kennedy Labor Board." Industrial relations

(3: 2), February 1964, p. 33-45. 1039

Hills, Roderick M.
"A Close Look at Three Administrative Policies." Industrial relations (3: 2), February 1964, p. 5-20.
(Concerning labor-management relations.) 1040

Stern, James
"The Kennedy Policy: a Favorable View." Industrial relations (3: 2), February 1964, p. 21-32.
(Concerning labor relations.) 1041

"A Symposium: Labor Relations and the Kennedy Administration." Industrial relations 3, February 1964, p. 1-45. 1042

Clifton, C.
"Kennedy, the Commander in Chief" (condensed from Army, January 1964). Catholic digest 28, April 1964, p. 30-32. 1043

"Minow Describes Kennedy's TV Habits, Views." Broadcasting 66, June 8, 1964, p. 40. 1044

Erskine, Hazel (Gaudet)
"The Polls: Kennedy as President." Public opinion quarterly (28: 2), Summer 1964, p. 334-342. 1045

Neustadt, Richard E.
"Kennedy in the Presidency: a Premature Appraisal." Political science quarterly 79, Summer 1964, p. 334-342. 1046

Booker, Simeon
"President Kennedy and the Negroes" (condensed from Ebony, February 1964). Catholic digest 28, June 1964, p. 19-21. 1047

Odem, J.
"J.F.K.'s Best Kept Secret." Jewish digest 9, July 1964, p. 31-32. 1048

Schlesinger, Arthur M.
"Schlesinger at the White House, Edited by H. Brandon." Harper's magazine, July 1964, p. 55-60. 1049

Roche, John P.
"How a President Should use the Intellectuals." New York Times magazine, July 26, 1964, p. 10. 1050

Meyer, Karl E.
"A Sense of History and Proportion" (reprint from Show). U.S. Catholic 30, August 1964, p. 54. 1051

Carleton, William G.
"Kennedy in History; an Early Appraisal." Antioch review 24, Fall 1964, p. 277-299. 1052

"Jubilee's Presidential Poll: Assessment of J.F. Kennedy, Johnson and Goldwater." Jubilee 12, September 1964, p. 7-15. 1053

"An Interview with John Roche: Kennedy's Use of Power." Yale political 4, Fall 1964, p. 10-11. 1054

"It's one Year After JFK: the Changes." U.S. news & world report 57, November 23, 1964, p. 60-66.   1055

1965
Sorensen, Theodore C.
"Dann Räumt Lyndon den Laden aus." (Uber Kennedys Verhältnis zu seinem Bruder Robert, Lyndon B. Johnson, Robert MacNamara und Dean Rusk." Hamburg, Der spiegel (19: 40), 1965, p. 76-77. ("Then Lyndon Leaves the Store: On Kennedy's Relationship to his Brother Robert, Lyndon B. Johnson, Robert MacNamara and Dean Rusk.")   1056

Riemer, Neal
"Kennedy's Grand Democratic Design." The review of politics 27, January 1965, p. 3-16.   1057

"Controversy on Showing of Kennedy Film in U.S." Congressional quarterly weekly report 23, May 7, 1965, p. 879-880.   1058

"JFK's Private Opinions of Prominent People." U.S. news & world report 59, August 9, 1965, p. 53-54.   1059

O'Brien, Lawrence F.
"From White House to Capitol, how Things get Done." U.S. news & world report 59, September 20, 1965, p. 68-73.   1060

Romulo, Carlos P.
"A Trilogy of Leaders: Magsaysay, Kennedy, Quezon." Manila, Philippine journal of public administration (IX: 4), October 1965, p. 301-307.   1061

Macleod, Iain
"Sorensen on President Kennedy." London, Spectator, October 22, 1965, p. 507.   1062

Roberts, Steven V.
"The Two Presidents: Word Pictures by Ten of the Kennedy Advisers who Left." Esquire (LXIV: 5), November 1965, p. 90.   1063

"...And This is What They Have to say, Edited by S.V. Roberts." Esquire 64, November 1965, p. 90-93.   1064

Sullivan, Donald F.
"The Civil Rights Program of the Kennedy Administration; a Political Analysis." Dissertation abstracts (26: 5), November 1965, p. 2850.   1065

Shannon, William V.
"Controversial Historian of the age of Kennedy." New York Times magazine, November 21, 1965, p. 30-31.   1066

Sinclair, Andrew
"The Time of Power." London, Spectator, November 26, 1965, p. 692-695.   1067

Dennis, N.
"Sorensen with Tears." Atlas 10, December 1965, p. 356-357.   1068

1966
Abosch, H.
"Problematischer Kennedy."

Munich, Werkhefte (20: 11), 1966, p. 375-378.
("The Problematical Kennedy.") 1069

Koch, Thilo
"Der Sogenannte Kennedy-Mythos." Stuttgart, Merkur (20: 10), 1966, p. 983-987.
("The So-called Kennedy Myth.") 1070

Riemer, Neal
"The Political Philosophy of John F. Kennedy." Vienna, Americana Austriaca (Beiträge zur Amerika-kunde, v. 1), 1966, p. 91-115. 1071

Friedel, Frank
"35th President, 1961-1963." National geographic magazine 129, January 1966, p. 100-109. 1072

Folliard, E.T.
"Reporter at the White House" (condensed from American ecclesiastical review, November 1965). Catholic digest 30, March 1966, p. 51-57. 1073

Sorensen, Theodore C.
"A Lawyer Looks at a President." Record of the Association of the Bar of the City of New York 21, April 1966, p. 198-212. 1074

Muggeridge, Malcolm
"Two Opposing Views on Kennedy as Leader: the Man and the Myth. A Man for the Ages, by Arthur M. Schlesinger, Jr." Toronto, Maclean's 79, April 16, 1966, p. 14-15. 1075

"Salinger's Book Tells TV Tales; Debates won Presidency, JFK Believed." Broadcasting 71, September 12, 1966, p. 67-68. 1076

1967

Luce, C.B.
"Sunday Painters: Churchill, Eisenhower and Kennedy." McCall's 94, January 1967, p. 12. 1077

Clemens, C.
"My Visit with John F. Kennedy." Hobbies 72, April 1967, p. 109. 1078

Rowan, Carl T.
"How Kennedy's Concern for Negroes led to his Death." Ebony 22, April 1967, p. 27-30. 1079

Passent, Daniel
"The Making of a Myth." Atlas 13, June 1967, p. 27-31. 1080

Tugwell, Rexford G.
"The President and his Helpers (Review Article)." Political science quarterly 82, June 1967, p. 253-267. 1081

1968

Elsnau, Mary
"Kennedy and Johnson, a Story in the Stars." Fate (21: 6), Issue #219, June 1968, p. 34-39. 1082

International Affairs in the Career of John F. Kennedy

Books

1957

Kennedy, John F.
Let the lady hold up her head: reflections on American immigration policy. New York, American Jewish Committee, 1957, 7p. 1083

Kennedy, John F.
Remarks of Senator John F. Kennedy, Democrat, Massachusetts, Chairman, Senate Foreign Relations Subcommittee on U.N. Affairs, July 2, 1957, on Algeria. Washington, Senate Office Bldg. Documents Room, 1957, 15p. 1084

1958

Kennedy, John F.
The choice in Asia: democratic development in India: speech in the Senate of the United States, March 25, 1958. Washington, Senate Office Bldg. Documents Room, 1958, 23p. 1085

Kennedy, John F.
Israel: a miracle of progress. An address at the Golden Jubilee Banquet of B'nai Zion, February 9, 1958. Washington, G.P.O., 1958, 6p. 1086

1960

Kennedy, John F.
Amerikas Weg in die Zukunft, by John F. Kennedy & Richard M. Nixon. Munich, Ner-Tamid Verlag, 1960, 48p. (America's way in the future.) 1087

Kennedy, John F.
A Democrat looks at foreign policy (In Jacobson, Harold K., ed. America's foreign policy. New York, Random House, 1960, p. 349-365). 1088

Kennedy, John F.
Good fences make good neighbors; convocation address, October 8th, 1957, the University of New Brunswick, Fredericton, N.B. Fredericton, University of New Brunswick, 1960, 11p. 1089

Kennedy, John F.
Lead: or get left behind (In Life, periodical. Great reading from Life: a treasury of the best stories and articles. New York, Harper, 1960, p. 287-298). 1090

1961

Khrushchev, Nikita S.
Comunicado oficial del gobierno soviético y mensajes del primer ministro de la URSS Nikita Jruschov al presidente de los Estados Unidos John F. Kennedy sobre la criminal agresión imperialista a Cuba, abril 1961. Havana, Impr. Nacional de Cuba, 1961, 15p.
(Official communiqué of the Soviet Government, and messages of the Prime Minister of the USSR, Nikita Khrushchev, to the President of the United States, John F. Kennedy, on the imperialist criminal aggression in Cuba,

April 1961.) 1091

Kennedy, John F.
Alliance for progress. Text of an address delivered at the White House, March 13, 1961. Washington, Pan American Union, 1961, 5p. 1092

Kennedy, John F.
Amerika in der Welt von Morgen; ansprachen. Frankfurt-am-Main, Ner-Tamid-Verlag, 1961, 52p.
(America in the world of tomorrow; speeches.) 1093

Kennedy, John F.
The Berlin crisis: a report to the American people on Tuesday, July 25, 1961. Washington, G.P.O., 1961, 8p.
(87th Congress, first session. Senate document 40.)
1094

Kennedy, John F.
The lesson of Cuba; address, April 20, 1961, made at Washington, D.C. before the American Society of Newspaper Editors. Dept. of State publication 7185. Washington, Dept. of State, 1961, 7p. 1095

Peron, Juan Domingo (President, Argentine Rep.)
Carta a Kennedy. Buenos Aires, Cono Sur, S.R.L., 1961, 16p.
(Letter to Kennedy.) 1096

U.S. Dept of State. Bureau of Public Affairs. Office of Public Services
The Berlin crisis: report to the nation by President Kennedy, July 25, 1961. Publication 7243. Washington, G.P.O., 1961, 21p. 1097

U.S. Dept. of State
Highlights of President Kennedy's new act for international development; publication 7211. Washington, Office of Public Services, Bureau of Public Affairs, Dept. of State, 1961, 2 plus 44p.
1098

U.S. Dept. of State
President Kennedy's report to the people on his trip to Europe, May 30-June 6, 1961; address. Publication 7213. Washington, Office of Public Services, Bureau of Public Affairs, Dept. of State, 1961, 2, 17p. 1099

U.S. President
Report to Congress on the mutual security program. Dec. 31, 1951-1960/61. 19v. Washington, G.P.O., 1951-1961. 1100

U.S. President, 1961-1963 (Kennedy)
Establishment of permanent Peace Corps. Message transmitting special message for the establishment of a permanent Peace Corps. Washington, G.P.O., 1961, 4p.
(87th Congress, first session. House of Representatives document 98). 1101

U.S. President, 1961-1963 (Kennedy)
Foreign affairs; publication 7140. Washington, Office of Public Services, Bureau of Public Affairs, Dept. of

State, 1961, 14p. 1102

U.S. President, 1961-1963
(Kennedy)
Foreign aid; message relative to foreign aid. Washington, G.P.O., 1961, 11p.
(87th Congress, first session. House of Representatives document 117). 1103

U.S. President, 1961-1963
(Kennedy)
International civil aviation. Message from the President of the United States, transmitting a protocol relating to an amendment to the convention on international civil aviation. Washington? G.P.O.? 1961, 4p. 1104

U.S. President, 1961-1963
(Kennedy)
New program for foreign aid. President Kennedy's message to the Congress. Washington, Office of Public Services, Bureau of Public Affairs, Dept. of State, 1961, 17p. 1105

U.S. President, 1961-1963
(Kennedy)
Survival of the United Nations. Address delivered to the General Assembly of the United Nations on Monday, September 25, 1961. Washington, G.P.O., 1961, 9p.
(87th Congress, first session. Senate document 60). 1106

U.S. President, 1961-1963
(Kennedy)
U.S. balance of payments and gold outflow from United States. Message relative to U.S. balance of payments and the gold outflow from the United States. Washington, G.P.O., 1961, 12p.
(87th Congress, first session. House of Representatives document 84). 1107

1962
Castro Ruz, Fidel
En nombre de Cuba, Fidel Castro le responde a Kennedy...Havana, Imp. en la Fábrica 1201 "Alfredo Lopez," Empresa Consol. de Artes Gráficas, Ministerio de Industrias, 1962, 23p.
(In the name of Cuba, Fidel Castro replies to Kennedy.) 1108

Fair Play for Cuba Committee
Kennedy's Cuban policy: a disaster... New York, 1962, 7p. 1109

Joost, Wilhelm
Herren über Krieg oder Frieden. Chruschtschow, de Gaulle, Kennedy, Macmillan, Nasser, Nehru, Tito, Mao Tse-tung. Düsseldorf, Econ.-Verlag, 1962, 493p.
(Men on war and peace: Khrushchev, de Gaulle, Kennedy, Macmillan, Nasser, Nehru, Tito, Mao-Tse-tung.) 1110

Kennedy, John F.
Amerika und Kuba: rede Präsident Kennedys vom 22. Oktober 1962... (America and Cuba: President Kennedy's speech of October 22, 1962, translated into German). Vienna, U.S. Information

Kennedy, John F.
Service, Austria, 1962, 23p. 1111

Kennedy, John F.
America's basic defense and arms-control policies (In Lefever, Ernest W., ed. Arms and arms control: a symposium. New York, Praeger, 1962, p. 59-65). 1112

Kennedy, John F.
The future trade of the United States; address, May 4, 1962 (Publication 7380). Washington, Dept. of State, 1962, 13p. 1113

Kennedy, John F.
Il potenziamento di Cuba come base offensiva (Translation into Italian of speech, The strength of Cuba as a base for aggression). Rome, Ediz. U.S.I.S. (Tip. Apollon), 1962, 20p. 1114

Kennedy, John F.
Indipendenza e interdipendenza, Philadelphia 4 luglio 1962 (Translation into Italian of speech, Independence and inter-dependence, July 4, 1962). Rome, Ediz. U.S.I.S. (Tip. Apollon), 1962, 20p. 1115

Kennedy, John F.
Kernversuche und Abrüstung: eine rede, 2 März, 1962 (Nuclear testing and disarmament: a speech, March 2, 1962, translated into German). Vienna, U.S. Information Service, Austria, 1962, 19p. 1116

Kennedy, John F.
Let us call a truce to terror (In Baird, A.C., ed. Representative American speeches, 1961-1962. New York, Wilson, 1962, p. 41-54). 1117

Kennedy, John F.
Nuclear testing and disarmament; radio-television address made March 2, 1962. Washington, U.S. Arms Control & Disarmament Agency, 1962, 20p. 1118

Kennedy, John F.
President Kennedy speaks on the Alliance for Progress: addresses and remarks--the first year. Washington, U.S. Dept. of State, Agency for International Development, 1962- 1119

Kennedy, John F.
Solemn words on the fateful challenge (In Baird, A.C., ed. Representative American speeches, 1961-1962. New York, Wilson, 1962, p. 7-26). 1120

Kennedy, John F.
Trade and the Atlantic partnership. Remarks by President Kennedy and Secretary of State Rusk. (Dept. of State publication 7386). Washington, Dept. of State, 1962, 23p. 1121

Kennedy, John F.
The U.S. response to Soviet military buildup in Cuba; report to the people, October 22, 1962. Dept. of State publication 7449. Washington, Dept. of State, 1962, 12p. 1122

Kennedy, John F.
Visita del Presidente John F. Kennedy a Colombia. Bogotá, Imp. Nacional, 1962, 41p.
(Visit of President John F. Kennedy to Colombia.) 1123

México. Secretaría de Gobernación
Entrevista de los Presidentes de México y los Estados Unidos de América en la Ciudad de México, junio-julio, 1962. Meeting of the Presidents of Mexico and the United States of America in Mexico City, June-July 1962. Mexico, 1962, 201p. 1124

Morgenthau, Hans J.
Kennedy's foreign policy: failure and challenge (In his The restoration of American politics: v. 3, Politics in the twentieth century. Chicago, University of Chicago Press, 1962, p. 308-314). 1125

Nasser, Gamal Abdel (President, United Arab Rep.)
The Palestinian problem; correspondence exchanged between President Gamal Abdel-Nasser and President John Kennedy on the subject of the Palestinian problem. Cairo, Information Dept., 1962? 15p. 1126

U.S. Arms Control & Disarmament Agency
Excerpts on disarmament and nuclear testing from President's press conference, February 7, 1962. Washington, 1962, 4p. 1127

U.S. Dept. of Defense.
Armed Forces Information & Education Office
Why we test, President Kennedy's somber decision, May 15, 1962. (Item 312-A. DOD pamphlets, v. 1, no. 21). Washington, 1962, 4p. 1128

U.S. 87th Congress. Second Session. House of Representatives. Ways & Means Committee
Trade expansion act of 1962. President's message along with section-by-section analysis and summary of H.R. 9900, as prepared by executive branch; March 13, 1962; Committee print. (Y 4.W 36:T67/18/962). Washington, 1962, 81p. 1129

U.S. Information Agency
To protect the peace (remarks of John F. Kennedy on Soviet missile bases in Cuba and extract of statement by Adlai E. Stevenson in Security Council, October 23, on Cuba). Washington, 1962, 36p. 1130

U.S. President, 1961-1963 (Kennedy)
Authorizing the purchase of United Nations bonds. Message from the President of the United States, transmitting a draft of a bill to promote the foreign policy of the United States by authorizing the purchase of United Nations bonds and the appropriation of funds therefor. Washington, G.P.O., 1962, 3p.

(87th Congress, 2d session.
House of Representatives
document 321). 1131

U.S. President, 1961-1963
(Kennedy)
Foreign affairs. Dept. of
State publication 7334. Washington, G.P.O., 1962, 20p.
1132

U.S. President, 1961-1963
(Kennedy)
International wheat agreement, 1962. Message...transmitting the International wheat agreement, 1962, formulated at the United Nations Wheat Conference which concluded at Geneva on March 10, 1962. Washington, G.P.O., 1962, 39p.
(87th Congress, 2d session. Senate. Executive D). 1133

U.S. President, 1961-1963
(Kennedy)
National Advisory Council on International Monetary and Financial Problems. Message from the President of the United States relative to special borrowing arrangements of the International Monetary Fund. Committee on Banking and Currency, House of Representatives, Eighty-seventh Congress, second session. Washington, G.P.O., 1962, 24p. 1134

U.S. President, 1961-1963
(Kennedy)
Reciprocal trade agreements program: message... Washington, 1962, 13p.
(87th Congress, 2d session. House of Representatives document 314). 1135

U.S. President, 1961-1963
(Kennedy)
Trade expansion act of 1962. President's message along with section-by-section analysis and summary of H.R. 9900, as prepared by the executive branch. Washington, G.P.O., 1962, 81p.
(At head of title: Committee print. Committee on Ways and Means, House of Representatives, 87th Congress, 2d session). 1136

Vargas MacDonald, Antonio
Cartas de un Mexicano al Presidente Kennedy. Letters from a Mexican to President Kennedy. Mexico City, 1962, 59p. (Concerning U.S.-Mexican relations). 1137

Venezuela. Presidencia.
Secretaría General
Alianza para el progreso; visita del Presidente Kennedy a Venezuela. Caracas, Impr. Nacional, 1962, 77p.
(Alliance for Progress: Visit of President Kennedy to Venezuela.)
(Speeches by President and Mrs. Kennedy on the Alliance for Progress.) 1138

Zabludowsky, Jacobo, ed.
J.F. Kennedy, López Mateos y América; resumen de tres días de visita del presidente J.F. Kennedy a México, 29 y 30 de junio y 1 de julio de 1962. Texto de los discursos. México City, Costa-Amic, 1962, 110p.

(J. F. Kennedy, Lopez Mateos and America; summary of three days of the visit of President J.F. Kennedy to Mexico, June 29th and 30th, and July 1, 1962. Text of the speeches.) 1139

1963
Berlin (West Berlin) Presse- und Informationsamt
Ein grosser Tag in der Geschichte unserer Stadt, 26. Juni 1963: John F. Kennedy in Berlin. Berlin, 1963, 48p.
(A great day in the history of our city, June 26, 1963: John F. Kennedy in Berlin.) 1140

Castro Ruz, Fidel
Cuarto aniversario de la revolución cubana: Desfile militar y concentración. Fidel Castro habla a su pueblo y al mundo y da cumplida respuesta a Kennedy. Havana, Ed. Nacional de Cuba, 1963, 16p.
(Fourth anniversary of the Cuban revolution: Military parade and communication. Fidel Castro speaks to his people and to the world, and gives a complete reply to Kennedy.) 1141

Dokumenty k otázce odzbrojeni z let 1960-1962. Prague, NPL, 1963, 254p.
(Documents on problems of disarmament, 1960-1962.) 1142

Stevenson, Adlai E.
Looking outward; years of crisis at the United Nations. Preface by John F. Kennedy. New York, Harper & Row, 1963, 295p. 1143

Ireland (Eire) Parliament
Joint sitting of Dáil Eireaan and Seanad Éireann on the occasion of the visit of John Fitzgerald Kennedy, President of the United States of America, Friday, 28th June, 1963. Dublin, Stationery Office, 1963, 29p. 1144

Kennedy, John F.
Die Zukunft des Westens. Rede Präsident Kennedys in der Frankfurter Paulskirche, 25. Juni 1963. Vienna, U.S. Information Service, 1963, 19p.
(The future of the West: President Kennedy's speech in St. Paul's Church, Frankfurt, June 25, 1963.) 1145

Kennedy, John F.
John F. Kennedy in Deutschland. Die Ansprachen in d. Frankfurter Paulskirche und in Berlin. Berlin, Presse- und Informationsamt d. Landes, 1963, 46p.
(John F. Kennedy in Germany: speeches in St. Paul's Church, Frankfurt, and in Berlin.) 1146

Kennedy, John F.
New opportunities in the search for peace; address made before the United Nations General Assembly, September 20, 1963. Dept. of State publication 7595. Washington, for sale by the Superintendent of Documents, G.P.O., 1963, 20p. 1147

Kennedy, John F.
Op zoek naar vrede (In

search of peace. Translation into Dutch of address before the General Assembly of the United Nations, September 20, 1963). The Hague, 1963, 5p.
(Supplement to Oost-West (2: 5), November-December 1963). 1148

Kennedy, John F.
A selection of speeches and statements on the United Nations by President John F. Kennedy. New York, American Association for the United Nations, 1963, 30p. 1149

Kennedy, John F.
A step toward peace; report to the people on the nuclear test ban treaty. Washington, U.S. Arms Control & Disarmament Agency; for sale by Superintendent of Documents, G.P.O., 1963, 20p. 1150

Kennedy, John F.
U.S. participation in the UN; report by the President to the Congress for the year 1962. Dept. of State publication 7610. Washington, G.P.O., 1963, 452p. 1151

Kennedy, John F., et al
Why foreign aid? Two messages by President Kennedy and essays by Edward C. Banfield, and others. Chicago, Rand McNally & Co., 1963, 140p. 1152

Larson, David L., ed.
The Cuban crisis of 1962; selected documents and chronology. Boston, Houghton, Mifflin, 1963, 333p. 1153

A memory of John Fitzgerald Kennedy; visit to Ireland, 26th-29th June 1963. Dublin, Wood Printing Works, 1963, 32p. 1154

Pachter, Henry M.
Collision course: the Cuban missile crisis and co-existence. New York, Praeger, 1963, 261p. 1155

Schwoebel, J.
Les deux K, Berlin et la paix. Paris, Julliard, 1963, 329p.
(The two K's, Berlin and peace.) 1156

Solar, Tony
Open letter to President Kennedy. (In his Chaos in the Caribbean. Miami, 1963, p. 137-146.) 1157

Sorensen, Theodore C.
Decision-making in the White House; the olive branch or the arrows. New York, Columbia University Press, 1963, 94p. 1158

Sorensen, Theodore C.
New directions under the Kennedy Administration (In Whitton, John B., ed. Propaganda and the Cold War. Washington, Public Affairs Press, 1963, chapter 7). 1159

Stebbins, Richard P.
World affairs through American eyes (In Documents on American foreign relations, 1962-1963; the United States in world affairs. v. 1. New York, Harper, 1963, p. 8-

56).

To protect the peace. Washington? 1963? 36p.
(Speeches of President Kennedy and Adlai E. Stevenson with respect to the Cuban Missile Crisis, October 1962.) 1161

U.S. Arms Control & Disarmament Agency
Step toward peace, report to people on nuclear test ban treaty (radio-television address) by President John F. Kennedy, July 26, 1963. Includes text of test ban treaty initialed at Moscow on July 25 by representatives of United States, United Kingdom and Soviet Union. (Item 125-A-5. AC1.12: K38/2). Washington, 1963, 2 plus 20p. 1162

U.S. Arms Control & Disarmament Agency
Toward strategy of peace, by President John F. Kennedy, June 1963 (publication 17). Text of address made at commencement exercises at American University, Washington, D.C., June 10, 1963. (Item 125-A-5. AC 1.12: K38). Washington, 1963, 2, 17p. 1163

U.S. Dept. of Defense. Armed Forces Information & Education Office
New opportunities in search for peace, President Kennedy's address before United Nations General Assembly, September 20, 1963 (Alert series: v. 3, no. 7). Item 312-C. Washington, 1963, 4p. 1164

U.S. President, 1961-1963 (Kennedy)
Foreign affairs. Dept. of State publication 7487. Washington, G.P.O., 1963, 19p. 1165

U.S. President, 1961-1963 (Kennedy)
New opportunities in the search for peace. Dept. of State publication 7595. Washington, G.P.O., 1963, 20p. 1166

U.S. President, 1961-1963 (Kennedy)
Our foreign assistance act; message. Washington, G.P.O., 1963, 15p.
(88th Congress, first session. House of Representatives document 94). 1167

U.S. President, 1961-1963 (Kennedy)
Reasons for this Government's decision not to prohibit the sale of surplus American wheat, wheat flour, feed grains, and other agricultural commodities for shipment to the Soviet Union and other Eastern European countries during the next several months. Communication from the President of the United States transmitting a report to the Congress. Washington, G.P.O., 1963, 11p.
(88th Congress, first session. House of Representatives document 163). 1168

U.S. President, 1961-1963 (Kennedy)
Special message on the balance of payments; mes-

sage... Washington, G.P.O., 1963, 12p. 1169

U.S. President, 1961-1963 (Kennedy)
Trade agreement negotiated with the United Kingdom and an agreement negotiated with Japan; message... Washington, G.P.O., 1963, 8p.
(88th Congress, first session. House of Representatives document 34). 1170

1964
Brandt, Willy
Begegnungen mit Kennedy. Munich, Kindler, 1964, 242p.
(Meetings with Kennedy.) 1171

Kennedy, John F.
An address to the United Nations (In Gross, Franz B., ed. The United States and the United Nations, by Waldo Chamberlin, et al. Norman, University of Oklahoma Press, 1964, p. 277-288). 1172

Kennedy, John F.
Enlarging the Peace Corps (In Madow, Pauline, ed. The Peace Corps. New York, Wilson, 1964, p. 96-99). 1173

Kennedy, John F.
John F. Kennedy and Poland, a selection of texts and documents. Edited by Jan Wszelaki. New York, Polish Institute of Arts & Sciences in America, 1964, 140p. 1174

Kennedy, John F.
A permanent Peace Corps (In Madow, Pauline, ed. The Peace Corps. New York, Wilson, 1964, p. 20-25). 1175

Kennedy, John F.
A step toward peace (In Baird, A.C., ed. Representative American speeches, 1963-1964. New York, Wilson, 1964, p. 20-29). 1176

Kennedy, John F.
Toward a strategy of peace (In Baird, A.C., ed. Representative American speeches, 1963-1964. New York, Wilson, 1964, p. 9-19). 1177

Kuberzig, Kurt
Für Frieden und Freiheit. Düsseldorf, Hoch Verlag, 1964, 255p.
(For peace and freedom.) 1178

Stebbins, Richard P.
America turns a page (In Documents on American foreign relations, 1963-1964; the United States in world affairs, 1963. New York, Harper, 1964, p. 8-47).1179

Thant, U
On John F. Kennedy (In his Toward world peace. New York, Yoseloff, 1964, p. 402-404). 1180

1965
Artus, O.M.
Präsident John F. Kennedy in Deutschland; eine Dokumentation. President John F. Kennedy in Germany; a documentation. Translations by Hermann Kusterer and Heinz Weber. Heiligenhaus, Bez. Düsseldorf, Richard-Barenfeld-Verlag, 1965, 187p.1181

Di'bis, 'Abd al-Jawwad Hamzah
Masra' Kinidi wa-al-sihyuniyah. Cairo, Al-dar al-Qawmiyyah li'taba'ah wa'l-nashr, 1965, 75p.
(The Fall of Kennedy and Zionism.) 1182

Kennedy, John F.
John F. Kennedy on Israel, Zionism and Jewish issues. Published for the Zionist Organization of America. Compiled by Ernest E. Barabash. New York, The Herzl Press, 1965, 69p. 1183

Paranjoti, Violet
President John F. Kennedy; creative statesmanship in the field of foreign affairs. New York, Carlton Press, 1965, 48p. 1184

Watson, Richard L., ed.
The United States in the contemporary world, 1945-1962. New York, The Free Press, 1965, 309p. 1185

1966
Abel, Elie
The missile crisis. Philadelphia, Lippincott, 1966, 220p. 1186

Besson, Waldemar
Die grossen Mächte; Strukturfragen der gegenwärt Weltpolitik. Freiburg-im-Breisgau, Rombach, 1966, 85p.
(The great powers: problems of the structure of future international politics.) 1187

Bugat, Jean M.
Kennedy, l'Amérique et nous. Paris, Eds. Temps Nouveaux, 1966, 54p.
(Kennedy, America and us.) 1188

Hennessey, Maurice N.
I'll come back in the springtime: John F. Kennedy and the Irish. New York, Ives Washburn, 1966, 109p. 1189

John F. Kennedy moves away from the Cold War concept (In Millis, Walter, ed. American military thought. New York, Bobbs-Merrill, 1966, p. 514-521). 1190

Kennedy, John F.
Kennedy et l'Afrique. Extraits de discours et écrits du Président John F. Kennedy. Translated by Pierre Nicolas. Paris, Istra, 1966, 200p.
(Kennedy and Africa: selections from speeches and writings of President John F. Kennedy.) 1191

Robinson, Edgar E., et al
Powers of the President in foreign affairs, 1945-1965: Harry S. Truman, Dwight D. Eisenhower, John F. Kennedy, Lyndon B. Johnson. San Francisco, Commonwealth Club of California, 1966, 279p. 1192

Nuclear testing and disarmament (In Kissinger, Henry A., ed. Problems of national strategy, a book of readings. New York, Praeger, 1966, p. 392-401). 1193

1967
Hilsman, Roger
To move a nation; the politics of foreign policy in the administration of John F. Kennedy. New York, Doubleday, 1967, 602p. 1194

1968
Semidei, Manuela
Kennedy et le problème cubain après la crise novembre 1962-novembre 1963 (In her Les Etats-Unis et la révolution cubaine. Paris, Armand Colin, 1968, p. 141-151).
(Kennedy and the Cuban problem after the crisis of November 1962-November 1963. In her The United States and the Cuban revolution.) 1195

Articles

1954
Kennedy, John F.
"The War in Indochina." Vital speeches 20, May 1, 1954, p. 418-424. 1196

Kennedy, John F.
"What Should the U.S. do in Indochina?" Foreign policy bulletin, May 15, 1954, p. 4-6. 1197

Kennedy, John F.
"Foreign Policy is the People's Business." New York Times magazine, August 8, 1954, p. 5. 1198

1956
Kennedy, John F.
"Statement on U.S. Immigration Policy." Congressional digest 35, January 1956, p. 18, 20. 1199

Kennedy, John F.
"America's Stake in Vietnam: Address, June 1, 1956." Vital speeches 22, August 1, 1956, p. 617-619. 1200

1957
Kennedy, John F.
"Comity and Common Sense in the Middle East: Address, February 24, 1957." Vital speeches 23, April 1, 1957, p. 359-361. 1201

Kennedy, John F.
"Should U.S. Give aid to Communist Countries: Letter, March 12, 1957." Foreign policy bulletin 36, April 15, 1957, p. 117. 1202

"Critic of France." U.S. news & world report 43, July 12, 1957, p. 16. 1203

Kennedy, John F.
"The World Around us." Arkansas law review 11, Summer 1957, p. 288. 1204

"Kennedy and Poland." New republic 137, September 2, 1957, p. 7. 1205

Kennedy, John F.
"A Democrat Looks at

Foreign Policy." Foreign affairs 36, October 1957, p. 44-59. 1206

Kennedy, John F.
"Algerian Crisis: a new Phase?" America 98, October 5, 1957, p. 15-17. 1207

1958
Kennedy, John F.
"If India Falls." Progressive 22, January 1958, p. 8-11. 1208

1960
Heindl, Gottfried
"Kennedy; die Civilcourage und der Ultraoceanismus." Vienna, Osterreichische monatshefte (16: 10), 1960, p. 19-22. ("Kennedy: Profile in Courage and Internationalism.")1209

"Kennedy zur Oder-Neisse-Frage. Für Selbstbestimmungsrecht und Wiedervereinigung Deutschlands." Lübeck, Unser Danzig (12: 23), 1960, p. 3-4.
("Kennedy on the Oder-Neisse Matter. For the Right of Sovereignty and Reunification of Germany.") 1210

Pächter, Heinz
"Kennedy nach Kuba und Wien." Berlin, Der monat (154: 13), 1960-61, p. 32-37.
("Kennedy After Cuba and Vienna.") 1211

Nixon, Richard M.
"On Disarmament: Disarmament can be won, by John F. Kennedy." Bulletin of the atomic scientists 16, June 1960, p. 217-219. 1212

Nash, C. K.
"How Kennedy Stands on Canada and World." Toronto, Financial post 54, July 23, 1960, p. 48. 1213

Kennedy, John F.
"How I'd Handle Khrushchev." Manila, Mirror, September 17, 1960, p. 16. 1214

Kennedy, John F.
"If the Soviets Control Space, they can Control Earth: Kennedy Proposals." Missiles & rockets 7, October 10, 1960, p. 12-13. 1215

Bowles, Chester
"The Foreign Policy of Senator Kennedy." America 104, October 15, 1960, p. 69-73. 1216

McNaught, K.
"Canada's Stake in the U.S. Election." Toronto, Saturday night 75, November 12, 1960, p. 11-13. 1217

Kennedy, John F.
"Where Democrats Stand on Gold and the Dollar." U.S. news & world report 49, November 14, 1960, p. 93-94. 1218

Andrade, V.
"Latin America and Mr. Kennedy." America 104, November 26, 1960, p. 288. 1219

Kalb, Bernard & Marvin L. Kalb
"How Mr. Kennedy Looks to the Russians." The reporter 23, December 8, 1960,

p. 51-52. 1220
1961
Albinowski, Stanislaw
  "Quadros i Kennedy." Warsaw, Zycie Warszawy (18: 43), 1961, p. 4, 7. ("Quadros and Kennedy.") 1221

Berger, Kurt M.
  "Präsident Kennedy." Heidelberg, Zeitschrift fur geopolitik 32, 1961, p. 18-21.
  ("President Kennedy.") 1222

Borch, Herbert von
  "Kennedys Nationaler Stil fur die Aussenpolitik." Stuttgart, Aussenpolitik 12, 1961, p. 9-15.
  ("Kennedy's Domestic Style in Foreign Affairs.") 1223

Burns, James MacG.
  "In the Eye of the Storm." London, New statesman & nation (61: 1559), 1961, p. 128-130. 1224

'Das Gesetz unserer Zeit und das Gesprach von Vien." Berlin, Einheit 16, 1961, p. 976-985.
("The Law of our Time and the Talk in Vienna.") 1225

Dasūquī, Salah al-
  "Afrīquiyā wal'l- Wilāyāt al-Muttahida 'l-Amrīkiyya." Cairo, al-majalla 51, 1961, p. 7-14.
  ("Africa and the United States": new U.S. African Policy, with Quotations from President John F. Kennedy.)
1226
Dasūquī, Salah al-
  "Al- Wilāyāt al-Muttahida bayn al-'Arab wa- Isra-īl." Cairo, al-majalla 52, 1961, p. 6-11.
  ("The United States Between the Arabs and Israel": Criticism of President Kennedy's Policy of Cordiality to Israel.) 1227

'Dopo il Vertice Kennedy-Krusciov." Rome, Nuova antologia 482, 1961, p. 89-94.
("After the Kennedy-Khrushchev Summit.") 1228

'Dopo Vienna." Florence, Rivista di studi politici internazionali (28: 2), 1961, p. 163-168.
("After Vienna.") 1229

Erwen, L.
  "Kennedy und Chruschtschow nach dem Wiener Treffen." Bonn, Internationale politik (12: 270-271), 1961, p. 7-9.
  ("Kennedy and Khrushchev After the Vienna Meeting.")
1230
Falls, Cyril
  "Fidel Castro and President Kennedy." London, Illustrated London news (238: 6354), 1961, p. 788. 1231

"Frieden der Gerechtigkeit: das Ziel der 'Neuen Amerikanischen Aussenpolitik' Kennedys." Uelsen, Germany, Riesengebirgsbote (13: 1), 1961, p. 1-2.
("Joys of Justice: the Aim of Kennedy's New U.S. Foreign Policy.") 1232

Gresham, M.
"Kennedy Opens the Tariff Battle." London, <u>Time & tide</u> (42: 50), 1961, p. 2103-2104. 1233

"John Fitzgerald: Mr. Kennedy and the Dollar." London, <u>Banker</u> 111, 1961, p. 157-162. 1234

Karol, K.S.
"Kennedy in Venezuela." London, <u>New statesman & nation</u> (62: 1605), 1961, p. 918-920. 1235

"Kennedy Muss sich Entscheiden." Berlin, <u>Deutsche aussenpolitik</u> 6, 1961, p. 9-15. ("Kennedy Must Come to a Decision.") 1236

"Kennedy's Challenge to Britain." London, <u>Time & tide</u> (42: 4), 1961, p. 116-117. 1237

"Kennedy's Latin Primer." London, <u>Time & tide</u> (42: 5), 1961, p. 154. 1238

Kruck v. Poturzyn, M.J.
"Am Rande der Wiener Tage: Treffen Kennedy und Chruschtschow." Freibourg-im-Breisgau, <u>Die kommenden</u> (15: 11), 1961, p. 2.
("On the Brink of the Day in Vienna: the Meeting of Kennedy and Khrushchev.") 1239

Lowenthal, Richard
"Kennedys Omvurdering af USAs Verdenspolitik." Copenhagen, <u>Fremtiden</u> (16: 8), 1961, p. 7-14.
("Kennedy's Reevaluation of U.S. Foreign Policy.") 1240

Matthias, L.L.
"Quo Vadis, Kennedy?" Düsseldorf, <u>Geist und zeit</u> 3, 1961, p. 133-136.
("Whither Goest thou, Kennedy?") 1241

Palmer, N.D.
"The Foreign Policy of the Kennedy Administration." Karachi, <u>Pakistan horizon</u> (14: 4), 1961, p. 280-290. 1242

Peyret, H.
"L'Expérience Kennedy." Paris, <u>Economie</u> 762, 1961, p. 1-2.
("The Kennedy Experiment.") 1243

Peyret, H.
"Paris et Vienne." Paris, <u>Economie</u> (17: 778), 1961, p. 1-2.
("Paris and Vienna.") 1244

"President and Chancellor Adenauer Hold Talks at Washington." <u>Dept. of State bulletin</u> 45, 1961, p. 967-968. 1245

"President and Greek Prime Minister Discuss Problems of Mutual Interest." <u>Dept. of State bulletin</u> 44, 1961, p. 724-727. 1246

"President Announces two new Programs to aid U.S. Exporters." <u>Dept. of State bulletin</u> 45, 1961, p. 837-838. 1247

"President Describes Role of Food-for-Peace Director." <u>Dept. of State bulle-</u>

tin 44, 1961, p. 216-218. 1248

"President Emphasizes Importance of EPC Meeting." Dept. of State bulletin 44, 1961, p. 648-649. 1249

"President Emphasizes U.S. Support for U.N. in the Congo." Dept. of State bulletin 44, 1961, p. 332-333. 1250

"President Kennedy and Chancellor Adenauer Hold Informal Talks." Dept. of State bulletin 44, 1961, p. 621-623. 1251

"President Kennedy and Prime Minister Macmillan Discuss Wide Range of World Problems." Dept. of State bulletin 44, 1961, p. 579-580. 1252

"President Kennedy Holds Talks with President of Argentina." Dept. of State bulletin 44, 1961, p. 719-720. 1253

"President Kennedy Holds Talks with President of Ghana." Dept. of State bulletin 44, 1961, p. 445-446. 1254

"President Kennedy Receives Representatives of the Belgrade Conference, Explains U.S. Position on Current World Situation." Dept. of State bulletin 44, 1961, p. 539-543. 1255

"President Kennedy's Inheritance in the Far East." London, Times review of industry (15: 169), 1961, p. 56-57. 1256

"President Makes State Visit to Paris, Meets Mr. Khrushchev at Vienna and Mr. Macmillan at London." Dept. of State bulletin 44, 1961, p. 991-999. 1257

"President Outlines Measures for Aiding Cuban Refugees." Dept. of State bulletin 44, 1961, p. 309-310. 1258

"President Sends Anniversary Greetings to Republic of Viet-Nam." Dept. of State bulletin 45, 1961, p. 810. 1259

Schappacher, Alfred
"Von Monroe bis Kennedy." Cologne, Begegnung 16, 1961, p. 93-95.
("From Monroe to Kennedy.") 1260

Silesius, pseud.
"Kennedy in der Feuerprobe." Recklinghausen, Der Schlesier (13: 8), 1961, p. 1-2.
("Kennedy in the Test of Fire.") 1261

"Soviet Reactions to President Kennedy's Isvestia Interview." Munich, Soviet affairs analysis service 13, 1961-62, p. 1-3. 1262

Sundermann, Helmut
"Kennedy, Adenauer und die Kommenden Prüfungen." Coburg, Nation Europa (4: 11), 1961, p. 43-48.
("Kennedy, Adenauer and the Coming Tests.") 1263

Takita, K.
"Blueprint for Kennedy-Ikeda 'Summit'." Hongkong, Far eastern economic review 32, 1961, p. 475.   1264

Kennedy, John F.
"Senator John F. Kennedy on the Cuban Situation: Presidential Campaign of 1960." Inter-American economic affairs 15, Winter 1961, p. 79-95.   1265

Riesman, David
"Dealing with the Russians over Berlin." American scholar (31: 1), Winter 1961-62, p. 1-27.   1266

"220 Kennedy Campaign Policy Declarations Listed." Congressional quarterly weekly report 19, January 13, 1961, p. 32-42.   1267

Sheerin, John B.
"President Kennedy's Foreign Policy." Catholic world 192, February 1961, p. 260-263.   1268

Kennedy, John F.
"History will be our Judge: Address, January 9, 1961." Vital speeches 27, February 1, 1961, p. 227-228.   1269

Drummond, Roscoe
"Mr. Kennedy's Calculated Risk: Presidential Press Conference on TV and Radio." Saturday review 44, February 11, 1961, p. 82-84.   1270

Kennedy, John F.
"Disarmament and Arms Control." Manila, Mirror, February 18, 1961, p. 26-27.   1271

Kennedy, John F.
"U.S. Balance of Payments and Gold Outflow from the United States: Message to Congress, February 6, 1961." Dept. of State bulletin 44, February 27, 1961, p. 287-295.   1272

"How JFK Made Diefenbaker Feel Good on Washington Trip." Toronto, Financial post 55, March 4, 1961, p. 10.   1273

Kennedy, John F.
"President Emphasizes U.S. Support for United Nations in the Congo: February 15, 1961." Dept. of State bulletin 44, March 6, 1961, p. 332-333.   1274

Kennedy, John F.
"President Pledges United States Support of NATO... February 15, 1961." Dept. of State bulletin 44, March 6, 1961, p. 333-334.   1275

Kennedy, John F.
"Address at a White House Reception for Latin American Diplomats, March 13, 1961." Congressional quarterly weekly report 19, March 17, 1961. p. 441-442.   1276

Kennedy, John F.
"President's Ten-Point Plan for a Decade of Progress." Buenos Aires, Review of the River Plate (129:

3417), March 17, 1961, p. 19-21. 1277

Kennedy, John F.
"Peace Corps Created on Pilot Basis; President Seeks Permanent Legislation, Message to Congress, March 1, 1961." Dept. of State bulletin 44, March 20, 1961, p. 400-403. 1278

Birnbaum, K.E.
"Kennedys Globala Sakerhetspolitik." Stockholm, Utrikespolitik (16: 2), April 1961, p. 41-46.
("Kennedy's Global Policies.") 1279

Zehrer, Hans
"A German Tribute to Kennedy. America and Israel. JFK's new Economic Frontiers." Atlas 1, April 1961, p. 57-60. 1280

Kennedy, John F.
"United States Aid to Latin America: March 13, 1961." Vital speeches 27, April 1, 1961, p. 354-356. 1281

Kennedy, John F.
"Alianza para Progreso." Dept. of State bulletin 44, April 3, 1961, p. 471-474. 1282

Kennedy, John F.
"If Laos Falls, all Southeast Asia Endangered: News Conference, March 23, 1961." U.S. news & world report 50, April 3, 1961, p. 81-82. 1283

Griffiths, E.
"Kennedy's Image Abroad: Free-world Leaders Speak their Minds." Newsweek 57, April 3, 1961, p. 42-44. 1284

"President Kennedy se Prizňává k 'Prohrané Partii'." Prague, Rudé právo, April 21, 1961, p. 3.
("President Kennedy Realizes that he Lost the Game.") 1285

"Kennedy Jednal s Eisenhowerem o Kubě." Prague, Rudé právo, April 23, 1961, p. 5.
("Kennedy Discussed Cuba with Eisenhower.") 1286

"Kennedy Learns About Personal Diplomacy." U.S. news & world report 50, April 24, 1961, p. 46-47. 1287

"President Kennedy's new Proposals on Taxation of American Firms and Individuals Abroad." Manila, American Chamber of Commerce of the Philippines journal (37: 5), May 1961, p. 195-196, 198, 200. 1288

Kennedy, John F.
"Pan American Day: Remarks, April 14, 1961." Dept. of State bulletin 44, May 1, 1961, p. 615-617. 1289

Niebuhr, Reinhold
"The President and Cuba: Mistaken Venture. United States Policy and Social Revolution, by Edward P. Morgan. Kennedy and Crises, by Tristram Coffin." New leader 44, May 1, 1961, p.

3-7. 1290

Kennedy, John F.
"President Recommends Participation in Effort to Save Nubian Monuments." Dept. of State bulletin 44, May 1, 1961, p. 643-645. 1291

Kennedy, John F.
"We do not Intend to Abandon Cuba to Communists: April 20, 1961." U.S. news & world report 50, May 1, 1961, p. 74-75. 1292

"United States and Soviet Union Exchange Messages in Regard to Events in Cuba." Dept. of State bulletin 44, May 8, 1961, p. 661-667. 1293

Kennedy, John F.
"Texto de los Mensajes Cambiados Entre el Presidente de los Estados Unidos de América, Excelentísimo Señor John F. Kennedy, y el Señor Presidente de la República, Dr. Manuel Prado (Información Oficial)." Lima, El peruano 6015, May 9, 1961, p. 1.
("Text of Messages Exchanged Between the President of the United States of America, his Excellency, Mr. John F. Kennedy, and Dr. Manuel Prado, President of the Republic of Peru.") 1294

West, A. P.
"The Day the new President Came Apart." Toronto, Saturday night 76, May 27, 1961, p. 12-13. 1295

Kennedy, John F.
"President Kennedy on International Educational Exchange." School & society 89, Summer 1961, p. 256. 1296

Kennedy, John F.
"O Programa de Ajuda ao Exterior dos Estados Unidos da América." Rio de Janeiro, Revista brasileira de política internacional (4: 14), June 1961, p. 154-169.
("The Foreign Aid Program of the U.S.A.") 1297

"Text of the President's May 26, 1961 Foreign Aid Request..." Congressional quarterly weekly report 19, June 2, 1961, p. 921-923. 1298

"The Power and la Gloire: Mr. Kennedy, on his way to Vienna, has had Talks with General de Gaulle." London, Economist 199, June 3, 1961, p. 977-978. 1299

Leon, Bernardo de
"Kennedy-Khrushchev Summit." Manila, Mirror, June 3, 1961, p. 6-7. 1300

"Advice De Gaulle Gives Kennedy on Dealing with Khrushchev." U.S. news & world report 50, June 5, 1961, p. 39-41. 1301

Kennedy, John F.
"Common Aims of Canada and the United States: Address, May 17, 1961, with Joint Communiqué." Dept. of State bulletin 44, June 5, 1961, p. 839-843. 1302

Kennedy, John F.
"Text of President Kennedy's June 6, 1961 Report to the Nation...on his European Trip." Congressional quarterly weekly report 19, June 9, 1961, p. 960-962. 1303

Snell, David
"In Paris and in Vienna." Life 50, June 9, 1961, p. 42-49. 1304

"Reassurance from Paris: President Kennedy's European Visit." Tablet 215, June 10, 1961, p. 549-550. 1305

Kennedy, John F.
"Freedom's cause: May 25, 1961." Vital speeches 27, June 15, 1961, p. 514-520. 1306

"After the Ball is Over (European Journey)." Commonweal 74, June 16, 1961, p. 291-292. 1307

Campion, D.R.
"Two Americans Abroad." America 105, June 17, 1961, p. 444-445. 1308

"JFK in the Old World." America 105, June 17, 1961, p. 434. 1309

Rovere, Richard H.
"Summit Diary." New Yorker 37, June 17, 1961, p. 95-100. 1310

Kennedy, John F.
"Text of President's June 16, 1961 Speech on Foreign Aid Program." Congressional quarterly weekly report 19, June 23, 1961, p. 1045-1046. 1311

Kennedy, John F.
"Un Juicio Sobre Fidel Castro." Havana, Universidad de La Habana (25: 151-153), July-December 1961, p. 218.
("An Opinion on Fidel Castro.") 1312

Silva Herzog, Jesús
"Reflexiones Sobre Política Internacional." Mexico City, Cuadernos americanos (117: 4), July-August 1961, p. 39-49.
("Thoughts on International Politics.") 1313

Sip, Emil
"'Vídeň v Zrcadle Amerického Tisku." Prague, Rudé právo, July 1, 1961, p. 5.
("Vienna in the Mirror of the U.S. Press.") 1314

Rusk, Dean & John F. Kennedy
"Foreign aid, an Opportunity in a Crucial Year." Dept. of State bulletin 45, July 3, 1961, p. 3-10. 1315

Kennedy, John F.
"President Sizes up Berlin Crisis...News Conference, June 28, 1961." U.S. news & world report 51, July 10, 1961, p. 52-53. 1316

Kennedy, John F.
"Berlin Shall Continue to have Freedom: News Conference, July 19, 1961." U.S. news & world report 51, July 31, 1961, p. 81-82. 1317

Alsop, Joseph
"The Most Important Decision in U.S. History, and how the President is Facing it." Saturday review 44, August 5, 1961, p. 7-9.   1318

"World Listens to a World Leader." America 105, August 5, 1961, p. 578. 1319

Kennedy, John F.
"President Submits New Legislation on Refugee aid Programs...July 21, 1961." Dept. of State bulletin 45, August 7, 1961, p. 255-257.
1320
"Message to the Punta del Este Conference." Buenos Aires, Review of the River Plate (130: 3431), August 11, 1961, p. 17-18.   1321

Brock, T.F.
"Again, the President asks for Sacrifice; Berlin Crisis Speech to American People." Ave Maria 94, August 12, 1961, p. 18.   1322

Kennedy, John F.
"Berlin Crisis." Vital speeches 27, August 15, 1961, p. 642-645.   1323

Folliard, E.T.
"Kennedy's Nerves and NATO: Berlin Crisis." America 105, September 16, 1961, p. 730.   1324

U.S. President (John F. Kennedy)
"Survival of the United Nations: Address Delivered to the General Assembly of the United Nations on September 25, 1961." Congressional quarterly weekly report 19, September 29, 1961, p. 1672-1675.   1325

Hyman, Sidney
"The Testing of Kennedy." New republic 145, October 2, 1961, p. 11-14.   1326

Kennedy, John F.
"President Kennedy Receives Representatives of Belgrade Conference, Explains U.S. Position on Current World Situation...September 13, 1961." Dept. of State bulletin 45, October 2, 1961, p. 539-543.   1327

Kennedy, John F.
"President Sends Message to Conference on Science and World Affairs." Dept. of State bulletin 45, October 2, 1961, p. 553.   1328

"Blessed are the Peacemakers: Kennedy's U.N. Address." Ave Maria 94, October 7, 1961, p. 16. 1329

"Race for Peace: Kennedy's UN Address." America 106, October 7, 1961, p. 7.   1330

McNaspy, C.J.
"Reading the Papers in Spain: Kennedy's UN Address." America 106, October 14, 1961, p. 36.   1331

Kennedy, John F.
"President Signs bill Creating U.S. Disarmament

Agency: September 26, 1961." Dept. of State bulletin 45, October 16, 1961, p. 646. 1332

Kennedy, John F.
"President Announces two new Programs to aid U.S. Exporters: October 27, 1961." Dept. of State bulletin 45, November 20, 1961, p. 837-838. 1333

"Text of Soviet Newspaper Isvestia's Interview with Kennedy." Wall Street journal 158, November 29, 1961, p. 20. 1334

Chiari Remón, Roberto F. (President of Panama)
"Nuestras Relaciones con Estados Unidos; Carta del Presidente Chiari, Sept. 1961." Panama, Lotería (6: 73), December 1961, p. 15-19.
("Our Relations with the United States: Letter of President Chiari, September 1961.") 1335

Kennedy, John F.
"Discurso Pronunciado en la Morita, Estado Aragua, Venezuela." Caracas, Política 19, December 1961, p. 126-128.
("Speech Delivered at La Morita, Aragua State, Venezuela.") 1336

"Our Vital Interests: Kennedy's Seattle Speech." Commonweal 75, December 1, 1961, p. 243-244. 1337

Kennedy, John F.
"Diplomacy and Defense: a Test of National Maturity: Address, November 16, 1961." Dept. of State bulletin 45, December 4, 1961, p. 915-917. 1338

"Text of President's Trade Speech Before N.A.M." Congressional quarterly weekly report 19, December 8, 1961, p. 1937-1941. 1339

Kennedy, John F.
"What Kennedy told the Russian People: Kennedy Adzhubei Interview." Time 78, December 8, 1961, p. 20. 1340

Kennedy, John F.
"What Common Market Means to the U.S.: Excerpts from News Conference, November 29, 1961." U.S. news & world report 51, December 11, 1961, p. 8. 1341

Kennedy, John F.
"Text of President's Trade Talk to AFL-CIO, December 7, 1961 Address to the Convention, Bal Harbour, Fla." Congressional quarterly weekly report 19, December 15, 1961, p. 1957-1959. 1342

Kennedy, John F.
"The Hour of Decision: a new Approach to American Trade Policy: December 6, 1961." Dept. of State bulletin 45, December 25, 1961, p. 1039-1047. 1343

1962

Alsop, Stewart
"Der Präsident und die Fische: Kennedys Weltpoli-

tische Konzeption." Hamburg, Der spiegel (16: 13), 1962, p. 64-69.
("The President and the Fish: Kennedy's Concept of International Politics.") 1344

"J.F. Kennedy Attend Beaucoup de la Nouvelle Loi Américaine sur l'Expansion du Commerce." Paris, Economie (18: 840), 1962, p. 4-5.
("J.F. Kennedy Expects Much from the new U.S. Law on Trade Expansion.") 1345

McGhee, George C.
"John Fitzgerald: the President's Trade Program--Key to the Grand Design." Dept. of State bulletin 46, 1962, p. 289-293. 1346

Paine, J.
"Kennedy and Europe." London, Time & tide (43: 30), 1962, p. 17. 1347

"The President and the 'Captive Nations Week'." Ukrainian quarterly 18, 1962, p. 101-109. 1348

"President Kennedy Reaffirms Views on Frame Work for Conduct of Disarmament Negotiations." Dept. of State bulletin 46, 1962, p. 465-470. 1349

Wesley, David
"Kennedy ou le Prestige de la Marque." Paris, Temps modernes (18: 199), 1962, p. 1052-1071.
("Kennedy, or the Prestige of the Mark.") 1350

"Foreign Policy of the Kennedy Administration." Current history (42: 245), January 1962, p. 1-48. 1351

"On Interview with U.S. President Kennedy." Current digest of the Soviet press 13, January 3, 1962, p. 3-5. 1352

Kennedy, John F.
"President and Mrs. Kennedy Visit Venezuela and Colombia: Remarks, December 16-17, with Address and Joint Communiqué." Dept. of State bulletin 46, January 15, 1962, p. 89-94. 1353

Kennedy, John F.
"Kennedy-Betancourt Communiqué." Current history (42: 246), February 1962, p. 114-115. 1354

"Kennedy Navrhuje Setkání Ministrú Zahranici na 12. Brezna." Prague, Rudé právo, March 7, 1962, p. 5.
("Kennedy Proposes a Meeting of Foreign Ministers for March 12.") 1355

Kennedy, John F.
"Text of the President's Address on Testing and Disarmament." Congressional quarterly weekly report 20, March 9, 1962, p. 413-415. 1356

"Momentous Step: Resumption of Atmospheric Nuclear Tests." Commonweal 75,

March 16, 1962, p. 631-632. 1357

Kennedy, John F.
"Nuclear Testing and Disarmament." Dept. of State bulletin 46, March 19, 1962, p. 443-448. 1358

"President Kennedy Reaffirms Views on Framework for Conduct of Disarmament Negotiations..." Dept. of State bulletin 46, March 19, 1962, p. 465-470. 1359

Newman, James R.
"Testing: What does Kennedy mean?" New republic 146, March 26, 1962, p. 11-13. 1360

"U.S. Plan to Resume Nuclear Testing Explained to Japanese Prime Minister..." Dept. of State bulletin 46, March 26, 1962, p. 497-498. 1361

Alsop, Stewart
"The two Grand Strategies: Talk with President Kennedy." London, Time & tide 43, March 29, 1962, p. 8-13. 1362

Kennedy, John F.
"Statement Reporting Nuclear Test ban Impasse Because of USSR Refusal to Accept international Inspection." New York times, March 30. 1962, p. 2, column 2. 1363

Alsop, Stewart
"Kennedy's Grand Strategy." Saturday evening post 235, March 31, 1962, p. 11-17. 1364

Kennedy, John F.
"Exchange of Messages on Question of Exploration and use of Outer Space." United Nations review 9, April 1962, p. 37-38. 1365

Wright, Esmond
"Foreign Policy Since Dulles." Edinburgh, The political quarterly 33, April 1962, p. 114-128. 1366

Kennedy, John F.
"Accomplishments of Alliance for Progress; Address, March 13, 1962." Vital speeches 28, April 1, 1962, p. 354-356. 1367

Kennedy, John F.
"Fulfilling the Pledges of the Alliance for Progress." Dept. of State bulletin 46, April 2, 1962, p. 539-542. 1368

Kennedy, John F.
"U.S. Presents Proposal to U.S.S.R. for Cooperation in Space Exploration: March 7, 1962." Dept. of State bulletin 46, April 2, 1962, p. 536-538. 1369

Kennedy, John F.
"President Repeats U.S. Desire for Effective Test ban Treaty: March 29, 1962." Dept. of State bulletin 46,

April 16, 1962, p. 624-625. 1370

'Ittihāmat li-Kīnidī min al-Kūbiyīn fī Amrīkā bi-Shā n al-Ghazw." Cairo, al-Akhbār, April 17, 1962, p. 2. ("Cubans in America Accuse Kennedy of the Invasion.") 1371

Kennedy, John F.
"President Reviews World Problems with Prime Minister Macmillan: Joint Communiqué, April 29, 1962." Dept. of State bulletin 46, May 14, 1962, p. 802-803. 1372

Kennedy, John F.
"Trade or Fade: Digest of Address." Toronto, Financial post 56, May 19, 1962, p. 6. 1373

Kennedy, John F.
"The Future Trade of the United States." Dept. of State bulletin 46, May 21, 1962, p. 823-826. 1374

Mexico. Secretaria de Relaciones Exteriores
"Visita del Presidente de los Estados Unidos de América, Excelentísimo Señor John F. Kennedy a Mexico." Mexico, México de hoy (14: 140), June 1962, p. 4-15.
("Visit of the President of the United States of America, his Excellency, Mr. John F. Kennedy to Mexico.") 1375

Kennedy, John F.
"Remarks Before the Conference on Trade Policy, May 17, 1962." Dept. of State bulletin 46, June 4, 1962, p. 906-909. 1376

Kennedy, John F.
"Trade and the Atlantic Partnership..." Dept. of State bulletin 46, June 4, 1962, p. 906-911. 1377

Kennedy, John F.
"President Congratulates Venezuela on Firm Defense of Democracy: Letter, June 5, 1962." Dept. of State bulletin 46, June 25, 1962, p. 1023. 1378

Brandon, D.
"Kennedy's Record in Foreign Affairs." Catholic world 195, July 1962, p. 219-227. 1379

"Intihā' Ziyārat Kinīdī lil-Miksīk." Cairo, al-Ahrām, July 2, 1962, p. 2.
("The End of Kennedy's Visit to Mexico.") 1380

Murray, P.
"The Kennedys in Mexico." Catholic messenger 80, July 12, 1962, p. 5. 1381

Kennedy, John F.
"President Talks with Group of Brazilian Students: Interview, July 31, 1962." Dept. of State bulletin 47, August 20, 1962, p. 289-291. 1382

Kennedy, John F.
"U.S. Participation in the United Nations During 1961: Letter Transmitting to Congress the Annual Report." Dept. of State bulletin 47, August 20, 1962, p. 293-294. 1383

Kennedy, John F.
"United States Reviews Position on test ban Treaty: August 1, 1962." Dept. of State bulletin 47, August 20, 1962, p. 283-284. 1384

Kennedy, John F.
"What Kennedy Wants: Digest of Address." Toronto, Financial post 56, August 25, 1962, p. 6. 1385

Rovere, Richard H.
"Letter from Washington." New Yorker 38, August 25, 1962, p. 101-107. 1386

Joel, K.
"Footnote to a Triumph: the Kennedys' Visit to Guadalupe Basilica." Columbia 42, September 1962, p. 26-27. 1387

Kennedy, John F.
"President Kennedy's Statement on the Taiwan Strait, June 27, 1962." Current history 43, September 1962, p. 178. 1388

"Amrīkā Tuhadid Rūsyā wa-Kūbā; Sahīfah Kūbīyah Tattahim Kīnidī bil-Tadakhul fī shu'ūn Kūbā." Cairo, al-Misa', September 6, 1962, p. 1.
("America Warns Russia and Cuba; Cuban Newspaper Accuses Kennedy of Interfering in Cuban Affairs.") 1389

Kennedy, John F.
"Text of the President's September 12, 1962 Speech on Space." Congressional quarterly weekly report 20, September, 14, 1962, p. 1550-1551. 1390

"Kennedy's Fateful Decision: the Night the Reds Clinched Cuba." U.S. news & world report 53, September 17, 1962, p. 41-42. 1391

Kennedy, John F.
"Latest Word From Kennedy on the Red Buildup in Cuba: News Conference, September 13, 1962." U.S. news & world report 53, September 24, 1962, p. 111. 1392

Kennedy, John F.
"President States U.S. Policy Toward Cuba." Dept. of State bulletin 47, October 1, 1962, p. 481-482. 1393

Kennedy, John F.
"The Space Challenge: September 13, 1962." Vital speeches 28, October 1, 1962, p. 738-740. 1394

Kennedy, John F.
"USA Zustaly Pozadu v Dobývání Kosmu." Prague, Rudé právo, October 3, 1962, p. 3.
("The United States Remains Behind in Winning World Favor.") 1395

"White House to Vatican: the President's Letter on the Council." America 107, October 13, 1962, p. 870. 1396

Kennedy, John F.
"Sharing the Financial Burdens of a Changing World:

September 20, 1962." Dept. of State bulletin 47, October 15, 1962, p. 573-575. 1397

Kennedy, John F.
"Text of President's Message to the Nation on Cuba: October 22, 1962 Speech on the Quarantine of Cuba." Congressional quarterly weekly report 20, October 26, 1962, p. 2058-2059. 1398

Rovere, Richard H.
"Letter from Washington: Cuban Crisis." New Yorker 38, November 3, 1962, p. 118-123. 1399

Kennedy, John F.
"Statement...Announcing USSR Missile Bases in Cuba are Being Dismantled." New York times, November 3, 1962, p. 7, column 4. 1400

Bell, Coral
"President Kennedy and Foreign Policy." Sydney, Australian quarterly 34, December 1962, p. 7-21. 1401

Lawrence, William H., et al, eds.
"Kennedy Talks About Red China, Cuba, Steel, a Second Term: Interview." U.S. news & world report 53, December 31, 1962, p. 54-63. 1402

1963
Birrenbach, K.
"Was will Kennedy? Der Amerikanisch-Sowjetische Dialog." Cologne, Die politische meinung (89: 8), 1963, p. 19-25.
("What Does Kennedy Want? The American-Soviet Dialog.") 1403

"Blicke in das Zeitgeschehn. Der 36. Präsident der USA--Zeitgewonnen--Angriff auf Chruschtschow." Freibourg-im-Breisgau, Die kommenden (17: 23), 1963, p. 3-4.
("A Backward Glance: the 36th President of the USA. Time won. Attack on Khrushchev.") 1404

"Bonn-Kennedy Besuch: JFK und die Deutschen." Hamburg, Der spiegel (17: 26), 1963, p. 15-24.
("Bonn-Kennedy Visit: JFK and the Germans.") 1405

"Bonn-Kennedy-Besuch: Kanzler schon da." Hamburg, Der spiegel (17: 20), 1963, p. 22.
("Bonn-Kennedy Visit: The Chancellor is Already Here.") 1406

"Bonn-Kennedy Reaktionen: Nichts dran Machen." Hamburg, Der spiegel (17: 8), 1963, p. 16-17.
("Bonn-Kennedy Reactions: Nothing of Consequence.") 1407

"La Défense du Dollar: Extraits du Message du Président Kennedy." Paris, Problèmes économiques 814, 1963, p. 6-9.
("The Defense of the Dollar: Excerpts from President Kennedy's Message.") 1408

Donhoff, Marion (Gräfin)
"Was wird Bleiben? John F. Kennedys Politik für die Welt von Morgen." Hamburg, Die zeit (18: 48), 1963, p. 1.
(What Will Remain? John F. Kennedy's Policy for the World of Tomorrow.") 1409

Dürrenmatt, Peter
"John F. Kennedys Konzeption." Zürich, Reformatio 12, 1963, p. 401-402.
("John F. Kennedy's Concept.") 1410

Dürrenmatt, Peter
"Kennedy in Europa." Zürrich, Reformatio 12, 1963, p. 398-400.
("Kennedy in Europe.") 1411

Edwards, Robert G.
"Wende in Washington? Einige Bemerkungen zu dem Deutschland-Besuch Kennedys." Göttingen, Archiv (17: 27), 1963.
("Turning Point in Washington? A few Remarks on Kennedy's Visit to Germany.") 1412

Epstein, Julius
"Amerikas Kriegsreserven für die Sowjets? Ein neuer Plan Präsident Kennedys." Hamburg, Der spiegel (17: 5), 1963, p. 54-55.
("America's War-reserves for the Soviets? A new Plan of President Kennedy.") 1413

Epstein, Julius
"Kennedy Wechselt den Kurs. Neue Politik Gegenüber Exilgruppen und Satellitenländern." Cologne, Rheinische merkur (18: 18), 1963, p. 8.
("Kennedy Changes his Course. New Policy Towards Exile Groups and Satellite Nations.") 1414

Erven, L.
"Zur Europareise Präsident Kennedys." Bonn, Internationale politik (14: 318-319), 1963, p. 15-17.
("President Kennedy's European Trip.") 1415

Fabian, Rainer
"Kennedy und die Deutschen." Cologne, Rheinische merkur (18: 26), 1963, p. 24.
("Kennedy and the Germans.") 1416

Falls, Cyril
"President and Chancellor." London, Illustrated London news (243: 6466), 1963, p. 8-11. 1417

Guttenberg, Karl T. zu
"Kennedys Entspannungspolitik und die Deutsche Frage." Cologne, Rheinische merkur (18: 37), 1963, p. 5.
("Kennedy's Policy of Relieving Tension and the German Question.") 1418

Herre, F.
"Kennedy in Deutschland." Cologne, Die politische meinung (85: 8), 1963, p. 3-6.
("Kennedy in Germany.") 1419

Inglis, Brian
"Kennedy in Ireland." London, Spectator 7045, 1963,

p. 6-7.   1420

Kaiser, Horst
"Die Deutschen in der Nachfolge Kennedy." Bad Godesberg, Gemeinschaft und politik 11, 1963, p. 343-344.
("Germans in Imitation of Kennedy.")   1421

"Kennedy-Besuch. Ko-Existenz: Demokrat auf dem Tiger." Hamburg, Der spiegel (17: 27), 1963, p. 15-16.
("Kennedy's Visit: Coexistence: Democrat on the Tiger.")
     1422

Kennedy, John F.
"Discurso Pronunciado... en San José de Costa Rica, el 18 de Marzo y con Motivo de la Inauguración en San José, de la Conferencia de Presidentes de las Repúblicas Centroamericanas y de Estados Unidos..." Caracas, Documentos (Revista de información política) 12, January-March 1963, p. 182-186.
("Speech Delivered... in San José, Costa Rica, March 18 (1963) upon the Inauguration in San José, of the Conference of the Presidents of the Central American Republics and of the U.S.A...")   1423

Kennedy, John F.
"Kennedy at the UN: Excerpts from Address, September 20, 1963." United Nations review 10, 1963, p. 9-10.
     1424
"Kennedys Zahlungsbilanz-Botschaft." Frankfurt am Main, Aussenhandelsdienst der Industrie- und Handelskammer und Wirtschaftsverbande 17, 1963, p. 612.
("Kennedy's Message on the Balance of Payments.")
     1425

Koch, Thilo
"Der Präsident. Vor dem Staatsbesuch: ein Politisches Porträt." Hamburg, Die zeit (18: 25), 1963, p. 16.
("The President. Upon the State Visit: a Political Portrait.")   1426

Leuchtenberg, William E.
"President Kennedy and the end of the Postwar World: the President was Succeeding in his Goal of Getting America 'Moving Again' in Foreign Affairs." Bologna, American review 3, Winter 1963, p. 18-29.   1427

Lohr, George
"Halbzeit für Kennedy." Berlin, Deutsche aussenpolitik 8, 1963, p. 264-274.
("Half-time for Kennedy.")
     1428
Miller, J.
"Präsident Kennedys Pressekonferenzen." Bad Godesberg, Zeitungs-verlag und zeitschriften-verlag 60, 1963, p. 2063.
("President Kennedy's Press Conferences.")   1429

"'Mr. President' in Berlin." Cologne, Polizei/polizei praxis 54, 1963, p. 231-236.   1430

"Nach dem Kennedy-Besuch." Coburg, Nation Europa (8: 13), 1963, p. 38-44.

("After the Kennedy Visit.")
                                    1431
Paetel, Karl O.
 "Kennedy und das 'Andere
Kuba'." Frankfurt-am-Main,
Geist und tat 18, 1963, p.
173-175.
 ("Kennedy and the 'Other
Cuba'.")   1432

Pesendorfer, Franz
 "Kennedy Spielt mit der
Sympathie der Verbündeten."
Salzburg, Berichte und infor-
mationen der Oesterreichischen
Forschungsinstitutes für Wirt-
schaft und Politik (18: 861),
1963, p. 1-3.
 ("Kennedy Plays on the Sym-
pathy of the Allies.")   1433

Pleyer, Wilhelm
 'Nach dem Kennedy-Besuch."
Munich, Schlesische rundschau
(15: 27), 1963, p. 5.
 ("After the Kennedy Visit.")
                                    1434
"Präsident Kennedy in Deutsch-
land." Bonn, Bulletin des
Presse- und Information-
samtes der Bundesregierung
108, 1963, p. 957.
 ("President Kennedy in Ger-
many.")   1435

"Präsident Kennedys Freindens-
Strategie." Hannover, Das
andere Deutschland 13, 1963,
p. 1.
 ("President Kennedy's Friendly
Strategy.")   1436

"Präsident Kennedys Letzter
Besuch bei den Vereinten
Nationen." Baden-Baden,
Vereinte nationen 11, 1963,
p. 185-186.

 ("President Kennedy's Last
Visit to the UN.")   1437

Samhaber, Ernst
 "Kennedys Hand in Süda-
merika." Cologne, Rheinische
merkur (18: 25), 1963, p. 6.
 ("Kennedy's Hand in South
America.")   1438

Seeberg, Axel
 "Partnerschaft--aber wie?"
Hamburg, Sonntagsblatt 48,
1963, p. 1-2.
 ("Partnership: but how?")
                                    1439
Sommer, Theo
 'Europa und Amerika: ein
Plädoyer für Kennedys
Grossen Plan." Hamburg,
Die zeit (18: 26), 1963, p.
8.
 ('Europe and America: a
Plea for Kennedy's Great
Plan.")   1440

Stain, Walter
 "Entspannung auf unsere
Kosten: Ist Kennedy Deutsch-
lands Präsident?" Munich,
Schlesische rundschau (15:
39), 1963, p. 3.
 ("The Easing of our Food
Supply: Is Kennedy Germany's
President?")   1441

Steinitz, Hans
 "Das Vertrauen der Deutschen Eröbert." Bad Reichenhall, Europa (14: 8), 1963,
p. 16.
 ("The Confidence of the
Germans is Obtained.") 1442

"USA-State Department:
Keine Zeit Nachzudenken."
Hamburg, Der spiegel (17:

9), 1963, p. 61-62.
("U.S. State Department: no Time for Afterthoughts.")   1443

Veiga Veiriz, M.
"Kennedy Visita a Europa." Lisbon, Brotéria (77: 1), 1963, p. 86-91.
("Kennedy Visits Europe.")   1444

Werner, Richard
"Kennedys neue Experimente zur militärischen NATO-Diskussion." Cologne, Blätter für deutsche und internationale politik (8: 5), 1963, p. 356-360.
("Kennedy's new Experiments on NATO's Military Discussions.")   1445

"Wie steht es um Berlin und Europa, Herr Präsident? Aus einem Interview mit Präsident Kennedy." Bochum, Germany, Gewerkschäftliche rundschau 16, 1963, p. 64-65.
("How are Things in Berlin and Europe, Mr. President? From an Interview with President Kennedy.")   1446

"As Kennedy Looks at U.S. and World: his Views for '63." U.S. news & world report 54, January 14, 1963, p. 35-38.   1447

"How President Kennedy Upset Cuban Invasion of April 1961." U.S. news & world report 54, February 4, 1963, p. 29-30.   1448

Fromm, J. & F.C. Painton
"U.S. Failing in Europe?" U.S. news & world report 54, March 25, 1963, p. 48-52.   1449

Kennedy, John F.
"President's March 18, 1963 Speech to Costa Rica Conference of Presidents: San Jose, Costa Rica." Congressional quarterly weekly report 21, March 29, 1963, p. 459-460.   1450

Kennedy, John F.
"Presidents' Meeting at San Jose: Statements, Addresses and Remarks, March 18-21, 1963." Dept. of State bulletin 48, April 8, 1963, p. 511-520.   1451

Kennedy, John F.
"Free-World Defense and Assistance Programs; Message to Congress, April 2, 1963." Dept. of State bulletin 48, April 22, 1963, p. 591-599.   1452

Kennedy, John F.
"Sir Winston Churchill Becomes Honorary Citizen of United States: Exchange of Remarks, April 9, 1963." Dept. of State bulletin 48, May 6, 1963, p. 715-716.   1453

"President Kennedy and Prime Minister Pearson of Canada Hold Talks: Text of a Joint Communiqué Issued on May 11, 1963 at the Close of Their Meetings at Hyannis Port, Mass., May 10-11." Dept. of State bulletin 48, May 27, 1963, p. 815-817.   1454

Kennedy, John F.
"President Kennedy's June 10, 1963 Address on World Peace: Remarks at American University, Washington, D.C." Congressional quarterly weekly report 21, June 14, 1963, p. 976-978. 1455

Halle, L.J.
"Appraisal of Kennedy as World Leader." New York times magazine, June 16, 1963, p. 7. 1456

Canavan, F.
"Peace on Earth: Parallels Between Pope John's Encyclical and President Kennedy's American University Speech." America 108, June 22, 1963, p. 876. 1457

"President Penelope." London, The economist 207, June 22, 1963, p. 1226-1227. 1458

"A European Barnstorm for Kennedy." Manila, Philippines herald magazine, June 29, 1963, p. 10-11. 1459

"Kennedy in Germany." London, The economist 207, June 29, 1963, p. 1347-1348. 1460

Kennedy, John F.
"Strategy of Peace: Address, June 10, 1963." Vital speeches 29, July 1, 1963, p. 558-561. 1461

"Why Wilson did not see Kennedy." London, Time & tide, July 4-10, 1963, p. 6. 1462

Inglis, Brian
"Kennedy in Ireland." London, Spectator, July 5, 1963, p. 6-7. 1463

"Kennedy Enraptures Germany, Challenges De Gaulle." Life 55, July 5, 1963, p. 30-31. 1464

Kennedy, John F.
"Transcript of President Kennedy's Speech on Unity: June 25th Speech in Frankfurt, Germany on Western Unity." Congressional quarterly weekly report 21, July 5, 1963, p. 1111-1113. 1465

MacNeice, Louis
"Great Summer Sale: Visit to Eire." London, New statesman 66, July 5, 1963, p. 10-12. 1466

"Old and New Frontiers: Kennedy's European Visit." Tablet 217, July 6, 1963, p. 725-726. 1467

"President Kennedy Visits the Land of his Ancestors." London, Illustrated London news 243, July 6, 1963, p. 9. 1468

"President Kennedy's Working Visit to the Federal German Republic." London, Illustrated London news 243, July 6, 1963, p. 11, 18-19. 1469

Kennedy, John F.
"President Urges Quest for East-West Settlement in Berlin Speech: Remarks of the

President, June 26, 1963 at Free University, West Berlin." Congressional quarterly weekly report 21, July 12, 1963, p. 1135-1136. 1470

Rovere, Richard H.
"Our Far-Flung Correspondents: Journal of a Pseudo-Event." New Yorker 39, July 13, 1963, p. 76-78. 1471

"Why Western Europe Cheered Kennedy." U.S. news & world report 54, July 15, 1963, p. 32-34. 1472

Kennedy, John F.
"President Kennedy Visits Europe: Texts of Joint Communiqués Released at Bonn, Birch Grove House, Sussex, and Rome, with Major Addresses and Remarks, June 23-July 2, 1963." Dept. of State bulletin 49, July 22, 1963, p. 114-137. 1473

"President Kennedy Visits Europe..." Dept. of State bulletin 49, July 22, 1963, p. 114-137. 1474

"Giving a Little: Concerning Mr. Kennedy's Speech at American University." New republic 149, July 6, 1963, p. 5. 1475

Kennedy, John F.
"Secretary Assigned Leadership in International Aviation Policy: Letter to Secretary Rusk, June 22, 1963." Dept. of State bulletin 49, July 29, 1963, p. 160-161. 1476

"President Recommends Expansion of Peace Corps: Text of a Letter from President Kennedy to Lyndon B. Johnson, President of the Senate & John W. McCormack, Speaker of the House of Representatives." Dept. of State bulletin 49, July 29, 1963, p. 170-172. 1477

Paul VI, Pope
"To President John F. Kennedy: Achievements of the U.S. in the Fields of Race Relations, Space Exploration, World Peace, Economic Assistance; Harmony of President Kennedy's Statements with Pope John's Pacem in Terris." Vatican City, Acta apostolicae sedis 55, August 1963, p. 650-651. 1478

Smith, Merriman
"Too Many Stops Drain Impact from Kennedy Travels Abroad." Nation's business 51, August 1963, p. 21-22. 1479

Kennedy, John F.
"The Nuclear Test ban Treaty: a Step Toward Peace." Dept. of State bulletin 49, August 12, 1963, p. 234-238. 1480

Kennedy, John F.
"Test Ban Treaty: Address, July 26, 1963." Vital speeches 29, August 15, 1963, p. 644-647. 1481

Kennedy, John F.
"President Recommends Revision of Immigration Laws: Letter, July 23, 1963." Dept. of State bulletin 49, August 19, 1963, p. 298-300. 1482

Kennedy, John F.
"President Kennedy's Remarks on Export Expansion, September 17, 1963, Before the White House Conference on Exports." Congressional quarterly weekly report 21, September 20, 1963, p. 1665-1666. 1483

Kennedy, John F.
"President Discusses Viet-Nam on CBS and NBC News Programs, September 2 and September 9, 1963." Dept. of State bulletin 49, September 30, 1963, p. 498-500. 1484

Kennedy, John F.
"Discurso ante la Sociedad Interamericana de Prensa (Florida, Noviembre 18, 1963)." Caracas, Documentos (Revista de información política) 15, October-December 1963, p. 93-98.
("Speech Before the Interamerican Press Association, Florida, November 18, 1963.") 1485

O'Broin, Leon
"Ireland as a Rostrum." London, Month 30, October 1963, p. 213-219. 1486

Kennedy, John F.
"Transcript of President Kennedy's Monetary Fund Speech." Congressional quarterly weekly report 21, October 4, 1963, p. 1738-1739. 1487

Kennedy, J.F., et al
"White House Holds Conference on Export Expansion: Texts of Three Addresses made on September 17 Before the White House Conference on Export Expansion, Which met at Washington, September 17-18, 1963." Dept. of State bulletin 49, October 14, 1963, p. 595-605. 1488

Kennedy, John F.
"Responsibilities of the United Nations: Address, September 20, 1963." Vital speeches 30, October 15, 1963, p. 2-5. 1489

"Text of President Kennedy's Letter Explaining Wheat Sale: October 10, 1963..." Congressional quarterly weekly report 21, October 18, 1963, p. 1834-1835. 1490

Kennedy, John F.
"Selling Wheat to Russia: Kennedy Gives his Reasons, October 9, 1963." U.S. news & world report 55, October 21, 1963, p. 53. 1491

Kennedy, John F.
"Strengthening the International Monetary System, Remarks September 30, 1963." Dept. of State bulletin 49, October 21, 1963, p. 610-613. 1492

Kennedy, John F.
"President Kennedy Assesses Improved East-West Re-

lations." Congressional quarterly weekly report 21, October 25, 1963, p. 1864-1865. 1493

Kennedy, John F.
"What Women can do now for Peace: Interview." McCall's 91, November 1963, p. 102-103. 1494

Kennedy, John F.
"President Kennedy Defends Foreign Aid Program." Congressional quarterly weekly report 21, November 15, 1963, p. 2005-2006. 1495

Kennedy, John F.
"Science and International Cooperation." Dept. of State bulletin 49, November 18, 1963, p. 778-782. 1496

Kennedy, John F.
"President Urges Hemisphere Progress on Four Fronts." Congressional quarterly weekly report 21, November 22, 1963, p. 2051-2053. 1497

"Kennedy to Explain U.S. Policy; to Address Weizmann Institute Dinner." London, Jewish observer 12, November 22, 1963, p. 5-6. 1498

Kennedy, John F.
"Our Obligation to the Family of Man: Address, November 8, 1963." Dept. of State bulletin 49, November 25, 1963, p. 806-810. 1499

Kennedy, John F.
"Five Speeches and a Reply to Questions at a News Conference, by J.F. Kennedy. Printed in the Jewish Observer and Introduced by Abba Eban under the Title, 'Kennedy's Bequest to the Middle East'." London, Jewish observer 12, November 29, 1963, p. 23-26. 1500

Kennedy, John F.
"Address to Convention by Film. Hadassah Convention Report: Opening Session." Hadassah magazine 44, December 1963, p. 8. 1501

Kennedy, John F.
"The Educated Citizen's Responsibility in an age of Change: an Address by the President of the United States Commemorating the Founding of the University." (In "Stability and Change Through Law." Vanderbilt law review 17, December 1963, p. 1-). 1502

Klutznick, Philip
"Kennedy and his ZOA Speech." American zionist 54, December 1963, p. 4. 1503

Kennedy, John F.
"Latin America: Necessity for Political Democracy and Stability: Address, November 18, 1963." Vital speeches 30, December 1, 1963, p. 102-105. 1504

Heikal, H.
"Kennedy and After; the Egyptian View." Reprinted from Cairo's al-Ahram. London, Jewish observer 12, December 6, 1963, p. 5. 1505

Kennedy, John F.
"Battle for Progress with Freedom in the Western Hemisphere: Address, November 18, 1963." Dept. of State bulletin 49, December 9, 1963, p. 900-904.   1506

Cleveland, Harlan
'Great Power and Great Diversity: the Perceptions and Policies of President Kennedy: Address, December 1, 1963." Dept. of State bulletin 49, December 23, 1963, p. 964-969.   1507

1964
Falk, Stanley L.
"The National Security Council under Truman, Eisenhower and Kennedy." Political science quarterly (79: 3), 1964, p. 403-434.   1508

Krafft-Delmari, Fr.
'Die Weltpolitik Drängt weiter- wohin Drängt sie? Kennedys Professorentrust und Johnsons Aufräumarbeit." Salzburg, Berichte und informationen der Oesterreichischen Forschungsinstitutes für Wirtschaft und Politik (19: 921), 1964, p. 1-3.
("International Politics Surges Forward: Whereto? Kennedy's Braintrust and Johnson's Cleanup.")   1509

Rendulic, Lothar
'Das Erbe nach Kennedy und die Krise des Westens." Salzburg, Berichte und informationen der Oesterreichischen Forschungsinstitutes für Wirtschaft und Politik (19: 917), 1964, p. 1-3.
("The Heritage of Kennedy and the Crisis of the West.")   1510

Kennedy, John F.
"Peace and Freedom Walk Together." Way 20, January-February 1964, p. 13-17.   1511

Kennedy, John F.
"President Kennedy's Address to the Oireachtas on 28 June, 1963." Dublin, Irish ecclesiastical record 101, January 1964, p. 60-66.   1512

Verrier, A.
"Kennedy and Europe: the end of a Chapter." London, The world today 20, January 1964, p. 39-46.   1513

"Kennedy Fellowships for Weizmann Institute." Jerusalem, Israel digest 7, January 3, 1964, p. 8.   1514

Luyks, B.
"President Kennedy and the Congo." America 110, January 4, 1964, p. 17.   1515

Kennedy, John F.
'Does America Have a Vocation to World Service?" (Excerpts from President Kennedy's Speeches, Read by Bishop Hannan at Conclusion of Funeral Mass). Shield 43, February-March 1964, p. 2-3.   1516

Bundy, McGeorge
"The Presidency and the Peace." Foreign affairs 42, April 1964, p. 353-365.   1517

Nieburg, H. L.
"John F. Kennedy and the Revival of Diplomacy." Meerut, International review of history & political science (1: 1), June 1964, p. 1-12. 1518

Kennedy, John F.
"1957 Kennedy Talk Stressed Spiritual Side of World Crisis (Excerpts)." Catholic Association for International Peace news 25, October 1964, p. 6-7. 1519

Nixon, Richard M.
"Cuba, Castro and John F. Kennedy." Reader's digest 85, November 1964, p. 281-284. 1520

Robbins, J.
"Visit to County Wexford, Ireland." Redbook 124, November 1964, p. 76-78. 1521

Roddy, Jon
"Ireland: the Kennedy cult: They Cried the Rain down that Night." Look 28, November 17, 1964, p. 66-72. 1522

1965
Gavin, James M.
"On Dealing With DeGaulle." Atlantic 215, June 4, 1965, p. 49-54. 1523

"J.F.K.'s Image in Poland." America 112, June 12, 1965, p. 844-845. 1524

Schlesinger, Arthur M.
"Bay of Pigs, a Horrible Expensive Lesson. Excerpts from A Thousand Days." Life 59, July 23, 1965, p. 62-70. 1525

Mahajani, U.
"Kennedy and the Strategy of Aid: the Clay Report and After." Western political quarterly (18: 3), September 1965, p. 656-668. 1526

No entry 1527

"John F. Kennedy on Israel, Zionism and Jewish Issues (review)." National Jewish monthly 80, October 1965, p. 34. 1528

Kuroda, Y.
"Japanese View of President Kennedy." Asian survey 5, November 1965, p. 552-557. 1529

"Kennedy's Near East Policy." Near East report 9, November 30, 1965, p. 96. 1530

Tobin, R. L.
"Kennedy on the Ould sode." Saturday review 48, December 11, 1965, p. 59. 1531

1967
Smith, Jean E.
"Kennedy and Defense: the Formative Years." Air University review 18, March-April 1967, p. 38-54. 1532

Eckhardt, William & Ralph K. White
"The Test of the Mirror-Image Hypothesis: Kennedy and Khrushchev." Journal of conflict resolution 11, September 1967, p. 325-332. 1533

Smith, Jean E.
"Kennedy and Defense: the

Formative Years." Kingston, Canada, Queen's quarterly 74, Winter 1967, p. 627-648. 1534

The Death of President John F. Kennedy

Assassination

(Note: The controversy concerning the book by William Manchester entitled Death of a president, published by the New York city firm of Harper and Row in 1967, is included in this section.)

Books

1963

Asesinato: el asesinato de Kennedy en todos sus detalles. Compiled by Ignacio Puche. 2d ed. Madrid, Gráfica Ruán, 1963, 80p.
 (Assassination: the assassination of Kennedy in all its details.) 1535

Bernières, Luc
 Le jour où Kennedy fut assassiné. Paris, Eds. du Gerfaut, 1963, 171p.
 (The day Kennedy was assassinated.) 1536

Castro Ruz, Fidel
 Comparecencia del Comandante Fidel Castro, ante el pueblo de Cuba sobre los sucesos relacionados con el asesinato del Presidente Kennedy. Havana, Comisión de Orientación Revolucionaria, Dirección Nacional del PURSC, 1963, 24p.
 (The appearance of Major Fidel Castro before the people of Cuba, with regard to the events concerned with the assassination of President Kennedy.) 1537

Four dark days in history: November 22, 23, 24, 25, 1963; a photo history of President Kennedy's assassination. Los Angeles, J. Matthews, 1963, 68p. 1538

Kristl, Zvonimir, et al
 Kennedy; drama u Dallasu. Zagreb, Novinsko Izdavačka Kuća "Stvarnost," 1963, 368p.
 (Kennedy: drama in Dallas.) 1539

Life Magazine
 John F. Kennedy memorial edition: all of Life's pictures and text on the most shocking event of our time, including his biography and his most enduring words. Chicago, Time, Inc., 1963, 85p. 1540

1964

Associated Press
 The torch is passed; the Associated Press story of the death of a president. New York, 1964, 100p. 1541

Bealle, Morris A.
 Guns of the regressive right; the only reconstruction of the Kennedy assassination that makes sense. Washington, Columbia Pub. Co., 1964, 124p. 1542

Bekessy, Jean (pseud.)
 Anatomy of hatred; the

wounded land, by Hans Habe.
Translated from the German
by Ewan Butler. London, G.G.
Harrap, 1964, 296p. 1543

Buchanan, Thomas G.
Who killed Kennedy? New
York, Putnam's, 1964, 207p.
1544
Carlos, Newton
A conspiração. 2d ed. Rio
de Janeiro, J. Alvaro, 1964,
172p.
(The conspiracy.) 1545

Cottrell, John
Assassination. The world
stood still. London, New English Library, 1964, 128p. 1546

Denegre Vaught, Livingston
La eterna antorcha de Arlington; reportajes de un periodista mexicano desde Washington, a la muerte de John
F. Kennedy. Mexico, Editorial Academia Literaria, 1964,
229p.
(The eternal torch of Arlington; reports from a Mexican
journalist in Washington, upon
the death of John F. Kennedy.)
1547
Denson, R.B.
Destiny in Dallas; on the
scene story in pictures. (R.B.
Denson, 8171 Hunnicut Street,
Dallas, Texas), 1964, 64p.
1548
Gun, Nerin E.
Red roses from Texas. London, Frederick Muller, Ltd.,
1964, 208p. 1549

Idris, Soewardi
Terbunuhnja Presiden Kennedy. Djakarta, Tekad, 1964,
71p.
(How President Kennedy
was assassinated.) 1550

Iorysh, Abram I.
Kuda vedut sledy. Moscow,
1964, 89p.
(Where the traces lead.)
1551
Murray, Norbert
Legacy of an assassination.
New York, Pro-people Press,
1964, 479p. 1552

New York Times
Assassination of a president. Reported from the New
York Times, November 23
to 28, 1963. New York, 1964,
variously paged. 1553

Pokorny, Dušan
Ulice jilmu. 1st ed.
Prague, MF, 1964, 193p.
(Elm Street.) 1554

Rojas, Robinson
Estos mataron a Kennedy!
Reportaje de un golpe de
estado. Santiago, Chile, Ediciones Arco, 1964, 168p.
(They killed Kennedy! Report of a coup d'état.) 1555

Sawai, Sirimongkon
Būanglang khāttakam prathānāthipbōdī Kēnnēdī. Bangkok, 1964, 235p.
(On the assassination of
President Kennedy.) 1556

Seter, 'Ido
Oz ya'uz neged rotshe
Kenedi. Tel Aviv, N. Twersky, 1964, 194p.
(Force will move against
Kennedy's murderers.) 1557

Texas. Attorney General's
Office
Texas supplemental report
on the assassination of President John F. Kennedy and the
serious wounding of Governor
John B. Connally, November
22, 1963, by Attorney General
Waggoner Carr. Austin, 1964,
20p.   1558

United Press International &
American Heritage
Four days: the historical
record of the death of President Kennedy. New York,
American Heritage Publishing
Co., 1964, 143p.   1559

Venkateswararao, Potluri
Kennedīhatya kēsu. Madras,
Balaji Pubs., 1964, 110p.
(The case of the assassination of Kennedy.)   1560

Warner, Dale G.
Who killed the President?
1st ed. New York, American
Press, 1964, 24p.   1561

Wise, David & Thomas B.
Ross
The day Kennedy died. San
Antonio, The Naylor Co.,
1964, 137p.   1562

1965
Baker, Dean C.
The assassination of President Kennedy: a study of the
press coverage. Ann Arbor,
Dept. of Journalism, University of Michigan, 1965, 107p.
                             1563
Fine, William M., ed.
That day with God. New
York, McGraw-Hill, 1965,
213p.   1564

Ford, Gerald R. & John R.
Stiles
Portrait of the assassin.
New York, Simon & Schuster,
1965, 508p.   1565

Fox, Sylvan
The unanswered questions
about President Kennedy's
assassination. New York,
Award Books, 1965, 221p.
                             1566
Greenberg, Bradley S. &
Edwin B. Parker, eds.
The Kennedy assassination
and the American public;
social communication in
crisis. Stanford, Stanford
University Press, 1965,
392p.   1567

Hartogs, Renatus & Lucy
Freeman
The two assassins. New
York, Crowell, 1965, 264p.
                             1568
John F. Kennedy, 22 november 1963. Samlet og odsendt af Danmark-Amerika
Fondets stipendiatsektion.
Copenhagen, Nyt Nordisk
Forlag, 1965, 24p.
(John F. Kennedy, November
22, 1963. A collection of
reports of the Danish-
American Foundation,
Scholarship Section.) 1569

U.S. Congress. House. Committee on the Judiciary
Preserving evidence pertaining to the assassination
of President Kennedy; report
to accompany H.R. 9545.
Washington, G.P.O., 1965,

Van Der Karr, Richard K.
Crisis in Dallas; an historical study of the activities of Dallas television broadcasters during the period of President Kennedy's assassination. Bloomington, 1965, 91p. 1571

Vuilleumier, John F.
Lincoln-Kennedy, eine tragische Parallele. Basel, Gute Schriften, 1965, 71p.
(Lincoln-Kennedy, a tragic parallel.) 1572

1966
Brooks, Stewart M.
Our murdered presidents: the medical story. New York, Frederick Fell, 1966, p. 175-202. 1573

Duhamel, Morvan
Les quatres jours du Dallas. Paris, Editions France-Empire, 1966, 191p.
(Four days in Dallas.) 1574

Howe, Irving
On the death of John F. Kennedy (In his Steady work: essays in the politics of democratic radicalism. New York, Harcourt, Brace & World, 1966, p. 187-194). 1575

Marcus, Raymond
The bastard bullet; a search for legitimacy for Commission exhibit 399. Los Angeles, Rendell Publications, 1966, 77p. 1576

National Broadcasting Company, Inc. NBC News
Seventy hours and thirty minutes, as broadcast on the NBC Television Network by NBC News. New York, Random House, 1966, 152p. 1577

Smith, William R.
Assassination by consensus: the story behind the Kennedy assassination. Washington, L'Avant Garde Pubs., 1966, 240p. 1578

Wolfenstein, Martha & Gilbert W. Kliman, eds.
Children and the death of a president; multidisciplinary studies. New York, Doubleday, 1966, 288p. 1579

1967
Itek Corporation, Lexington, Mass.
Life-Itek Kennedy assasination film analysis. Lexington, 1967, 24p. 1580

Gosset, P. & R. Gosset
L'homme qui crut tuer Kennedy. Paris, Presses de la Cité, 1967.
(The man who thought of killing Kennedy.) 1581

James, Rosemary & Jack D. Wardlaw
Plot or politics? The Garrison case and its cast. New Orleans, Pelican Pub. Co., 1967, 167p. 1582

Manchester, William R.
The death of a president, November 20-November 25, 1963. New York, Harper, 1967, 710p. 1583

Marks, Stanley J.
Murder most foul! The conspiracy that murdered President Kennedy; 975 questions and answers. Los Angeles, Bureau of International Relations, 1967, 149p.   1584

Mayo, John B.
Bulletin from Dallas: the President is dead. New York, Exposition Press, 1967, 157p.   1585

Morin, Relman
Assassination: the death of President John F. Kennedy. New York, New American Library, 1967, 227p.   1586

Rajski, Raymond B., ed.
A nation grieved; the Kennedy assassination in editorial cartoons. Rutland, Tuttle, 1967, 134p.   1587

Rand, Michael, comp., et al
The assassination of President Kennedy; compiled and designed by Michael Rand, Howard Loxton and Len Deighton. London, Cape, 1967, unpaged.   1588

Roberts, Charles W.
The truth about the assasination. New York, Grosset & Dunlap, 1967, 128p.   1589

Thompson, Josiah
Six seconds in Dallas. New York, Bernard Geis Associates, 1967, 344p.   1590

Van Gelder, Lawrence
The untold story: why the Kennedys lost the book battle. New York, Award Books, 1967, 128p.
(Controversy concerning book, The death of a president, by William Manchester.)   1591

1968

Hepburn, James (pseud.)
L'Amérique brûle. Paris, Nouvelles Frontières, 1968, 412p.
(America burns. This book is also available in English translation under the title, Farewell America.)   1592

Michel, Armand
L'assassinat de John Kennedy, le Rapport Warren et ses critiques. [n.p.] Trinckvel, 1968, 189p.
(The assassination of John Kennedy, the Warren Report and its critics.)   1593

1969

Epstein, Edward J.
Counterplot. New York, Viking Press, 1969, 182p.   1594

Flammonde, Paris
The Kennedy conspiracy; an uncommissioned report on the Jim Garrison investigation. New York, Meredith Press, 1969, 348p.   1595

Articles

1963

"Das Teuflische Spiel um den Kennedy-Mord. Der Trick des Weltkommunismus

Durchschaut und Missglückt." Munich, Schlesische rundschau (15: 49), 1963, p. 1, 3.
("The Diabolical Game Concerning the Death of Kennedy. The Trick of International Communism is Observed and Fails.") 1596

"Der Mord von Dallas Mähnt die Welt." Berlin, Begegnung (12: 3), 1963, p. 1-2.
("The Assassination in Dallas Admonishes the World.") 1597

"Hvem Myrdede Hven og Hvorfor?" Copenhagen, Frit Danmark (22: 11), 1963-64, p. 3-5.
("Who Murdered Whom and Why?") 1598

Koch, Thilo
"Der Tod des Präsidenten." Hamburg, Die zeit (18: 48), 1963, p. 2.
(The Death of the President.") 1599

Kurnoth, Rudolf
"Gedanken um den Tod John F. Kennedys." Lengerich, Frankenstein-Munsterberger heimatblatt (10: 12), 1963, p. 2.
("Thoughts About the Death of John F. Kennedy.") 1600

Lerner, Max
"The World Impact." London, Illustrated London news (66: 1707), 1963, p. 769. 1601

"L'Occidente e la Morte di Kennedy." Florence, Rivista di studi politici internazionali (30: 3), 1963, p. 323-326.
("The West and the Death of Kennedy.") 1602

Meyer, Karl E.
"Echoes of Dallas." London, Illustrated London news (66: 1709), 1963, p. 868-870. 1603

Meyer, Karl E.
"History as Tragedy." London, Illustrated London news (66: 1707), 1963, p. 766-768. 1604

Schüler, Alfred
"Im 'Carousel' Sitzen FBI-Agenten. Dallas nach dem Kennedy-Mord." Hamburg, Der spiegel (17: 50), 1963, p. 76.
("FBI Agents Sit in a Carousel: Dallas After the Kennedy Assassination.") 1605

"USA-Attentat-Aufklärung: Weisser Mann Gesucht." Hamburg, Der spiegel (17: 49), 1963, p. 83-86.
("USA: Explanation of the Assassination: White Man Sought.") 1606

"USA-Kennedy-Attentat: Mord in der Sonne." Hamburg, Der spiegel (17: 49), 1963, p. 77-83.
("USA: Kennedy Assassination: Murder in Broad Daylight.") 1607

"USA-Präsidentenschutz: Fenster zu." Hamburg, Der spiegel (17: 49), 1963, p. 86-87.

("Protection of the U.S. President: Close the Window.") 1608

"Editor's Shop Talk." Antioch review 23, Winter 1963-64, p. 403-404. 1609

"Death of President Kennedy: Statements by Sir Robert Menzies and Sir Garfield Barwick on 23d November." Canberra, Current notes on international affairs 34, November 1963, p. 38-39. 1610

"Kennedy Assassination-Communist Version." Communist affairs 1, November-December 1963, p. 3-6. 1611

Budimac, Budimir
"Zlocin u Teksasu." Novi Sad, Dnevnik 22, November 23, 1963, p. 6124.
("Crime in Texas.") 1612

Milić, Živko
"Ubijen Predsednik SAD Dzon Kenedi." Belgrade, Borba 28, November 23, 1963, p. 324.
("U.S. President John Kennedy Killed.") 1613

"President Kennedy Assassinated." London, The times, November 23, 1963, p. 8. 1614

Radojčić, Miroslav
"Kako je Amerika Primila Vest o Zlocinu u Teksasu." Belgrade, Politika LX, November 23, 1963, p. 18010.
("How the United States Accepted the News About the Crime in Texas.") 1615

Barbieri, Frane
"Dva Atentata." Belgrade, Vjesnik 24, November 24, 1963, p. 6024.
("Two Assassination Attempts.") 1616

Milić, Živko
"Stravicna Hronika 22. Novembra." Belgrade, Borba 28, November 24, 1963, p. 325.
("Horrifying Chronicle of November 22.") 1617

Mihovilović, Ive
"Snajperski Metak na Savijest Amerike." Zagreb, Vjesnik u srijedu, November 27, 1963, p. 604.
("Sniper's Bullet on America's Conscience.") 1618

Cooke, Alistair
"Death of the Young Warrior." London, Listener 70, November 28, 1963, p. 863-864. 1619

Mayes, Stanley
"What They are Saying." London, Listener 70, November 28, 1963, p. 868. 1620

"A Chronology of Tragedy." London, Time & tide, November 28-December 4, 1963, p. 7-9. 1621

"The Shot That Changed our Future." London, Time & tide, November 28-December 4, 1963, p. 4. 1622

"Death of a modern." London, Spectator, November 29, 1963, p. 681. 1623

Lerner, Max
"The World Impact." London, New statesman 66, November 29, 1963, p. 769. 1624

"The World and the White House." London, New statesman 66, November 29, 1963, p. 765. 1625

"After the Tragedy." Tablet 217, November 30, 1963, p. 1181-1182. 1626

"The Death of the President." London, Illustrated London news 243, November 30, 1963, p. 889-899. 1627

Friedman, R.
"Pictures of Assassination." Editor & publisher 96, November 30, 1963, p. 16-17. 1628

"Funeral of John Fitzgerald Kennedy." London, Illustrated London news 243, November 30, 1963, p. 890-893. 1629

"I Just Heard Some Shots: 3 Shots." Editor & publisher 96, November 30, 1963, p. 14-15. 1630

"President Assassinated by a Gunman at Dallas." London, Illustrated London news 243, November 30, 1963, p. 887, 889, 895. 1631

"This is a Great Nation." London, The economist 209, November 30, 1963, p. 901-902. 1632

"A Nation Grieves." Interracial review 36, December 1963, p. 232. 1633

Hart, L.
"The Death of President Kennedy." Columbia 43, December 1963, p. 3. 1634

"The Hatred That Consumes ..." Address of November 24 by Chief Justice E.G. Warren on the Assassination of the President." Hadassah magazine 44, December 1963, p. 32. 1635

"Pity of it" (editorial). Jewish frontier 30, December 1963, p. 3. 1636

Milić, Živko
"Amerika je Povela Istragu nad Samom Sobom." Belgrade, Borba (XI: 29-30), December 1, 1963, p. 330. ("America Investigates Itself.") 1637

"Assassination Gives Impetus to Dodd's gun Bill." Advertising age 34, December 2, 1963, p. 1-2. 1638

Radojčić, Miroslav
"Zasto je Amerika Cutala?" Belgrade, Politika, December 2, 1963, p. 18017. ("Why was America Silent?") 1639

"World Listened and Watched; Radio-TV Meets Greatest Challenge in Wake of JFK Tragedy..." Broadcasting 65, December 2, 1963, p. 36-61. 1640

Carunungan, C.A.
"Grave Dangers Beset Presidents." Manila, Weekly graphic (30: 24), December 4, 1963, p. 3, 86. 1641

"Who Killed President Kennedy: Soviet Condolences." Moscow, New times, December 4, 1963, p. 5-7. 1642

Cooke, Alistair
"After the President's Assassination." London, Listener 70, December 5, 1963, p. 907-908. 1643

Levin, Bernard
"The Bell Tolls in Dallas." London, Listener 70, December 5, 1963, p. 914. 1644

Murray, P.
"Report from Mexico on Reaction to John Kennedy's Tragic Death." Catholic messenger 82, December 5, 1963, p. 12. 1645

"Death of the President." Commonweal 79, December 6, 1963, p. 299-301. 1646

"Johnson Names Commission to Probe Assassination." Congressional quarterly weekly report 21, December 6, 1963, p. 2122-2123. 1647

"Paris: le Coup de Dallas." London, New statesman 66, December 6, 1963, p. 817. ("Paris: the Blow at Dallas.") 1648

Allarey, Monina
"When Night Fell on the U.S." Manila, Philippines herald magazine, December 7, 1963, p. 12. 1649

Joaquin, Nick
"An American Tragedy." Manila, Philippines free press (56: 49), December 7, 1963, p. 2-3, 75. 1650

"Who was to Blame?" London, The economist 209, December 7, 1963, p. 1022. 1651

"The Assassination of President John F. Kennedy." Current digest of the Soviet press 15, December 11, 1963, p. 3-15. 1652

Holmes, W.A.
"One Thing Worse Than This: Sermon Delivered at Northaven Methodist Church, Dallas, November 24, 1963." Christian century 80, December 11, 1963, p. 1555-1556. 1653

Izakov, Boris
"The Dallas Investigation." Moscow, New times, December 11, 1963, p. 10-12. 1654

Cameron, J.
"Humane and Sane." Commonweal 79, December 13, 1963, p. 338-339. 1655

Langer, E.
"Kennedy's Assassination: Study Organized by Social Scientists." Science 142, December 13, 1963, p. 1446-1447. 1656

"Martyred President and a Nation's Journey." Recon-

Breig, J.
"Assassination of a People." Ave Maria 98, December 14, 1963, p. 10.   1658

Tobin, Richard L.
"If you can Keep Your Head When all About you: Television and News Magazine Coverage of the Kennedy Assassination Story." Saturday review 46, December 14, 1963, p. 53-54.   1659

"The World Resounds: Reactions to the President's Murder, a Symposium: New York, by W. Wells. Tokyo, by J. Blewett. Rome, by D. Campion. Washington, by S. Quinlan. Bogota, by V. Andrade. Milwaukee, by Q. Quade. Toulouse, by F. Becheau. London, by A. Boyle." America 109, December 14, 1963, p. 767-771.   1660

"The World Resounds: Symposium." America 109, December 14, 1963, p. 767-771.   1661

"Soviet Press Comment Following Kennedy's Death." Current digest of the Soviet press 15, December 18, 1963, p. 3-7.   1662

Eller, J.
"Winter, 1963: a Time for Quiet Voices." America 109, December 21, 1963, p. 787.   1663

Minnis, J. & S. Lynd
"Seeds of Doubt: Some Questions About the Assasination." New republic 149, December 21, 1963, p. 14-17.   1664

Carney, Frederick S.
"Crisis of Conscience in Dallas: Soul-Searching vs. 'New Faith in Dallas.' Thoughts on the day of the Funeral, by Tom F. Driver." Christianity & crisis 23, December 23, 1963, p. 235-241.   1665

"Collective Guilt in the U.S. ? Take a Look at the World: with Excerpts from Address by Thruston B. Morton." U.S. news & world report 55, December 23, 1963, p. 72-74.   1666

Pacis, Vicente A.
"Hate Campaign did it." Manila, Weekly graphic (30: 27), December 25, 1963, p. 2-3, 98.   1667

"On the Far Right: the Assassination." Commonweal 79, December 27, 1963, p. 384-385.   1668

"Where the Shots Came From." New republic 149, December 28, 1963, p. 7.   1669

1964

Bachmann, Ida
"Praesident Johnsons Mordkommission." Copenhagen, Frit Danmark (23: 2), 1964-65, p. 4-6.
("President Johnson's Commission on the Assassina-

tion.")   1670

Besson, Waldemar
"Die Schusse von Dallas. War eine Verschwörung des Hasses am Werk?" Hamburg, Die zeit (19: 33), 1964, p. 6.
("The Shooting in Dallas. Was There a Conspiracy of Hate at Work?")   1671

"Die Hintergründe des Kennedy-Morde." Hannover, Das andere Deutschland 3, 1964, p. 7.
("The Background of the Kennedy Assassination.") 1672

Dunson, J.
"Sad Day in Texas." Sing out (14: 4), 1964, p. 26-27.
                                 1673

Gordon, W.E.
"The Assassination of President Kennedy." London, Contemporary review 205, 1964, p. 8-13.   1674

Götte, Fritz
'Nach John F. Kennedys Tod." Stuttgart, Die drei 34, 1964, p. 143-145.
("After the Death of John F. Kennedy.")   1675

Greenberg, Bradley S.
"Diffusion of News of the Kennedy Assassination." Public opinion quarterly (28: 2), 1964, p. 225-232.   1676

Habe, Hans
'Die Hälfte der Wahrheit; der Mörder Gefundender Mord Ungeklärt." Zürich, Weltwoche (32: 1614), 1964, p. 13.
("The Half of the Truth: the Murderer Found, the Murder Unexplained.")   1677

Hermann, Kai
"Wer war Kennedys Mörder?" Hamburg, Die zeit (19: 15), 1964, p. 7.
("Who was Kennedy's Murderer?")   1678

Kempton, Murray
"Looking Back on the Anniversary." London, Spectator 7119, 1964, p. 778-779.
                               1679

Korolovszky, Lajos
"Fanatizmus és Vallásosság. Gondolatok a Kennedy Gyilkosság Hátteréról." Budapest, Világosság (5: 2), 1964, p. 80-87.
("Fanaticism and Piety: Thoughts on the Background of the Assassination.") 1680

McNaspy, C.J.
'Après la Mort de Kennedy: l'Amérique Devant Elle-Même." Paris, Etudes: Revue Catholique d'intérêt général 320, 1964, p. 27-37.
("After the Death of Kennedy: America Facing Itself.")   1681

Robert, Peter
"Tragicna pot Stirih Predsednikov." Ljubljana, Obzornik (64: 8), 1964, p. 573-578.
("Tragic Road for Four Presidents.")   1682

Sauvage, Leo
"Detektiven Thomas Buchanan." Copenhagen, Perspektiv, det danske magasin (12: 7), 1964-65, p. 7-15.

("Detective Thomas Buchanan.") 1683

Schwelien, Joachim
"Der Mord von Dallas."
Hamburg, Die zeit (19: 40), 1964, p. 3.
("The Murder in Dallas.") 1684

Sheatsley, Paul B. & Jacob J. Feldman
"The Assassination of President Kennedy. A Preliminary Report on Public Reactions and Behavior." Public opinion quarterly (28: 2), 1964, p. 189-215. 1685

Thomas, J.
"Le 'Monde Libre' et le Crime de Dallas." Paris, La nouvelle revue internationale (7: 1), 1964, p. 83-88.
("The Free World and the Crime of Dallas.") 1686

Ahler, J. & J. Tamney
"Some Functions of Religious Ritual in a Catastrophe: Kennedy Assassination." Sociological analysis 25, Winter 1964, p. 212-230. 1687

"The Assassination: the Reporters' Story; What was Seen and Read: Television, Newspapers, Magazines; Journalism's Role; Unresolved Issues." Columbia journalism review 2, Winter 1964, p. 5-31. 1688

Apollonia, L. d'
"Reflexions sur une Tragédie." Montreal, Relations 24, January 1964, p. 27.
("Thoughts About a Tragedy.") 1689

"The Assassination of President Kennedy." East Europe 13, January 1964, p. 25-26. 1690

Bar-David, M.
"Diary of an Israel Housewife." Hadassah magazine 45, January 1964, p. 21-22. 1691

"BB (i.e., B'nai Brith) Overseas Mourn JFK; BBYO's 40th Anniversary Service Dedicated to JFK; Hillel Directors Place Wreath at Tomb of President." National Jewish monthly 78, January 1964, p. 24-26. 1692

"Four Days." Television 21, January 1964, p. 27-33. 1693

Gordon, William E.
"The Assassination of President Kennedy." London, Contemporary review 205, January 1964, p. 8-13. 1694

Hart, L.
"A Year of Progress with a Sorrowful Close." Columbia 44, January 1964, p. 16. 1695

Nardi, S.S.
"And All that Mighty Heart..." Hadassah magazine 45, January 1964, p. 24. 1696

Nelson, W.H.
"Assassination." Toronto, Canadian forum 43, January 1964, p. 219-220. 1697

Breig, J.
"President Kennedy's Death: Why?" Ave Maria 99, January 11, 1964, p. 9. 1698

Allarey, Monina
"That day in Washington." Manila, Philippines herald magazine, January 25, 1964, p. 23-25. 1699

Stone, I. F.
"We all had a Finger on That Trigger." Sydney, Outlook 8, February 1964, p. 8-9. 1700

Buchanan, Thomas C.
"Pravo Porocilo o Umoru v Dallasu." Belgrade, Delo 6, February 27-29, 1964, p. 56-58.
("The Rights of Man and Death in Dallas.") 1701

Brienberg, Mordecai
"The Riddle of Dallas." London, Spectator 6, March 1964, p. 305-306. 1702

Dies, Martin
"Assassination and its Aftermath." American opinion 7, March 1964, p. 1-10; April 1964, p. 33-40. 1703

Lauzon, A.
"Au Banc Accusés, une Ville: Dallas." Montreal, Le magazine Maclean 4, March 1964, p. 13-15, 56-58.
("The Accused in the Dock: a City, Dallas.") 1704

Dunning, John L.
"The Kennedy Assassination as Viewed by Communist Media." Journalism quarterly (41: 2), Spring 1964, p. 163-169. 1705

Mendelsohn, Harold
"Broadcast vs. Personal Sources of Information in Emergent Public Crises: the Presidential Assassination." Journal of broadcasting 8, Spring 1964, p. 147-156. 1706

Brienberg, Mordecai
"The Riddle of Dallas." London, Spectator 212, March 6, 1964, p. 305-306. 1707

"In Jurul Procesului de la Dallas. Răsfoind Presa Străină." Bucharest, Scînteia (33: 6191), March 9, 1964, p. 4.
("In the Jury Trial at Dallas: Looking Through the Foreign Press.") 1708

Cruz, J. V.
"RM and JFK: Twins of Fate." Manila, Philippines herald magazine, March 14, 1964, p. 42, 44, 67, 72. 1709

Hegyi, Károly
"A Dallasi Itélethirdetés Után." Bucharest, Előre (18: 5092), March 17, 1964, p. 3.
("After the Sentence was Delivered at Dallas.") 1710

Ushakov, G.
"Dallas Merry-go-Round." Moscow, New times, March 18, 1964, p. 27-29. 1711

Poznanska, A.
"Procès à Dallas." Montreal, Cité libre 15, April

1964, p. 26-28.
("Trial in Dallas.")   1712

"JFK's Murder: Sowers of Doubt." Newsweek 63, April 6, 1964, p. 22-24.   1713

"Dallasi Detektivhistoria." Bucharest, Előre (18: 5113), April 10, 1964, p. 3. ("Dallas Detective Story.")   1714

Lineberry, William
"The Lingering 'Plot': Foreign Opinion and the Assassination." New leader 47, April 27, 1964, p. 21-22.   1715

Banta, Thomas J.
"The Kennedy Assassination: Early Thoughts and Emotions." Public opinion quarterly 28, Summer 1964, p. 216-224.   1716

Greenberg, Bradley S.
"Diffusion of News of the Kennedy Assassination." Public opinion quarterly 28, Summer 1964, p. 225-232.   1717

Hill, Richard J. & Charles M. Bonjean
"News Diffusion: a Test of the Regularity Hypothesis." Journalism quarterly (41: 3), Summer, 1964, p. 336-342.   1718

Sheatsley, Paul B. & Jacob J. Feldman
"The Assassination of President Kennedy: a Preliminary Report on Public Reactions and Behavior." Public opinion quarterly 28, Summer 1964, p. 189-215.   1719

Sassa, Atsuyuki
"New Light on the Assassination: a Secret Agent's Story." U.S. news & world report 56, June 8, 1964, p. 38-39.   1720

Gellner, J.
"Who Killed John Kennedy?" Toronto, Saturday night 79, July 1964, p. 11-14.   1721

Kavanaugh, J.
"A Visit to the Grave." Catholic digest 28, July 1964, p. 8-11.   1722

"Compendium of Curious Coincidences: Parallels in the Lives and Deaths of A. Lincoln and J.F. Kennedy." Time 84, August 21, 1964, p. 19.   1723

Sauvage, Leo
"Thomas Buchanan, Detective." New leader 47, September 28, 1964, p. 10-15.   1724

Baxandall, Lee
"The Kennedy Assassination." London, Views 6, Autumn 1964, p. 90-93. 1725

"Inquest on Dallas: the Right to Bear Arms." Tablet 218, October 3, 1964, p. 1101-1102.   1726

"New York Times Runs 48 Pages of Report." Editor & publisher 97, October 3, 1964, p. 61.   1727

"So it Can't Occur Again; Safeguarding the President." Business week, October 3,

1964, p. 34.   1728

"The Assassination." Manila, Philippines herald magazine, October 10, 1964, p. 26-30.   1729

"A Dallasi Tragédia." Budapest, Magyar Szovjet közgazdasági szemle (21:2), October 14, 1964, p. 273-285.
("Tragedy in Dallas.")   1730

Cuffaro, H.K.
"Reaction of Pre-school Children to the Assassination of President Kennedy." Young children 20, November 1964, p. 100-105.   1731

McLaughlin, M.
"Paris, November 22nd, 1963." Immaculate Heart crusader 28, November-December 1964, p. 8-9.   1732

Sauvage, Leo
"As I was Saying." New leader 47, November 9, 1964, p. 8-13.   1733

"If it all Happened Again." Editor & publisher 97, November 21, 1964, p. 9-10.   1734

"Anniversary of an Assassination" (editorial). Reconstructionist 30, November 27, 1964, p. 6.   1735

"And Then it was November 22 Again." Newsweek 64, November 30, 1964, p. 25-28.   1736

Spitzer, Stephen P.
"Mass Media vs. Personal Sources of Information About the Presidential Assassination: a Comparison of Six Investigations." Journal of broadcasting (9: 1), Winter 1964-65, p. 45-50.   1737

"The Death of a President: Told in Direct Testimony, Excerpts." U.S. news & world report 57, December 7, 1964, p. 68-70.   1738

"What they saw that Dreadful day in Dallas: Testimony and Evidence Published." Newsweek 64, December 7, 1964, p. 28-30.   1739

"Policaj Ubil Kennedija?" Sarajevo, Vecernji Sarajevski list (12: 22), December 24, 1964, p. 298-300.
("Did Police Kill Kennedy?")   1740

1965
Saint-Jean, Claude
"Histoire d'un Crime." Paris, Revue 1, 1965, p. 275.
("History of a Crime.")   1741

Ludwig, J.
"New York." Partisan review 32, Winter 1965, p. 63-69.   1742

Possony, S.T.
"Clearing the air." National review 17, February 9, 1965, p. 113-114.   1743

"Death of a President: the Established Facts." Atlantic 215, March 1965, p. 112-118.   1744

Montgomery, R.
"Crystal Ball: Condensation from Gift of Prophecy." Reader's digest 87, July 1965, p. 235-242.   1745

Schreiber, F.R. & M. Herman
"November 22, 1963, a Psychiatric Evaluation." Science digest 58, July 1965, p. 39-41.   1746

"Death of a President: Excerpt From the Introduction to the Annual Report of the Librarian of Congress for the Fiscal Year Ending June 30, 1964." Library journal 90, August 1965, p. 3173-3176.   1747

Antoninus, Brother
"Death has Pounced: Excerpt from Tongs of Jeopardy." Dominicana 50, September 1965, p. 9-12.   1748

Stewart, C.J.
"The Pulpit in Time of Crisis: 1865 and 1963." Speech monographs 32, November 1965, p. 427-434.   1749

Saltz, E. & J. Wickey
"Resolutions of the Liberal Dilemma in the Assassination of President Kennedy." Journal of personality 33, December 1965, p. 636-648.   1750

Spitzer, S.P. & N.K. Denzin
"Levels of Knowledge in an Emergent Crisis." Social forces 44, December 1965, p. 234-237.   1751

1966

Epstein, Edward J.
"Der Tod kam bei Bild 313: eine neue Untersuchung des Kennedy-Mordes." Hamburg, Der spiegel (20: 29), 1966, p. 63-67.
("Death Came at Picture 313: a new Investigation of the Kennedy Assassination.")   1752

Janssen, Karl-Heinz
"Wer Ermordete Kennedy? Fakten und Phantome: Suche Nach dem Zweiten Attentäter." Hamburg, Die zeit (21: 48), 1966, p. 7.
("Who Murdered Kennedy? Facts and Phantoms: Search for the Second Assassin.")   1753

Joesten, Joachim
"Der Kennedy-Mord als 'Politische Warhreit'." Frankfurt am Main, Frankfurte hefte, zeitschrift für kultur und politik (21: 8), 1966, p. 534-540.
("The Kennedy Assassination as 'Political Truth'.")   1754

O'Brien, Conor C.
"The Life and Death of Kennedy." London, New statesman (71: 1818), 1966, p. 50-51.   1755

Fox, Sylvan
"Unanswered Questions About President Kennedy's Assassination (review by M.S. Evans)." National review 18, January 11, 1966, p. 34-37.   1756

"Assassination, a new Book (by Sylvan Fox) Poses

Some Unanswered Questions." Toronto, Maclean's magazine 79, April 16, 1966, p. 18-19. 1757

Kopkind, Andrew
"The Kennedy Mystery Reopened." London, New statesman 72, July 29, 1966, p. 163. 1758

"Kennedy's Death: How the Controversy was Reborn." London, Sunday times, August 21, 1966, p. 6. 1759

Wiznitzer, L.
"Que s'est-il Passé à Dallas?" Toronto, Maclean's magazine 6, September 1966, p. 2-3.
("What Happened in Dallas?") 1760

Cooke, Alistair
"Man at Large: the Evidence on the Assassination of President Kennedy." Manchester, Manchester guardian, September 22, 1966, p. 8. 1761

Thomas, Harford
"Chance or Design?" Manchester, Manchester guardian, September 28, 1966, p. 18. 1762

"Who Killed Kennedy? The Crucial Evidence." London, Sunday times magazine, October 9, 1966, p. 7-21. 1763

Love, Ruth (Leeds)
"Television and the Kennedy Assassination." London, New society, October 13, 1966, p. 567-571. 1764

Berezhkov, V.
"More Light on the Kennedy Assassination (book review of Die Wahrheit über den Kennedy-Mord: wie und warum der Warren-report lügt, by Joachim Joesten)." Moscow, New times, October 26, 1966, p. 28-32. 1765

Trevor-Roper, Hugh
"Ki Ölte meg Kennedy-t?" Cluj, Korunk (25: 11), November 1966, p. 1601-1609.
("Who Killed Kennedy?") 1766

Muggeridge, Malcolm
"A new Kennedy Theory." London, New statesman 72, November 18, 1966, p. 735. 1767

"Pilgrimages to Grave of President Kennedy: Shadow Still Cast over White House." London, The times, November 23, 1966, p. 8. 1768

Mironescu, Emil
"Enigma de la Dallas și Semnele ei de Întrebare." Bucharest, Pentru apărarea păcii 12, December 1966, p. 19-21.
("Enigma of Dallas and the Vestiges of the Problem.") 1769

"Vrae Wat nog Hinder na Kennedy-Moord." Pretoria, Huis en haard (42: 2331), December 2, 1966, p. 18-21.
("A Question Which Still is an Obstacle in the Kennedy Assassination.") 1770

Brand, Sergiu
  "Și Totusi Cine?" Bucharest, Cronica (1: 45), December 17, 1966, p. 12. ("And Yet, Who?") 1771

Cooke, Alistair
  "Mrs. Kennedy Suffers Grief she Sought to Avoid." Manchester, Manchester guardian, December 21, 1966, p. 7. 1772

Izakov, Boris
  "Echo of Dallas." Moscow, New times, December 21, 1966, p. 29-31. 1773

Kopkind, Andrew
  "The Kennedy Book Battle." London, New statesman 72, December 30, 1966, p. 956. 1774

1967

Goodhart, A.L.
  "The Mysteries of the Kennedy Assassination and the English Press." London, Law quarterly review 83, January 1967, p. 22-23. 1775

"L'Affaire Manchester." Triumph 2, January 1967, p. 7. 1776

Welsh, David & David Lifton
  "The Case for Three Assassins." Ramparts 5, January 1967, p. 77-100. 1777

"Growing Rift of LBJ and Kennedy: Behind the Furor over a Book, Concerning the Death of a President, by William Manchester." U.S. news & world report 62, January 2, 1967, p. 22-27. 1778

Wills, Gary
  "Dallas: out There." National Catholic reporter 3, January 4, 1967, p. 10. 1779

"The Kennedy Book." Commonweal 85, January 6, 1967, p. 361-362. 1780

McGrory, Mary
  "A Controversy that has only just Begun." America 116, January 7, 1967, p. 10. 1781

Wyndham, Francis
  "Manchester and the Kennedys." London, Sunday times, January 15, 1967, p. 10. 1782

"Mrs. Kennedy Reaches Accord with Harper & Row and William Manchester." Publishers weekly 191, January 23, 1967, p. 222. 1783

Cooke, Alistair
  "Fresh Shots in Kennedy Book Battle." Manchester, Manchester guardian, January 24, 1967, p. 9. 1784

"Feud Over Death of a President Intensifies as Manchester Attacks Kennedy Family and Aids." Publishers weekly 191, January 30, 1967, p. 88-89. 1785

Smith, R.H.
  "Suppression Business." Publishers weekly 191, January 30, 1967, p. 93. 1786

Snider, A.J.
  "Assassination, a new

Medical Opinion." Science digest 61, February 1967, p. 35-36.   1787

"How to Lose a war: Long-running row Over Manchester's Book." Newsweek 69, February 6, 1967, p. 34-35.   1788

Hughes, E.J.
"Trials of Government-in-Exile; Graceless Battle Between the Kennedy Family and W. Manchester." Newsweek 69, February 6, 1967, p. 20.   1789

"To Help you Keep the Record Straight About That Book; Concerning The Death of a President, by W. Manchester." U.S. news & world report 62, February 6, 1967, p. 66-67.   1790

Churchill, Randolph S.
"The Manchester Book." London, The times, February 13, 1967, p. 13; February 14, 1967, p. 11.   1791

Wills, Gary
"The Assassin Seekers." National Catholic reporter 3, February 15, 1967, p. 8.   1792

"In the Hours After Dallas: the Book and the Testimony: Concerning The Death of a President by William Manchester." U.S. news & world report 62, February 20, 1967, p. 51-52.   1793

"Garrison Under Fire." London, The economist 222, February 25, 1967, p. 730.   1794

Jones, Penn
"Mysterious Deaths in the Long Aftermath of Dallas." London, The times, February 25, 1967, p. 11.   1795

Irons, Evelyn
"'Several Plots' Claims District Attorney." London, Sunday times, February 26, 1967, p. 6.   1796

Gingrich, A.
"Truth as Private Property." Esquire 67, March 1967, p. 6.   1797

"Bourbon Street Rococo; J. Garrison's Investigation." Time 89, March 3, 1967, p. 26.   1798

"Carnival in New Orleans: J. Garrison's Investigation." Newsweek 69, March 6, 1967, p. 32.   1799

Smith, Merriman
"Jim Garrison and his Sources of Evidence." Manchester, Manchester guardian, March 18, 1967, p. 7.   1800

"Taste for Conspiracy: European Newsmen are Leery of Garrison's Investigation." Newsweek 69, March 20, 1967, p. 76.   1801

'D.A. Wins a Round: Jim Garrison's Investigation." Time 89, March 24, 1967, p. 17-18.   1802

"Tales of Garrison." London,

The economist 222, March 25, 1967, p. 1145. 1803

Wills, Gary
"Manchester's Upheaval."
National Catholic reporter 3, March 29, 1967, p. 10. 1804

"Sifting Fact From Fantasy: use of Truth Drugs in Jim Garrison's Investigation." Time 89, March 31, 1967, p. 41. 1805

Kaplan, John
"The Assassins." American scholar 36, Spring 1967, p. 271-286. 1806

Collins, R.S.
"Kennedy vs. Look, Manchester, Harper & Row; an Informal Glossary of Press Relations Techniques." Public relations journal 23, April 1967, p. 13-15. 1807

Cafiero, L.H.
"Manchester Book Alleges Com Lag Day JFK Killed." Electronic news 12, April 3, 1967, p. 22. 1808

"Charge of Conspiracy." Newsweek 69, April 3, 1967, p. 36-37. 1809

Manchester, William
"William Manchester's own Story." Look 31, April 4, 1967, p. 62-66. 1810

"Two Mrs. Kennedys." National review 19, April 4, 1967, p. 335-336. 1811

Cohen, J. & N.C. Chriss
"New Orleans: Act I."
The reporter 36, April 6, 1967, p. 17-20. 1812

"Manchester Book: Despite Flaws and Errors, a Story That is Larger Than Life or Death." Time 89, April 7, 1967, p. 22-23. 1813

Froncek, T.
"An American View."
Tablet 221, April 8, 1967, p. 382-383. 1814

"New Orleans Plot?" Senior scholastic, teachers edition 90, April 14, 1967, p. 18-19. 1815

Cunliffe, Marcus
"A Courtier's Obsequies (Review of Death of a President, by William Manchester)." London, New society, April 20, 1967, p. 580-581. 1816

Churchill, Randolph S.
"Shivs, Kazzazza and Code 4." London, Spectator, April 21, 1967, p. 447-449. 1817

Tomalin, Nicholas
"Just Read the News, Mr. Manchester." London, New statesman 73, April 21, 1967, p. 547-548. 1818

Dirix, B.
"Why was JFK Shot?"
Atlas 13, May 1967, p. 10-13. 1819

Kempton, Murray
"Rage Greater Than Grief."
The Atlantic 219, May 1967,

p. 98-100. 1820

Orren, K. & P. Peterson
"Presidential Assassination: a Case Study in the Dynamics of Political Socialization." The journal of politics 29, May 1967, p. 388-404. 1821

"Second Primer of Assassination Theories." Esquire 67, May 1967, p. 104-107. 1822

Phelan, J.
"Plot to Kill Kennedy? Rush to Judgment in New Orleans." Saturday evening post 240, May 6, 1967, p. 21-25. 1823

"Sleight of Hand: Jim Garrison's Assassination Investigation Extended to FBI and CIA." Newsweek 69, May 22, 1967, p. 40. 1824

"Shadow on a Grassy Knoll: Photographic-Analysis Shows no new Evidence." Time 89, May 26, 1967, p. 21. 1825

Breslow, Paul
"The Second Assassination." London, Nova, June 1967, p. 66-67. 1826

Powledge, F.
"Is Garrison Faking?" New republic 156, June 17, 1967, p. 13-18. 1827

"Lenta Disparitie din Scena a lui Jim Garrison." Bucharest, Lumea (5: 26), June 22, 1967, p. 97-100. ("Slow Disappearance from the Scene by Jim Garrison.")
1828

Epstein, Edward J.
"Manchester Unexpurgated: from Death of Lancer to The Death of a President. Comparative Study of Successive Versions of Book." Commentary 44, July 1967, p. 25-31. 1829

"Pathologist Sleuth Reopens Kennedy Controversy: Suggests JFK Suffered From Addison's Disease." Science news 92, July 22, 1967, p. 79-80. 1830

Berendt, John
"If They've Found Another Assassin, let them Name Names and Produce their Evidence." Esquire 68, August 1967, p. 80-82. 1831

Logan, A.
"JFK: the Stained-Glass Image." American heritage 18, August 1967, p. 4-7.
1832

"Outdoor Life and The Death of a President: William Manchester Charges Outdoor Life with Hard-boiled Callousness Toward a National Tragedy." Outdoor life 140, October 1967, p. 32-33. 1833

Roddy, Jon
"Did this man Happen upon John Kennedy's Assassins?" Toronto, Maclean's magazine 80, November 1967, p. 2-3.
1834

"Back to Dallas: Theories of J. Thompson and J. Connally." Time 90, November 24, 1967, p. 54-55. 1835

Connally, John B.
"Why Kennedy Went to Texas." Life 63, November 24, 1967, p. 86A-86B. 1836

"November 22, 1963, Dallas: Photos by Nine Bystanders." Life 63, November 24, 1967, p. 87-97. 1837

Thompson, Josiah
"The Cross Fire that Killed President Kennedy: Excerpt from Six Seconds in Dallas." Saturday evening post 240, December 2, 1967, p. 27-31. 1838

1968
Turner, William W.
"Garrison Commission on the Assassination of President Kennedy..." Ramparts magazine 5, January 1968, p. 43-56. 1839

Karp, Irwin
"Debate over Dallas: Theories of John Sparrow and Sylvia Meagher." Saturday review 51, March 9, 1968, p. 113-114. 1840

Wise, David
"Secret Evidence on the Kennedy Assassination." Saturday evening post, April 6, 1968, p. 70-73. 1841

Motion Pictures

1968
A child's eyes: November 22, 1963 (motion picture). Group VI Productions, 1968. Released by Pathé Contemporary Films. 1842

The Oswald Affair

Books

1964
Joesten, Joachim
Oswald: assassin or fall guy? New York, Marzani & Munsell, Inc., 1964, 158p. 1843

1965
Kaplan, John & Jon R. Waltz
The trial of Jack Ruby. New York, Macmillan, 1965, 392p. 1844

Pottecher, Frédéric
Grands procès: Dallas. v. 2. Paris, Arthaud, 1965, 294p.
(Great trials: Dallas.)1845

Pottecher, Frédéric
Le procès de Dallas. Paris, Librairie Jules Tallandier, 1965, 283p.
(The trial at Dallas.) 1846

Thornley, Kerry W.
Oswald. Chicago, New Classics House, 1965, 126p. 1847

1966
Popkin, Richard H.
The second Oswald. New York, Avon Books, 1966, 147p. 1848

Sauvage, Leo
The Oswald affair: an examination of the contradictions and omissions of the Warren report. Cleveland, World Pub. Co., 1966, 418p. 1849

Stafford, Jean
 A mother in history. London, Chatto & Windus, 1966, 98p. 1850

1967

Chapman, Gil & Ann Chapman
 Was Oswald alone? San Diego, Publishers Export Co., 1967, 160p. 1851

Joesten, Joachim
 Marina Oswald. London, Dawnay, 1967, 165p. 1852

Joesten, Joachim
 Oswald: the truth. London, Dawnay, 1967, 372p. 1853

Mihilović, Ive
 Tko je ubio Kennediyja. Zagreb, "Stvarnost," 1967, 457p. (Who killed Kennedy.) 1854

Stern, R.
 Le procès Ruby-Dallas. Kapellen (Belgium), Beckers, 1967.
 (The trial of Ruby in Dallas.) 1855

1968

Wills, Gary & Ovid Demaris
 Jack Ruby. New York, New American Library, 1968, 266p. 1856

Articles

1963

Bachmann, Ida
 "Hvem Myrdede Praesident Kennedy? Et Defensorat for Oswald Indleveret." Copenhagen, Frit Danmark (22: 10), 1963-64, p. 1-3.
 ("Who Murdered President Kennedy? A Defense of Oswald's Identification.") 1857

Cooke, Alistair
 "Oswald had Psychopathic Personality: no Evidence of Conspiracy." Manchester, Manchester guardian, November 27, 1963, p. 11. 1858

"Radio-TV Barred from Ruby Trial." Broadcasting 65, December 23, 1963, p. 56. 1859

"Public Relations Firm Sets Press Rules for Judge at Ruby's Trial." Editor & publisher 96, December 28, 1963, p. 9. 1860

1964

Sauvage, Leo
 "Oswald in Dallas: a Few Loose Ends." The reporter 30, January 2, 1964, p. 24-26. 1861

"If Oswald had Lived, Could Impartial Jury Have Been Found to try him?" Broadcasting 66, January 6, 1964, p. 52-53. 1862

Bloom, S.
 "Tells his Public Relations Role in Ruby Case." Editor & publisher 97, February 1, 1964, p. 58. 1863

Popa, Stefan
 "Dallas: Procesul Ruby." Bucharest, Lumea 8, Feb. 20, 1964, p. 10-11; Feb. 27, 1964, p. 8-9. ("Dallas: Ruby's Trial.") 1864

Sauvage, Leo
 "The Oswald Affair." Com-

mentary 37, March 1964, p. 55-65. 1865

Tupa, Stefan
"Dallas: Declaraţii şi Ipoteze." Bucharest, Lumea 11, March 12, 1964, p. 9-10.
("Dallas: Statements and Hypotheses.") 1866

Lauzon, A.
"Oswald a-t-il tué Kennedy?" Montreal, Le magazine Maclean 4, March 1964, p. 1-2.
("Did Oswald Kill Kennedy?") 1867

"Radio-TV Newsmen Testify in Ruby Trial." Broadcasting 66, March 16, 1964, p. 74. 1868

"Ruby Death Verdict: a TV Spectacular." Editor & publisher 97, March 21, 1964, p. 11. 1869

Popa, Stefan
"Dallas 'Paziţi-l Bine pe Ruby'." Bucharest, Lumea (2: 13), March 26, 1964, p. 10-11.
("Dallas Guarding Ruby's Rights.") 1870

"Oswald Diary Publication Stirs Furor." Editor & publisher 97, July 4, 1964, p. 14. 1871

Joesten, Joachim
"Lazni Osvald." Belgrade, Oslobodenje (21: 3), November 13, 1964, p. 5927-5938.
("Fake Oswald.") 1872

1965
Sparrow, John H. A.
"Making Mysteries About Oswald." Atlas 9, March 1965, p. 173-174. 1873

"Was Oswald Guilty? A Judicial Summing-up of the Warren Report." London, New statesman 69, March 12, 1965, p. 399-403. 1874

Snyder, L.
"Lee Oswald's Guilt: How Science Nailed Kennedy's Killer." Popular science 186, April 1965, p. 68-73. 1875

Sauvage, Leo
"Afera Oswald." Zagreb, Vjesnik u srijedu 18, August 25, 1965, p. 694-695.
("The Oswald Affair.") 1876

Sauvage, Leo
"L'Affaire Oswald (review by J. Amalric)." Atlas 10, October 1965, p. 249-250. 1877

Stafford, Jean, ed.
"The Strange World of Marguerite Oswald." McCall's 93, October 1965, p. 112-113. 1878

1966
"Ruby and the King of Torts." London, Times literary supplement, March 17, 1966, p. 221. 1879

O'Brien, Conor C.
"No one Else but him." London, New statesman 72, September 30, 1966, p. 479-481. 1880

"Can Ruby Tell?" London, Sunday times, October 9, 1966, p. 8. 1881

Kempton, Murray
"Ruby, Oswald and the State." London, Spectator, October 21, 1966, p. 506-507. 1882

1967

Kempton, Murray
"The Disposable Jack Ruby." London, Spectator, January 13, 1967, p. 35. 1883

"New Orleans and the Cubans: who was Ready to Help Oswald?" London, The times, February 20, 1967, p. 12. 1884

"Theory of an Oswald Conspiracy." Life 62, March 3, 1967, p. 33. 1885

Graham, J.
"Acquittal for Oswald." Commonweal 86, April 21, 1967, p. 149-151. 1886

Roberts, G.
"The Case of Jim Garrison and Lee Oswald." New York times magazine, May 21, 1967, p. 32-35. 1887

1969

Epstein, Edward J.
"Final Chapter in the Assassination Controversy?" New York times magazine, April 20, 1969, p. 30-31. 1888

The Warren Report

Books

1964

Crawford, Curtis, et al
Critical reactions to the Warren report. New York, Marzani & Munsell, 1964, 64p. 1889

Thomson, George C.
The quest for truth; a quizzical look at the Warren report; or, How President Kennedy really was assassinated. Glendale, Calif., G.C. Thomson Engineering Co., 1964, 50p. 1890

U.S. 88th Congress. Public Law 202
S.J. Res. 137, joint resolution authorizing Commission established to report upon assasination of President John F. Kennedy to compel attendance and testimony of witnesses and production of evidence. Approved December 13, 1963. Washington, 1964, 2p. 1891

U.S. House of Representatives. 88th Congress
House report 1013, authorizing subpoena power for Commission on Assassination of President John F. Kennedy. Report from Committee on Judiciary to accompany H.J. Res. 852. December 10, 1963. Washington, House Document Room, 1964, 3p. 1892

U.S. President's Commission on the Assassination of

President Kennedy
A concise compendium of the Warren Commission report on the assassination of John F. Kennedy. New York, Popular Library, 1964, 637p.
1893

U.S. President's Commission on the Assassination of President Kennedy
Investigation of the assassination of President John F. Kennedy; hearings before the President's Commission on the Assassination of President Kennedy. 26v. Washington, G.P.O., 1964. 1894

U.S. President's Commission on the Assassination of President Kennedy
Report of the Warren Commission on the assassination of President Kennedy...with added material prepared by the New York Times exclusively for this edition. New York, McGraw-Hill, 1964, 726p. 1895

1965

U.S. President's Commission on the Assassination of President Kennedy
The Warren report; report of the Commission. New York, Associated Press, 1965, 366p.
1896

U.S. President's Commission on the Assassination of President Kennedy
The witnesses--selected and edited from the Warren Commission's hearings by the New York Times. New York, McGraw-Hill, 1965, 634p. 1897

Weisberg, Harold
The report on the Warren Report; or, The six wise men of Industan. [n.p.] 1965, 188p. 1898

Weisberg, Harold
Whitewash: the report on the Warren Report. Hyattstown, Md., 1965, 224p. 1899

1966

Epstein, Edward J.
Inquest; the Warren Commission and the establishment of truth. New York, Viking Press, 1966, 224p.
1900

Joesten, Joachim
Die Wahrheit über den Kennedy-Mord; wie und warum der Warren-Report lügt. Zürich, Schweizer Verlagshaus, 1966, 355p.
(The truth about the Kennedy murder; how and why the Warren Report is lying.)
1901

Jones, Penn
Forgive my grief; a critical review of the Warren Commission report on the assassination of John F. Kennedy. v. 1. Midlothian, Texas, Midlothian Mirror, 1966, 188p. 1902

Lane, Mark
Rush to judgment; a critique of the Warren Commission's inquiry into the murders of President John F. Kennedy, Officer J.D. Tippit, and Lee Harvey Oswald. New York, Holt, Rinehart & Winston, 1966, 478p.
1903

Macdonald, D.
A critique of the Warren Report (In Walker, Gerald, ed. Best magazine articles, 1966. New York, Crown, 1966, p. 19-53). 1904

Meagher, Sylvia
Subject index to the Warren report and hearings and exhibits. New York, Scarecrow Press, 1966, 150p. 1905

The Warren Commission on the Assassination of President Kennedy; the Warren Commission Report on the role of the press in the assassination of President John F. Kennedy (In Gross, Gerald, ed. The responsibility of the press. New York, Fleet Pub., 1966, p. 50-82). 1906

Weisberg, Harold
Whitewash II: the FBI-Secret Service cover-up. Hyattstown, Md., 1966, 250p. 1907

1967
Lewis, Richard W.
The scavengers and critics of the Warren Report; the endless paradox. Based on an investigation by Lawrence Schiller. New York, Delacorte Press, 1967, 188p. 1908

Meagher, Sylvia
Accessories after the fact; the Warren Commission, the authorities and the report. Indianapolis, Bobbs-Merrill, 1967, 477p. 1909

1968
Lane, Mark
A citizen's dissent: Mark Lane replies. New York, Holt, Rinehart & Winston, 1968, 290p. 1910

Sparrow, John H. A.
After the assassination; a positive appraisal of the Warren report. New York, Chilmark Press, 1968, 77p. 1911

Smith, William R.
A hog story; from the aftermire of the Kennedy assassination. Washington, L'Avant Garde Pubs., 1968, 55p. 1912

White, Stephen
Should we now believe the Warren Report? New York, Macmillan, 1968, 309p. 1913

Articles

1964
Osvald, Frank
"Kan man Stole pa Warren?" Copenhagen, Verdens gang 18, 1964, p. 274-279. ("Can One Trust Warren?") 1914

"Sonderkommission Untersucht Kennedy-Attentat." Cologne, Polizei-polizeipraxis 55, 1964, p. 159-160. ("Special Commission Investigates the Kennedy Assasination.") 1915

Meyer, Karl E. & N. MacKenzie
"Spotlight on Warren." London, New statesman 68, October 2, 1964, p. 474-476. 1916

"Text of Summary of Warren Commission Report." Congressional quarterly weekly report 22, October 2, 1964, p. 2332-2340. 1917

Rivers, C.
"Warren Report Slaps Press and Calls for Ethics Code; News Media Share in Blame for Killing JFK's Assassin." Editor & publisher 97, October 3, 1964, p. 13. 1918

"Poročilo Warrenove Komisije." Ljubljana, Ljubljanski dnevnik (14: 1), October 8, 1964, p. 268-275.
("Report of the Warren Commission.") 1919

Meyer, Karl E.
"The Warren Report: the Triumph of Caliban. The Other Witnesses, by George Nash & Patricia Nash." New leader 47, October 12, 1964, p. 4-9. 1920

Montagu, Ivor
"The Warren Report." London, Labour monthly 46, November 1964, p. 499-503. 1921

Clifford, G.
"Warren Report: a new Boost for the Kennedy Memorabilia Industry." Toronto, Maclean's magazine 77, November 2, 1964, p. 3. 1922

Ellis, W.
"The Warren Report." Jubilee 12, December 1964, p. 24-27. 1923

1965

Mühlen, Norbert
"Mord und Legende. Die Kritiker des Warren-Reports." Frankfurt am Main, Der monat (17: 199), 1965, p. 14-28.
("Murder and Legend: the Critics of the Warren Report.") 1924

Schoenmann, Ralph
"Ist der Warren-Bericht über den Tod Präsident Kennedys Glaubwürdig?" Frankfurt am Main, Frankfurter hefte (20: 1), 1965, p. 15-24.
("Is the Warren Report on the Death of President Kennedy Credible?") 1925

Scobey, Alfredda
"A Lawyer's Notes on the Warren Commission Report..." American Bar Association journal 51, January 1965, p. 39-43. 1926

Jacobson, Dan
"Mean Street: Warren Commission Report." London, New statesman 69, January 15, 1965, p. 76-77. 1927

Trevor-Roper, Hugh R.
"Slovenly Warren Report." Atlas 9, February 1965, p. 115-118. 1928

Macdonald, Dwight
"A Critique of the Warren

Report." Esquire (LXIII: 3), March 1965, p. 59.   1929

Salandria, Vincent J.
"The Warren Report? A Philadelphia Lawyer Analyzes the President's Back and Neck Wounds..." Liberation 10, March 1965, p. 14-32.   1930

"Symposium on the Warren Commission Report." New York University law review 40, May 1965, p. 404-524.   1931

1966

Howard, Anthony
"Warren Commission Storm: the Clamour Rises for Kennedy X-rays." London, Observer, August 7, 1966, p. 10.   1932

Gibbons, R.
"The Warren Commission." Ave Maria 104, September 17, 1966, p. 16-17.   1933

Cline, R.A.
"Warren in the Dock: who Killed Kennedy?" London, Spectator, September 23, 1966, p. 371-372.   1934

Cohen, Jacob
"The Warren Commission Report and its Critics." Frontier 18, November 1966, p. 5-20.   1935

Sauvage, Leo
"Professor Bickel and the Warren Commission. Leo Sauvage and the Warren Commission, by Alexander M. Bickel. As I was Saying, by Leo Sauvage." New leader 49, November 21, 1966, p. 19-22.   1936

McReynolds, D.
"New York Letter: Macbeth in the White House." Toronto, Saturday night 81, December 1966, p. 22-23.   1937

1967

Cline, R.A.
"Postscript to Warren." London, Spectator, January 27, 1967, p. 99.   1938

Towne, Anthony
"The Assassination, the Warren Report and the Public Trust." Motive 27, February 1967, p. 6-14.   1939

Bickel, Alexander M.
"Failure of the Warren Report." Commentary 43, April 1967, p. 7-8.   1940

"55 People Given Credit for 9-month News Probe." Editor & publisher 100, July 8, 1967, p. 56.   1941

Bickel, Alexander M.
"CBS on the Warren Report." New republic 157, July 15, 1967, p. 29-30.   1942

Shayon, Robert L.
"Persistent Devils: CBS News Inquiry: the Warren Report." Saturday review 50, July 22, 1967, p. 46.   1943

"'Warren Report Wrong,' College Teacher Says." Los Angeles Times, November 17, 1967 (part I), p. 18.   1944

1968
Cook, Fred J.
"The Warren Report and the Irreconcilables: Theories of Josiah Tompson and Sylvia Meagher." The nation 206, February 26, 1968, p. 277-281. 1945

Eulogies

Books

1963
Bravo, Francisco
John Fitzgerald Kennedy, el mártir de la esperanza; discurso. Cuenca, 1963, 14p.
(John Fitzgerald Kennedy, martyr of hope; speech.) 1946

Mansfield, Michael J.
John Fitzgerald Kennedy, eulogies to the late President delivered in the rotunda of the United States Capitol, November 24, 1963, by Mike Mansfield, Earl Warren and John W. McCormack. Washington, G.P.O., 1963, 6p. 1947

McGrory, Mary
In memoriam: John Fitzgerald Kennedy. Washington, Evening Star Newspaper Co., 1963, unpaged. 1948

U.S. President, 1963-
(Lyndon B. Johnson)
Message to the Congress; address delivered before a joint session of the Senate and the House of Representatives. Washington, G.P.O., 1963, 4p. (88th Congress, first session. House of Representatives Document no. 178). 1949

Uruguay. Biblioteca del Poder Legislativo
John Fitzgerald Kennedy: 1917-1963; noticia biográfica en ocasión de su fallecimiento. Montevideo, 1963, 4p.
(Uruguay. Library of Congress
John Fitzgerald Kennedy: 1917-1963; biographical notice on the occasion of his death.) 1950

1964
Alonso Pujos, Guillermo
The world before a tomb. Barcelona, 1964, 24p. 1951

Brodie, Israel
Tribute to the late President John Fitzgerald Kennedy ...at the Marble Arch Synagogue, London...1963. London, Office of the Chief Rabbi, 1964, 7p. 1952

Daetwyler, Hans W., ed.
In memoriam John F. Kennedy. Aus dem Leben eines grossen Staatsmannes. 3d. ed. Zürich, Römerhof-Verlag, 1964, 32p. 1953

Kentucky. University
In memoriam: John Fitzgerald Kennedy, 1917-1963, President of the United States of America; memorial convocation at the University of Kentucky, Lexington, Kentucky, November the twenty-fifth, nineteen hundred and sixty-three. Lexington? 1964, unpaged. 1954

King, Martin Luther
  Die rede bei d. Gedenkfeier für John F. Kennedy anlässl. d. Eröffnung d. Berliner Festwochen, 1964. Vienna, U.S. Information Service, 1964, 6p.
  (Speech at the commemorative celebration for John F. Kennedy, on the occasion of the opening of Berlin Festival Week, 1964.)   1955

Durant, John & Alice Durant
  Pictorial history of American presidents. 4th rev. ed. New York, A.S. Barnes, 1965, p. 302-319.   1956

Mansfield, Michael J.
  Eulogies to the late President John Fitzgerald Kennedy delivered in the rotunda of the United States Capitol, November 24, 1963. New Britain, Conn., J.L. Kapica, 1964, 30p.   1957

Salinger, Pierre E.G. & Sandor Vanocur, eds.
  A tribute to John F. Kennedy. Chicago, Encyclopaedia Britannica Press, 1964, 162p.   1958

Schmidt, Sister M. Bernadette, comp.
  The trumpet summons us... John F. Kennedy. New York, Vantage Press, 1964, 195p. 1959

Stevenson, Adlai E.
  Tributes to John F. Kennedy (In Baird, A.C., ed. Representative American speeches, 1963-1964. New York, Wilson, 1964, p. 30-33).   1960

Stewart, Charles J. & Bruce Kendall, eds.
  A man named John F. Kennedy; sermons on his assassination. Glen Rock, N.J., Paulist Press, 1964, 208p.   1961

That Was the Week That Was (BBC Television Program)
  "That was the week that was," a tribute to John Fitzgerald Kennedy, 23 November 1963. London, British Broadcasting Corp., 1964? 18p.   1962

United States Committee for the United Nations
  Homage to a friend; a memorial tribute by the United Nations for President John F. Kennedy. New York, 1964, 93p.   1963

U.S. 88th Congress, Second session, 1964
  Memorial addresses in the Congress of the United States and tributes in eulogy of John Fitzgerald Kennedy, late a President of the United States. Washington, G.P.O., 1964, 911p.   1964

1965

La Gente (Television Program)
  Funeral cívico por Alfredo L. Palacios; Funeral cívico

por John F. Kennedy. Buenos Aires, Editorial La Gente, 1965, 153p. (Civil funeral service for Alfredo L. Palacios; civil funeral service for John F. Kennedy.) 1965

Reyes Monroy, José L., ed. Ramo de orquídeas; la bella flor nacional de Guatemala, a la memoria del gran presidente de los Estados Unidos dè América, señor John F. Kennedy. Guatemala, Tip. Nacional, 1965, 354p. (A branch of orchids; the beautiful national flower of Guatemala, to the memory of the great President of the United States of America, Mr. John F. Kennedy.) 1966

U.S. Dept. of Commerce Remarks by Under Secretary of Commerce Franklin D. Roosevelt, Jr., in connection with posthumous presentation of Franklin D. Roosevelt Four Freedoms Award to John Fitzgerald Kennedy, New York City, May 25, 1965. Washington (Cl.18: G36/965), 1965, 3p. 1967

U.S. Post Office Department Address by John A. Gronouski, Postmaster General, at State convention of National Association of Postmasters of United States, Fond du Lac, Wisconsin, June 10, 1965. Washington (Information Service: General release 71), P 1.27: G 89/59, 1965, 6p. 1968

1966
Kennedy, John F. A John F. Kennedy memorial miniature. 4v. New York, Random House, 1966. 1969

1968
Henderson, Bruce & Sam Summerlin 1:33 in memoriam: John F. Kennedy. New York, Cowles Education Corp., 1968, 256p. 1970

Articles

1963
"President Kennedy: an Appreciation." Wellington, External affairs review 13, November 1963, p. 1-9. 1971

"President's Death Mankind's Loss." Catholic Association for International Peace news 24, October-November 1963, p. 3. 1972

"Statement of CAIP on the Death of President John F. Kennedy." Catholic Association for International Peace news 24, October-November 1963, p. 1. 1973

Vanier, G.P. "Canada's Tribute to President Kennedy." Ottawa, External affairs 15, November 1963, p. 382-383. 1974

Chile. Laws, statutes, etc. "Decreto no. 2,144: Declara Duelo Oficial en Todo el Territorio de la República, con Motivo del Falle-

cimiento del Excelentísimo Señor Presidente de los Estados Unidos de América, Don John Fitzgerald Kennedy." Santiago, Diário oficial (86: 25,698), November 23, 1963, p. 2565.
("Decree No. 2,144: Official Mourning is Declared Throughout the Republic due to the Death of the President of the United States of America, John Fitzgerald Kennedy.") 1975

Mexico. Laws, statutes, etc.
"Decreto que Dispone que Durante Tres Días, a Partir del 23 de Noviembre en Curso, se Observe Luto Oficial en Homenaje a la Memoria del Presidente de los Estados Unidos de América, Señor John F. Kennedy." Mexico, Diario oficial (261: 19), November 23, 1963, p. 1.
("Decree Stating that for Three Days, Beginning November 23, Official Mourning will be Observed in Respect to the Memory of the President of the United States of America, Mr. John F. Kennedy.") 1976

Peru. Laws, statutes, etc.
"Día de Duelo Oficial por la Muerte del Presidente Kennedy. Decreto Supremo." Lima, El peruano 6764, November 23, 1963, p. 1.
("Official Day of Mourning for the Death of President Kennedy: Supreme Decree.") 1977

Vrhovec, J.
"Kennedy je Bio Vjeran Miru." Belgrade, Vjesnik 24, November 23, 1963, p. 6023.
("Kennedy was Devoted to Peace.") 1978

"Zum Tode J.F. Kennedys." Bonn, Aufrüstung (11: 23), 1963, p. 9.
("On the Death of J.F. Kennedy.") 1979

Budimac, Budimir
'Nesrecan Kraj 'Deteta Srece'." Ljubljana, Dnevnik, November 24, 1963, p. 6125.
("Sad Child of Fortune.") 1980

Nenadović, Aleksandar
"Secanja i Obaceze." Belgrade, Politika LX, November 24, 1963, p. 324.
("Memories and Sadness.") 1981

Vrhovec, J.
"Kennedy: Covjek i Drzavnik." Belgrade, Vjesnik 24, November 24, 1963, p. 6024.
("Kennedy: Man and Statesman.") 1982

Brazil. Laws, statutes, etc.
"Decreto no. 52,918--de 22 de Novembro de 1963. Declara Luto Oficial em Todo o País, em Sinal de Pesar Pelo Falecimento do Presidente John F. Kennedy." Brasília, Diário oficial (102: 224), November 25, 1963, p. 9891.
("Decree No. 52,918, of November 22, 1963. Official Mourning is Declared Throughout the Country, as a Sign of Mourning of the Death of President John F. Kennedy.") 1983

Douglas-Home, Alec, et al
"Tributes to President Ken-

nedy." London, Listener 70, November 28, 1963, p. 865-866. 1984

"President Mourned at Council." Catholic messenger 82, November 28, 1963, p. 1. 1985

Eban, Abba
"Kennedy's Bequest to the Middle East." London, Jewish observer 12, November 29, 1963, p. 23. 1986

"National Mourning in Peru for Death of President Kennedy." Lima, Peruvian times (23: 1197), November 29, 1963, p. 1. 1987

"The Presidency: 'The Government Still Lives'." Time 82, November 29, 1963, p. 21-32. 1988

Hollis, C.
"The First Catholic in the White House." Tablet 217, November 30, 1963, p. 1184-1185. 1989

"Leader of the West." London, The economist 209, November 30, 1963, p. 881-886. 1990

Locsin, Teodoro M.
"The Legacy (Editorial)." Manila, Philippines free press (56: 48), November 30, 1963, p. 1, 8. 1991

"Mourning for Kennedy." Tablet 217, November 30, 1963, p. 1302. 1992

"Notes and Comment: Kennedy in Miami." New Yorker 39, November 30, 1963, p. 49-51. 1993

"Towards Their Going: Requiem Masses Offered." Tablet 217, November 30, 1963, p. 1290. 1994

"The Vigorous JFK." Manila, Philippines herald magazine, November 30, 1963, p. 22-23. 1995

"The World's Loss." Tablet 217, November 30, 1963, p. 1183-1184. 1996

Zumel, Antonio
"The Loss was ours, too." Manila, Philippines herald magazine, November 30, 1963, p. 4-5. 1997

"Amigo de los Hombres (Murió John F. Kennedy ....") Madrid, Indice de artes y letras (16: 179), December 1963, p. 1. ("The Friend of Men John F. Kennedy has Died...") 1998

"And the Light Shineth in Darkness (Editorial)." Fredericton, Canada, Atlantic advocate 54, December 1963, p. 14-15. 1999

"Ave Atque Vale; B'nai Brith Mourns President Kennedy; Pledges Cooperation to President Johnson." National Jewish monthly 78, December 1963, p. 8. 2000

"Beileidsbekundungen zum Tode John F. Kennedys." Bonn, Die Sowjetunion heute (23: 8), 1963, p. 4-

5.
("Manifestestations of Condolence upon the Death of John F. Kennedy.") 2001

Berger, Kurt M.
"Das Ende einer 'Führungsmacht'." Bad Godesberg, Gemeinschaft und politik 11, 1963, p. 339-342.
("The End of a Strong Leadership.") 2002

Câmara, José A.
"John F. Kennedy." Fortaleza, Brazil, Revista do Instituto do Ceará 77, January-December 1963, p. 5-8. 2003

Díaz Casanueva, Humberto
"Homenaje al Presidente de Estados Unidos, John F. Kennedy." Concepción, Chile, Atenea (152: 402), October-December 1963, p. 8-10.
("Homage to the President of the United States, John F. Kennedy.") 2004

Dodson, J.M.
"John Fitzgerald Kennedy, 35th President of the United States of America." Kentucky school journal 42, December 1963, p. 7. 2005

Druskovic, Drago
"John Fitzgerald Kennedy." Belgrade, Naši razgledi (12: 23), 1963, p. 449. 2006

"Ein Bedeutender Staatsmann." Berlin, Begegnung (12: 3), 1963, p. 19.
("An Outstanding Statesman.") 2007

Erhard, Ludwig
"Zuverlässiger Huter der Freiheit und Sicherheit." Bonn, Bulletin des Presse- und Informationsamtes der Bundesregierung 208, 1963, p. 1841-1842.
("Unfailing Guardian of Freedom and Security.")2008

"In Memoriam, a 'Profile in Courage'." Pioneer woman 38, December 1963, p. 2. 2009

"John F. Kennedy." Buenos Aires, El príncipe (4: 27-28), November-December 1963, p. 225-226.2010

"John Fitzgerald Kennedy." Land and life 22, December 1963, p. 2. 2011

"John Fitzgerald Kennedy: 1917-1963." AAUP bulletin 49, December 1963, p. 307. 2012

"John Fitzgerald Kennedy: Text of Funeral Eulogy." Jewish spectator 28, December 1963, p. 3. 2013

Johnson, H.
"President John F. Kennedy." Social justice review 56, December 1963, p. 265-266. 2014

Johnson, Lyndon B.
"Im Geist und nach dem Willen Kennedys." Bonn, Bulletin des Presse- und Informationsamtes der Bundesregierung 211, 1963, p. 1869-1870.
("In the Spirit and Wish of Kennedy.") 2015

"Kennedy and Lincoln (Review Article)." Fredericton, Canada, Atlantic advocate 54, December 1963, p. 65-66. 2016

"Kennedys Tausend Tage." Hamburg, Der spiegel (17: 48), 1963, p. 24-29. ("Kennedy's Thousand Days.") 2017

Korfmacher, W.
"Champion of Youth: JFK." Classical bulletin 40, December 1963, p. 24. 2018

Kramarsky, L.
"In Memoriam: John Fitzgerald Kennedy, 1917-1963." Hadassah magazine 44, December 1963, p. 2. 2019

Licuanan, Francisco H.
"After Kennedy, What?" Manila, Philippine journal of education (42: 6), December 1963, p. 454-455. 2020

Lohmar, Ulrich
"Kennedys Vermächtnis." Gutersloh, Kirche und mann (16: 12), 1963, p. 2. ("Kennedy's Legacy.") 2021

Perez Herrera, Carlos
"Homenaje a John Fitzgerald Kennedy." Panama, Lotería (8: 97), December 1963, p. 9-11.
("Homage to John Fitzgerald Kennedy.") 2022

Rauschning, Hermann
"In Memoriam John Fitzgerald Kennedy. 35. Präsident der Vereinigten Staaten von Amerika." Cologne, Blätter für deutsche und internationale politik (8: 12), 1963, p. 914-925.
("In Memoriam, John Fitzgerald Kennedy, 35th President of the United States of America.") 2023

Remus, Bernard
"Erinnerung an John F. Kennedy." Zürich, Weltwoche (31: 1568), 1963, p. 1, 3. ("Remembrance of John F. Kennedy.") 2024

Rubin, Berthold
"Vor dem Toten den Degen Senken. Ein Nachruf auf den Tod des US-Präsidenten John Kennedy." Munich, Schlesische rundschau (15: 48), 1963, p. 3.
("Lowering the Sword Before the Warrior. An Obituary on U.S. President John Kennedy.") 2025

Sociedad Bolivariana del Ecuador
"Homenaje a la Memoria de John Fitzgerald Kennedy." Quito, El libertador 129, July-December 1963, p. 43-50.
("Homage to the Memory of John Fitzgerald Kennedy.") 2026

"Sorrow and Hope." London, World Jewry 6, November-December 1963, p. 6. 2027

Tanner, Werner
"John F. Kennedy." Basel, Kirchenblatt für die reformierte Schweiz 119, 1963, p. 377-378. 2028

"Tributes to President John

F. Kennedy." United Nations review 10, December 1963, p. i-iv.   2029

Tschäppät, R.
"Das Geistige Erbe Kennedys." Zürich, Schweizerisches kaufmännisches zentralblatt (67: 48), 1963, p. 1.
("Kennedy's Spiritual Legacy.")   2030

Wagman, Frederick H.
"Tribute." ALA bulletin 57, December 1963, p. 994.   2031

"What John F. Kennedy Stood for." Lamp 61, December 1963, p. 16-17.   2032

"ZOA Members Observe Traditional '30 Days' for Late President." American Zionist 54, December 1963, p. 1.   2033

"Zum Tode von Präsident John F. Kennedy." Cologne, Blätter für deutsche und internationale politik (8: 12), 1963, p. 904-905.
("On the Death of President John F. Kennedy.")   2034

Forbes, M.S.
"Firm Experienced Hand." Forbes 92, December 1, 1963, p. 9-10.   2035

Ecuador. Laws, statutes, etc.
"Declárase Ocho Días de Duelo Nacional por el Fallecimiento del Excelentísimo Señor John F. Kennedy, Presidente de los Estados Unidos de América. Decreto no. 1017." Quito, Registro oficial (1: 119), December 2, 1963, p. 1073.
("Eight Days of National Mourning are Declared due to the Death of His Excellency, Mr. John F. Kennedy, President of the United States of America. Decree No. 1017.")   2036

"Foreign Countries too Mourn First Citizen of the World." U.S. news & world report 55, December 2, 1963, p. 48-49.   2037

"In Memoriam: John F. Kennedy." Congress bi-weekly 30, December 2, 1963, p. 1.   2038

"A man and his Milestones." Newsweek 62, December 2, 1963, p. 39-42.   2039

Cushing, Richard J.
"Eulogy for President" (text). Catholic messenger 82, December 5, 1963, p. 8.   2040

"Cables of Condolences from Israeli Leaders." Jerusalem, Israel digest 6, December 6, 1963, p. 2.   2041

Hamblin, D.J.
"President Kennedy is Laid to Rest." Life 55, December 6, 1963, p. 38-49.   2042

"Israel's Leaders and People Mourn President Kennedy." Jerusalem, Israel digest 6, December 6, 1963, p. 2-3.   2043

"Sorrow Rings a World: Tributes to President Ken-

nedy." Life 55, December
6, 1963, p. 117-126. 2044

Sover, Z.
"Late President and Israel."
Jerusalem, Israel digest 6,
December 6, 1963, p. 3. 2045

Cousins, Norman
"The Legacy of John F. Kennedy." Saturday review 46,
December 7, 1963, p. 21-27.
2046

"From Death, Life." Ave
Maria 98, December 7, 1963,
p. 16-17. 2047

"The Kennedy Legacy." Tablet
217, December 7, 1963, p.
1309-1310. 2048

"May he Rest in Peace."
America 109, December 7,
1963, p. 728-729. 2049

"St. Paul's Cathedral During
the Memorial Service for
President Kennedy." London,
Illustrated London news 243,
December 7, 1963, p. 937.
2050

Daguio, Amador T.
"Kennedy: 20th Century Perfection." Manila, Examiner,
77th issue, December 8, 1963,
p. 10-11. 2051

Estrada, Nina
"Death of a man: Life of an
Ideal." Manila, Examiner, 77th
issue, December 8, 1963, p.
9, 19. 2052

Flores, A.O.
"Kennedy Invested the U.S.
Presidency with the Vigor of
Youth and the Wisdom of Maturity." Manila, Sunday times
magazine, December 8, 1963,
p. 20-22. 2053

Goloy, Gloria G.
"John Fitzgerald Kennedy."
Manila, Sunday times magazine, December 8, 1963, p.
19. 2054

Lorredo, Jorge
"Kennedy's Legacy: a Sense
of History." Manila, Examiner, 77th issue, December 8,
1963, p. 11. 2055

Patacsil, Artemio C.
"A Profile in Courage."
Manila, Examiner, 77th issue,
December 8, 1963, p. 8, 28.
2056

Argentine Republic. Laws,
statutes, etc.
"Duelo Nacional: Declárase
por el Fallecimiento del
Señor Presidente de los Estados Unidos de Norteamérica, John F. Kennedy. Decreto no. 907." Buenos Aires,
Boletín oficial (71: 20,291),
December 9, 1963, p. 1.
("National Mourning: Declared due to the Death of the
President of the United States
of America, John F. Kennedy. Decree No. 907.")
2057

"As the World Wept." U.S.
news & world report 55,
December 9, 1963, p. 51-57. 2058

"Foreign Dignitaries Attend
Funeral of President Kennedy: List." Dept. of State
bulletin 49, December 9,
1963, p. 895-899. 2059

"May the Angels, Dear Jack, Lead you Into Paradise." Newsweek 62, December 9, 1963, p. 30-33. 2060

"UN General Assembly Holds Memorial Meeting: Statements of C. Sosa-Rodriguez, U. Thant, Adlai E. Stevenson." Dept. of State bulletin 49, December 9, 1963, p. 892-895. 2061

"World Leaders Pay Tribute to President Kennedy: Messages of Condolence Sent to President Johnson and Mrs. Kennedy." Dept. of State bulletin 49, December 9, 1963, p. 884-891. 2062

Burnham, W.D.
"After JFK, What?" Commonweal 79, December 13, 1963, p. 340-343. 2063

Honduras. Laws, statutes, etc.
'Decreto Número 16. Decreta: Declarar Duelo Nacional por Tres Días, a Contar de Esta Fecha, por el Fallecimiento del Excmo. Sr. John F. Kennedy, Durante los Cuales Permanecerá Izado a Media asta el Pabellón Nacional, en los Edificios Públicos." Tegucigalpa, La gaceta (88: 18,150), December 13, 1963, p. 1-2.
("Decree Number 16. Decrees: Declare National Mourning for Three Days From This Date due to the Death of His Excellency, Mr. John F. Kennedy, During Which the National Emblem will Fly at Half-mast on Public Buildings.")2064

"The Kennedy Legacy, the People's Task." Commonweal 79, December 13, 1963, p. 335-336. 2065

Shannon, William V.
"The Mood in Washington." Commonweal 79, December 13, 1963, p. 339-340. 2066

Fischer, E.
"The Great Script Dares What Lesser Scripts Dare Not." Ave Maria 98, December 14, 1963, p. 15. 2067

Hughes, H.S.
"A Most Unstuffy man." The nation 197, December 14, 1963, p. 408-409. 2068

Lasky, Melvin J.
"Thoughts After Kennedy." Manila, Philippines herald magazine, December 14, 1963, p. 12-13. 2069

McGrory, Mary
"After Great Pain, a Formal Feeling." America 109, December 14, 1963, p. 764. 2070

"Memorial: New York City's Memorial Service for President Kennedy, on Steps of City Hall." New Yorker 39, December 14, 1963, p. 45-46. 2071

Schlesinger, Arthur M.
'Eulogy: John Fitzgerald Kennedy." Saturday evening post 236, December 14, 1963, p. 32-32A. 2072

Polier, S.
"Kennedy's Impact on

American Freedom." Congress bi-weekly 30, December 16, 1963, p. 6-8.   2073

"Homenaje a Kennedy." Mexico, Trinchera (1: 3), December 20, 1963, p. 3-4. ("Homage to Kennedy.")   2074

"President Johnson's Appreciation." Jerusalem, Israel digest 6, December 20, 1963, p. 2.   2075

Kennedy, W.
"The Military Legacy: Kennedy's Contribution to our National Strength." America 109, December 21, 1963, p. 790.
2076

Calderón, Cicero D.
"Kennedy: Citizen of the World." Manila, Examiner, 79th issue, December 22, 1963, p. 15, 19.   2077

Riesman, David, et al
"Reflections on the Fate of the Union: Kennedy and After." New York review of books 1, December 26, 1963, p. 3-11.
2078

1964

Bailey, S.K.
"Looking Backward and Forward: the Lessons of the Assassination." Educational record 45, Winter 1964, p. 5-10.
2079

Borch, Herbert von
"Wird Kennedys Erbe Uberleben?" Stuttgart, Aussenpolitik 15, 1964, p. 1-4.
("Will Kennedy's Heritage Survive?")   2080

Craig, G.M.
"John Fitzgerald Kennedy." Toronto, International journal 19, Winter 1963-64, p. 1-6.
2081

Eckstein, Günther
"John F. Kennedy." Cologne, Gewerkschaftliche monatshefte 15, 1964, p. 3-4.   2082

Eisendrath, Maurice N.
"Mourning is not Enough." American Judaism 13, Winter 1963-64, p. 7.   2083

Hannan, P.
"Eulogy of President Kennedy." Lasallian digest 6, Winter 1964, p. 3-4.   2084

Harpprecht, Klaus
"John F. Kennedy." Berlin, Der monat (184: 16), 1963-64, p. 9-14.   2085

"John F. Kennedy zum Gedächtnis." Aschaffenburg, Katholischer digest 18, 1964, p. 10-12.
("John F. Kennedy in Memory.")   2086

Johnson, Lyndon B.
"The Lighting of the National Christmas Tree. U.S. Marks Final Day of Mourning for President Kennedy." Dept. of State bulletin (50: 1281), 1964, p. 38-39.   2087

Kahler, Otto
"John F. Kennedy, Staatsmann und Bildungsreformer." Darmstadt (nebst Beil), Hessische lehrer-zeitung 17, 1964, p. 5-6.

("John F. Kennedy, Statesman and Educational Reformer.") 2088

Kahler, Otto
"John F. Kennedy: Staatsmann und Kulturpolitiker." Munich, Die bayrische schule 17, 1964, p. 7-9.
("John F. Kennedy: Statesman and Politician of Cultural Affairs.") 2089

Kraft, Joseph
"Präsident-Sein als Metier." Berlin, Der monat (184: 16), 1963-64, p. 15-19.
("The Presidency as a Profession.") 2090

LaSalle, Brother
"Tribute to John Fitzgerald Kennedy." Catholic business education review 15, Winter 1964, p. 4. 2091

Mann, Golo
"John F. Kennedy." Frankfurt am Main, Die neue rundschau (75: 1), 1964, p. 9-14. 2092

Oraze, S.
"We Must Pray for our President." Divine Love 7, Winter 1963-64, p. 2-3. 2093

Pouillon, Jean
"De l'Assassinat à l'Enterrement." Paris, Temps modernes (2: 218), 1964, p. 184-192.
("From the Assassination to the Burial.") 2094

Schram, S.R.
"Adieu au Président Kennedy." Paris, Christianisme social (72: 1-2), 1964, p. 113.
("Farewell to President Kennedy.") 2095

Schroers, Rolf, et al
"John F. Kennedy." Stuttgart, Merkur 18, 1964, p. 63-77. 2096

Seaborg, Glenn T.
"John F. Kennedy: Some Recollections..." Nucleonics (22: 1), 1964, p. 41-44. 2097

Vorspan, Albert
"Why Did I Weep?" American Judaism 13, Winter 1963-64, p. 6. 2098

Wollenberg, Otto
"John F. Kennedy." Cologne, Gewerkschaftliche monatshefte 15, 1964, p. 1-2. 2099

Alberse, J.
"In Memoriam; November 22, 1963." Friar 21, January 1964, p. 39-41. 2100

Barbeau, C.
"John F. Kennedy." Way 20, January-February 1964, p. 2-10. 2101

Cargas, H.
"Two Men Named John." Queen's work 56, January 1964, p. 3. 2102

Carr, A.
"J.F.K." Homiletic & pastoral review 64, January 1964, p. 368. 2103

Cushing, Richard J.
"Aus der Gedenkrede von Kardinal Cushing auf Präsident Kennedy." Freiburg-im-Breisgau, Germany, Herder-korrespondenz 18, January 1964, p. 169-170.
("From the Spoken Thoughts of Cardinal Cushing on President Kennedy.") 2104

Cushing, Richard J.
"John Fitzgerald Kennedy (1917-1963): Sermon at Requiem Mass, November 24, 1963." Catholic mind 62, January 1964, p. 4-7. 2105

Echánove, A.
"La Emoción Kennedy." Madrid, Razón y fé 169, January 1964, p. 85-91.
("The Kennedy Emotion.") 2106

Gallagher, R.
"John Fitzgerald Kennedy." Catholic charities review 48, January 1964, p. 1. 2107

Gorman, R.
"JFK." Sign 43, January 1964, p. 8. 2108

Gray, R.
"Meditation in Arlington." Mary 25, January-February 1964, p. 48-53. 2109

Hanley, J.
"Reclaiming our High Hopes." Today 19, January 1964, p. 9-11. 2110

Hayoul, M.
"La Succession de John Kennedy." Tournai, Belgium, Revue nouvelle 39, January 1964, p. 74-84.
("The Succession of John Kennedy.") 2111

Hochwalt, F.
"In Memoriam to John F. Kennedy" (a prayer). Catholic school journal 64, January 1964, p. 29. 2112

"In Memoriam." Toronto, World affairs 29, January 1964, p. 3, 9. 2113

"John F. Kennedy Mourned: Moetzet Hapoalot." Pioneer woman 39, January 1964, p. 18. 2114

"John Fitzgerald Kennedy." Journal of nursing education 19, January 1964, p. 66. 2115

Keenan, J.
"A Sprig of Lilac." Four quarters 13, January 1964, p. 1-2. 2116

"Kenyan Tribute to Kennedy." Overseas 3, January 1964, p. 30. 2117

Kirk, S. A.
"John Fitzgerald Kennedy." Exceptional children 30, January 1964, p. 193. 2118

"Korean Farmer's Tribute." Mission digest 22, January 1964, p. 27. 2119

"Leader of his Generation (Editorial)." Don Mills, Canada, Executive 6, January 1964, p. 21. 2120

McNaught, K.
"Kennedy Legacy and Ideal for a Pragmatic Heir." Toronto, Saturday night 79, January 1964, p. 9-11. 2121

Mary Maureen, Sister
"Dear Jack." Marist 20, January-February 1964, p. 10-13. 2122

Minifie, J.M.
"Legacy of John F. Kennedy." Montreal, Montrealer 38, January 1964, p. 18-20. 2123

Molz, K.
"November 22, 1963." Wilson library bulletin 38, January 1964, p. 408. 2124

Muirhead, P.P.
"The Kennedy Legacy." Higher education 20, January 1964, p. 5-7. 2125

O'Connor, J.
"The Magnificat's Comment." Magnificat 112, January 1964, p. 8-10. 2126

"Resolution of Condolence." Social justice review 56, January 1964, p. 320. 2127

Sclanders, Ian
"The Legacy of John Kennedy and how Congress can Live up to it." Toronto, Maclean's magazine 77, January 4, 1964, p. 2-3. 2128

Sheen, F.
"JFK: Victim for a Better World." Pastoral life 12, January 1964, p. 4. 2129

Sheerin, John B.
"John F. Kennedy and the New Catholic Image." Catholic world 198, January 1964, p. 203. 2130

Sweezey, Paul M.
"Kennedy: the Man and the President." Monthly review 15, January 1964, p. 511-515. 2131

Wechsler, James A.
"John F. Kennedy: a Retrospect." Progressive 28, January 1964, p. 11-15. 2132

Wendell, F.
"A Man Passed This Way." Torch 48, January 1964, p. 1. 2133

"What was Kennedy's Greatest Accomplishment? Symposium." Americas 16, January 1964, p. 2-3. 2134

Johnson, Lyndon B.
"In Memory of President Kennedy: Address, December 22, 1963." Vital speeches 30, January 1, 1964, p. 162. 2135

"Two Presidents and the Jewish Community." World over 25, January 3, 1964, p. 4. 2136

"Earliest Kennedy Memorial Service: Temple Emanu-El, Weldon, N.C." World over 25, January 17, 1964, p. 5. 2137

Maslog, Crispin
"The Kennedy I Knew." Manila, Weekly graphic (30:

31), January 22, 1964, p. 13. 2138

Colombia. Laws, statutes, etc.
"Decreto no. 2823, 1963 (nov. 22) por el cual el Gobierno de Colombia Rinde Homenaje a la Memoria del Presidente John F. Kennedy." Bogotá, Diario oficial (100: 31,275), January 23, 1964, p. 74-75.
("Decree no. 2823, November 22, 1963, Whereby the Colombian Government Renders Homage to the Memory of President John F. Kennedy.") 2139

"Words of Sorrow: Memorial Praise (in English and Hebrew)." World over 25, January 31, 1964, p. 5. 2140

Booker, Simeon
"How JFK Surpassed Abraham Lincoln." Ebony 19, February 1964, p. 25-28. 2141

"John Fitzgerald Kennedy." Columbia 44, February 1964, p. 4. 2142

"John Fitzgerald Kennedy." Mission digest 22, February 1964, p. 22. 2143

McDowell, J.
"Our JFK: Reflections." Catholic educator 34, February 1964, p. 549-550. 2144

Misiego, M.
"President Kennedy." Overseas 3, February 1964, p. 3. 2145

Payet, G.
"John Fitzgerald Kennedy." Madrid, Razón y fé 169, February 1964, p. 177-192. 2146

Zimmerman, A. H.
"John Fitzgerald Kennedy, 1917-1963." Music educators journal 50, February 1964, p. 33. 2147

Tebbel, J.
"Remembering the President." Saturday review 47, February 8, 1964, p. 50-51. 2148

Leach, R.
"A Fitting Memorial: President Kennedy's Plan to Get Rid of Urban Blight." America 110, February 8, 1964, p. 186-188. 2149

Stewart, C.
"Pulpit Reaction: Study of Sermons on Kennedy's Death: Reply." America 110, February 8, 1964, p. 177. 2150

Jameson, Conrad
"Kennedy: an American Gentleman." Manchester, Manchester guardian, February 20, 1964, p. 12. 2151

Kennedy, Robert F.
"Robert Kennedy's Tribute to JFK." Look 28, February 25, 1964, p. 37-38. 2152

Grosvenor, M. B.
"The Last Full Measure: the World Pays Tribute to President Kennedy." National geographic magazine 125, March 1964, p. 307-355. 2153

Colombia. Laws, statutes, etc.
"Ley 160, 1963 (Dic. 31) por la cual se Honra la

Memoria de John F. Kennedy, Ciudadano Ejemplar de América." Bogotá, Diário oficial (100: 31326), March 24, 1964, p. 873.
("Law 160, December 31, 1963, in Honor of the Memory of John F. Kennedy, Exemplary Citizen of the Americas.") 2154

Johnson, E.A.
"On the Proclamation of President Johnson, November 23, 1963." Social studies 55, April 1964, p. 127-129. 2155

Syer, W.B.
"Notes from our Correspondents: Service in Boston's Holy Cross Cathedral." High fidelity 14, April 1964, p. 17. 2156

White, Theodore M.
"For President Kennedy: an Epilogue" (reprint from Life). Catholic digest 28, April 1964, p. 27-29. 2157

Cogley, J.
"J.F.K.: a Final Word." Commonweal 80, May 8, 1964, p. 190-191. 2158

McElrath, D.
"John Fitzgerald Kennedy: a Witness to Christian Humanism." Interest 2, Summer 1964, p. 33-35. 2159

"One Man can Make the Difference." Ave Maria 99, June 13, 1964, p. 17. 2160

Sorensen, Theodore C.
"The Sound of a Voice that is Still." Sign 43, July 1964, p. 10-12. 2161

Antoninus, Brother
"The Tongs of Jeopardy" (Reprint from Season, Winter 1963). Ramparts 2, September 1964, p. 3-9. 2162

Hebblethwaite, Frank P.
"John Fitzgerald Kennedy, 1917-1963." Inter-American review of bibliography (14: 3), July-September 1964, p. 257-261. 2163

Costa Rica. Laws, statutes, etc.
"No. 3395 (Se Autoriza a las Instituciones Autónomas y Semiautónomas del Estado para que de Acuerdo con sus Posibilidades Contribuyan para la Construcción de un Monumento en Memoria del Presidente John F. Kennedy)." San José, La gaceta (86: 221), September 29, 1964, p. 3567.
("No. 3395, Autonomous and Semi-Autonomous Institutions of the Government are Authorized to Contribute, in Accordance with Their Means, for the Construction of a Monument in Memory of President John F. Kennedy.") 2164

Dodd, Thomas
"Anniversary." Friar 22, November 1964, p. 3-6. 2165

"In Memory of John F. Kennedy." Redbook 124, November 1964, p. 68-81. 2166

Ragan, L.
"Thoughts on the Day Fol-

lowing John F. Kennedy's Funeral." New city 2, November 15, 1964, p. 16. 2167

"Arlington." Look 28, November 17, 1964, p. 81-83. 2168

"Year After the Assassination the U.S. Recalls John F. Kennedy." Newsweek 64, November 30, 1964, p. 26-27. 2169

"Mass for President Kennedy." Jerusalem, Israel digest 7, December 4, 1964, p. 3. 2170

Besson, Waldemar
"Kennedys Erbe." Frankfurt am Main, Der monat (17: 194), 1964-65, p. 16-24. ("Kennedy's Heritage.") 2171

Wild, H.
"J. F. Kennedy." Immensee (Switzerland), Civitas (20: 3), 1964-65, p. 106-113. 2172

1965
Ryan, P.
"Africa Remembers JFK." America 112, February 27, 1965, p. 288. 2173

Skipworth, J. T.
"Many will say the President was not a Cowboy." Esquire 63, March 1965, p. 84-85. 2174

"Ideal man: They Remember JFK: Kennedy Image Among College Students." Newsweek 65, March 22, 1965, p. 47. 2175

Hirshberg, A.
"Jack Kennedy was my Best Friend" (condensed from Saga, 1965). Catholic digest 30, November 1965, p. 138-146. 2176

Fairlie, H.
"He was a man of Only one Season." New York Times magazine, November 21, 1965, p. 28-29. 2177

"JFK: Anniversary." Ave Maria 102, November 27, 1965, p. 16-17. 2178

Brandon, H.
"JFK Remembered." Saturday review 48, December 11, 1965, p. 58-59. 2179

Special Inter-American Conference. 2d, Rio de Janeiro, 1965
"The Common Quest for Freedom and Prosperity in the American Republics (Address by Secretary Rusk; Eulogy to President Kennedy; the Act of Rio de Janeiro, an Economic and Social Act)." Dept. of State bulletin (53: 1382), December 20, 1965, p. 985-1001. 2180

1966
Harriman, W. Averell
"The Legacy of Franklin D. Roosevelt and John F. Kennedy." Dept. of State bulletin (55: 1413), 1966, p. 137-140. 2181

Sclanders, Ian
"The Kennedy Legend." Toronto, Maclean's magazine 79, April 16, 1966, p. 10-13, 44. 2182

Kateb, G.
"Kennedy as Statesman."
Commentary 41, June 1966,
p. 54-60.   2183

1967

Sorensen, Theodore C.
"May 29, 1967 Would Have
Been John Kennedy's Fiftieth
Birthday." McCall's 94, June
1967, p. 58-59.   2184

Johnson, Lyndon B.
"U.S.S. John F. Kennedy:
Remarks, May 27, 1967."
Dept. of State bulletin 56,
June 26, 1967, p. 959-960.
                                 2185
Logan, Andy
"JFK: the Stained-glass Image." American heritage 18,
August 1967, p. 4-7.   2186

Greeley, A.
"John Fitzgerald Kennedy,
Doctor of the Church." Critic
26, October-November 1967,
p. 40-44.   2187

Memorials

Books

1959

U.S. John F. Kennedy Center
  for the Performing Arts
  (Smithsonian Institution)
  The National Cultural Center,
  chartered by the 85th Congress, 1958. Washington, 1959?
  16p.   2188

1963

U.S. Congress. Senate. Committee on Public Works
  Providing for renaming the
  National Cultural Center as
  the John F. Kennedy Center
  for the Performing Arts, and
  authorizing an appropriation
  therefor. Report to accompany S.J. Res. 136. Washington, G.P.O., 1963, 14p.
                                 2189

1964

Bunte Illustrierte. Munchner/
  Frankfurter
  John F. Kennedy: ein
  Gedenkband. Sonderdruck der
  Bunten Illustrierten. Offenburg, Burda Druck und Verlag, 1964, 206p.
  (John F. Kennedy, a memorial volume.)   2190

Macfadden-Bartell Corp.
  (firm)
  A John F. Kennedy memorial, by the editors, Macfadden-Bartell Corporation.
  New York, 1964, 157p. 2191

Paris. Conseil Municipal
  Inauguration officielle de
  l'Avenue du Président Kennedy...16 mars 1964. Paris,
  Imp. Municipale, 1964, 27p.
  (Official inauguration of
  Avenue President Kennedy...
  March 16, 1964.)   2192

Studer, Hans K., ed.
  John F. Kennedy, der
  grosse Mensch und Staatsmann; ein Gedenkbuch. Kilchberg/Zürich, Internationale
  Bildreportage, 1964, 205p.
  (John F. Kennedy, the
  great man and statesman; a
  memorial volume.)   2193

U.S. Bureau of the Budget
  Proposed supplemental ap-

propriations involving increases for the John F. Kennedy Center for the Performing Arts and the National Capital Planning Commission. Communication from the President of the United States transmitting proposed supplemental appropriations for the fiscal year 1964 involving increases in the amount of $15,500,000 for the John F. Kennedy Center for the Performing Arts; and $3,300,000 for the National Capital Planning Commission. Washington, G.P.O., 1964, 3p. 2194

U.S. 88th Congress. House of Representatives. Public Works Committee
John F. Kennedy Center for Performing Arts, hearings before joint session of Committee on Public Works, House, and Committee on Public Works, Senate, 88th Congress, 1st session, on H.J. Res. 828, S.J. Res. 136, and H.J. Res. 871, December 12 and 16, 1963. (Item 1024, Y4.P 96/11:88). Washington, 1964, 114p. 2195

U.S. 88th Congress. House of Representatives. Report on Public Bill 1050
John F. Kennedy Center act. Report from Committee on Public Works to accompany H.J. Res. 871. December 17, 1963. Washington, House Document Room, 1964, 13p. 2196

U.S. 88th Congress. House of Representatives. Report on Public Bill 1050 (part 2)
John F. Kennedy Center act. Minority views from Committee on Public Works to accompany H.J. Res. 871. January 8, 1964. Washington, House Document Room, 1964, 5p. 2197

U.S. 88th Congress. Second session. Public Works Committee
Compilation of existing laws relating to John F. Kennedy Center for Performing Arts; March 25, 1964; Committee print 18. Washington, 1964, 5p. 2198

U.S. 88th Congress. Senate
Memorial addresses in Congress of United States and tributes in eulogy of John Fitzgerald Kennedy, late President of United States. Washington, for sale by Superintendent of Documents, 1964, 7 plus 911p. (Document 59). 2199

U.S. Laws, statutes, etc.
Compilation of existing laws relating to the John F. Kennedy Center for the Performing Arts. March 25, 1964. Washington, G.P.O., 1964, 5p. 2200

U.S. Post Office Department
Address by John A. Gronouski, Postmaster General, at dedication of John Fitzgerald Kennedy memorial stamp, Boston, Mass., May 29, 1964 (General release 112; Information Service). P 1.27: G89/14. Washington, 1964, 6p. 2201

U.S. Post Office Department
Address by John A. Gronouski, Postmaster General, at fund raising dinner for John Fitzgerald Kennedy Library, Webster, Mass., May 18, 1964. (Information Service, General release 101). Washington, 1964, 7p.   2202

1966

Garduno, Joseph A.
Museum for a president, John F. Kennedy. New York, Carlton, 1966, 55p.   2203

U.S. House of Representatives. Government Operations Committee
John Fitzgerald Kennedy Library, hearing before subcommittee, 89th Congress, 2d session, on H.J. Res. 1207, July 26, 1966. Washington, G.P.O., 1966, 60p.   2204

U.S. John F. Kennedy Center for the Performing Arts (Smithsonian Institution)
Footlight. Washington, 1966- (monthly)   2205

U.S. 89th Congress (Public Laws)
H.J. Res. 1207, joint resolution to authorize Administrator of General Services to accept title to John Fitzgerald Kennedy Library, and for other purposes. Approved August 27, 1966. Washington, Superintendent of Documents, 1966, 1p.   2206

U.S. 89th Congress. Senate
Report 1456: authorizing Administrator of General Services to accept title to John Fitzgerald Kennedy Library, and for other purposes. Report from Committee on Government Operations to accompany H.J. Res. 1207. August 11, 1966. Washington, U.S. Senate Document Room, 1966, 21p.   2207

1967

U.S. Senate. Committee on Interior & Insular Affairs. Subcommittee on Arts & Recreation
John Fitzgerald Kennedy historic site: hearing, March 20, 1967, on S. 1161, a bill to establish the John Fitzgerald Kennedy national historic site in the Commonwealth of Massachusetts. Washington, 1967, 9p.
(90th Congress. 1st session).   2208

Articles

1963

"Remembering Kennedy: Memorials in Israel." London, Jewish observer 12, December 6, 1963, p. 17-18.   2209

Sacher, M.M.
"Kennedy Memorial (Letter)." London, Jewish observer 12, December 6, 1963, p. 23.   2210

"As Honors Grow for John F. Kennedy." U.S. news & world report 55, December 9, 1963, p. 4.   2211

"'Victory' School to be Named After Kennedy."

Catholic messenger 82, December 12, 1963, p. 1. 2212

"Land of Kennedy: Renaming of Plazas, Bridges, Parks, etc." Time 82, December 13, 1963, p. 27. 2213

"Cape Canaveral Renamed for the Late President." Science newsletter 84, December 14, 1963, p. 375. 2214

"Memorial Fever." London, The economist 209, December 14, 1963, p. 1167. 2215

"Peace Corps Placing Kennedy Libraries Abroad." Publishers weekly 184, December 16, 1963, p. 22. 2216

"Kennedy Park Inaugurated at Miraflores." Lima, Peruvian times (23: 1201), December 27, 1963, p. 9. 2217

"Kennedy University." London, The economist 209, December 28, 1963, p. 1325. 2218

"Memorial Boom." Newsweek 62, December 30, 1963, p. 49-50. 2219

1964

"Image Distilled from 800 Pictures: Bronze Head by R. Berks." Life 56, January 3, 1964, p. 28-31. 2220

"Kennedy Libraries Drive Collects Over 4000 Books." Publishers weekly 185, January 6, 1964, p. 57. 2221

Rudin, E.
"Kennedy Library at Harvard University." Library journal 89, January 15, 1964, p. 300. 2222

McGrory, Mary
"The Kennedy Memorial Library, Harvard." America 110, March 14, 1964, p. 333. 2223

Hansen, B. K.
"Kennedy Center for the Performing Arts." Quarterly journal of speech 50, April 1964, p. 212-213. 2224

"Visitors to the Kennedy Grave, an Endless Line." U.S. news & world report 56, May 25, 1964, p. 79-81. 2225

De Kooning, E.
"Painting a Portrait of the President." Art news 63, Summer 1964, p. 37. 2226

McMullen, E. W.
"Cape Canaveral and Chicago." Names 12, June 1964, p. 128-129. 2227

Cameron, E.
"John F. Kennedy Library Exhibit: First Display of Tour." Wilson library bulletin 39, September 1964, p. 63-65. 2228

Davis, T.
"Discourtesy and Destruction by Grave Visitors." America 111, September 19, 1964, p. 270. 2229

"To John F. Kennedy: Homage by Artists." Art in America 52, October 1964, p. 90-95. 2230

"John Fitzgerald Kennedy, a Reader's Memorial: Symposium." Ebony 20, November 1964, p. 180-188. 2231

"New JFK Memorial Playground." Ebony 20, November 1964, p. 190-194. 2232

Haworth, David
"Oral History and Political Hygiene." Manchester, Manchester guardian, November 13, 1964, p. 12.
(Concerning Kennedy Institute of Politics, Harvard University.) 2233

"Simplicity of Mr. Kennedy's Grave." London, The times, November 17, 1964, p. 9. 2234

"Tomb for JFK." Time 84, November 20, 1964, p. 96. 2235

Breslin, J.
"Still they come to the Hillside: Arlington National Cemetery." Saturday evening post 237, November 21, 1964, p. 22-23. 2236

"Runnymede Memorial to President Kennedy." London, The times, November 23, 1964, p. 10. 2237

"John F. Kennedy Grave a Discreet, Respectful Design by J.C. Warnecke." Progressive architecture 45, December 1964, p. 185-187. 2238

"The J.F.K. Grave." America 111, December 5, 1964, p. 732. 2239

1965
"Kennedy-Biographien: Wettstreit zu Dritt." Hamburg, Der spiegel (19: 41), 1965, p. 145-148.
("Kennedy's Biographies: Contest in 3's.") 2240

"Kennedy Memorial Hall, Dublin, Ireland." Stuttgart, Architektur und wohnform, innendekoration (73: 5), 1965, p. 250-257. 2241

"Kennedy Grave Design is Disclosed." Architectural record 137, January 1965, p. 12-13. 2242

Vinterhalter, Vilko
"Govor na Otvaranju Izlozbe Posvecene Dzonu F. Kenediju." Belgrade, Borba 30, February 14, 1965, p. 43.
("Speech on the Occasion of the Opening of the Exposition in Honor of John F. Kennedy.") 2243

"What's Being Done About FDR and JFK Memorials." U.S. news & world report 58, April 12, 1965, p. 11. 2244

"Memorial Questions." London, The economist 215, May 15, 1965, p. 766. 2245

"England Builds a Monument to JFK: Tribute at Runnymede." Life 58, May 28, 1965, p. 75-78. 2246

Rusk, Dean
"Memorial to President Kennedy at Runnymede." Dept. of State bulletin 52, June 7, 1965, p. 897-898. 2247

Heckscher, P.H.
"Kennedy Center: Harvard Report." The Harvard review 3, Fall 1965, p. 89-96. 2248

Jellicoe, G.A.
"Landscape Memorial at Runnymede to the Late President Kennedy." London, The architectural review 138, October 1965, p. 286-287. 2249

"Empty Room: Kennedy Memorial, Dallas." Time 86, December 24, 1965, p. 38. 2250

1966
"A National Cultural Centre for the U.S." London, Illustrated London news 248, April 16, 1966, p. 17. 2251

"Kennedy Memorial Built near Jerusalem." Jerusalem, Israel digest 9, June 17, 1966, p. 3. 2252

1967
"At Consecration of Kennedy Gravesite." U.S. news & world report 62, March 27, 1967, p. 12. 2253

"Harvard's Kennedy Complex." London, The economist 224, August 5, 1967, p. 496-497. 2254

Tuohy, William
"'Kennedy Street' Dedicated by ex-First Lady." Los Angeles Times, November 7, 1967, part I, p. 18. 2255

"President John F. Kennedy's Grave." Architectural record 142, December 1967, p. 128-130. 2256

1968
Ace, Goodman
"Happy Birthday to Whomever: New York State Assembly Approves Bill Requiring Public Schools to Hold Memorial Services on the Birthday of JFK." Saturday review 51, March 2, 1968, p. 9. 2257

Memorabilia

Books

1964
Minkus Publications, Inc. (firm)
John F. Kennedy world wide memorial stamp album. New York, 1964- 2258

U.S. 88th Congress
Public law 256. H.R. 9413, act to provide for coinage of 50 cent pieces bearing likeness of John Fitzgerald Kennedy. Approved December 30, 1963. Washington, 1964, 1p. 2259

1965
Hamilton, Charles
The robot that helped to make a president; a reconnaissance into the mysteries of John F. Kennedy's signature. New York, Charles Hamilton Autographs, Inc.,

1965, 63p. 2260

1966

Mayhew, Aubrey
 The world's tribute to John F. Kennedy in medallic art; medals, coins and tokens; an illustrated standard reference. New York, Morrow, 1966, 197p. 2261

Rochette, Edward C.
 The medallic portraits of John F. Kennedy; a study of Kennediana, with historical and critical notes and a descriptive catalogue of the coins, medals, tokens and store cards struck in his name. Iola, Wisconsin, Krause Pub., 1966, 188p. 2262

Articles

1961

"Signatures of Mr. Kennedy." Reader's digest 79, October 1961, p. 186. 2263

1964

"By Loewy: JFK Stamp." Printer's ink 287, May 8, 1964, p. 18. 2264

Kennedy, Jacqueline (Bouvier)
 "These are the Things I Hope Will Show how he Really was: Exhibit of Mementos." Life 56, May 29, 1964, p. 32-34A. 2265

Montgomery, H. & M. Montgomery
 "The Kennedy Half Dollar." Catholic digest 28, July 1964, p. 79-81. 2266

Gannon, T.
 "The Kennedy Memorabilia: Traveling Exhibit." America 111, September 19, 1964, p. 304-306. 2267

Chamberlin, A.
 "Commercialization of JFK Tawdry Souvenirs." Saturday evening post 237, November 21, 1964, p. 20-21. 2268

1967

"John Kennedy Plane Makes Final Flight." Los Angeles Times, November 18, 1967 (part I), p. 9.
(Concerning The Caroline, President Kennedy's Private Airplane.) 2269

Poetry Written in Honor of President John F. Kennedy

Books

1961

Frost, Robert
 Dedication (and) The gift outright. The inaugural address of John Fitzgerald Kennedy, Washington, D.C., January the twentieth, 1961. New York, Holt, Rinehart & Winston, 1961, 19p. 2270

1963

Kazan, Molly (Thacher)
 Kennedy. New York, Stein & Day, 1963, 19p. 2271

Levy, Clifford V., comp.
 Twenty-four personal eulogies on the late President John F. Kennedy, 1917-1963.

San Francisco, 1963, 18p. 2272

Marten, Paul
Kennedy requiem. Toronto, Weller Pub., 1963, 36p. 2273

1964

Armour, Richard
Our presidents. New York, Norton, 1964, p. 78. 2274

Berry, Wendell
November twenty-six, nineteen hundred sixty-three; poem. 1st ed. New York, Braziller, 1964, 31p. 2275

Commemorative anthology. Los Angeles? 1964, 128p. 2276

Geer, Candy
Six white horses; an illustrated poem about John-John. Ann Arbor, M & W Quill Publishing Co., 1964, unpaged. 2277

Glikes, Erwin A. & Paul Schwaber, eds.
Of poetry and power; poems occasioned by the Presidency and by the death of John F. Kennedy. New York, Basic Books, Inc., 1964, 155p. 2278

Gomes, Abeylard Pereira
Elegia para John Fitzgerald Kennedy, cidadão do mundo. 2d ed. rev. & enl. Rio de Janeiro, Livraria São José, 1964, 120p.
(Elegy for John Fitzgerald Kennedy, citizen of the world.) 2279

Johnson, Percy E.
Sean Pendragon requiem. Poetrical texture by Percy Edward Johnston. Artistical texture by William A. White. 1st ed. New York, Dasein-Jupiter Hammon, 1964, 27p. 2280

McCarrell, Stuart
The assassinations 1963 (In Lowenfels, Walter, ed. Poets of today: a new American anthology. New York, International Publishers, 1964, p. 88-89). 2281

Moscoso Dávila, Isabel
A Jacqueline. Cuenca, Casa de la Cultura Ecuatoriana, Núcleo del Azuay, 1964, 13p.
(To Jacqueline.) 2282

Vilnis, Aija
Bearer of the star-spangled banner. In memory of President John Fitzgerald Kennedy. Tr. by Lilija Pavars. New York, Robert Speller & Sons, 1964, 31p. 2283

Waas, Johannes B.
Requiem für John Fitzgerald Kennedy. Bad Oeynhausen, Germany, Verlag zum Turm der Alten Mutter, 1964, 23p.
(Requiem for John Fitzgerald Kennedy.) 2284

1965

Lasić, Bozo
Kennedy, smrt u Dalasu; pjema. Mostar, Jugoslavia, 1965, 23p.
(Kennedy: death in Dallas; poem.) 2285

1967

Keinz, Virginia P.
Poems in memory of President John F. Kennedy. [n.p.]

1967, 32p. 2286

Articles

1963

Peguy, C.
"In Memoriam: J.F.K."
(poem). Catholic messenger
82, November 28, 1963, p. 1.
2287

Squirru, Rafael
"Death has Taken Away a
Friend." Americas (15: 12),
December 1963, p. 1. 2288

Carter, M.A.
"November 22, 1963: World
Stage: Monometal: Assassin:
Clay Figure." Christian century 80, December 11, 1963,
p. 1540. 2289

Berry, Wendell
"November 26, 1963." The
nation 197, December 21,
1963, p. 437. 2290

1964

Squirru, Rafael
"A Deeper Reality." Americas 16, January 1964, p. 1.
2291

Mina, B.
"And he Shall be Like a
Tree" (poem). Sacred Heart
messenger 99, February 1964,
p. 5. 2292

Coppinger, E.
"Lines on the Passing of
the President" (poem). American Catholic Historical Society
records 75, March 1964, p.
3-5. 2293

Coxe, L.
"Friday, November 22,
1963." Poetry 104, April
1964, p. 30. 2294

Byrd, C.W.
"How Silent the Forest."
American forests 70, April
1964, p. 6. 2295

Jones, B.
"Special Delivery from
Heaven" (poem). Sign 43,
May 1964, p. 20. 2296

Rockwell, Norman
"New Kennedy Painting."
Look 28, July 14, 1964, p.
60-61. 2297

"392 Verses on Death of
JFK Wins a Sicilian top
Balladeer Honors in Italy."
Variety 235, August 5,
1964, p. 2. 2298

Griffiths, B.
"An Elegy for John F.
Kennedy" (poem). London,
(New) Blackfriars 45, September 1964, p. 387. 2299

Phelps, E.
"To John F. Kennedy."
Seventeen 23, September
1964, p. 43. 2300

Menard, E.
"He Sleeps: in Memory of
President John F. Kennedy,
November 22, 1963." Negro
history bulletin 28, November 1964, p. 48. 2301

"In Memoriam: Seven Poems."
Redbook 124, November
1964, p. 79-80. 2302

McKee, W.
"November 22, 1963" (poem). Liguorian 52, November 1964, p. 34-35. 2303

Chiarella, M.
"Thoughts of a Lovely Lady" (poem). Sacred Heart messenger 99, November 1964, p. 24. 2304

Stanislaus, Sister
"When he Shall die: 13 Poems." Sign 44, November 1964, p. 16. 2305

Therese, Sister
"Where the Dogwood Weeps" (Poem). America 111, November 21, 1964, p. 663. 2306

1965
Holland, J.
"Let it be Said." Columbia 45, November 1965, p. 22. 2307

Fiction

1964
Fiore, Ilario
Il kennediano, romanzo. Milan, Lerici Editori, 1964, 315p.
(The Kennediad, novel.) 2308

1966
Cabral, Nelson Lustoza
Uma cruz para Kennedy; novela. Rio de Janeiro, Editora Leitura, 1966, 71p.
(A cross for Kennedy; novel.) 2309

Bibliography

Books

1964
Jenkins Company (firm)
John F. Kennedy; a catalogue of books, articles, autographs, memorabilia. Austin, Texas, 1964? unpaged. 2310

U.S. Library of Congress. General Reference and Bibliography Division. Bibliography and Reference Correspondence Section
John Fitzgerald Kennedy, 1917-1963; a chronological list of references. Washington, for sale by Superintendent of Documents, G.P.O., 1964, 68p. 2311

Articles

1964
Gropp, Arthur E.
"Books: a Kennedy Bibliography." Americas (16: 1), January 1964, p. 40-41. 2312

1967
Dollen, Charles
"The J.F.K. Books: Bibliography." Catholic library world 38, April 1967, p. 520-522. 2313

John Fitzgerald Kennedy

Manuscript Materials
on the Career of
President John F. Kennedy

(Note: either the number of items of research materials is mentioned, e.g. "500 items," or in some instances the amount of shelf space is noted, e.g., "48 ft.," housing the materials.)

1961

Edelman, John W., 1893-
  Papers, 1926-63. 48ft.
In Wayne State University, Labor History Archives, Detroit.

Labor union official, journalist, and national legislative representative for the Textile Workers Union of America. Correspondence, clippings, and documents relating to Edelman's work as a legislative representative, to housing reform, civil liberties, and other public service activities. Correspondents include...John F. Kennedy...

Unpublished finding aid in the repository.

Information on literary rights available in the repository. Gift of Mr. Edelman, 1961-64. **2314**

Palmer, Paul, 1900-
  Correspondence, 1929-60
(ca. 500 items)
  In Yale University Library.
Journalist and editor. Palmer's professional correspondence with such prominent figures as...John F. Kennedy... Material is related to the library's Walter Lippman and Charles A. Lindbergh collections.
Catalogued individually in the library.
Information on literary rights available in the library.
Gift of Mr. Palmer, 1961. **2315**

Schary, Dore, 1905-
  Papers, 1950-61. 3 ft.
In State Historical Society of Wisconsin collections.
Playwright and producer. Correspondence and other papers. Chiefly mss. outlines and scripts for plays and screenplays including The devil's advocate (1961), For special occasions (1962), and Sunrise at Campobello (1957). Includes scripts and production photos for 7 plays, together with screenplays and stills of 12 productions. Correspondents include...
John F. Kennedy...
Unpublished inventory in the repository. Information on literary rights available in the library.
Gift of Mr. Schary, 1961. **2316**

1962

Mitchell, Hugh Burnton, 1907-
  Papers, 1945-52. 49 ft.
In University of Washington Library (Seattle).
Business executive, U.S. Senator and Representative from Washington. Chiefly correspondence relating to electric power in the Pacific Northwest and industrial relations in Alaska and Washington and to politics. Includes extensive correspond-

ence with federal and state government units and labor organizations. Correspondents include...John Fitzgerald Kennedy...
Unpublished inventory and guide in the library. Information on literary rights available in the library. Permission to use the collection must be obtained from Mr. Mitchell. Gift of Mr. Mitchell, 1962.   2317

Spence, Brent, 1874-
Papers, 1937-62. 60 ft. (ca. 37,500 items)
In University of Kentucky Library.
U.S. Representative from Kentucky, Democrat. Correspondence from constituents; files on service academy appointments, service cases, and Veterans Administration records; material on general legislation; and correspondence, hearings, reports and public laws concerning legislation on price control, housing, banking, monetary affairs, and other business of the Committee on Banking and Currency of which Spencer was chairman almost continuously from 1943-62. Correspondents include...John F. Kennedy...
Unpublished inventory, list & index in the library. Correspondence service files, Veterans Administration files and railroad retirement cases (1959-62) restricted. Gift of Mr. Spencer, 1962-63.   2318

Wilson, Edith (Bolling) Galt, 1872-1961
Papers, 1833-1961. 27 ft. (ca. 19,000 items)
Wife of Woodrow Wilson, President of the United States (1856-1924). Family and general correspondence, diary notes, drafts and correspondence concerning Mrs. Wilson's ("My Memoir," 1938), financial and legal papers, genealogical materials, memorabilia, and printed matter. Most of the correspondence is of a social nature from leaders in American political and social life. Correspondents include...Jacqueline Kennedy, John F. Kennedy...
Unpublished finding aid in the Library. Information on literary rights available in the Library. Gifts of Mrs. Wilson, 1957-60, and the Woodrow Wilson House, Washington, D.C., 1962-65. 2319

1963

Alexander, Holmes Moss, 1906-
Papers, 1929-63. 2 boxes.
In West Virginia University Library.
Author and gentleman farmer. Correspondence, literary mss., and photos primarily concerned with Alexander's literary and publishing activities. Other subjects include his interest in livestock raising, a proposed birth control law and moving picture censureship in Maryland. Correspondents include...John F. Kennedy...
Gift of Mr. Alexander,

Flanders, Ralph Edward,
1880-
Papers, 1923-58. ca. 70 ft.
and 12 reels of microfilm
(negative).
In Syracuse University Library.
Microfilm copies (negative) of original Flanders' papers (1951-57) consisting chiefly of correspondence relating to Senator Joseph R. McCarthy, in the State Historical Society of Wisconsin.
Business executive, author, inventor, mechanical engineer, and U.S. Senator from Vermont. Correspondence (ca. 50,000 items), records relating to engineering resources (1903-32) and patent materials (1920-38), Vermont broadcasts (1949-58), voting record notebooks (1947-58), and a personal record file containing articles, speeches, literary mss., scrapbooks, photos, clippings, genealogical materials and other papers relating to Flanders' career. Includes general and business correspondence, letters relating to screw threads and gear cutting standardization, to the Vermont Planning Board, and to Flanders' term as U.S. Senator (1946-58). Correspondents include...John F. Kennedy... Register published by the library in 1964.
Information on literary rights available in the library.
Gift of Senator Flanders, 1963. 2321

Carroll, Gladys (Hasty),
1904-
Papers, 1915-64. 9 ft.
In Boston University Library.
Author and trustee of Bates College, Lewiston, Maine. Personal and professional correspondence; 152 Mss. of Mrs. Carroll's short stories and articles, including 15 of her novels and some juvenilia; clippings and other publicity material consisting of 8 scrapbooks and one carton on all of her works, including the motion picture and folk play versions of As the earth turns (1933). Includes a file of correspondence (1934-64) relating to Bates College; and letters from... President John F. Kennedy... Inventory, partially catalogued, available in the library. Information on literary rights available in the library. Deposited by Mrs. Carroll, 1964. 2322

Knebel, Fletcher, 1911-
Papers, 1960-63 (ca. 1100 items)
In Boston University Library.
Author and journalist. Correspondence with publishers and with prominent political figures; and typescripts of Knebel's works. Includes a 4-page letter from Jacqueline Kennedy detailing the interests of her husband, John F. Kennedy. Correspondents include...John F. Kennedy...
Inventory, with annotations

by Knebel, in the library. Information on literary rights available in the library. Gift of Mr. Knebel, 1964. Additions to the collection are anticipated. 2323

1965
Waldron, James R.
<u>8818</u>. New York, Pageant Press, 1965, 54p.
(A large part of the book consists of the correspondence which took place between the author and Senator John F. Kennedy.) 2324

Biographies of John F. Kennedy

Youth

Books

1962
Bissell, Richard P.
<u>You can always tell a Harvard man</u>. New York, McGraw-Hill, 1962, 282p. 2325

1967
Damore, Leo
<u>The Cape Cod years of John F. Kennedy</u>. Englewood Cliffs, Prentice-Hall, 1967, 262p. 2326

Articles

1961
Walker, G. & D.A. Allan
"Jack Kennedy at Harvard." <u>Coronet</u> 50, May 1961, p. 82-95. 2327

1964
"Maryglade College, Memphis, Michigan, Houses Altar Piece for Which President Kennedy Posed as Model for an Angel." <u>Marian era</u> 5, 1964, p. 83. 2328

1966
Muheim, E.
"When JFK was Rich, Young and Happy." <u>Esquire</u> 66, August 1966, p. 65-66. 2329

Service During World War II

Books

1961
Donovan, Robert J.
<u>PT 109; John F. Kennedy in World War II</u>. New York, McGraw-Hill, 1961, 247p. 2330

1962
Donovan, Robert J.
<u>The wartime adventures of President John F. Kennedy</u>. London, Anthony Gibbs & Phillips, Ltd., 1962, 160p. 2331

Tregaskis, Richard W.
<u>John F. Kennedy: war hero</u>. New York, Dell Pub. Co., 1962, 223p. 2332

Whipple, Chandler
<u>Lt. John F. Kennedy--expendable!</u> New York, Universal Pub. & Distributing Corp., 1962, 160p. 2333

1964
Duino, Michel
<u>Le lieutenant Kennedy</u>.

Verviers, Belgium, Gérard,
1964, 160p.
(Lieutenant Kennedy.) 2334

1965
Shepard, Tazewell T.
John F. Kennedy, man of the sea. New York, Morrow, 1965, 161p. 2335

1966
Fay, Paul B.
The pleasure of his company. New York, Harper & Row, 1966, 262p. 2336

Articles

1944
Hersey, John
"Survival: Lieutenant John F. Kennedy, a PT Skipper in the Solomons." Reader's digest 45, August 1944, p. 75-80. 2337

Adult Life and Career

Books

1960
Burns, James MacG.
John Kennedy, a political profile. New York, Harcourt, Brace & World, Inc., 1960, 309p. 2338

Joesten, Joachim
Präsident Kennedy. Stuttgart, Deutsche Verlags Anstalt, 1960, 233p.
(President Kennedy.) 2339

Lasky, Victor
John F. Kennedy: what's behind the image? Washington, Free World Press, 1960, 300p. 2340

Narbona González, Francisco
Kennedy. Madrid, S.A.E. Gráficas Espejo, 1960, 63p. 2341

Vigil, Manuel
El valeroso Kennedy. Barcelona, Eds. Civitas, 1960, 133p.
(The brave Kennedy.) 2342

1961
Ben-Gurion, David
David und Goliath in unserer Zeit. Foreword: "Kennedy über Israel." Postscript: by Robert St. John. Munich, Ner-Tamid Verlag, 1961, 280p.
(David and Goliath in our time.) 2343

Gandolfo, Giampaolo
John F. Kennedy. 1st ed. Rome, Opere Nuove, 1961, 151p. 2344

Haskin Service
The Presidents and their wives, from Washington to Kennedy. Washington, 1961, 66p. 2345

Lowe, Jacques
Portrait; the emergence of John F. Kennedy. New York, McGraw-Hill, 1961, 223p. 2346

Markmann, Charles L. & Mark Sherwin
John F. Kennedy; a sense of purpose. New York, St.

Martin's Press, 1961, 346p. 2347

Persson, Per
  Kennedy. Stockholm, Raben & Sjögren, 1961, 32p. 2348

Sanghvi, Ramesh
  John F. Kennedy; a political biography. Bombay, Perennial Press, 1961, 200p. 2349

Sigless, Thomas
  Kennedy und seine Mannschaft. Karlsruhe, Condor-Verlag, 1961, 64p.
  (Kennedy and his manliness.) 2350

1962

Manchester, William R.
  Portrait of a president: John F. Kennedy in profile. Boston, Little, Brown & Co., 1962, 238p. 2351

1963

Narbona González, Francisco
  Kennedy, el Lincoln del siglo XX. Madrid, S.A.E. Gráficas Espejo, 1963, 91p.
  (Kennedy: twentieth-century Lincoln.) 2352

Lasky, Victor
  John F. Kennedy: the man and the myth. New York, Macmillan, 1963, p. 599-636. 2353

Schwarz, Urs
  John F. Kennedy, 1917-1963. Lausanne, Eds. Rencontre, 1963, 212p. 2354

Siegler, Heinrich
  Kennedy oder de Gaulle? Bonn, Siegler, 1963, 161p.
  (Kennedy or de Gaulle?) 2355

Spaan, J.B.T.
  John Fitzgerald Kennedy. President van moed en karakter. Amsterdam, Stichting Ivio, 1963, 16p.
  (John Fitzgerald Kennedy: courageous President.) 2356

U.S. Information Agency
  The President of the United States of America. Washington, U.S. Information Service, 1963? unpaged. 2357

United Press International & Chase Studios, Ltd.
  John F. Kennedy, from childhood to martyrdom. Washington, Tatler Pub., 1963, 102p. 2358

1964

Akmentinš, Osvalds
  Džons F. Kenedijs un latvieši. John F. Kennedy and the Latvian people. Boston (Dorchester), Vaidava, 1964, 133p. 2359

Bradlee, Benjamin
  That special grace. Philadelphia, Lippincott, 1964, 27p. 2360

Chacón, Jorge
  John F. Kennedy. Quito, "La Prensa Católica," 1964, 34p. (In Spanish) 2361

Cordaro, Philip
  Kennedy (Translated into Spanish by Domingo Pruna). Barcelona, Plaza & Janés, 1964, 286p. 2362

Dikshita, Syama Bihari Lala
  Amerika ke pentisuveṃ

rāshtrapaṭi Jauna Phiṭsajeralḍa Kaineḍī. Delhi, Dharambhumi Prakashan, 1964, 240p.
(John F. Kennedy, 35th President of the United States.) 2363

Meister, Knud
Klokken 12:31, John F. Kennedys saga. Copenhagen, Erichsen, 1964, 164p.
(12:31 o'clock, John F. Kennedy's saga.) 2364

Naki (pseud.)
Maṉitarul mannikam Keṉṉati. Madras, Vāṉati Patippakam, 1964, 111p.
(Kennedy, a man among men.) 2365

Pereira, Arthur P.
President Kennedy, the man who defied defeat. Bombay, Macmillan, 1964, 96p. 2366

Shannon, William V.
President John F. Kennedy (In his The American Irish. New York, Macmillan, 1964, p. 392-413). 2367

Shikhare, Damodar Narhar
Dhīrodātta Keneḍī. Bombay, Jagannath Prakashan, 1964, 6 plus 104p.
(Brave, generous Kennedy.) 2368

Steiner, Paul
175 little-known facts about JFK. New York, Citadel Press, 1964, 48p. 2369

Steinmetz, Eigil & Sune Kempe, eds.
John F. Kennedy, Människan och statsmannen. Stockholm, Seelig, 1964, 205p.

(John F. Kennedy, man and statesman.) 2370

Sukla, Narasimha Rama
Amarīkī rāshṭrapati Keneḍī. 2d ed. Allahabad, 1964, 128p.
(Kennedy, President of the United States.) 2371

The thousand days, John Fitzgerald Kennedy as President. New York, Citadel Press, 1964, 124p. 2372

Walsh, William G., ed.
Children write about John F. Kennedy. Brownsville, Texas, Springman-King Pub. Co., 1964, 178p. 2373

Warren, Sidney
John Fitzgerald Kennedy; unfinished achievement (In his The president as world leader. Philadelphia, Lippincott, 1964, p. 417-429). 2374

Wicker, Tom
Kennedy without tears; the man beneath the myth. New York, Morrow, 1964, 61p. 2375

1965

Chase, Harold W. & Allen H. Lerman, eds.
Kennedy and the press. New York, Thomas Y. Crowell, 1965, 555p.
(Kennedy press conferences). 2376

Dollen, Charles
John F. Kennedy, American. Jamaica Plain, Mass., Daughters of St. Paul, 1965, 244p. 2377

Lincoln, Evelyn
My twelve years with John F. Kennedy. New York, McKay, 1965, 371p. 2378

Sidey, Hugh
John F. Kennedy; portrait of a president. Baltimore, Penguin Books, 1965, 421p. 2379

Sorensen, Theodore C.
Kennedy. New York, Harper & Row, 1965, 783p. 2380

Volek, Jindrich
Meze odvahy; politicky profil J.F. Kennedyho. 1st edition. Prague, Nakl. Politicke Literatury, 1965, 182p.
(The limits of courage; a political profile of John F. Kennedy.) 2381

1966
Cárcano, Miguel A.
Churchill, Kennedy. Buenos Aires, Eds. Pampa y Cielo, 1966, 69p. (In Spanish) 2382

Kittler, Glenn
The young knight (In his The wings of eagles; portraits of six great Catholics of the twentieth century. Garden City, Doubleday, 1966, p. 45-84). 2383

Salinger, Pierre E.G.
With Kennedy. New York, Doubleday, 1966, 391p. 2384

Weil, Ursula & Otto Weil
John F. Kennedy. Der 35. Präsident d. USA. Berlin, Buchverlag der Morgen, 1966, 255p.

(John F. Kennedy, 35th President of the United States.) 2385

Werther, Maurice
John Fitzgerald Kennedy. Paris, Seghers, 1966, 192p. 2386

1967
Jaszuński, Grzegorz
Życie i śmerć Johna Kennedy' ego. Warsaw, Iskry, 1967, 287p.
(The life and death of John Kennedy.) 2387

1968
Frank, Elke
John F. Kennedy. Berlin, Colloquium Verlag, 1968, 94p.
(In German) 2388

Lincoln, Evelyn
Kennedy and Johnson. New York, Holt, Rinehart & Winston, 1968, 201p. 2389

Humor

Books

1964
Harris, Leon A.
John F. Kennedy (In his The fine art of political wit. New York, Dutton, 1964, p. 255-276). 2390

Articles

1961
Evans, Rowland
"That wit in the White House." Saturday evening post 234, September 2, 1961,

1962

"Did you Hear they Changed the New Frontier to One Man's Family?" Newsweek 60, July 16, 1962, p. 16-17.   2392

"I Come from a Small town in Massachusetts." Life 53, September 28, 1962, p. 129-131.   2393

"Suck in that gut, America." Esquire 58, November 1962, p. 82-85.   2394

Bunzel, Peter
"Kennedy Spoof Full of Vigah: The First Family." Life 53, December 1962, p. 83-84.   2395

"Good Night, Jackie; Good Night, Bobby: First Family Phonograph Record." Newsweek 60, December 3, 1962, p. 29.   2396

1963

"Report to the Bourgeoisie." Esquire 59, January 1963, p. 41-47.   2397

Intellectual Life

Books

1961

John Fitzgerald Kennedy...su filosofía...sus ideas en sus discursos y escritos. Madrid, Casa Americana, 1961? 44p.
(John Fitzgerald Kennedy...his philosophy...his ideas in his speeches and writings.)   2398

1962

Clemens, Cyril
Mark Twain and John F. Kennedy. Kirkwood, Mo., Mark Twain Journal, 1962, 4p.   2399

Kazin, Alfred
The President and other intellectuals (In his Contemporaries. Boston, Little, Brown, 1962, p. 447-465).   2400

1965

Wood, Playstead & Editors of Country Beautiful Magazine
The life and words of John F. Kennedy. Dayton, Scholastic Pub., 1965, 79p.   2401

1966

Schlette, Heinz R. & Ingo Hermann
Revolution der vernunft; philosophie des politischen bei John F. Kennedy. Munich, Kösel, 1966, 67p.
(The revolution of the intellect; the political philosophy of John F. Kennedy.)   2402

1967

Meyers, Joan (Simpson), ed.
John Fitzgerald Kennedy; as we remember him. Edited and produced under the direction of Goddard Lieberson; art director, Ira Teichberg. Compiled from documents, letters, speeches, photographs, quotations from, and conversations with Charles Bartlett, et al. New York,

Macmillan, 1967, 241p. 2403

Articles

1960

"Nixon, Kennedy view Music and the Arts." Musical America 80, October 1960, p. 8. 2404

Schonberg, H.C.
"Candidates on Culture." New York times 110, Section 2, October 30, 1960, p. 9. 2405

"Jack's Choice for Inaugural: Classical Fare." The billboard music week 72, December 31, 1960, p. 8. 2406

1961

"Thank you, Mr. President." Music educators' journal (48: 2), 1961, p. 33-36. 2407

Saxe, S.
"New Administration Gives Recognition to the Arts." Musical courier 163, February 1961, p. 5. 2408

Sidey, Hugh
"The President's Voracious Reading Habits." Life 50, March 17, 1961, p. 55-56. 2409

Parmenter, R.
"The World of Music." New York times 110, Section 2, March 19, 1961, p. 13. 2410

Collins, Frederic W.
"The Mind of John F. Kennedy." New republic 144, May 8, 1961, p. 15-20. 2411

Cater, Douglass
"Kennedy Look in the Arts." Horizon 4, September 1961, p. 4-17. 2412

Kazin, Alfred
"The President and Other Intellectuals." American scholar 30, Autumn 1961, p. 498-516. 2413

"Anniversary Season (President Praises Brevard)." Musical America 81, October 1961, p. 18-19. 2414

Britton, A.P.
"Thank you, Mr. President." Music educators journal 48, November 1961, p. 33-36. 2415

1962

Brandon, H.
"Washington's Struggle for Culture." The Saturday review 45, January 6, 1962, p. 16-17. 2416

Carpenter, L.
"JFK Intent on Cultural Pitch." Variety 225, January 10, 1962, p. 4. 2417

Gelb, A. & B. Gelb
"Culture Makes a hit at the White House." New York times 111, Magazine Section, January 28, 1962, p. 9. 2418

"Government and the Arts." Music magazine 164, May 1962, p. 8-9. 2419

Fuller, E.
"Where is President Leading us in Education?" The nation's schools 70, July

1962, p. 70.   2420

"Even JFK Finds D.C. Cultural Center a Tough VIP Sell at $1,000 a Table." Variety 228, November 21, 1962, p. 1.   2421

Kempton, Murray
"President Kennedy as Social Historian." London, Spectator, November 30, 1962, p. 849-850.   2422

"Jazz at the White House." Down beat 29, December 6, 1962, p. 13.   2423

1963
Pastreich, P.
"President Kennedy Greets Central Kentucky Youth Symphony." ASOL newsletter (14: 3), 1963, p. 12.   2424

"The Paul Winter Sextet at the White House." Down beat 30, January 3, 1963, p. 18-19.   2425

Carpenter, L.
"Washington Asks: Is Kennedy Truly a Theatre Buff?" Variety 229, January 9, 1963, p. 3.   2426

Wilson, G.C.
"Interlochen Visits the White House." The school musician 34, March 1963, p. 48-49.   2427

"Institute Citation to President Kennedy." Journal of the American Institute of Architecture 40, July 1963, p. 110-111.   2428

"JFK Puts Muscle into Fund Drive for Washington Center." Variety 232, October 16, 1963, p. 55.   2429

1964
Walter, V.
"John Fitzgerald Kennedy on the Arts." Musart 16, January 1964, p. 5.   2430

Goodfriend, J.
"Editorial (President Kennedy's Influence on American Attitude Toward Music)." Listen 1, February 1964, p. 12.   2431

Brophy, L.
"The Catholic Intellectual and J.F.K." Friar 22, November 1964, p. 55-59. 2432

1965
O'Hara, W.T.
"President Kennedy and Education." School & society 93, November 27, 1965, p. 444-450.   2433

Children's Books

1961
Sammis, Edward R.
John Fitzgerald Kennedy, youngest President. New York, Scholastic Book Services, 1961, 62p.   2434

1962
Hoopes, Roy
What the President does all day: a typical office day in the presidency, presented through photos and brief text. New York, John Day Co.,

1962, 64p.   2435

Tregaskis, Richard W.
 All about President Kennedy's wartime adventure.
 London, W.H. Allen & Co., Ltd., 1962, 139p.   2436

Tregaskis, Richard W.
 John F. Kennedy and PT109.
 New York, Random House, 1962, 192p.   2437

Wilkins, Frances
 President Kennedy. London, Cassell & Co., Ltd., 1962, 118p.   2438

1963

Schoor, Gene
 Young John Kennedy. New York, Harcourt, Brace & World, Inc., 1963, 253p. 2439

1964

Frisbee, Lucy (Post)
 John F. Kennedy: young statesman. Indianapolis, Bobbs-Merrill, 1964, 200p.   2440

Frolick, S.J.
 Once there was a president. New York, Kamrom, Inc., 1964-   2441

Lee, Bruce
 Boy's life of John F. Kennedy; memorial edition. New York, Sterling Publishing Co., 1964, 196p.   2442

Lee, Bruce
 JFK: boyhood to White House. Rev. ed. Greenwich, Conn., Fawcett Publications, 1964, 160p.   2443

Lee, Bruce
 The life of John F. Kennedy; school edition. New York, Globe Book Co., Inc., 1964, 217p.   2444

Levine, Israel E.
 Young man in the White House; John Fitzgerald Kennedy. New York, Messner, 1964, 192p.   2445

Martin, Patricia (Miles)
 John Fitzgerald Kennedy: a see and read beginning to read biography. New York, Putnam's, 1964, 64p.   2446

Strousse, Flora
 John Fitzgerald Kennedy: man of courage. New York, P.J. Kenedy & Son, 1964, 189p.   2447

Webb, Robert N.
 The living JFK: with a tribute by Lyndon B. Johnson. New York, Grosset & Dunlap, 1964, 93p.   2448

1965

Graves, Charles P.
 John F. Kennedy, new frontiersman. Champaign, Ill., Garrard Pub. Co., 1965, 80p.   2449

Hanff, Helene
 John F. Kennedy: young man of destiny; prepared with the cooperation of the American Geographical Society. Garden City, Doubleday, 1965, 64p.   2450

Miers, Earl S.
 The story of John F. Ken-

nedy. New York, Grosset &
Dunlap, 1965, 48p.   2451

White, Nancy (Bean)
  Meet John F. Kennedy. New
York, Random House, 1965,
85p.   2452

1966
Fiedler, Jean
  Great American heroes.
New York, Hart, 1966, p.
181-192.   2453

Shapp, Martha & Charles
  Shapp
  Let's find out about John
Fitzgerald Kennedy. New York,
Watts, 1966, 53p.   2454

Vinton, Iris
  The story of President Kennedy. New York, Grosset &
Dunlap, 1966, 180p.   2455

1967
Flavius, Brother
  In virtue's cause; a story of
John F. Kennedy. Notre Dame,
Dujarie Press, 1967, 96p.
      2456
Reidy, John P.
  The true story of John Fitzgerald Kennedy, U.S. President. Chicago, Childrens
Press, 1967, 144p.   2457

Schoor, Gene
  Courage makes the champion.
Princeton, Van Nostrand, 1967,
p. 132-142.   2458

Portraits, Photographs and Caricatures of John F. Kennedy

Books

1961
Life Magazine
  Inaugural spectacle, by
the editors of Life. Souvenir
edition. New York? 1961,
unpaged.   2459

1963
Faith, Samuel J.
  See Jack run. Illustrated
by Bob Lev. Newark, Deanebra Co., 1963, unpaged.
      2460
Life Magazine
  John F. Kennedy memorial
edition, including his biography and his most enduring
words. All of Life's pictures
and text on the most shocking event of our time. Chicago, Time, Inc., 1963, unpaged.   2461

Look Magazine
  Kennedy and his family in
pictures, by the editors of
Look. With the exclusive pictures from the files of Look.
New York? 1963, unpaged.
      2462
U.S. Dept. of Defense.
  Naval Weapons Bureau
  November 16, 1963 (Polaris firing). Photographic
record of the late President
John F. Kennedy's visit to
USS Observation Island prepared as a salute to him by
Navy Polaris team. (Item
408-B-1; D 217.2: P75/2).
Washington, 1963, 2, 12,

1p.   2463

Wortman, Eugene, ed.
 The New Frontier joke book.
New York, Macfadden Books,
1963, 112p.   2464

1964

Altiery, Mason
 John F. Kennedy in Hawaii.
Honolulu? 1964, 31p.   2465

Block, Herbert
 Straight Herblock. New York,
Simon & Schuster, 1964, 224p.
                                  2466
Dobbins, James J.
 Dobbins' diary of the New
Frontier; cartoons. Boston,
Bruce Humphries, Inc., 1964,
182p.   2467

Ferraro, Lance
 One hour in our history;
October 14, 1960. Photos by
Lance Ferraro and the Kala-
mazoo Gazette. Kalamazoo,
1964, 36 plus 2p.   2468

Harris, Patricia (Howard)
  comp.
 An Austin scrapbook of John
F. Kennedy. Compiled from
United Press International
Newspapers, Inc., and others.
Austin, Pemberton Press,
1964, unpaged.   2469

In color; the illustrated story
 of John F. Kennedy, champion of freedom. New York?
 1964, unpaged.   2470

Look Magazine
 JFK memorial book; new
color pictures of his family,
a color visit to his Ireland,
pages from a family album,
the unknown JFK. Des
Moines, 1964, 79p.   2471

The New York Times
 The Kennedy years. Photographs by Jacques Lowe, and
others... with contributions
by John Corry, and others.
New York, Viking Press,
1964, 327p.   2472

Saunders, Doris E., ed.
 The Kennedy years and the
Negro; a photographic record.
Chicago, Johnson Publishing
Co., 1964, 143p.   2473

Silverman, Al, ed.
 John F. Kennedy memorial
album. New York, Macfadden-
Bartell Corp., 1964, 80p.
                                  2474
Spina, Tony
 This was the President;
text and photographs. New
York, A.S. Barnes, 1964,
190p.   2475

Steinmetz, Eigil & Sune
  Kempe, eds.
 John F. Kennedy; mennesket
og statsmander. Helsinki,
Skandinavisk Kultursamling,
1964, 205p.
 (John F. Kennedy, man
and statesman.)   2476

1965

Bergquist, Laura
 A very special president.
Photos by Stanley Tretick.
Designed by Leonard Jossel.
1st ed. New York, McGraw-
Hill, 1965, 203p.   2477

The President nobody knew.

v. 1, no. 1. New York,
P.S.L. Pub. Corp., 1965?
48p.   2478

1967
Duhème, Jacqueline
John F. Kennedy: a book of paintings. New York, Atheneum, 1967-   2479

1968
Quinion, Jean C.
Ubu land. (French text by Jean C. Quinion; drawings by François Monet). Paris, J. Martineau, 1968, unpaged.   2480

Articles

1940
"John Fitzgerald Kennedy (Portrait)." Time 36, August 12, 1940, p. 64.   2481

1961
"Official Color Photograph." Life 50, March 31, 1961, p. 14-15.   2482

"25 Faces of JFK." Editor & publisher 94, April 1, 1961, p. 15. (cartoons).   2483

1962
Bissell, Richard P.
"Carefree Harvard days of Three Presidents: Excerpts from You can Always tell a Harvard man." McCall's 90, October 1962, p. 89-91.   2484

1963
"Late President's Early Life and Family." London, Illustrated London news 243, November 30, 1963, p. 898-899.   2485

1964
Schoor, Gene & Mina Wetzig
"Jack Kennedy, Schoolboy." Manila, Mirror, January 4, 1964, p. 3-4; January 11, 1964, p. 30; January 18, 1964, p. 10-11; January 25, 1964, p. 4; February 1, 1964, p. 31; February 8, 1964, p. 30; February 15, 1964, p. 31; February 22, 1964, p. 10.   2486

1966
"John F. Kennedy: Portrait." Toronto, Maclean's magazine 6, December 1966, p. 65.   2487

Music

Articles

1962
"The ballad of JFK." Newsweek 59, February 5, 1962, p. 57.   2488

1963
"Music and Disk Industry Bringing our Memorial Tributes to President Kennedy." Variety 233, December 4, 1963, p. 61.
                                2489

1964
Sloane, L.
"Memorial Disks." New York times 113, Section 2, January 5, 1964, p. 16. 2490

"RCA Cuts Nonprofit LP of Boston Symphony and Chorale Memorial Mass for JFK." Variety 233, January 22, 1964, p. 71. 2491

"Irish Concert to Honor Kennedy." <u>Variety</u> 233, February 12, 1964, p. 2. 2492

"Stravinsky Ode to JFK After Verse of Auden." <u>Variety</u> 234, March 11, 1964, p. 2. 2493

"When a Just man Dies: Song by I. Stravinsky." <u>Newsweek</u> 63, April 20, 1964, p. 75. 2494

Scores and Songs

1963
Hurd, Danny, arranger
<u>Sing along with Jack; hit songs from the New Frontier</u>, arranged for voice, piano, guitar--and pure fun! Original lyrics by Milton M. Schwartz. Illustrated by David Gantz. [n.p.] Bonny Pub. Corp. (1963). 2495

1964
Auden, Wystan H. & Igor F. Stravinskii
<u>Elegy for J.F.K.</u> [n.p.] Boosey & Hawkes, c1964. 2496

Austin, Larry
<u>In memoriam: John Fitzgerald Kennedy; for concert band</u>. Berkeley, Calif., Berkeley Pub. Co., c1964. 2497

Stravinskii, Igor F.
<u>Elegy for J.F.K. Baritone solo</u>. [n.p.] Boosey & Hawkes, c1964. 2498

Stravinskii, Igor F.
<u>Elegy for J.F.K. Mezzo soprano solo</u>. [n.p.] Boosey & Hawkes, c1964. 2499

1965
Danburg, Russell
<u>Let us go forth; for mixed chorus with piano or organ accompaniment</u>. Park Ridge, Ill., N.A. Kjos Music Co., (1965). 2500

Recordings

1966
Harris, Roy
<u>Epilogue to Profiles in courage: JFK</u>. Louisville, Louisville Orchestra (1966). LS 666. 2501

Documentary
Phonograph Records

1961
<u>John F. Kennedy--Inaugural address, 1961</u>. Spoken Arts 827. ($5.95) 2502

<u>Kennedy inauguration address, and Eisenhower farewell address</u>. Spoken Word 130 (Footnotes of History) ($5.98) 2503

1962
<u>The First family</u>. Cadence Records CLP 3060, 3065 (1962-63). 2504

<u>Kennedy-Nixon debates</u> (April 1962). Spoken Word A-26. (Footnotes of History) (3 records: $5.98 each) 2505

Sahl, Mort
<u>New frontier</u>. Reprise 9-5002. ($5.98) 2506

John Fitzgerald Kennedy

1963
American Broadcasting Company
November 22nd, 1963. New York (1963). Matrix no. ABC-JFK A-D. 2507

JFK the man, the President. New York, Documentaries Unlimited (1963). Matrix no. 101-102. 2508

1964
Kennedy in Germany. Narrated by Howard K. Smith. Produced by Lou Reizner. Eindhoven (Netherlands), Philips Monaural PCC-210 (April 1964). ($5.98) 2509

Kennedy, John F. His last 24 hours, President John Fitzgerald Kennedy's three speeches in Texas and his inaugural address. Dallas, State Democratic Executive Committee of Texas, 1964, JFK 1963. 2510

Memorial tribute to President John F. Kennedy, Women's National Democratic Club, December 2, 1963. Washington, (1963) MM-111. 2511

The actual voices and events of four days that shocked the world, November 22, 23, 24, 25, 1963; the complete story. Colpix Records, CP 2500 (1964). 2512

John F. Kennedy, a documentary: the presidential years, 1960-1963. Recorded by Fox Movietone News. New York, Twentieth Century Fox Records, Monaural TFM 3127, 1964? 2513

Kennedy, John F. John F. Kennedy. Diplomat 10000 (1964). 2514

Kennedy, John F. The Kennedy wit. RCA Victor VDM 101 (1964). ($5.98) 2515

Kennedy nos habla (April 1964) - Harmonia 3006 ($3.98) (Kennedy speaks to us.) 2516

Kennedy speaks (April 1964) - Harmonia 3005 ($3.98) 2517

The making of the President 1960 - Soundtrack (April 1964) - United Artists UXS-59 (2 records: $5.98 each) 2518

A profile of courage. Regina LPR 303 (1964). ($4.98) 2519

Self-portrait (May 1964) - Caedmon 2021 (2 records: $5.95 each) 2520

Stereo tribute: John F. Kennedy. John F. Kennedy's dynamic speeches, documents of freedom... Produced by Foy Willing, et al. Hollywood, Tribute? [n.d.] 2521

That was the week that was (February 1964) - Decca 79116 ($5.79) 2522

Trilogia en la muerte (by Casado): Trilogy in death

(in Spanish) - Concert Classics 4150 ($3.98) 2523

Washington, D.C. Radio Station WQMR
Four dark days in November, a presentation of WQMR news. Washington, Connie R. Gay Broadcasting Corp. (1964). Matrix no. PB 1495-1496. 2524

The wit of John F. Kennedy at the press conference. Challenge, CH618. ($3.79) 2525

Westinghouse Broadcasting Company, Inc.
November 22, dialogue in Dallas. New York (1964) Matrix no. N-WBC 2692-2693. 2526

1965
Of poetry and power, poems occasioned by the Presidency and by the death of John F. Kennedy. New York, Folkway Records FL 9721 (1965). (2 records: $5.79 each) 2527

That day with God (Henry Fonda) - (December 1965) RCA Victor VDM-105 ($5.79) 2528

1966
Herschensohn, Bruce
John F. Kennedy, years of lightning day of drums. Capitol T 2486 (1966). ($4.79) 2529
John F. Kennedy--As we remember him (January 1966) (2 records), Columbia L2L-1017 ($19.95 with book) 2530

1967
Schiller, Lawrence
The controversy. Capitol KAO 2677 (1967).
(Concerning the book, Death of a president, by William Manchester.) 2531

Motion Pictures and Filmstrips

1957
PT-109 (Motion picture). Gallu Productions. Released by CBS Films (1957). 2532

1961
Hemisphere mission (Motion picture). CBS News (1961). 2533
The inauguration of John F. Kennedy-35th President of the United States (Motion picture). U.S. Information Agency, 1961. Made by Fox-Movietone News. Released for public educational use in the United States through the U.S. Office of Education (1961). 2534

The President on tour (Motion picture). CBS News (1961). 2535

1962
Kennedy and Congress (Motion picture). CBS News (1962). 2536

The President at missile sites (Motion picture). CBS News (1962). 2537

1963

John F. Kennedy, 1917-1963 (Motion picture). U.S. Dept. of the Air Force (1963). 2538

John F. Kennedy, the man and the President (Motion picture). Castle Films (1963). 2539

1964

Adventures on the New Frontier (Motion picture). Time-Life Broadcast, 1961. Made by Bob Drew Associates. Released by Peter M. Robeck & Co. (1964). 2540

The burden and the glory of John F. Kennedy (Motion picture). CBS News. Released by Carousel Films (1964). 2541

Four days in November (Motion picture). Wolper Productions. Released by United Artists (1964). 2542

JFK, 1917-1963 (Motion picture). Movietonews. Made & released by Encyclopaedia Britannica Films (1964). 2543

John Fitzgerald Kennedy (Filmstrip). Society for Visual Education (1964). 2544

John Fitzgerald Kennedy (Motion picture). Hearst Metrotone News. Made by Capital Film Laboratories. Released by Star Film Co. (1964). 2545

John F. Kennedy remembered (Motion picture). National Broadcasting Co. (1964). 2546

The last full measure of devotion (Motion picture). National Funeral Directors Association. Made and released by North American Communications Corp. (1964). 2547

Primary (Motion picture). Time-Life Broadcast, 1960. Made by Bob Drew Associates. Released by Peter M. Robeck & Co. (1964). 2548

A thousand days: a tribute to John F. Kennedy (Motion picture). Wolper Productions. Released by Wolper Television Sales Co. (1964). 2549

Trip of the President (Motion picture). U.S. Bureau of Reclamation (1964). 2550

1965

John Fitzgerald Kennedy, 1917-1963 (Motion picture). Chicago, Encyclopaedia Britannica Films (1965). 2551

Some small part of each of us (Motion picture). Jewish Theological Seminary of America, & National Broadcasting Co. Made by National Broadcasting Co. Released by National Academy for Adult Jewish Studies of the United Synagogue of America (1965). 2552

U.S. Senate (Public Bill 647: Report)
USIA film John F. Kennedy, years of lightning, day of

drums. Report from Committee on Foreign Relations to accompany S.J. Res. 106. August 25, 1965. Washington, 1965, 3p.   2553

1966
James A. Michener greeting John F. Kennedy (Motion picture). James A. Michener (1966).   2554

Kennedy--what is remembered is never lost (Motion picture). National Broadcasting Co. Made and released by Encyclopaedia Britannica Films (1966).   2555

The Kennedy wit (Motion picture). American Broadcasting Co. (1966). Made by Dolphin Enterprises.   2556

1967
Age of Kennedy. Part 1: The early years. Part 2: The Presidency. (Motion picture). NBC News. Released by McGraw-Hill Book Co. (1967).   2557

John F. Kennedy: the childhood years, a memoir for television by his mother, October 31, 1967. (Motion picture). New York, CBS Television, 1967.   2558

Jacqueline Lee (Bouvier) Kennedy

Mrs. Jacqueline Lee Bouvier Kennedy was born in Southampton, Long Island, New York on July 28, 1929, the daughter of John Vernon Bouvier III and Mrs. Janet (Lee) Bouvier. In her childhood her ability in writing was easily noticeable, and she enjoyed horseback riding as a sport. In 1947 Jacqueline Bouvier attended Miss Porter's School in Farmington, Connecticut, and during the 1947-48 school year studied at Vassar College. In 1949 she was a student at the Sorbonne (University of Paris), France, where she took courses in languages and art, both of which were destined to be her strong interests as First Lady. In 1951 Jacqueline Bouvier received her A.B. degree from George Washington University, Washington, D.C., and in the same year was awarded Vogue Magazine's Prix de Paris.

The Washington Times-Herald employed Jacqueline Bouvier as a reporter-photographer in 1952. Her assignments included an interview with Senator John F. Kennedy of Massachusetts, and it was this first meeting which culminated eventually in their marriage, on September 12, 1953.

As a senatorial wife, Mrs. Kennedy assisted her husband in his campaigns and greatly inspired him during his hospitalization for back injuries in the years 1954-55. Writing was their common interest, and undoubtedly both the quality and number of the President's books were the direct results of Mrs. Kennedy's inspiration. Mrs. Kennedy became a celebrity in her own right, for her youth and beauty, unique for a First Lady, were enhanced by comparison with almost all of her predecessors in the White House. On trips to Latin America, Canada and France, Mrs. Kennedy would deliver speeches in flawless Spanish or French, adding significantly to the presidential impact, and improved American goodwill among the peoples of the nations visited.

Jacqueline Kennedy sponsored concerts and was a prominent organizer of the First Inter-American Music Conference, held in Washington in 1961. Also in 1961 she formed the Fine Arts and Special Paintings Committees for the purpose of fostering public cooperation in supplying to the White House paintings, antiques and other furnishings characteristic of its heritage. During the following year Mrs. Kennedy appeared on television to point out items received in response to her requests, for as she stated, the White House really belongs to the people. As a result of the telecast, which was actually a White House tour, she received the 1962 "Emmy" Award for Public Service, given annually by the TV industry.

Mrs. Kennedy was also instrumental in saving many ancient and historically (as well as culturally) significant buildings in Washington, which would otherwise have been destroyed, and in restoring them. She asked Mrs. Eisenhower to join with her in a program to create a national cultural center in Washington, since it seemed logical to her that Washington should be a center for all of the arts. Following the assassination of President Kennedy, Congress passed legislation changing the center's name to the John F. Kennedy Center for the Performing Arts. During the Kennedy administration, interest in the arts and education throughout the nation as a whole flourished, due in great measure to the example of a President who was an author and Pulitzer Prize winner, and to his wife who was a great patron of the arts. White House members and guests from all of the arts and literature, as well as from universities were in evidence; indeed, Mrs. Kennedy is still a trustee of the Whitney Museum of American Art.

After the assassination of her husband, Jacqueline Kennedy requested that the funeral be as similar to that of President Lincoln as possible, and in the funeral procession she walked at its head, from the White House to St. Matthews Cathedral. At Arlington National Cemetery she lit the eternal flame on his grave.

In the autumn of 1964 Mrs. Kennedy and her children moved to New York City from their home in Georgetown, a Washington, D.C. suburb. One of Mrs. Kennedy's major interests is the John F. Kennedy Memorial Library at Harvard University.

Jacqueline Lee (Bouvier) Kennedy

Articles by Mrs. Jacqueline (Bouvier) Kennedy

1960
Kennedy, Jacqueline (Bouvier)
 "Our Thanksgiving, What it Means to us. Edited by J. Younger." Ladies' home journal 77, November 1960, p. 55.   2559

1963
Kennedy, Jacqueline (Bouvier)
 "Christmas Message." Look 27, December 31, 1963, p. 14-15.   2560

1964
Kennedy, Jacqueline (Bouvier)
 "Mrs. Kennedy says Thank you to 800,000 Friends." Life 56, January 24, 1964, p. 32B-32C.   2561

Kennedy, Jacqueline (Bouvier)
 "Mrs. Kennedy Thanks President Shazar." Jerusalem, Israel digest 7, February 14, 1964, p. 6.   2562

Kennedy, Jacqueline (Bouvier)
 "Mrs. Kennedy Thanks Israel for Sympathy and J.F. Kennedy Memorials." World over 25, April 24, 1964, p. 4.   2563

Kennedy, Jacqueline (Bouvier)
 "These are the Things I hope Will Show how he Really was." Life 56, May 29, 1964, p. 32-34A.   2564

Kennedy, Jacqueline (Bouvier)
 "Memoir." Look 28, November 17, 1964, p. 36.   2565

Kennedy, Jacqueline (Bouvier)
 "The Words JFK Loved Best." Look 28, November 17, 1964, p. 84-90.   2566

Books about Mrs. Jacqueline (Bouvier) Kennedy

1961
Heller, Deane & David Heller
 Jacqueline Kennedy: the complete story of America's glamorous first lady. Derby, Conn., Monarch Books, 1961, 139p.   2567

McConnell, Jane (Tompkins) & Burt M. McConnell
 Our first ladies from Martha Washington to Jacqueline Lee Bouvier Kennedy. New York, Crowell, 1961, p. 336-347.   2568

Thayer, Mary (Van Rensselaer)
 Jacqueline Bouvier Kennedy. New York, Doubleday, 1961, 127p.   2569

1962
Curtis, Charlotte
 First lady. New York, Pyramid Books, 1962, 158p.   2570

Petersen, Peter
 Jacqueline Kennedy, First Lady der USA. Nach zeitgenössischen Quellen frei bearb. von Peter Petersen. Düsseldorf, Deutsche Buchvertriebs- und Verlags-Gesellschaft, 1962, 350p.   2571

Rhea, Mini & Frances (Spatz) Leighton
 I was Jacqueline Kennedy's dressmaker. New York,

Fleet Pub. Corp., 1962, 334p.
2572
U.S. 87th Congress. Senate
Films recording Mrs. John
F. Kennedy's visit to India
and Pakistan. Report from
Committee on Foreign Relations to accompany S. Con.
Res. 84. August 16, 1962.
Washington, 1962, 5p. (Report
1883). 2573

Wolff, Perry S.
A tour of the White House
with Mrs. John F. Kennedy.
New York, Doubleday, 1962,
258p. 2574

1963
Bair, Majorie
Jacqueline Kennedy in the
White House. Art director:
Rolf Erikson. New York,
Paperback Library, 1963, 128p.
2575
Heller, Deane & David Heller
Jacqueline Kennedy; the
warmly human life story of
the woman all Americans have
taken to their heart. New enl.
ed. Derby, Conn., Monarch
Books, 1963, 222p. 2576

1964
Hall, Gordon L. & Ann Pinchot
Jacqueline Kennedy, a biography. New York, Frederick
Fell, Inc., 1964, 275p. 2577

Hawley, Earl, ed.
A salute to Jacqueline Kennedy, the bravest woman in
the world; the highlights and
shadows in her life, from inauguration to Arlington. Los
Angeles, J.P. Matthews,
1964, 62p. 2578

Jacqueline Kennedy, woman
of valor. Jack J. Podell,
editorial director; Claire
Safran, editor; Kenneth
Cunningham, art director,
and Marion Will, assistant
art director. New York,
Macfadden-Bartell, 1964,
80p. 2579

Moscoso Dávila, Isabel
A Jacqueline. Cuenca,
Ecuador, Casa de la Cultura
Ecuatoriana, Nucleo del
Azuay, 1964, 13p.
(To Jacqueline: poem.)
2580
Palmén, Aili & Kirsti Korpi
Jacqueline Kennedy. Helsinki, Otava Kustannus, 1964,
96p. 2581

Prindiville, Kathleen
First ladies. 2d ed. New
York, Macmillan, 1964, p.
1-18.
(Children's book). 2582

U.S. 88th Congress. Public
Law 195
H.R. 9291, act to provide
office space, supplies, equipment, and franking privileges
for Mrs. Jacqueline Bouvier
Kennedy, to authorize appropriations for payment of expenses incident to death and
burial of former President
John Fitzgerald Kennedy, and
for other purposes. Approved
December 11, 1963. Washington, 1964, 2p. 2583

U.S. Smithsonian Institution
Gown of Mrs. John F. Kennedy, as displayed in National Museum, Smithsonian In-

stitution; by Margaret Brown Klapthor. SI 3.2: D 81/supp. -2. Washington, 1964, 5p.   2584

1965

Dareff, Hail
Jacqueline Kennedy, a portrait in courage. New York, Parents' Magazine Press, 1965, 192p.   2585

Rathi, Baldev S.
Mrs. Kennedy; the negative force of human reverence... Bikaner, India, 1965, 205p.   2586

Ridha, Muhd
Jacqueline Kennedy. Djakarta, Pustaka Negara, 1965, 91p.   2587

Riess, Curt
Zehn Jahre und ein Tag; Jacqueline Kennedy, Glück und Leid. Munich, Lichtenberg, 1965, 283p.
(Ten years and one day; Jacqueline Kennedy, joy and sorrow.)   2588

Truett, Randle (Bond)
First ladies in fashion. New York, Hastings House, 1965, p. 82-83.   2589

1966

Adler, Bill, ed.
Common sense wisdom of three first ladies. New York, Citadel Press, 1966, 160p.   2590

Harding, Robert T. & A.L. Holmes
Jacqueline Kennedy, a woman for the world. New York, Encyclopedia Enterprises, Inc., 1966, 128p.   2591

1967

Carpozi, George
The hidden side of Jacqueline Kennedy. New York, Pyramid Books, 1967, 239p.   2592

Corry, John
The Manchester affair. New York, Putnam's, 1967, 223p.   2593

Lincoln, Anne H.
Kennedy White House parties. New York, Viking Press, 1967, 168p.   2594

Malkus, Alida (Sims)
The story of Jacqueline Kennedy. New York, Grosset & Dunlap, 1967, 179p.   2595 (children's book)

Articles about Mrs. Jacqueline (Bouvier) Kennedy

1953

"Life Goes Courting with a U.S. Senator." Life 35, July 20, 1953, p. 96-99.   2596

"A Senator Weds." Life 35, September 28, 1953, p. 45-46.   2597

1954

"Senator's Wife Goes Back to School." McCall's 82, October 1954, p. 50-51.   2598

1959

"John Kennedy's Lovely Lady." Life 47, August 24, 1959, p. 75-81.   2599

1960

Young, A.A.
"Meet Mrs. Jack Kennedy."

Information 74, July 1960, p. 2-11. 2600

"Jackie Kennedy: First Lady at 30? A closeup View of the big Kennedy Family." U.S. news & world report 49, July 25, 1960, p. 60-62. 2601

"Lovely Aspirants for Role of First Lady." Life 49, October 10, 1960, p. 150-157. 2602

Howard, Mortimer
"The Woman Behind the man who may be the Next U.S. President." Manila, Mirror, October 15, 1960, p. 22-23. 2603

"Important Women in Their Lives." Newsweek 56, October 17, 1960, p. 31-34. 2604

"Beauty in the White House." U.S. news & world report 49, November 21, 1960, p. 78-79. 2605

"Kennedy on way to see son." Life 49, December 5, 1960, p. 35-39. 2606

1961

Brogan, Denis W.
"Jacqueline Bouvier: Court Gossip." London, Spectator 6930, 1961, p. 548-549. 2607

"Jackie: First Lady of the Land." Time 77, January 20, 1961, p. 18-20. 2608

Joaquin, Nick
"The new U.S. First Lady." Manila, Philippines free press (54: 3), January 21, 1961, p. 33-34. 2609

Thomas, Helen & Jane Bell
"The Girl who has Everything." Manila, Weekly graphic (27: 38), March 15, 1961, p. 8-11, 34. 2610

Thomas, Helen & Jane Bell
"Marriage and Children." Manila, Weekly graphic (27: 39), March 22, 1961, p. 8-9. 2611

Thomas, Helen & Jane Bell
"Old-fashioned Mother." Manila, Weekly graphic (27: 40), March 29, 1961, p. 14, 23, 25, 59. 2612

"America's First Lady: Jacqueline Kennedy." Reader's digest 78, April 1961, p. 50-54. 2613

Thomas, Helen & Jane Bell
"Epitome of Modern Living." Manila, Weekly graphic (27: 41), April 5, 1961, p. 14-15. 2614

Thomas, Helen & Jane Bell
"Jazz at the White House." Manila, Weekly graphic (27: 42), April 12, 1961, p. 18-19. 2615

Thomas, Helen & Jane Bell
"The Kennedys at Home." Manila, Weekly graphic (27: 43), April 19, 1961, p. 14-15, 19, 23. 2616

Lisagor, Peter
"First Lady to the First Lady." McCall's 88, June 1961, p. 96-97. 2617

Marple, Allen
"Off the Cuff." The writer 74, June 1961, p. 3-4. 2618

"New White House Mood." Manila, Weekly graphic (27: 50), June 7, 1961, p. 12-13. 2619

Lansdown, S.
"JFK's Crutches and Cassocks by Dior." America 105, June 24, 1961, p. 457. 2620

"Kennedys: a Private View at Hyannis Port." Vogue 138, July 1961, p. 50-57. 2621

"What Mrs. Kennedy Could Learn from Queen Elizabeth." Manila, Sunday times magazine (16: 49), July 16, 1961, p. 32-33. 2622

"Jackie Kennedy: Glamor in the White House." Manila, Saturday herald magazine, August 26, 1961, p. 20-23. 2623

"Jacqueline Kennedy and a Reaffirmation of the American Image." American fabrics 54, Fall 1961, p. 15-17. 2624

Cater, Douglass
"The Kennedy Look in the Arts." Horizon 4, September 1961, p. 4-17. 2625

"First Lady Brings History and Beauty to the White House." Life 51, September 1, 1961, p. 54-65. 2626

McKnight, B.S.
"Jacqueline Kennedy Look in Flowers for the White House."
American home 64, October 1961, p. 11-14. 2627

"Bright day, Blue day." Newsweek 58, October 9, 1961, p. 23-24. 2628

"A Week in the life of JFK's Wife." Life 51, November 24, 1961, p. 32-40. 2629

Carleton, W.G.
"Cult of Personality Comes to the White House." Harper's magazine 223, December 1961, p. 63-68. 2630

"Family Thanksgiving." Time 78, December 1, 1961, p. 12. 2631

1962

Lambert, Gilles
"Jackie Kennedy und ihr 'Museum'." Zürich, Weltwoche (30: 1511), 1962, p. 39.
("Jackie Kennedy and her 'Museum';") 2632

"Jacqueline Kennedy." Newsweek 59, January 1, 1962, p. 31-35. 2633

"Man of the Year." Time 79, January 5, 1962, p. 9-14. 2634

"Simply Everywhere." Time 79, February 23, 1962, p. 24-25. 2635

"First-rate Junket for a First Lady." Life 52, March 23, 1962, p. 42-44. 2636

"First Lady at the Vatican."

America 106, March 24, 1962, p. 807. 2637

"Jackie Leaves her Mark on India and Pakistan." Life 52, March 30, 1962, p. 24-31. 2638

"First Lady Tops Annual Award Poll." Travel 117, April 1962, p. 29-31. 2639

Stark, J.T.
"Jacqueline Kennedy Inspires the International Look." Look 26, June 5, 1962, p. 73-78. 2640

Mailer, Norman
"An Evening with Jackie Kennedy." Esquire (LVIII: 1), July 1962, p. 56. 2641

"Glamorous First Ladies." Ebony 17, August 1962, p. 21-24. 2642

"The Kennedy Dynasty and Jacqueline." London, Time & tide 43, August 2-9, 1962, p. 13. 2643

"As First Lady and Caroline Took Italy by Storm." U.S. news & world report 53, August 20, 1962, p. 12-13. 2644

Cassini, I.
"How the Kennedy Marriage has Fared." Good housekeeping 155, September 1962, p. 68-69. 2645

"Don't Forget Vacation in Ravello, Italy." Time 80, September 7, 1962, p. 16. 2646

"First Lady and the White House." Newsweek 60, September 17, 1962, p. 71-78. 2647

"Jacqueline Kennedy, b.b.c." Reader's digest 81, October 1962, p. 157-158. 2648

"Hunt-country Retreat for the Kennedys." U.S. news & world report 53, November 12, 1962, p. 8. 2649

"Christmas with the Kennedys." Redbook 120, December 1962, p. 54-55. 2650

1963

McGrory, Mary
"First Lady has a Style all her own." America 108, February 23, 1963, p. 249. 2651

Kane, J.
"The First Family Record." Marriage 45, March 1963, p. 34-38. 2652

Plimpton, George
"Newport Notes; the Kennedys and Other Salts." Harper's magazine 226, March 1963, p. 39-47. 2653

Kempton, Murray
"First Family Business." London, Spectator, March 15, 1963, p. 314-315. 2654

Smith, M.
"First Family has Everything but Privacy." Nation's business 51, May 1963, p. 23-24. 2655

Braden, J., ed.
"Exclusive Chat with Jackie

Kennedy: Interview." Saturday evening post 235, May 12, 1963, p. 85-89. 2656

"Arabian Nights: Visit to Morocco." Time 82, October 25, 1963, p. 24-25. 2657

"Caesar's Wife." Newsweek 62, October 28, 1963, p. 20-21. 2658

Haines, A.
"First Lady in her own Right." Torch 47, November 1963, p. 16-19. 2659

"Christmas Paintings of Jacqueline Kennedy." McCall's 91, December 1963, p. 98-99. 2660

"Profile in Courage." America 109, December 7, 1963, p. 722. 2661

"A new Profile of Courage." Manila, Weekly graphic (30: 27), December 25, 1963, p. 3. 2662

1964

Levy, L.
"Jacqueline Kennedy, Woman of Valor." Pioneer woman monthly 39, January 1964, p. 5-6. 2663

Carunungan, C.A.
"What the new Year Holds for Jacqueline." Manila, Weekly graphic (30: 28), January 1, 1964, p. 8-9, 70. 2664

"Kennedy's Estate, 7.6 million, after Taxes?" U.S. news & world report 56, January 6, 1964, p. 4. 2665

"A House for Jacqueline." Manila, Philippines herald magazine, January 18, 1964, p. 18-19. 2666

Carunungan, C.A.
"The Brave new World of Jacqueline Kennedy." Quezon City, Weekly graphic, January 8, 1964, p. 16-17, 70; January 22, 1964, p. 12-13, 70; January 29, 1964, p. 10-11; February 12, 1964, p. 12-13, 78. 2667

Bergquist, Laura
"Valiant is the Word for Jacqueline." Look 28, January 28, 1964, p. 72-74. 2668

"Mrs. John Fitzgerald Kennedy: Resolution Presented to NCC." Catholic mind 62, February 1964, p. 40. 2669

Smith, Norman
"Salute to a new American Artist." Manila, Weekly graphic (30: 33), February 5, 1964, p. 14-15. 2670

Romulo, Virginia (Llamas)
"My Impressions of Mrs. Kennedy." Manila, Weekly graphic (30: 35), February 19, 1964, p. 4-5. 2671

Knebel, Fletcher
"After the Shots: the Ordeal of Lyndon Johnson." Look 28, March 10, 1964, p. 26-28. 2672

"Jacqueline Kennedy: a Postscript." Manila, Weekly

graphic (30: 42), April 8, 1964, p. 8-9; (30: 43), April 15, 1964, p. 8, 82. 2673

"Children's Letters to Jacqueline Kennedy and her Children." Redbook 123, May 1964, p. 50-51. 2674

Hoogterp, D.
"For Mrs. Jacqueline Kennedy" (poem). Our Lady's digest 19, May 1964, p. 17. 2675

Thomas, Helen
"Six Months After: the no. 1 Widow." Manila, Philippines herald magazine, June 13, 1964, p. 24. 2676

Stolley, Richard B.
"Work, Memories, old Friends." Manila, Sunday times magazine, July 26, 1964, p. 63. 2677

Shannon, William V.
"Jacqueline Kennedy" (condensed from Good housekeeping). Catholic digest 28, August 1964, p. 108-111. 2678

Meares, P.
"I Helped with Mrs. Kennedy's Mail." Catholic digest 28, September 1964, p. 19-22. 2679

Duncan, Eileen
"Jacqueline Kennedy: the Woman who Must Live." Manila, Sunday times magazine, September 20, 1964, p. 54-56. 2680

"New Family in Town: New Life in New York." Newsweek 64, September 28, 1964, p. 31-32. 2681

Steinem, Gloria
"Mrs. Kennedy at the Moment." Esquire (LXII: 4), October 1964, p. 125. 2682

Walsh, L.
"What Makes Women Lovely?" (condensed from Sacred Heart messenger). Our Lady's digest 19, October-November 1964, p. 138-142. 2683

1965
Shannon, William V.
"Jackie Kennedy and her Children" (condensed from Good housekeeping, November 1964). Catholic digest 29, February 1965, p. 55-58. 2684

"Callas Fan Brightens Opera Night." Life 58, April 2, 1965, p. 105-106. 2685

"Tiny Party on Fifth Avenue." Time 85, April 30, 1965, p. 80. 2686

"From Jackie to Lady Bird: Letter That Caused an Uproar." U.S. news & world report 58, May 31, 1965, p. 10-11. 2687

"Graceful Entrance: Social Week." Time 85, October 1, 1965, p. 32. 2688

"Dancing at the Dove." Newsweek 66, October 4, 1965, p. 28-29. 2689

Jacqueline Lee (Bouvier) Kennedy

1966

Breslin, C.
"Jacqueline Kennedy, Keeper of a Legend: her Triumph and Ordeal." Toronto, Maclean's magazine 79, April 16, 1966, p. 17, 36-37.   2690

1967

Birmingham, S.
"How the Remarkable Auchincloss Family Shaped the Jacqueline Kennedy Style." Ladies' home journal 84, March 1967, p. 91-93.   2691

Brothers, Joyce
"Jacqueline Kennedy: the Magic and the Myth." Good housekeeping 164, March 1967, p. 60.   2692

Levy, A.
"Jackie Kennedy: a View From the Crowd." Saturday evening post 240, March 11, 1967, p. 19-23.   2693

"Jackie Exclusive: Concerning Interview in New York World Journal Tribune." Time 89, March 24, 1967, p. 63-64.   2694

Bender, Marylin
"How Jacqueline Kennedy influences the way you look." Redbook 129, August 1967, p. 52.   2695

Dudar, Helen
"Jackie Kennedy: What People Close to her Think About her now." Good housekeeping 165, October 1967, p. 90-91.   2696

"Jackie's Next Trip: Cambodia Visit on Again." U.S. news & world report 63, October 16, 1967, p. 20.   2697

"Living Theatre." Newsweek 70, November 13, 1967, p. 57-58.   2698

"Mrs. Kennedy Cannot Escape From Limelight." Los Angeles times, November 19, 1967 (section H), p. 8-9.   2699

"The Travels of Jackie." Newsweek 70, November 20, 1967, p. 76-77.   2700

1968

Kalb, Bernard & Marvin Kalb
"Jacqueline Kennedy's Secret Message to Asia." McCall's 95, June 1968, p. 60-61.   2701

Photographs and Portraits

1960

"Milestones in the life of a First-Lady-to-be and a Mother." Life 49, December 5, 1960, p. 38-39.   2702

1967

"Mrs. John F. Kennedy: Photographs." Vogue 149, May 1967, p. 176-177.   2703

Motion Pictures

1961

The President and the First Lady in Latin America (Motion picture). CBS News (1961).   2704

1962
Jackie's journey to India (Motion picture). CBS News
(1962). 2705

A tour of the White House with Mrs. John F. Kennedy (Motion picture). Columbia Broadcasting System. Released by McGraw-Hill Book Co. (1962). 2706

The world of Jacqueline Kennedy (Motion picture). NBC-TV (1962). 2707

1963
Invitation to India (Motion picture). U.S. Information Agency, 1962. Made by Hearst Metrotone News. Released for public educational use through U.S. Office of Education (1963). 2708

Invitation to Pakistan (Motion picture). U.S. Information Agency, 1962. Made by Hearst Metrotone News. Released for public educational use through U.S. Office of Education (1963). 2709

Jacqueline Kennedy's Asian journey (Motion picture). U.S. Information Agency, 1962. Made by Hearst Metrotone News. Released for public educational use through U.S. Office of Education (1963). 2710

The Children of John F. Kennedy

Books

1964
Shaw, Mark
  The John F. Kennedys. New York, Farrar, Strauss & Co., 1964, 159p. 2711

1966
Shaw, Maud
  White House nannie; my years with Caroline and John Kennedy, Jr. New York, New American Library, 1966, 205p. 2712

1967
Sadler, Christine
  Children in the White House. New York, Putnam's, 1967, p. 295-303. 2713

U.S. Congress. House
  Secret Service protection for widow and minor children of former President. Report no. 813 to accompany H.R. 13165, October 24, 1967. Washington, House Document Room, Capitol, 1967, 2p. 2714

Articles

1960
"John Jr." Time 76, December 5, 1960, p. 11-13. 2715
"Life with Father." Time 76, December 12, 1960, p. 19. 2716
"High Point in a Notable Week: Christening of John F. Kennedy's son." Life

Jacqueline Lee (Bouvier) Kennedy

49, December 19, 1960, p. 29. 2717

1961

"You Don't Have to Look Hard to see Another Jackie." Life 50, January 20, 1961, p. 16-23. 2718

Montgomery, Ruth
 "Jackie Kennedy Tells: How I'm Raising my Children in the White House." Good housekeeping 152, June 1961, p. 54-57. 2719

Anderson, Jack
 "The Little Girl in the White House." Manila, Mirror, July 22, 1961, p. 20-21. 2720

Bergquist, Laura
 "Caroline." Look 25, September 26, 1961, p. 76-82. 2721

"Like Papa." New republic 145, October 23, 1961, p. 2. 2722

"Impish Heir's Birthday Picture." Life 51, November 24, 1961, p. 34-39. 2723

1962

"Caroline's Wonderful Summer." Manila, Mirror, September 15, 1962, p. 32-35. 2724

"John, Jr. Helps Welcome a Dignitary: Ben Bella." U.S. news & world report 53, October 29, 1962, p. 12. 2725

1963

Buchmueller, A.D.
 "Two is the age of Firsts." McCall's 90, July 1, 1963, p. 27-29. 2726

"With a new Kind of Loneliness: Birth and Death of the Kennedy Baby." Newsweek 62, August 19, 1963, p. 17-18. 2727

Thomas, Helen
 "Caroline's Wonderful Little White House School." Good housekeeping 157, October 1963, p. 84-85. 2728

Thomas, Helen
 "The President Calls him John-John." Manila, Philippines herald magazine, October 5, 1963, p. 19. 2729

"A Look Inside the White House School." U.S. news & world report 55, October 7, 1963, p. 70-72. 2730

Bergquist, Laura
 "The President and his Son." Look 27, December 3, 1963, p. 26-34. 2731

1967

"Mini Trend Setter." Time 90, August 11, 1967, p. 43. 2732

1968

Cameron, Gail
 "Caroline and John F. Kennedy, Jr.: the Happy Years are now." Ladies home journal 85, June 1968, p. 54. 2733

John F. Kennedy Family: Photographs and Portraits

Books

1963

Doud, Earle, et al
The First Family photo album. Greenwich, Conn., Fawcett Publications, 1963, unpaged. 2734

First family album. Jack J. Podell, editorial director. New York, Macfadden-Bartell Corp., 1963, 79p. 2735

Articles

1960

"Ex-fotog Shoots her own pix of Newsy Vacation." Life 49, August 1, 1960, p. 82-83. 2736

1961

"J.F.K. Picks a Picture for a Great Occasion." Life 50, January 20, 1961, p. 88-89. 2737

"Pictorial Highlights of his Career and Family Life." Extension 55, February 1961, p. 12-13. 2738

"New Folks at Home." Time 77, February 10, 1961, p. 14-15. 2739

"A day with John F. Kennedy: Photographs." New York times magazine, February 19, 1961, p. 10-13. 2740

Bergquist, Laura
"Informal Visit with our new First Family." Look 25, February 28, 1961, p. 100-101. 2741

"Glimpse at Life in Today's White House." U.S. news & world report 50, April 3, 1961, p. 63-66. 2742

"Study in Contrasts: The Summiteers." New York times magazine, June 4, 1961, p. 8-9. 2743

"Kennedys on Vacation." Ladies' home journal 78, August 1961, p. 32-37. 2744

Tames, George
"When the President Goes to the People." New York times magazine, November 26, 1961, p. 26-27. 2745

1962

"Key Moods of the First Year." New York times magazine, January 14, 1962, p. 10-11. 2746

Brown, N.B.
"JFK Touch in Office Decor." New York times magazine, April 8, 1962, p. 38-39. 2747

"The Happy World of Caroline and John, Jr." U.S. news & world report 53, December 3, 1962, p. 15. 2748

1964

Lowe, J.
"JFK: a Personal Memoir" (photo essay). Sign 43, February 1964, p. 11-19. 2749

"Pages from a Family Album."
 Look 28, November 17,
 1964, p. 103-105.   2750

            1965
Durniak, J.
 "More a Kaleidoscope Than
 a Still Picture: G. Tames'
 Photograph." Popular photog-
 raphy 57, November 1965, p.
 154-155.   2751

"Full Happy Life of John F.
 Kennedy; Paintings by J.
 Duhème; With Comments by
 Robert Kennedy." Ladies'
 home journal 82, November
 1965, p. 100-105.   2752

Rose Marie Kennedy

Rose Marie Kennedy was born in Brookline, Massachusetts on September 13, 1918. A loveable, attractive child, Rose Marie could not keep up with her brothers and sisters in the energetic, rough-and-tumble play of a large household. A loving family took special care of their child and their sister who, they later learned, had been a victim of the cruel effects of mental retardation. Mrs. Kennedy often played the piano and sang to Rose Marie, who was encouraged to enjoy her childhood with her siblings.

Rose Marie accompanied the family to London, England, and prior to her father's entry upon his three-year ambassadorship to Great Britain, Rose Marie and her sisters were presented to the Queen of England. No efforts were spared to afford Rose Marie the opportunities of a normal childhood, aided by a continuous search for the finest medical attention available.

For years the family determined to have their eldest daughter remain at home with them. Because of progressive deterioration of Rose Marie's condition they finally, but sadly, realized that Rose Marie might be in need of regular professional care. Thus it was that Rose Marie Kennedy took up permanent residence at St. Coletta's, a Roman Catholic institution in Jefferson, Wisconsin.

The Joseph P. Kennedy, Jr. Foundation, long active in research and care of children who are victims of mental retardation, has been construed by some not only as a tribute to Rose Marie's brother, who was lost over Europe serving as a Navy pilot during World War II, but also as a living symbol of the Kennedy family's devotion to its oldest daughter. Active in the same field are the Kennedy Child Study Center, located in New York City, and the Kennedy Institute, with headquarters in Washington, D.C.

Kathleen (Kennedy) Cavendish

Kathleen Kennedy was born in Brookline, Massachusetts on February 20, 1920. As a student Kathleen attended the Sacred Heart convent school in Noroton, Connecticut. In the autumn of 1935 she accompanied her parents on a tour of western Europe, and during the years 1937-40 (when Joseph P. Kennedy served as American Ambassador to Great Britain), she attended the Sacred Heart convent school in Roehampton, England. As the daughter of the American Ambassador, Kathleen was privileged to attend many fashionable social events. "Kick" was the nickname given her by her brothers and sisters.

In 1941, after previously returning to the United States, Kathleen obtained a position with the Washington Times-Herald. She left this position in early 1943 to return to London as a Red Cross worker, in order to do her part in the war effort. It was here that a flame was rekindled, for while she resided with her family in London during the ambassadorship of her father, one of her friends was William Cavendish, the Marquess of Hartington. She had remembered him as a gay youth, but at their 1943 meeting he was an officer in the Coldstream Guards. Their courtship resulted in their marriage in London, in May of 1944. It was during this period that Lieutenant Joseph P. Kennedy, Jr., her brother, stationed in England with the U.S. Naval Air Corps, was a source of guidance to Kathleen. One month after their marriage, the groom left to rejoin his unit for the invasion of France, and Kathleen returned to her parents' home in the United States.

On August 12, 1944, they were informed that Lieutenant Joseph P. Kennedy, Jr. had been killed in an airplane accident. This wound was made much more painful for Kathleen, who was informed only two weeks later, that her husband had been killed in action. Kathleen returned to London, and grew very close to her in-laws, the Duke and Duchess of Devonshire, living in the memory of her lost love. Kathleen was however, to be reunited with him, for in May of 1948, the airplane in which she was flying over France crashed, and she was killed. Kathleen was buried next to the grave of her husband in Chatsworth, England.

Eunice (Kennedy) Shriver

Mrs. Eunice (Kennedy) Shriver was born in Brookline, Massachusetts on July 10, 1921. As a child she attended the Sacred Heart convent school in Noroton, Connecticut, and during the period (1937-40) in which her father, Joseph P. Kennedy served as U.S. Ambassador to England, attended the Sacred Heart convent school in Roehampton, England. She chose to major in Sociology at Stanford University, and was graduated with a B.S. degree in 1943 (after having previously studied at Manhattanville College of the Sacred Heart).

Shortly after World War II, Eunice Kennedy worked for the Department of State in the task of orientation of American prisoners of war who returned to the United States after being liberated from German prison camps. In 1947 she assisted Robert Sargent Shriver in setting up the National Conference on Juvenile Delinquency under the aegis of the Department of Justice in Washington, D.C. Her work took in various aspects of juvenile delinquency, and in her position she made contact with state and city agencies working in this field.

Beginning in 1950 Eunice Kennedy began to appear before audiences throughout the United States to arouse interest in released prisoners, so that they would more easily find their proper places in society. The field of juvenile delinquency was to become a key activity of Eunice Kennedy in future years; indeed, her next position was with the House of the Good Shepherd in Chicago, working with teen-age delinquents.

On May 23, 1953 Eunice was married to Robert Sargent Shriver, Jr. They now have five children: Robert Sargent, III; Maria; Timothy; Mark Kennedy; and Paul Fitzgerald Kennedy. Although they consider the city of Chicago as home (for thirteen years, until 1961, Mr. Shriver managed the Merchandise Mart in Chicago, one of the Kennedy family holdings), Washington had been the site of the Shriver family's activities from 1961 to the spring of 1968, a period during which Sargent Shriver served first as Director of the

Peace Corps and subsequently as Director of the Office of Economic Opportunity (popularly known as "the poverty program"). Paris, France became the new home of the Shrivers, for in April of 1968 President Lyndon B. Johnson appointed Mr. Shriver as American Ambassador to France.

Highly efficient Eunice (Kennedy) Shriver serves as Executive Vice President of the Joseph P. Kennedy, Jr. Foundation, which operates in the area of mental retardation of children. As a result of her speaking tours throughout the United States, and the support she has enlisted from civic groups and teachers, she has been able to improve the national attitude toward mentally-retarded children.

At the beginning of its existence, the Joseph P. Kennedy, Jr. Foundation built a 125-bed rehabilitation hospital for children in Massachusetts, as well as homes and schools. In later years the Kennedy Child Study Center, and the Kennedy Institute were established, in New York City and in Washington, D.C., respectively.

Eunice Shriver fosters such activities as physical education and summer camp experience for retarded children; she has assisted in the realization of a program which includes retarded children in games. During recent summers many retarded children, assisted by the Shrivers' own children, have enjoyed the advantages of attending the Shriver Summer Day Camp. Mrs. Shriver fully believes that most retarded children can be amalgamated into society, and she has asserted that they have as much right to enjoy life as do more fortunate youngsters.

Another of Mrs. Shriver's projects concerns the granting by schools of course credits in child care, and in effect, the recognition of motherhood as a profession. It is her opinion that motherhood is one of the most critical and significant of the world's professions, yet is not so considered in educational institutions, many of which grant credits and degrees in fields of far less importance. She believes that women today at all levels must have a sense of purpose and commitment, to achieve significantly.

Eunice Shriver formerly was a member of the National Advisory Child Health and Human Development Council, and a consultant to the President's Panel on Retardation (which was originally appointed by President John F. Kennedy). She was also a member of the Board of Governors of the Menninger

Foundation. In 1966 she received the Albert Lasker Public Service Award in Health for her assistance in regard to legislation passed by Congress in the fight against mental retardation. The Award was granted "in recognition of her leadership in encouragement of national legislation against retardation and the new hope she has brought to blighted lives of millions."

An extremely efficient, dedicated and hard-working individual, Eunice Shriver is the heart and soul of the Kennedy Foundation, which she has been operating since its activities grew too cumbersome and varied for her father, Joseph P. Kennedy to manage, some years ago. For her efforts in behalf of humanity, Eunice Kennedy Shriver was awarded honorary doctoral degrees by Regis College (Weston, Massachusetts), D'Youville College (Buffalo, New York), Manhattanville College of the Sacred Heart, and the University of Santa Clara. Despite all of the effort devoted to her profession, Eunice Shriver found time to aid her brother, John F. Kennedy, in his first congressional campaign in 1946, as well as in his later efforts to win the presidency.

Articles by Mrs. Eunice (Kennedy) Shriver

1962
Shriver, Eunice (Kennedy)
  "Hope for Retarded Children." Saturday evening post 235, September 22, 1962, p. 71-75.　　　　　2753

1965
Shriver, Eunice (Kennedy)
  "Answer to the Attacks on Motherhood." McCall's 92, June 1965, p. 88-89.　　2754

1968
Shriver, Eunice (Kennedy)
  "When Pregnancy Means Heartbreak, is Abortion the Answer?" McCall's 95, April 1968, p. 60-61.　　2755

Articles about Mrs. Eunice (Kennedy) Shriver

1947
"Eunice M. Kennedy: Portrait." Parents' magazine 23, August 1948, p. 77; Newsweek 29, January 27, 1947, p. 29.　　2756

1968
Devlin, Polly
  "Eunice Shriver Kennedy, the Spark." Vogue 151, March 1, 1968, p. 160-162.
　　　　　　　　　2757

Robert Sargent Shriver, Jr.

Robert Sargent Shriver, Jr., husband of Eunice Kennedy Shriver, was born in Westminster, Maryland, on November 9, 1915. He prepared for Yale University at the Canterbury School, New Milford, Connecticut, graduating from Yale in 1938 (cum laude), and receiving his LL.B. degree from Yale Law School in 1941.

He enlisted in the United States Navy in 1940 as a seaman, and when mustered out of service in 1945, he had achieved the rank of Lieutenant-Commander. Prior to entering the Navy he had worked as an attorney for the law firm of Winthrop, Stimson, Putnam and Roberts. In 1941 he was admitted to practice before the New York State bar, and Illinois granted him the same permission in 1959.

Mr. Shriver was employed as an Editor for Newsweek Magazine during the years of 1945-46; in 1946 he became associated with the Joseph P. Kennedy Enterprises. During the year of 1947 Sargent Shriver assisted Eunice Kennedy in establishing the National Conference on Juvenile Delinquency, in Washington, D.C., and worked closely with the Attorney-General. From 1948 to 1961 he held the position of Assistant General Manager of the Merchandise Mart, Chicago, Ill., one of the holdings of the Kennedy family.

During the 1960 presidential campaign of John F. Kennedy, Shriver served as an adviser. In 1961 President Kennedy appointed him as first Director of the Peace Corps, a post which took him all over the world in implementation of Peace Corps policy. In September of 1961, Congress placed the Peace Corps on a permanent basis, appropriating funds on a regular basis.

President Lyndon B. Johnson appointed Sargent Shriver first Director of the Office of Economic Opportunity in 1966, by virtue of the keen administrative insight he displayed in the overwhelming success of the Peace Corps. He held this position until April of 1968, and during his two-year tour of duty he was able to bring the problems of the poor before

Robert Sargent Shriver, Jr.   253

government officials as well as before the rank-and-file of
American citizens. It was his aim that the poor become involved in programs leading to their own betterment, that
they should become active in local community activities, as
well as in local politics.

In April of 1968 President Johnson appointed Sargent
Shriver U.S. Ambassador to France. The appointment was
heralded as a coup for President Johnson, in view of the fact
that French President de Gaulle highly regarded members of
the Kennedy family.

Robert Sargent Shriver, Jr., and Eunice Kennedy were
married on May 23, 1953. Their children are Robert Sargent, III; Maria; Timothy; Mark Kennedy; and Paul Fitzgerald
Kennedy. The Shrivers maintain a residence in Washington,
D.C., but since the Spring of 1968 they have resided in
Paris, France, where Mr. Shriver has been serving as U.S.
Ambassador to France.

While he resided in Chicago and in Washington, D.C.,
Sargent Shriver was active in the civil affairs of both cities.
He has also been Executive Director of the Joseph P. Kennedy, Jr. Foundation. A veritable host of colleges and universities have awarded him honorary doctoral degrees, among
them St. Louis University, Brandeis, Notre Dame, Duquesne,
Fordham, Yale and Georgetown.

A prolific author of periodical articles on the Peace
Corps and the war on poverty, Sargent Shriver wrote a book
(published by Harper and Row in 1964) incisively detailing
the development and accomplishments of the Peace Corps,
entitled The Point of the Lance.

Books by Robert Sargent Shriver

1962
Shriver, Robert S.
  Meet the press: guest, Sargent Shriver, Director, the
Peace Corps. Washington,
Merkle Press, 1962, 11p.
                                              2758

1964
Shriver, Robert S.
  The first year was tough
(In Madow, Pauline, ed. The
Peace Corps. New York,
Wilson, 1964, p. 57-67).
                                              2759

Shriver, Robert S.
  Meet the press: guest,
Sargent Shriver, Director,
the Peace Corps. Washington,
Merkle Press, 1964, 11p. 2760

Shriver, Robert S.
The Peace Corps' strength (In Madow, Pauline, ed. The Peace Corps. New York, Wilson, 1964, p. 158-163). 2761

Shriver, Robert S.
Peace Corps successes (In Madow, Pauline, ed. The Peace Corps. New York, Wilson, 1964, p. 99-104). 2762

Shriver, Robert S.
The point of the lance. New York, Harper & Row, 1964, 240p. 2763

Shriver, Robert S.
Some questions and answers (In Madow, Pauline, ed. The Peace Corps. New York, Wilson, 1964, p. 146-148). 2764

1965
Shriver, Robert S.
Meet the press: guest, Sargent Shriver, Director, Office of Economic Opportunity. Washington, Merkle Press, 1965, 11p. 2765

1966
Shriver, Robert S.
Poverty in the United States: what next? (In Goodman, Leonard H., ed. Economic progress and social welfare; papers presented at a workshop organized by the Bureau of Social Science Research under contract with the Welfare Administration, Dept. of Health, Education and Welfare, in December 1965. Published for the National Conference on Social Welfare. New York, Columbia University Press, 1966, p. 55-66). 2766

1967
Shriver, Robert S.
Meet the press: guest, Sargent Shriver, Director, Office of Economic Opportunity. Washington, Merkle Press, 1967, 11p. 2767

Articles by
Robert Sargent Shriver

1961
Shriver, Robert S.
"The Peace Corps: its Director Tells What to Expect." U.S. news & world report 50, April 3, 1961, p. 90. 2768

Shriver, Robert S.
"The Peace Corps Needs Farm Men and Women." Successful farming 59, July 1961, p. 17. 2769

1962
Shriver, Robert S.
"The Job was Tough. Address, March 6, 1962." Vital speeches 28, April 15, 1962, p. 407-411. 2770

Shriver, Robert S.
"A Blow for Freedom." I.U.D. digest 7, Fall 1962, p. 3-13. 2771

1963
Shriver, Robert S.
"When Peace Corps Teachers Return." NEA journal 52, March 1963, p. 13-15. 2772

Shriver, Robert S.
"Peace Corps Lawyers:

Building Emerging African Societies: Need for Volunteer Lawyers." American Bar Association journal 49, May 1963, p. 456-459. 2773

Shriver, Robert S.
"I Have the Best Job in Washington." New York times magazine, June 9, 1963, p. 34-35. 2774

Shriver, Robert S.
"Peace Corps: Frontier for Youth." Parents' magazine 38, July 1963, p. 46-47. 2775

Shriver, Robert S.
"Two Years of the Peace Corps." Foreign affairs 41, July 1963, p. 694-707. 2776

1964

Shriver, Robert S.
"A Close Look at the Peace Corps and its Volunteers." U.S. news & world report 56, January 6, 1964, p. 38-41. 2777

Shriver, Robert S.
"A new Breed of American." Occupational outlook quarterly 8, February 1964, p. 1-4. 2778

Shriver, Robert S.
"Message to American Librarians." Wilson Library bulletin 38, June 1964, p. 833. 2779

Shriver, Robert S.
"Public Service and the Voluntary Spirit." Good government 81, Summer 1964, p. 12-16. 2780

Shriver, Robert S.
"Frontier of Service: Address Delivered June 8, 1964." America 111, July 4, 1964, p. 14-16. 2781

Shriver, Robert S.
"Ambassadors of Goodwill: the Peace Corps." National geographic magazine 126, September 1964, p. 297-345. 2782

Shriver, Robert S.
"The Challenge with a Difference." Saturday review 47, December 5, 1964, p. 30. 2783

1965

Shriver, Robert S.
"How Goes the War on Poverty?" Look 29, July 27, 1965, p. 30-32. 2784

Shriver, Robert S.
"The Dispute over Blame for the Los Angeles Riots." U.S. news & world report 59, August 30, 1965, p. 16. 2785

Shriver, Robert S.
"The OEO and Legal Services" (In "Availability of Legal Services: a Symposium." American Bar Association journal 51, November 1965, p. 1064-). 2786

1966

Shriver, Robert S.
"The New Radicalism: Round IV." Partisan review 33, Winter 1966, p. 56-60. 2787

Shriver, Robert S.
"First-hand Report on Poverty War." U.S. news & world report 60, February 28, 1966, p. 64-69. 2788

Shriver, Robert S.
"Excerpt from Address, December 6, 1965." Congressional digest 45, March 1966, p. 80.   2789

Shriver, Robert S.
"The War on Poverty (United States): a 'Giant Stride' Forward." AFL-CIO American federationist 73, April 1966, p. 6-9.   2790

Shriver, Robert S.
"Five Years with the Peace Corps." Saturday review 49, April 23, 1966, p. 14-15.
                                              2791
Shriver, Robert S.
'National Policy' (In "Symposium on Legal Service to the Poor: the Poverty Program." Journal of the State Bar of California 41, May-June 1966, p. 214-).   2792

Shriver, Robert S.
"The War is on Poverty." American county government 31, September 1966, p. 22-24.   2793

Shriver, Robert S.
"Symposium on Legal Aid: Opportunity or Octopus? Foreword." Washington & Lee law review 23, Fall 1966, p. 235.
                                              2794
Shriver, Robert S.
'How Lawyers can Break the Poverty Barrier." Illinois Bar journal 55, October 1966, p. 118.   2795

Shriver, Robert S.
"Change of Emphasis for the Poverty War?" U.S. news & world report 61, December 5, 1966, p. 10.   2796

Shriver, Robert S.
"The Moral Basis of the War on Poverty." Christian century 83, December 14, 1966, p. 1531-1533.   2797

1967
Shriver, Robert S.
"Towards a National Purpose: the War on Poverty." Public relations journal 23, January 1967, p. 10-12. 2798

Shriver, Robert S.
'Rural Poverty: the Problem and the Challenge' (In "Symposium: the War on Poverty, Legal Services and the Rural Poor." Kansas law review 15, May 1967, p. 401-).   2799

Shriver, Robert S.
'Observations of an Optimist." America 117, November 18, 1967, p. 594-595.
                                              2800

Books about
Robert Sargent Shriver

1961
Evening Star (periodical), Washington, D.C.
New frontiersmen. Washington, Public Affairs Press, 1961, p. 212.   2801

U.S. Congress. Senate. Committee on Foreign Relations Nomination of Robert Sargent Shriver, Jr. to be Director of the Peace Corps. Hearings before the Commit-

Robert Sargent Shriver, Jr.   257

tee, U.S. Senate, 87th Congress, first session...March 21, 1961. Washington, G.P.O., 1961, 60p. 2802

1964
Liston, Robert A.
Sargent Shriver: a candid portrait. New York, Farrar, Straus & Giroux, 1964, 209p. 2803

U.S. Congress. Senate. Labor & Public Welfare Committee
Nomination, hearing, 88th Congress, 2d session, on Robert Sargent Shriver, to be Director of Office of Economic Opportunity; September 9, 1964. Washington, 1964, 12p. 2804

1965
Webb, Robert N.
Leaders of our time. New York, Watts, 1965, p. 91-101. (Children's book). 2805

Articles about Robert Sargent Shriver

1961
Knebel, Fletcher
"On Trial: Sargent Shriver and the Peace Corps." Look 25, November 7, 1961, p. 34-37. 2806

Braestrup, P.
"Peace Corpsman Number 1: a Progress Report." New York times magazine, December 17, 1961, p. 11. 2807

1962
"People are Talking about Mr. & Mrs. Robert Sargent Shriver, Jr." Vogue 140, October 1, 1962, p. 150-151. 2808

1963
"It is Almost as Good as its Intentions." Time 82, July 5, 1963, p. 18-22. 2809

1964
"Robert Sargent Shriver." Congressional quarterly, January 1964, p. 71. 2810

"Field Marshall in Poverty War." Business week, March 7, 1964, p. 28-29. 2811

"Where $1 Billion Will go: LBJ's Anti-poverty Program." Business week, March 21, 1964, p. 29-30. 2812

Kempton, Murray
"The Essential Sargent Shriver." New republic 150, March 28, 1964, p. 12-14. 2813

Stolley, Robert B.
"Shriver of the Peace Corps: Handsome, Busy, hot Government Property." Life 56, May 1, 1964, p. 41-42. 2814

Mothner, I.
"What Next for Sargent Shriver?" Look 28, June 16, 1964, p. 77-78. 2815

Raskin, A.H.
"Generalissimo of the War on Poverty." New York times magazine, November 22, 1964, p. 39. 2816

1965
Spivak, Jonathan
"Spotlight on Shriver."

Wall Street journal 165, June 4, 1965, p. 1. 2817

"Just one job for Shriver? How LBJ Plans to end Furor." U.S. news & world report 58, June 21, 1965, p. 22. 2818

"People of the Week." U.S. news & world report 58, June 21, 1965, p. 22. 2819

"Progress, Protest and Politics." Time 86, July 16, 1965, p. 19-20. 2820

"Shriver and the War on Poverty." Newsweek 66, September 13, 1965, p. 22-26. 2821

Haddad, William F.
"Mr. Shriver and the Savage Politics of Poverty." Harper's magazine 231, December 1965, p. 43-50. 2822

1966

"One Man, One Job." Newsweek 67, January 31, 1966, p. 22-23. 2823

"Shriver Leaves the Peace Corps." America 114, February 5, 1966, p. 186. 2824

"Grilled Shriver." Time 87, April 22, 1966, p. 21. 2825

"By or for the Poor?" New republic 154, April 30, 1966, p. 5-6. 2826

Carter, B.
"Sargent Shriver and the Role of the Poor." The reporter 34, May 5, 1966, p. 17-20. 2827

"War Within the War." Time 87, May 13, 1966, p. 25-29. 2828

Lens, Sidney
"Shriver's Limited War." Commonweal 84, July 1, 1966, p. 412-414. 2829

"Too Many Abuses in a big Poverty Project?" U.S. news & world report 61, November 7, 1966, p. 14-15. 2830

"Shriving Shriver." Christian century 83, November 23, 1966, p. 1431-1432. 2831

"Little by Little, Less and Less of the OEO." New republic 155, December 10, 1966, p. 10-11. 2832

1967

Mothner, I.
"Nickel Revolution." Look 31, June 13, 1967, p. 34-35. 2833

1968

"Still on the Johnson Team: Sargent Shriver." U.S. news & world report 64, April 1, 1968, p. 8. 2834

Patricia (Kennedy) Lawford

Patricia Kennedy was born in Brookline, Massachusetts, on May 6, 1924. While her father, Joseph P. Kennedy, served as the American Ambassador to Great Britain during the years 1937-40, Patricia attended the Sacred Heart convent school in Roehampton, England. Rosemont College was the institution which granted Patricia her A.B. degree in 1947; in the same year she obtained a position as an assistant in the National Broadcasting Company's production department, in New York City. Continuing her interest in theatrical activities, Patricia moved to California in 1951 to work in script preparation and general production of the radio and television programs of the Family Theater, under the direction of Father Patrick Peyton.

On April 25, 1954 Patricia Kennedy and actor Peter Lawford were married in the Church of St. Thomas More, in New York City. The marriage was the culmination of a friendship of over two years' standing. Christopher, the Lawford's first child, was born on April 5, 1955, and since then two daughters arrived, Sydney, and Victoria Francis. Mr. and Mrs. Lawford purchased the palatial estate of the late Hollywood tycoon, Louis B. Mayer, in Santa Monica, California. Among their friends were many of the movie idols, including Frank Sinatra, Judy Garland, Dean Martin, Tony Curtis and Sammy Davis, Jr. Mr. and Mrs. Lawford established their own firm to produce films for television. Patricia Lawford was prominent in Democratic political activities in the state of California; during the Democratic National Convention at Los Angeles in 1960, the Lawford residence was headquarters for the Kennedy family. Patricia herself aided in the very first election campaign of President Kennedy, when he ran as a Congressional candidate from Massachusetts in 1946.

After the couple's divorce in the mid-1960's, Patricia Kennedy Lawford established residence in New York City with her children.

Articles about Mrs. Patricia (Kennedy) Lawford

1953
"Haitian Holiday." House & garden 104, July 1953, p. 38.   2835

1954
"Wedding Season." Vogue 123, June 1954, p. 80-81.   2836

1964
"Barred from 117 East 72nd Street." Newsweek 63, April 20, 1964, p. 44.   2837

1966
"Catholic Church Opposes Divorce Reform." Christian century 83, February 16, 1966, p. 197.   2838

Robert Francis Kennedy

Robert Francis Kennedy was born in Brookline, Massachusetts on November 20, 1925. He prepared for college at Milton Academy, Milton, Massachusetts, from which he was graduated in 1943. After studying at Harvard for one year, he enlisted in the United States Navy. While in officer's training school, he requested re-assignment to serve as a seaman on the Joseph P. Kennedy, Jr., a destroyer named in honor of his brother who was killed as a Navy pilot over Europe during World War II. In 1946 he returned to Harvard, graduating with a bachelor's degree. In 1948 Robert covered the Arab-Israeli War as a correspondent for the Boston Post. He later attended the University of Virginia Law School, graduating with an LL.B. degree in 1950. On June 17, 1950 Robert married Ethel Skakel of Greenwich, Connecticut. In 1967 their tenth child, Douglas, was born to them, and their first nine children are Kathleen H., Joseph P., Robert F., Jr., David A., Mary C., Michael L., Mary K., Christopher G., and Matthew M.T. Rory, their youngest daughter, was born in December of 1968 some six months after her father's death, and is also his namesake.

The Massachusetts bar admitted Robert F. Kennedy to practice before it in 1951, and in 1955 the Supreme Court did likewise. In 1954 the United States Chamber of Commerce chose him as one of its ten outstanding young men.

Robert's first professional post was in the Criminal Division of the U.S. Dept. of Justice. He then served as chief counsel for the minority (i.e., Democratic Party) of the Permanent Subcommittee on Investigations of the Government Operations Committee of the Senate; in 1957 he became chief counsel of the Senate Select Committee to Investigate Improper Activities in Labor-Management Relations. As a result of his work, Robert was able to demonstrate proof of corruption in the Laundry, Cleaning and Dyehouse, and the Bakery and Confectionery Workers International Unions, as well as in the International Teamsters Union, all of which were later expelled from the AFL-CIO.

Active in all of President John F. Kennedy's political campaigns, Robert resigned his position in the autumn of

1959 to manage the 1960 presidential campaign of his brother. Many factors combined to present John F. Kennedy with a campaign victory in 1960, not the least of these being Robert's managerial ability, innate political sense, and a selfless involvement in his work above and beyond the call of duty. In January 1961 Robert F. Kennedy was appointed (and subsequently approved by the Senate) as Attorney-General.

As Attorney-General Robert dealt with the matters of antitrust legislation, civil rights, organized crime and labor racketeering. In antitrust activities, the Justice Dept. succeeded in its request that Congress pass the Antitrust Civil Process Act, whereby corporations must supply evidence in antitrust investigations of a civil nature. Likewise, the Justice Dept. was successful in passage, by Congress, of legislation with respect to gambling and racketeering, as well as narcotics control. Mail fraud, misbranded and unfit food and drugs were additional matters handled by the Justice Dept. in very-greatly increased instances since 1961, after which time Robert F. Kennedy instituted an intelligence unit in its Criminal Division.

In the civil rights activities of the Kennedy administration, Robert played a leading role. His involvement in protecting the "freedom riders," who sought equal rights in transportation for Negroes in the South, and his efforts in securing the entrance of the first Negro student at the University of Mississippi are but two of the many instances in which he displayed his beliefs in civil rights. The feeling was not perfunctory, for in 1961 he resigned from the Metropolitan Club in Washington, D.C., due to its refusal to accept Negroes as members.

Robert F. Kennedy demonstrated his belief in the importance of preventing and controlling juvenile delinquency. Based partly on his testimony and assistance, Congress appropriated funds for training juvenile delinquency specialists. In various articles, Robert had written about "half-way houses," which aid youths paroled from prisons in readjusting to a normal, useful way of life.

In the Spring of 1962 Robert testified before the House of Representatives' Commerce Committee in support of a bill for public control of a corporation to operate a worldwide satellite-communications system, in opposition to monopoly ownership by the American Telephone and Telegraph Company. He argued that the general public is entitled to obtain profits from such a public corporation, since the bill specified dividend payments and voting rights for the stock-owning public, while communication company-owned shares would pay neither dividends nor allow such companies voting rights.

An inveterate traveller, Robert F. Kennedy made several trips to various world areas (in 1955 he accompanied Justice William O. Douglas on a walking tour of six Asian republics of the Soviet Union). On many of these trips he addressed student groups, and in Johannesburg, South Africa, in the summer of 1966, he spoke on civil rights matters before university students and the local bar association. In addition to civil rights he assisted President John F. Kennedy in dealing with the Bay of Pigs matter, advising that a quarantine on shipping to Cuba would avoid possible hostilities.

Robert F. Kennedy was the first brother of a President ever to have been a cabinet member. He had written many articles in the field of law and on political topics, and was the author of four outstanding works: The Enemy Within (based on his work as a Justice Dept. attorney, published in 1961); Just Friends and Brave Enemies, a 1962 book, which discusses international problems; The Pursuit of Justice, edited by Theodore J. Lowi and issued in 1964; and To Seek a Newer World, a 1967 work detailing in depth the solutions to many of the problems in the domestic as well as international spheres facing America in the late 1960's. In addition, his speeches were edited by Thomas A. Hopkins (in a book published in 1964 by Bobbs-Merrill) entitled Rights for Americans; speeches.

After the assassination of President John F. Kennedy, Robert continued as Attorney-General. He resigned in 1964, however, to campaign for (and eventually to win) a Senate seat from New York. As a senator he demonstrated unusual political acumen and forthrightness. He served on the Senate Committees for Government Operations, Labor and Public Welfare, and the District of Columbia. His frequent, meaty magazine articles, and his distinctive speeches on radio and television on both domestic and international matters placed him in the forefront of Senate leaders.

Robert F. Kennedy was a member of the Board of Visitors of the University of Virginia Law School, the Advisory Council of the University of Notre Dame Law School, of the Federal, New York and American Bar Associations, the Veterans of Foreign Wars, and the American Legion. He was also President of the Foundation for All Africa. In 1958 the University of Notre Dame presented him with its Patriotism Award, and he held honorary doctoral degrees from Assumption College, Mt. St. Mary's College, Manhattan College, Fordham, Marquette and Tufts Universities, as well as from Nihon University of Japan, the University of the Philippines, and the Free University of Berlin.

Following the assassination of his brother in 1963, his quality of belief in fate became pronounced. This belief was spelled out, in early spring of 1968 (when he decided to campaign for the presidency), when in reply to a suggestion that he wait until 1972, he answered: "How does any of us know that he'll be around in 1972?" In his campaign work and on countrywide tours, he campaigned and won primary elections in many states, including Indiana, South Dakota and California. In the early hours of June 5, 1968, just after he made a victory speech carried over television from the Ambassador Hotel in Los Angeles, California, he was shot and critically wounded. Frantic efforts to save his life were in vain, and he died at approximately 1:40 A.M., June 6, 1968. On the same day his family and close friends (including Pierre Salinger, Kenneth O'Donnell and others on his campaign staff who had worked for President John F. Kennedy) accompanied his body by airplane to New York City, where it lay in state. On June 8, a mass was said at St. Patrick's Cathedral in New York City, and immediately afterward the same group accompanied the body by train to Washington, D.C., where Robert F. Kennedy was buried the night of June 8, 1968 at Arlington National Cemetery, beside his assassinated brother, President John F. Kennedy.

In the tradition of his brother, the President, Robert F. Kennedy tried to right the wrongs he saw in society, to help those who were underprivileged, to fight for the right. In his eulogy to Robert F. Kennedy, delivered on June 8, 1968 at St. Patrick's Cathedral, his brother, Senator Edward M. Kennedy of Massachusetts quoted Robert F. Kennedy's often-repeated remark: "Some men see things as they are and ask why. I dream things that never were and say why not."

Books by Robert F. Kennedy

1960

Kennedy, Robert F.
The enemy within. New York, Harper, 1960, 338p.
2839

Kennedy, Robert F.
The enemy within. New York, Popular Library, 1960, 320p.
2840

Kennedy, Robert F.
El enemigo en casa (The enemy within, translated into Spanish by J. Ferrer Aleu). Barcelona, Plaza & Janés, 1962, 442p.
2841

Kennedy, Robert F.
Gangster drängen zur macht (The enemy within, translated into German). 1st ed. Bern, Scherz Verlag, 1964, 263p.
2842

Kennedy, Robert F.
Naibu no teki (The enemy within, translated into Japanese by Yozô Hatano & Yokobori Yôichi). 5th ed. Tokyo, Nihon Gaisei Gakkai, 1964, 457p.
2843

Kennedy, Robert F.
Ma lutte contre la corruption (The enemy within, translated into French by Gloria de Cherisey Phillips). Paris, Laffont, 1965, 408p.
2844

Kennedy, Robert F.
Den indre fjende (The enemy within, translated into Danish). Copenhagen, Samleren, 1966, 287p.
2845

1962

Kennedy, Robert F.
"We must meet our duty and convince the world that we are just friends and brave enemies." 1st ed. New York, Harper & Row, 1962, 211p.
2846

Kennedy, Robert F.
Dongeng dan Kenjataan; lapuran perdjalanan keliling dunia, oleh Robert F. Kennedy ("We must meet our duty and convince the world that we are just friends and brave enemies," translated into Indonesian). Djakarta, Kantor Penerangan Amerika Serikat, 196- , 27p.
2847

Kennedy, Robert F.
Devemos convincer o mundo de que somos amigos leais e bravos inimigos (Just friends and brave enemies, translated into Portuguese). Rio de Janeiro, Record, 1962, 196p.
2848

Kennedy, Robert F.
Jiyû no hata no moto ni (Just friends and brave enemies, translated into Japanese by Yûzo Hatano). Tokyo, Nihon Gaisei Gakkai, 1962, 288p.
2849

Kennedy, Robert F.
Jeog-gwa dongji (Just friends and brave enemies, translated into Korean by Gyu-jeong Kim). Seoul, Sintaeyangsa, 1964, 342p. 2850

Kennedy, Robert F.
Epith opith (Just friends

and brave enemies, translated into Bengali by Farida Khatoon). Dacca, Khosroze Kitab Mahal, 1965, 198p. 2851

1964
Kennedy, Robert F.
Rights for Americans; speeches. Ed. & with commentary by Thomas A. Hopkins. Indianapolis, Bobbs-Merrill, 1964, 262p. 2852

Kennedy, Robert F.
The pursuit of justice. Ed. by Theodore J. Lowi. New York, Harper, 1964, 148p. 2853

Kennedy, Robert F.
The pursuit of justice. Ed. by Theodore J. Lowi. London, H. Hamilton, 1965, 149p. 2854

Kennedy, Robert F.
Em busca da justiça (The pursuit of justice, translated into Portuguese by Pinheiro de Lemos). Rio de Janeiro, Record, 1965, 151p. 2855

1967
Kennedy, Robert F.
The quotable Robert F. Kennedy. Comp. & ed. by Sue G. Hall & the staff of Quote. Indianapolis, Maxwell Droke, 1967, 208p. 2856

Kennedy, Robert F.
To seek a newer world. Garden City, Doubleday, 1967, 233p. 2857

1968
Kennedy, Robert F.
A new day. New York, New American Library, 1968, 157p. 2858

Reviews of Books by Robert F. Kennedy

1960
Kennedy, Robert F.
The enemy within. New York, Harper, 1960, 338p.
Reviewed in:
America 102, March 26, 1960, p. 770.
ALA booklist & subscription books bulletin 56, March 15, 1960, p. 438.
Bookmark 19, July 1960, p. 258.
Critic 18, May 1960, p. 29.
Christian Science monitor, February 24, 1960, p. 2.
Foreign affairs 38, July 1960, p. 687.
Library journal 85, February 1, 1960, p. 671.
New republic 142, February 29, 1960, p. 15.
New York herald tribune book review, February 28, 1960, p. 5.
New York times book review, February 28, 1960, p. 22.
Saturday review 43, February 27, 1960, p. 21. 2859

1962
Kennedy, Robert F.
Just friends and brave enemies. New York, Harper, 1960, 211p.
Reviewed in:
ALA booklist & subscription books bulletin 59, September 1, 1962, p. 10.
Best sellers 22, September 15, 1962, p. 240.
Bookmark 22, October 1962, p. 5.

Christian Science monitor,
August 23, 1962, p. 7.
Extension 57, October 1962,
p. 10.
Bulletin, Virginia Kirkus service (30), July 15, 1962,
p. 657.
Library journal 87, October
1, 1962, p. 3459.
New York herald tribune book
review, August 26, 1962,
p. 6.
New York times book review,
August 26, 1962, p. 34.
Saturday review 45, September 8, 1962, p. 22.
Sign 42, November 1962, p.
69. 2860

1964-65
Kennedy, Robert F.
The pursuit of justice. Ed.
by Theodore J. Lowi. New
York, Harper, 1964,
148p.
Reviewed in:
Book week, November 1, 1964,
p. 4.
Critic 23, February-March
1965, p. 77.
Library journal 89, December
1, 1964, p. 4821.
Times literary supplement
(London), September 9,
1965, p. 773. 2861

Kennedy, Robert F.
Rights for Americans: the
speeches of Robert F. Kennedy. Ed. by Thomas A. Hopkins. Indianapolis, Bobbs-Merrill, 1964, 262p.
Reviewed in:
ALA booklist & subscription
books bulletin 61, January
15, 1965, p. 448.
Choice 2, November 1965,
p. 610.
Christian century 81, December 9, 1964, p. 1537.
Library journal 89, November 1, 1964, p. 4366.
Quarterly journal of speech
51, April 1965, p. 220.
 2862

1967-68
Kennedy, Robert F.
To seek a newer world.
Garden City, Doubleday,
1967, 233p.
Reviewed in:
America 118, January 13,
1968, p. 42.
Book world, March 10, 1968,
p. 6.
Christian Science monitor,
December 28, 1967, p. 5.
Bulletin, Virginia Kirkus
service (35), November 1,
1967, p. 1352.
Library journal 93, January
1, 1968, p. 88.
New republic 157, December
2, 1967, p. 29.
New York times book review, December 17, 1967,
p. 12.
Publishers weekly 192, October 30, 1967, p. 47. 2863

Speeches and Statements
of Robert F. Kennedy

1961
Kennedy, Robert F.
Addresses by Robert F.
Kennedy, attorney general of
the United States. [n.p.]
1961- 2864

Kennedy, Robert F.
Meet the press: guest,
Robert F. Kennedy, the Attorney-General. Washington,
Merkle Press, 1961, 9p. 2865

1963
Kennedy, Robert F.
Aggada u-meziut (Legend
and reality, translated into
Hebrew). Tel Aviv, Serut haHasbara šel Arzot ha-Berit,
1963, 27p. 2866

Kennedy, Robert F.
An anticonspiracy law (In
East, Sara T., ed. Law in
American society. New York,
Wilson, 1963, p. 85-88). 2867

Kennedy, Robert F.
Meet the press: guest,
Robert F. Kennedy, Attorney
General of the United States.
Washington, 1963, 10p. 2868

Kennedy, Robert F.
Remarks by Attorney-General Robert F. Kennedy before
the National Congress of American Indians, Grand Pacific
Hotel, Bismarck, North Dakota, September 13, 1963. Washington, Dept. of Justice, 1963,
6p. 2869

1964
Kennedy, Robert F.
Meet the press: guest,
Robert F. Kennedy, Democratic candidate for senator
from the state of New York.
Washington, Merkle Press,
1964, 11p. 2870

1965
Kennedy, Robert F.
Kennedy contesta a universitarios. Caracas? 1965?
22p.
(Interview with university
students of various political
parties in Caracas, Venezuela, November 30, 1965).
2871
Kennedy, Robert F.
Meet the press: guest,
Senator Robert F. Kennedy,
New York, Democrat. Washington, Merkle Press, 1965,
11p. 2872

1966
Kennedy, Robert F.
The Alliance for Progress:
symbol and substance. Speech
...in the Senate of the United
States, May 9 and 10, 1966.
Washington, 1966, 20p. 2873

1968
Kennedy, Robert F.
Thirteen days: a memoir
of the Cuban Missile Crisis.
Introduction by Robert S. McNamara and Harold Macmillan. New York, Norton,
1968, 224p. 2874

Articles by
Robert F. Kennedy

1955
Kennedy, Robert F.
"Look Behind the Russian
Smiles: Interview, with Biographical Sketch." U.S. news
& world report 39, October
21, 1955, p. 62-67. 2875

1956
Kennedy, Robert F.
"The Soviet Brand of Colonialism." New York times
magazine, April 8, 1956,

p. 9. 2876

1959
Kennedy, Robert F.
"Gangster Invasion of Business Grows: Interview." Nation's business 47, May 1959, p. 41. 2877

Kennedy, Robert F.
"Urgent Reform Plan." Life 46, June 1, 1959, p. 114. 2878

1960
Kennedy, Robert F.
"The Enemy Within (Condensation)." Reader's digest 76, March 1960, p. 90-97. 2879

Kennedy, Robert F.
"On Labor Racketeering." Information 74, May 1960, p. 20-24. 2880

1961
Kennedy, Robert F.
"Robert Kennedy Examines the Electric Company Scandals." Life 50, February 24, 1961, p. 30-32. 2881

Kennedy, Robert F.
"Robert Kennedy Speaks out: Interview, with Biographical Sketch, Edited by Peter Maas." Look 25, March 28, 1961, p. 23-26. 2882

Kennedy, Robert F.
"Attorney General Speaks." America 105, May 20, 1961, p. 304. 2883

Kennedy, Robert F.
"Civil Rights: Address, May 6, 1961." Vital speeches 27, June 1, 1961, p. 482-485. 2884

Kennedy, Robert F.
"Attorney-General: Interview." New Yorker 37, June 24, 1961, p. 19-21. 2885

Kennedy, Robert F.
"Robert Kennedy Talks of Government and Business: Interview." U.S. news & world report 51, September 25, 1961, p. 40-45. 2886

Kennedy, Robert F.
"More Light on the 'Freedom Rides'..." U.S. news & world report 51, October 30, 1961, p. 70-71. 2887

Kennedy, Robert F.
"Government and Business: Robert Kennedy Gives his View." U.S. news & world report 51, November 27, 1961, p. 106-107. 2888

Kennedy, Robert F.
"Justice is Found in the Hearts and Minds of Free Men." Federal probation 25, December 1961, p. 3. 2889

Kennedy, Robert F.
"Vigorous Antitrust Enforcement Assists Business: Address, November 13, 1961." Vital speeches 28, December 15, 1961, p. 134-136. 2890

1962
Kennedy, Robert F.
"Respect for Law." American Bar Association journal 48, January 1962, p. 31. 2891

Kennedy, Robert F.
"Address by Attorney General Robert F. Kennedy."

Fordham law review 30, February 1962, p. 437. 2892

Kennedy, Robert F.
"Buying it back from the Indians." Life 52, March 23, 1962, p. 17. 2893

Kennedy, Robert F.
"The Baleful Influence of Gambling." The Atlantic 209, April 1962, p. 76-79. 2894

Kennedy, Robert F.
"Attorney-General Explains U.S. Goals to People of Japan, Indonesia and Germany." Dept. of State bulletin 46, May 7, 1962, p. 761-764. 2895

Kennedy, Robert F.
"Communism in the U.S.: the Facts; Interview." Sign 41, June 1962, p. 7-10. 2896

Kennedy, Robert F.
"Misinformation and Misunderstanding About the United States: Address, April 23, 1962." Vital speeches 28, June 1, 1962, p. 495-497. 2897

Kennedy, Robert F.
"Attorney-General's Opinion on Wiretaps." New York times magazine, June 3, 1962, p. 21. 2898

Kennedy, Robert F.
"Address." Federal rules & decisions 30, August 1962, p. 422. 2899

Kennedy, Robert F.
"Three Weapons Against Organized Crime." Crime & delinquency 8, October 1962, p. 321- 2900

"From Robert Kennedy: Tough Talk in Brazil." U.S. news & world report 53, December 31, 1962, p. 11. 2901

1963
Kennedy, Robert F.
"The Program of the Dept. of Justice on Organized Crime." (In "Interstate Organized Crime Symposium." Notre Dame lawyer 38, Symposium 1963, p. 627-).2902

Kennedy, Robert F.
"Robert Kennedy Speaks his Mind About the First two Years of his Brother's Administration, and Looks into the Future." U.S. news & world report 54, January 28, 1963, p. 54-65. 2903

Kennedy, Robert F.
"Setting the Record Straight: What U.S. News & World Report Said About air Support at the Bay of Pigs." U.S. news & world report 54, February 4, 1963, p. 31. 2904

Kennedy, Robert F.
"Free Trade in Ideas: Excerpts from Address." Saturday review 46, February 16, 1963, p. 43-44.2905

Kennedy, Robert F.
"The Antitrust Aims of the Justice Dept." (In "Symposium on Antitrust." New York law forum 9, March 1963, p. 1-). 2906

Kennedy, Robert F.
"What About a Peace Corps Spirit at Home?" Saturday review 46, May 25, 1963, p. 20-21.　　　　　　　2907

Kennedy, Robert F.
"Criminal Law: a Symposium, Foreword." University of Florida law review 16, Fall 1963, p. 143.　　　　　2908

Kennedy, Robert F.
"Robert Kennedy Defines the Menace." New York times magazine, October 13, 1963, p. 15.　　　　　　　　2909

"Lawyer's Duty in 'Civil Rights,' pro and con: Are Lawyers who Take Cases that Challenge Civil Rights Statutes and Court Decisions 'Professionally Irresponsible'? The Sanctity of the Law is in Jeopardy, by Robert F. Kennedy..." U.S. news & world report 55, October 14, 1963, p. 120-123.　　　　　　　　2910

Kennedy, Robert F.
"The Sanctity of the Law is in Jeopardy: Address, September 27, 1963." U.S. news & world report 55, October 14, 1963, p. 120-122.　　2911

Kennedy, Robert F.
"Letter from Attorney-General to the Secretary of State Concerning Legal Questions Raised by the Proposed Wheat Sales to the Soviet Union and Eastern European Countries." Dept. of State bulletin 49, October 28, 1963, p. 661-667.　　　　　　　　　2912

Kennedy, Robert F.
"Civil Rights and the South: a Symposium. Introduction." North Carolina law review 42, December 1963, p. 1- .
　　　　　　　　　　2913

1964
Kennedy, Robert F.
"Criminal Justice." William & Mary law review 5, 1964, p. 167.　　　　2914

Kennedy, Robert F.
"The Dept. of Justice and the Indigent Accused." (In Reardon, P.C. "New England Defender Conference: a Summary Report." Journal of the American Judicature Society 47, January 1964, p. 159-).
　　　　　　　　　　2915

Kennedy, Robert F.
"Halfway Houses pay off." Crime & delinquency 10, January 1964, p. 1.　　2916

Kennedy, Robert F.
"Robert Kennedy's Tribute to JFK." Look 28, February 25, 1964, p. 37-38.　　2917

Kennedy, Robert F.
"Bold Proposal for American Sport." Sports illustrated 21, July 27, 1964, p. 12-15.　　　　　　　　　2918

Kennedy, Robert F.
"Amateur Sports Face Crisis" (condensed from Sports illustrated, July 27, 1964). Catholic digest 29, November 1964, p. 70-72.
　　　　　　　　　　2919

1965
Kennedy, Robert F.
"Law Day Address." University of Florida Law School record 13, Winter, 1965, p. 24. 2920

Kennedy, Robert F.
"Robert Kennedy Answers Some Blunt Questions. Edited by O. Fallaci." Look 29, March 9, 1965, p. 60-63. 2921

Kennedy, Robert F.
"Our Climb up Mt. Kennedy." Life 58, April 9, 1965, p. 22-27. 2922

Kennedy, Robert F.
"Educational Television in Canada and Abroad." Toronto, Canadian education & research digest 5, June 1965, p. 122-132. 2923

Kennedy, Robert F.
"A Peak Worthy of the President." National geographic magazine 128, July 1965, p. 5-9. 2924

Kennedy, Robert F.
"Counterinsurgency: Political Action Required, Address, July 9, 1965." Vital speeches 31, August 15, 1965, p. 649-652. 2925

Kennedy, Robert F.
"Senate Election seen as Repudiation of Jewish Vote." Issues 19, September 1965, p. 42-43. 2926

Kennedy, Robert F.
"How LBJ was Chosen: Robert Kennedy's Version." U.S. news & world report 59, September 6, 1965, p. 15. 2927

Kennedy, Robert F.
"Los Angeles Riots: Handling the Topic in Class, Excerpts from Address, August 18, 1965." Senior scholastic, teachers' edition 87 (supplement), October 7, 1965, p. 16-17. 2928

"Bobby on the Bomb." Newsweek 66, October 25, 1965, p. 30-31. 2929

Kennedy, Robert F.
"Why Can't we Make Cars Safer?" Popular science 187, November 1965, p. 63-67. 2930

1966
Kennedy, Robert F.
"Kolonialkriget Hemma." Stockholm, Clarté (39: 1), 1966, p. 5-10. ("Colonial Warfare at Home.") 2931

Kennedy, Robert F.
"We Can Build Safer Cars" (condensed from Popular science, November 1965). Catholic digest 30, March 1966, p. 27-30. 2932

Kennedy, Robert F.
"Vietnam: pro and con of Kennedy's Peace Plan." U.S. news & world report 60, March 7, 1966, p. 104-107. 2933

Kennedy, Robert F.
"Senator Robert Kennedy Explains his Position: Inter-

view on Communist Role in Vietnam." U.S. news & world report 60, March 14, 1966, p. 68-70. 2934

Kennedy, Robert F. "Address to the Johannesburg Bar." Johannesburg, South African law journal 83, August 1966, p. 273-277. 2935

Kennedy, Robert F. "Suppose God is Black." Look 30, August 23, 1966, p. 44-46. 2936

Kennedy, Robert F. "The Alliance for Progress: Symbol and Substance." Bulletin of the atomic scientists 22, November 1966, p. 28-34. 2937

Kennedy, Robert F. "Some Observations on Africa and the World." Africa report 11, November 1966, p. 46-47. 2938

1967
Kennedy, Robert F. "If Men do not Build, how Shall they Live?" Pratt planning papers 4, January 1967, p. 22-26. 2939

Kennedy, Robert F. "Problems of the Cities." Pratt planning papers 4, January 1967, p. 7-21. 2940

Kennedy, Robert F. "RFK's New Moves to Stand Apart from LBJ: Excerpts from Address, February 8, 1967." U.S. news & world report 62, February 20, 1967, p. 21. 2941

Kennedy, Robert F. "What can the Young Believe?" New republic 156, March 11, 1967, p. 11-12. 2942

Kennedy, Robert F. "Vietnam, two Views on Bombing." National Catholic reporter 3, March 15, 1967, p. 5. 2943

Kennedy, Robert F. "Crime in the Cities: Improving the Administration of Criminal Justice." Journal of criminal law 58, June 1967, p. 142-154. 2944

Kennedy, Robert F. "Government Injustice to Business." Nation's business 55, June 1967, p. 70-72. 2945

Kennedy, Robert F. "Redbook Dialogue." Redbook 129, September 1967, p. 74-75. 2946

Kennedy, Robert F. "Crisis in our Cities: Excerpt from The Church and the Urban Racial Crisis, Edited by M. Ahmann and P. Roach." Critic 26, October-November 1967, p. 60-63. 2947

1968
Kennedy, Robert F. "What our Young People are Really Saying (Excerpt from To Seek a Newer World)." Ladies' home journal 85, January 1968, p. 35. 2948

Kennedy, Robert F. "Kennedy on Vietnam: an Unwinnable War." U.S. news

& world report 64, February 19, 1968, p. 10. 2949

Kennedy Robert F.
"Happy Hunting Ground." Pageant (24: 3), September 1968, p. 37-52. (Discusses the under-privileged.) 2950

Kennedy, Robert F.
"Thirteen Days, a Story About how the World Almost Ended." McCall's (XCVI: 2), November 1968, p. 6-9, 148-152, 164-173. 2951

Books about
Robert F. Kennedy

1961
U.S. Congress. Senate. Committee on the Judiciary
Robert F. Kennedy, Attorney-General-designate. Hearings before the Committee on the Judiciary, United States Senate, Eighty-seventh Congress, first session...January 13, 1961. Washington, G.P.O., 1961, 39p. 2952

1962
Gordon, Gray
Robert F. Kennedy, assistant President; the dramatic life story of the second most powerful man in Washington. Derby, Conn., Monarch Books, 1962, 132p. 2953

Thompson, Robert E. & Hortense Myers
Robert F. Kennedy; the brother within. New York, Macmillan, 1962, 224p. 2954

1963
Jacobs, Paul
Extracurricular activities of the McClellan Committee (In his The state of the unions. New York, Atheneum, 1963, p. 71-87). 2955

1965
Gardner, Gerald C.
Robert Kennedy in New York. New York, Random House, 1965, 202p. 2956

Silver, Lily (Jay)
Profiles in success; 40 lives of achievement. New York, Fountainhead Pubs., 1965, p. 193-217. 2957

Thimmesch, Nick & William O. Johnson
Robert Kennedy at 40. New York, Norton, 1965, 304p. 2958

Waters, Bob
Bobby Kennedy, next President of the United States; the inside story on how Bobby Kennedy will succeed President Johnson. Rockville Centre, N.Y., G.C. London Pub. Corp., 1965, 66p. 2959

1966
Adler, Bill, ed.
Dear Senator Kennedy. New York, Dodd, Mead, 1966, 128p. 2960

Brubaker, Herb
Extremism in America today; an interview with Clifford P. Case, Morris B. Abram, and Robert F. Kennedy. Ed. & produced by the

Robert Francis Kennedy

Publication Service of the American Jewish Committee. New York, American Jewish Committee, Institute of Human Relations, 1966, 28p. 2961

1967

DeToledano, Ralph
 Robert F. Kennedy, the man who would be President. New York, Putnam's, 1967, 381p. 2962

Nilson, Ulf
 Robert Kennedy. Malmö, Forsberg, 1967, 158p. (In Swedish). 2963

Nicholas, William
 The Bobby Kennedy nobody knows. Greenwich, Fawcett Pubs., 1967, unpaged. 2964

Schaap, Dick
 RFK. Picture editor: Michael O'Keefe. New York, New American Library, 1967, 201p. 2965

Shannon, William V.
 Heir apparent: Robert Kennedy and the struggle for power. New York, Macmillan, 1967, 309p. 2966

1968

Kimball, Penn
 Bobby Kennedy and the new politics. Englewood Cliffs, Prentice-Hall, 1968, 214p. 2967

Laing, Margaret
 The next Kennedy. New York, Coward-McCann, 1968, 320p. 2968

Quirk, Lawrence J.
 The life story of Robert Francis Kennedy, 1925-1968. Los Angeles, Holloway House Pub., 1968, 312p. 2969

Ross, Douglas
 Robert F. Kennedy, apostle of change. New York, Trident Press, 1968, 600p. 2970

Zeiger, Henry A.
 Robert F. Kennedy; a biography. New York, Meredith Press, 1968, 152p. (Children's book) 2971

1969

Halberstam, David
 The unfinished odyssey of Robert Kennedy. New York, Random House, 1969, 211p. 2972

Witcover, Jules
 85 days; the last campaign of Robert Kennedy. New York, Putnam, 1969, 338p. 2973

Articles about Robert F. Kennedy

1957

"Young man with Tough Questions." Life 43, July 1, 1957, p. 81-82. 2974

Healy, Philip F.
 "Bob Kennedy, Investigator in a Hurry." Sign 37, August 1957, p. 11-14. 2975

"The Rise of the Brothers Kennedy." Look 21, August 6, 1957, p. 18-24. 2976

"Robert F. Kennedy: Portrait." New York times magazine, August 11, 1957, p. 1. 2977

Flannery, Harry W.
"The Other Kennedy." Ave Maria 86, August 31, 1957, p. 12-15. 2978

1958

"Debut into a Burgeoning Family." Life 44, April 21, 1958, p. 132-134. 2979

1959

Healy, Philip F.
"He's Rough on Racketeers." Extension 53, January 1959, p. 20-21. 2980

Martin, John B.
"The Struggle to get Hoffa." Saturday evening post 231, June 27, 1959, p. 19-21. 2981

"The Other Kennedy." U.S. news & world report 47, August 31, 1959, p. 74-76. 2982

1960

"Inside Story of the big Probe: Robert Kennedy's new book, The Enemy Within, Gives First-hand Account of McClellan Committee's Investigation of Labor Corruption." Business week, February 20, 1960, p. 140. 2983

Riesel, Victor
"The State of the Unions." Saturday review 43, February 27, 1960, p. 21. 2984

"Enter Bobby Kennedy: new Man-to-see in Changing Washington." Newsweek 56, November 21, 1960, p. 32-34. 2985

Scorza, Carlo
"Los 35 Años de Robert Kennedy." Buenos Aires, Dinámica social (11: 122), December 1960, p. 2-3. ("The 35 Years of Robert Kennedy.") 2986

"Robert Kennedy." New republic 143, December 12, 1960, p. 5-6. 2987

1961

"Kennedy-Kabinett: Bruder Bobby." Hamburg, Der spiegel (15: 1), 1961, p. 30-32. ("Kennedy Cabinet: Brother Bobby.") 2988

Bickel, Alexander M.
"Robert F. Kennedy: the Case Against him for Attorney-General." New republic 144, January 9, 1961, p. 15-19. 2989

"No Politics in Antitrust." America 104, January 28, 1961, p. 559-560. 2990

Young, A.A.
"Bob Kennedy: Energetic new Attorney General." Information 75, May 1961, p. 2-7. 2991

"Role of Robert Kennedy: no. 2 man in Washington." U.S. news & world report 51, July 10, 1961, p. 42-45. 2992

Chamberlin, A.
"The President's Brother Takes a Trip." Life 51, August 18, 1961, p. 28-35. 2993

"The Brothers Kennedy."
Manila, Sunday times magazine (17: 7), September 24, 1961, p. 26-30. 2994

Booker, Simeon
"Mr. Civil-Rights goes to Africa." Ebony 16, October 1961, p. 88-92. 2995

"President's Brother Leads." Interracial review 34, October 1961, p. 248-249. 2996

"Untold Story of the 'Freedom Rides' (Record of Telephone Call Between Attorney General Kennedy and the Manager of the Greyhound Bus Terminal, Birmingham, Alabama, May, 1961: Mr. Kennedy's Explanation of the Call)." U.S. news & world report 51, October 23, 1961, p. 76-79. 2997

1962

Améry, Jean
"Der 'Kleiner' Hört zu. Amerikas Justizminister Robert Kennedy." Cologne, Rheinische merkur (17: 47), 1962, p. 4.
("The Kid Brother Listens: U.S. Attorney-General Robert Kennedy.") 2998

Gresman, Hans
"Kleiner Bruder des Grossen Jack." Hamburg, Die zeit (17: 8), 1962, p. 2.
("Kid Brother of Big Jack.") 2999

"Kennedy-Besuch: Kalt in Deutschland." Hamburg, Der spiegel (16: 9), 1962, p. 34.
("Kennedy-Visit: Cold in Germany.") 3000

"Robert F. Kennedy: mein Bruder und ich." Hamburg, Der spiegel (16: 7), 1962, p. 46-64.
("Robert F. Kennedy: My Brother and I.") 3001

Velie, Lester
"Showdown Ahead for Major-League Crime." Reader's digest 80, January 1962, p. 122-127. 3002

O'Neil, Paul
"Number 2 man in Washington." Life 52, January 26, 1962, p. 76-78. 3003

Beecher, William
"Brother Bobby: World Trip may Signal more Responsible Role for Younger Kennedy..." Wall Street journal 159, February 6, 1962, p. 1. 3004

"More than a Brother." Time 79, February 16, 1962, p. 16-21. 3005

"Young, Tough, Trusted: Robert F. Kennedy; President's Brother, as Attorney General, is Juggling a Triple Role." Business week, February 17, 1962, p. 132-134. 3006

"Bobby Kennedy: is he the 'Assistant President'?" U.S. news & world report 52, February 19, 1962, p. 48-52. 3007

McGrory, Mary
"Having Wonderful Time, Bobby; Role as Goodwill Ambassador." America 106, February 24, 1962, p. 674. 3008

Barr, John
"Typhoon Bobby was Here." New republic 146, February 26, 1962, p. 12-13. 3009

Childs, Marquis
"Bobby and the President." Good housekeeping 154, May 1962, p. 80-81, 162, 164, 167, 169. 3010

Lomax, Louis E.
"Kennedys Move in on Dixie." Harper's magazine 224, May 1962, p. 27-33. 3011

McGrory, Mary
"Bobby's Dog has Congressmen Aflutter." America 107, September 1, 1962, p. 664. 3012

"Washington's Young man in a Hurry." Manila, Sunday times magazine (18: 7), September 23, 1962, p. 12-15. 3013

"Men Around President Kennedy." London, Illustrated London news 241, November 24, 1962, p. 833. 3014

1963

"Robert Kennedy at the Berlin Wall" (excerpt from Just friends and brave enemies). Catholic digest 27, January 1963, p. 69-74. 3015

Herbers, John
"He is Top-priority." Manila, Philippines herald magazine, February 2, 1963, p. 18. 3016

Coffin, Tristram
"Department of Justice." Holiday 33, March 1963, p. 94-95. 3017

Vidal, Gore
"Bobby Kennedy in '68: the Buildup has Begun." U.S. news & world report 54, March 4, 1963, p. 19. 3018

Sclanders, Ian
"Crowd Around the Loneliest man in the World." Toronto, Maclean's magazine 76, March 9, 1963, p. 27, 41-44. 3019

Lewis, Anthony
"What Drives Bobby Kennedy." New York times magazine, April 7, 1963, p. 34. 3020

Knebel, Fletcher
"Bobby Kennedy, he Hates to be Second." Look 27, May 21, 1963, p. 91-94. 3021

"The man Behind the President, Bobby Kennedy: the Attorney-General who Cooked Hamburgers in his Office." London, Time & tide (16: 12), June 1963, p. 7-8. 3022

"Nine Young Men in Charge of Integrating America." U.S. news & world report 55, July 29, 1963, p. 58-61. 3023

Kraft, Joseph
"Riot Squad for the New

Frontier." Harper's magazine 227, August 1963, p. 69-75. 3024

1964

"Attorney-General Completes Mission in Far East." Dept. of State bulletin (50: 1286), 1964, p. 239-243. 3025

Jones, Robert
'New York's Young Hopefuls." London, Statist (186: 4523), 1964, p. 411-413. 3026

Kempton, Murray
"His Brother's Keeper." London, Spectator 7078, 1964, p. 734-736. 3027

Kraft, J.
'Der US-Justizminister Tritt in die Fussstapfen Seines Bruders." Hamburg, Die zeit (19: 26), 1964, p. 6.
("The U.S. Attorney-General Walks in the Footsteps of his Brother.") 3028

'Robert Kennedy in Heidelberg." Heidelberg, Ruperto-Carola (16: 36), 1964, p. 262. 3029

"USA--Kennedy-Mission: Blick in die Sterne." Hamburg, Der spiegel (18: 6), 1964, p. 62.
("USA: Kennedy Mission: a Glance at the Stars.") 3030

"Why Another Kennedy Could Easily be the Next U.S. President." Manila, Sunday times magazine, January 5, 1964, p. 16-17. 3031

'Ruthless Robert Kennedy: an American Indictment." London, Time & tide (6: 12), February 1964, p. 19-20. 3032

Pope, J. M.
"Bobby was here." Manila, Sunday times magazine, February 2, 1964, p. 22-23. 3033

"Shell Game: Peacemaking Trip Through Southeast Asia." Time 83, February 7, 1964, p. 31-32. 3034

Arroyo, Nimia P.
"A Day in Manila." Manila, Mirror, February 8, 1964, p. 24-25. 3035

Hart, James
"Those left on Stage." Manila, Sunday times magazine, February 9, 1964, p. 14-15. 3036

"As the Buildup Begins for Robert Kennedy to get the Democratic Vice-Presidential Nomination this Year." U.S. news & world report 56, February 10, 1964, p. 38. 3037

Kempton, Murray
'Robert F. Kennedy." New republic 150, February 15, 1964, p. 9-11. 3038

Otten, Alan L.
"The Bobby Kennedy Dilemma: his Political Support Presents a Problem for Johnson." Wall Street journal 163, March 13, 1964, p. 8. 3039

"Kennedy on the Ticket?"

London, *The economist* 210, March 14, 1964, p. 992. 3040

"Robert Kennedy." *Forbes* 93, March 15, 1964, p. 12. 3041

"Bobby Kennedy on LBJ's '64 Ticket?" *U.S. news & world report* 56, March 23, 1964, p. 42-44. 3042

Maas, Peter
"What will RFK do Next?" *Saturday evening post* 237, March 28, 1964, p. 17-21. 3043

Mollenhoff, Clark R.
"Behind the Plot to Assasinate Robert Kennedy." *Look* 28, May 19, 1964, p. 49-50. 3044

Buckley, William F.
"Bobby for President?" *National review* 16, June 16, 1964, p. 481. 3045

Potter, Philip
"How LBJ got the Nomination." *The reporter* 30, June 18, 1964, p. 16-20. 3046

Ajemian, Robert
"Man's Week to Reckon." *Life* 57, July 3, 1964, p. 24-31. 3047

"What's Bobby Going to do? An Informal Talk with RFK." *Newsweek* 64, July 6, 1964, p. 24-26. 3048

"From Poland with Love: Visit to Poland." *America* 111, July 11, 1964, p. 35. 3049

"Goodbye Bobby: President Johnson Against Kennedy as Vice-Presidential Candidate." *Time* 84, August 7, 1964, p. 18-19. 3050

Kraft, Joseph
"The Ambitions of Bobby Kennedy." *Look* 28, August 25, 1964, p. 22-28. 3051

"Can a Kennedy Beat the Republicans in New York?" *U.S. news & world report* 57, August 31, 1964, p. 31-33. 3052

"Politics of State." London, *The economist* 212, September 5, 1964, p. 918. 3053

Kempton, Murray
"The Kennedy Squeal." London, *Spectator* 213, September 11, 1964, p. 329-330. 3054

Kempton, Murray
"Hosts of Unreason: Kennedy vs. Keating in New York State." *New republic* 151, September 12, 1964, p. 11-12. 3055

"The Kennedy Brothers' Dream: a new Chapter: far More than a Senate Seat is at Stake in Robert Kennedy's New York Race." *U.S. news & world report* 57, September 14, 1964, p. 33-35. 3056

"Kennedy? Why?" *Christian century* 81, September 16, 1964, p. 1134-1135. 3057

McGrory, Mary
"A Kennedy in New York

Politics." *America* 111, September 19, 1964, p. 284. 3058

"Why Robert Kennedy?" *New republic* 151, September 19, 1964, p. 3-4. 3059

Cooke, Alistair
"Robert Kennedy as Carpetbagger...the 'Locality Rule' in U.S. Politics." London, *Listener* 72, September 24, 1964, p. 452-453. 3060

"Campaigning." *New Yorker* 40, October 24, 1964, p. 50-51. 3061

Maas, Peter
"Can Kennedy Take New York?" *Saturday evening post* 237, October 31, 1964, p. 32-34. 3062

"Barry and Bobby: the Bold Buccaneers." Montreal, *Montrealer* 38, November 1964, p. 23-28. 3063

Chamberlain, John
"Political Powerhouse in Action." *Reader's digest* 85, November 1964, p. 189-190. 3064

Feiffer, J.
"A Matter of Conscience." *Commentary* 38, December 1964, p. 52-54. 3065

1965
"The Kennedys: White House Prospects of Senators Bob, Ted Stir new Speculation; Many see Humphrey Heading Ticket After Johnson, but few Rule out Brothers." *Wall Street journal* 165, January 7, 1965, p. 1. 3066

"What Burned Bobby: Charge of Planting in *Life* Magazine a Derogatory Story About Jimmy Hoffa." *Time* 85, March 12, 1965, p. 23-23A. 3067

Smith, Terry
"Bobby's Image." *Esquire* 63, April 1965, p. 62-63. 3068

Connelly, Dolly
"How did I get Myself into this?" *Sports illustrated* 22, April 5, 1965, p. 56-58. 3069

Golden, Harry
"The Bobby Twins Revisited." *Esquire* (LXIII: 3), June 1965, p. 42. 3070

Weaver, Warren
"Will the Real Robert Kennedy Stand up?" *New York times magazine*, June 20, 1965, p. 8-9. 3071

Wechsler, James A.
"Robert F. Kennedy: a Case of Mistaken Identity." *Progressive* 29, July 1965, p. 1-4. 3072

"Kennedy Bomb." London, *Jewish observer* 14, July 2, 1965, p. 6-7. 3073

"Kennedy and China." *New republic* 153, July 3, 1965, p. 5-6. 3074

Kempton, Murray
"Kennedy and Lindsay." London, *Spectator*, November 5, 1965, p. 568-569. 3075

Armstrong, Richard
"Bobby Kennedy and the Fight for New York." Saturday evening post 238, November 6, 1965, p. 29-31.   3076

"Roberto South of the Border." National review 17, December 14, 1965, p. 1144-1146.   3077

1966

Kopkind, Andrew
"Kennedy ends the Consensus." London, New statesman (71: 1823), 1966, p. 250-252.   3078

Muhlen, Norbert
"Der Politiker: Robert Kennedy." Stuttgart, Christ und welt (19: 52), 1966, p. 24. ("The Politician: Robert Kennedy.")   3079

Uyse, Stanley
"After Kennedy, the Screw." London, New statesman (71: 1840), 1966, p. 868-869.   3080

"Kennedy Caper: RFK in van of a new, Anti-LBJ bloc of Peace Democrats." Newsweek 67, March 7, 1966, p. 24-25.   3081

Shannon, William V.
"Bob Kennedy's Future." Commonweal 83, March 18, 1966, p. 686-687.   3082

Kopkind, Andrew
"He's a Happening." New republic 154, April 2, 1966, p. 18-22.   3083

Glass, Andrew J.
"Compulsive Candidate." Saturday evening post 239, April 23, 1966, p. 36-38.   3084

Brandon, Henry
"Robert Kennedy Feels his way to Power." London, Sunday times, April 24, 1966, p. 2.   3085

"Kennedy in New York." New Yorker 42, May 14, 1966, p. 39-42.   3086

Weaver, Warren
"Front Runners for '72." New York times magazine, May 22, 1966, p. 26-27.   3087

"Kennedy's Prescription for Latin America." New republic 154, May 28, 1966, p. 8-10.   3088

"Kennedy's Progress." London, The economist 219, June 4, 1966, p. 1082.   3089

"Kennedy Reception." New republic 154, June 11, 1966, p. 13-14. (Visit to South Africa.)   3090

"New Life for Liberals." London, The economist 219, June 11, 1966, p. 1176.   3091

"Senator Kennedy in South Africa." Tablet 220, June 18, 1966, p. 690.   3092

"Kennedy in Africa: Holy Johannesburg." Editor & publisher 99, June 25, 1966, p. 14.   3093

"Another Kennedy Seeks the Presidency." U.S. news & world report 60, June 27,

1966, p. 56-61. 3094

Alexander, Holmes
"RFK: How he's Building his own Party." Nation's business 54, July 1966, p. 38-39. 3095

"Kennedy on Africa." New Yorker 42, July 9, 1966, p. 19-21. 3096

Roberts, Steven V.
"Bobby Kennedy's Shadow Cabinet." Esquire (LXVI: 3), September 1966, p. 168. 3097

"The Making of the President, 1972?" Newsweek 68, September 5, 1966, p. 17-18. 3098

Kempton, Murray
"Robert Kennedy: ever or Never?" London, Spectator, September 9, 1966, p. 307-308. 3099

"What Party Leaders Think of Bobby Kennedy's Future." U.S. news & world report 61, September 26, 1966, p. 54-56. 3100

Minifie, James M.
"President Needs Victory and Soon." London, Canada, Business quarterly 31, Fall 1966, p. 8, 89. 3101

Kiker, Douglas
"Robert Kennedy and the What if Game." Atlantic 218, October 1966, p. 66-70. 3102

Rosen, Gerald R.
"Bobby Kennedy and the Businessmen." Dun's review 88, October 1966, p. 32-33. 3103

Shannon, William V.
"The Making of President Robert Kennedy." Harper's magazine 233, October 1966, p. 62-68. 3104

Donaldson, Gordon
"Bobby's Off: Running at Full Gallop." Toronto, Maclean's magazine 79, October 1, 1966, p. 1-2. 3105

Witcover, Jules
"Robert Kennedy on Tour." New republic 155, October 1, 1966, p. 9-10. 3106

"Robert Kennedy as Mexico's Reds see him." U.S. news & world report 61, October 10, 1966, p. 18. 3107

Miller, Helen (Hill)
"Kennedy in '68?" New republic 155, October 15, 1966, p. 11-13. 3108

"Bobby Kennedy Replies with the Words of a Dove." Toronto, Maclean's magazine 79, October 15, 1966, p. 4. 3109

"Senator Kennedy at Berkeley." America 115, November 5, 1966, p. 531. 3110

"On the Campaign Trail with Robert Kennedy." U.S. news & world report 61, November 7, 1966, p. 40-41. 3111

Newfield, Jack
"The Bobby Phenomenon."

The nation 203, November 14, 1966, p. 505-507. 3112

"Washington: Ten of its Most Powerful Men." Vogue 148, November 15, 1966, p. 156-157. 3113

"What is Robert Kennedy up to?" Life 61, November 18, 1966, p. 34-43. 3114

Cipes, Robert M.
"Wiretap War: Kennedy, Johnson and the FBI." New republic 155, December 24, 1966, p. 16-22. 3115

"Who Knew About 'Bugging'? RFK's Story, and the FBI's." U.S. news & world report 61, December 26, 1966, p. 32-35. 3116

1967

Witcover, Jules
"Robert F. Kennedy: the Making of an Electorate." Progressive 31, January 1967, p. 17-20. 3117

"Did LBJ Make John Kennedy President?" U.S. news & world report 62, January 16, 1967, p. 42-46. 3118

Kennedy, Jacqueline (Bouvier)
"The Real Robert F. Kennedy." Ladies' home journal 84, February 1967, p. 75. 3119

Scheer, Robert
"A Political Portrait of Robert Kennedy." Ramparts 5, February 1967, p. 11-16. 3120

"Kennedysmo on the Road: Tour of Western European Capitals." Time 89, February 10, 1967, p. 19-20. 3121

Howard, Anthony
"LBJ Carpets Robert Kennedy." London, Observer, February 12, 1967, p. 4. 3122

Reeves, Richard
"The People Around Bobby." New York times magazine, February 12, 1967, p. 25. 3123

"Why it will be a Johnson-Humphrey Ticket Again in '68." U.S. news & world report 62, February 13, 1967, p. 40-43. 3124

"Swinging Senator." The nation 204, February 20, 1967, p. 226-227. 3125

Weintal, Edward
"Other War: Middleman in Peace Relay." Newsweek 69, February 20, 1967, p. 31-32. 3126

"Bobby's Spring Offensive." National review 19, February 21, 1967, p. 180-182. 3127

Ascoli, Max
"Kennedy's Diplomacy." The reporter 36, February 23, 1967, p. 14. 3128

Brandon, Henry
"Dramatic Changes in Europe: Robert Kennedy Talks about American Failure to act." London, Sunday times, February 26, 1967, p. 10. 3129

Howard, Anthony
"Kennedy's Speech Finishes him with Johnson." London, Observer, March 5, 1967, p. 6. 3130

Wills, Gary
"Two of R.F.K.'s Many Sides." National Catholic reporter 3, March 8, 1967, p. 8. 3131

Kempton, Murray
"Up Bobs Bobby." London, Spectator, March 10, 1967, p. 273-274. 3132

Kopkind, Andrew
"Johnson vs. Kennedy." London, New statesman 73, March 10, 1967, p. 315. 3133

Rovere, Richard H.
"Letter from Washington." New Yorker 43, March 18, 1967, p. 176-178. 3134

"Charges Johnson...Raised U.S. Price for Halt in Bombing," New York times, March 22, 1967, p. 1, column 8. 3135

"Young Man on a Democratic Trapeze." London, The economist 222, March 25, 1967, p. 1141-1142. 3136

"Robert Kennedy: Portrait." Toronto, World affairs 32, April 1967, p. 20. 3137

"Will Bobby's Friends Trip up LBJ in '68?" U.S. news & world report 62, April 10, 1967, p. 53-54. 3138

Sypher, Alden H.
"Of Grasshoppers, Ho and Bobby." Nation's business 55, May 1967, p. 31-32. 3139

"Ronnie-Bobby Show." Newsweek 69, May 29, 1967, p. 26. 3140

Alsop, Stewart
"Bobby Kennedy's Best Chance." Saturday evening post 240, June 3, 1967, p. 20. 3141

Brandon, Henry
"Kennedy Returns to the Fold." London, Sunday times, June 11, 1967, p. 3. 3142

"Powdery air: Investigates air Pollution." New Yorker 43, July 15, 1967, p. 21-23. 3143

Semple, Robert B.
"Slum Planners." New republic 157, July 22, 1967, p. 8-10. 3144

"The Public Record of Robert F. Kennedy." Congressional quarterly weekly report 25, August 4, 1967, p. 1353-1363. 3145

Winter, A.
"Kennedy says Killing in war Makes Riots More Acceptable." National Catholic reporter 3, August 23, 1967, p. 1. 3146

"Is Robert Kennedy Trying to Upset LBJ in '68?" U.S. news & world report 63, October 2, 1967, p. 39-40. 3147

Shannon, William V.
"The Heir Apparent (Book Review by P.R. Wieck)."

New republic 157, October 21, 1967, p. 23-26. 3148

Moore, T.
"A Bit of the way With RFK." Ave Maria 106, October 28, 1967, p. 6-9. 3149

Martin, Dean
"Dean Martin Talks About his Drinking, the Mafia, Frank Sinatra, Women, Bobby Kennedy. Interview, Edited by Oriana Fallaci." Look 31, December 26, 1967, p. 78-85. 3150

1968
"Bobby: To Be or Not To Be." Newsweek 71, January 29, 1968, p. 18-19. 3151

Shannon, William V.
"Heir Apparent (Book Review by F. Getlein)." Commonweal 87, February 2, 1968, p. 543-544. 3152

"Revitalization." New Yorker 43, February 17, 1968, p. 26-27. 3153

"The Conscience of RFK." The reporter 38, February 22, 1968, p. 12. 3154

Reichley, A. J.
"He's Running Himself out of the Race." Fortune 77, March 1968, p. 112-114. 3155

"Kennedy Candidacy." Christian century 85, March 27, 1968, p. 380-381. 3156

Kopkind, Andrew
"The Importance of Kennedy." London, New statesman 75, March 29, 1968, p. 403-404. 3157

Newfield, Jack
"Kennedy Lays out a gut Campaign." Life 64, March 29, 1968, p. 28-31. 3158

Reeves, Richard
"The Making of a Candidate, 1968." New York times magazine, March 31, 1968, p. 25-27. 3159

"Inside Story of the Latest Bobby-LBJ Break." U.S. news & world report 64, April 1, 1968, p. 30-32. 3160

"Socking it to 'em: Travels with Bobby." Time 91, April 5, 1968, p. 22-23. 3161

Kerby, Phil
"Kennedy in Disneyland." The nation 206, April 8, 1968, p. 464-465. 3162

Riesman, David
"McCarthy and Kennedy." New republic 158, April 13, 1968, p. 22-23. 3163

Rogers, Warren
"Bobby's Decision." Look, April 16, 1968, p. 72-80. 3164

"Does Bobby Kennedy Have a Chance?" Saturday evening post 241, April 20, 1968, p. 88. 3165

Jeffries, Jean
"Why Vietnam is Kennedy's War." National review 20, April 23, 1968, p. 396-397. 3166

"If it's Nixon vs. Kennedy: the Odds." U.S. news & world report 64, April 29,

1968, p. 28-30. 3167

Higdon, Hal
"Indiana: a Test for Bobby." New York times magazine, May 5, 1968, p. 32-33. 3168

"Bobby Kennedy Record." U.S. news & world report 64, May 6, 1968, p. 50-54. 3169

Yoakum, Robert
"Kennedy and McCarthy: 1965-67 Voting Record." New republic 158, May 11, 1968, p. 23-27. 3170

Osborne, John
"Nebraska Primary, the ifs, ands and buts." New republic 158, May 18, 1968, p. 7-9. 3171

Schlesinger, Arthur M.
"Why I am for Kennedy." New republic 158, May 18, 1968, p. 39-40. 3172

O'Lessker, Karl
"Down the Primary Stretch, from Indiana to Oregon." The nation 206, May 27, 1968, p. 682-684, 686-690. 3173

Wise, David
"How Bobby Plans to win it." Saturday evening post 241, June 1, 1968, p. 23-27. 3174

"Win or Lose, the Primary Players." Life 64, June 7, 1968, p. 35-41. 3175

Wieck, Paul R.
"The Oregon Primary." New republic 158, June 8, 1968, p. 14-15. 3176

Halberstam, David
"Travels with Bobby Kennedy." Harper's magazine 237, July 1968, p. 51-61. 3177

"Robert F. Kennedy and the Negro." Ebony 23, July 1968, p. 29-32. 3178

Hilsman, Roger
"R.F.K. on Cuba: an Insider's Analysis." Commonweal 89, November 22, 1968, p. 273-275. 3179

The Assassination of Robert F. Kennedy

Books

1968

Editors of United Press International & Cowles
Assassination: Robert F. Kennedy, 1925-1968. Ed. by Francine Klagsbrun & David C. Whitney. New York, Cowles Education Crop., 1968, 272p. 3180

United in grief: three widows share their sorrow. Washington, Metro Pub. Reps., 1968, 60p. 3181

Three mothers: their life stories; how tragedy made them sisters. New York, Macfadden-Bartell Corp., 1968, 80p. 3182

Articles

1968

Kihss, Peter
"Suspect Called Calm and Lucid...Sirhan Describes Himself as Jordanian Born in Jerusalem." New York times, June 6, 1968, p. 1, 21.   3183

Reich, Ken
"McCarthy Suspends Political Activities, Asks Prayer Vigil." Los Angeles times, June 6, 1968, P.B, 18.   3184

Townsend, Dorothy
"Witness Reports Girl Said 'We Shot Him'." Los Angeles times, June 6, 1968, p. 11.   3185

Hill, Gladwin
"Kennedy State 'Extremely Critical'; Suspect, Arab Immigrant, Arraigned; President puts Guard on Candidates." New York times, June 6, 1968, p. 1, 20.   3186

Dougherty, Richard
"New Yorkers Weep as Family, Friends Return with Body." Los Angeles times, June 7, 1968, p. 1, 12.   3187

Einstoss, Ron
"First Court Appearance: Suspect Gives Impression of Cocky, Arrogant Confidence." Los Angeles times, June 7, 1968, p. 1, 15.   3188

Kendall, John
"Kennedy Made Each of his 42 Years Count." Los Angeles times, June 7, 1968, p. 2, 16.   3189

Lambert, Tom
"President Sets Sunday as Day for Mourning." Los Angeles times, June 7, 1968, p. B.   3190

Nelson, Harry
"If Kennedy had Survived: Life in Respirator Might Have Been his Fate." Los Angeles times, June 7, 1968, p. 1, 19.   3191

"Once Again, Once Again." Newsweek 71, June 17, 1968, p. 20-40.   3192

"The Accused: Ray and Sirhan." Life (64: 25), June 21, 1968, p. 24-34.   3193

Frankel, Charles
"The Meaning of Political Murder." Saturday review, June 22, 1968, p. 17-18.   3194

Horowitz, Irving L.
"Kennedy's Death, Myths and Realities." Trans-Action 5, July 1968, p. 3-5.   3195

Emmett, Christopher
"Media and the Assassinations." National review 20, July 30, 1968, p. 748-749.   3196

Scheer, Robert
"The Night Bobby Died." Ramparts magazine 7, August 10, 1968, p. 56-58.   3197

Howard, Anthony
"Logistics of the Funeral." Esquire 70, November 1968, p. 119-122.   3198

1969

"Incredible Year of '68: Year of Shock." Life 66, January 10, 1969, p. 30-37. 3199

"Assassins: Who did it and why?" Newsweek 73, March 24, 1969, p. 28-29. 3200

Poems

1968

Kenedy, Thomas B.
"The Fire of Your Love (June 5, 1968)." America 118, June 15, 1968, back cover. 3201

Lowell, Robert
"RFK; Poem." New republic 158, June 22, 1968, p. 27. 3202

"June 5, 1968" (a Poem). See, October 1968, p. 12-13. 3203

Eulogies of Robert F. Kennedy

1968

Goldman, John J.
"Brother Delivers Eulogy for 'Good and Decent Man'." Los Angeles times, June 9, 1968, p. 1, 22. 3204

"For Perspective and Determination; Life on the way to Death." Time 91, June 14, 1968, p. 15-18. 3205

"Friendly Pause on the way to a Rostrum; with Reports by L. Wainwright and T.H. White." Life 64, June 14, 1968, p. 32-42-D. 3206

Rovere, Richard H.
"Letter from Washington." New Yorker 44, June 15, 1968, p. 90-96. 3207

"Kennedys Thank Nation for Providing Them with Strength and Hope." New York times, June 16, 1968, p. 1, 34. 3208

"The Kennedy Cause." New republic, June 15, 1968, p. 3-4. 3209

"Notes and Comment." New Yorker 44, June 15, 1968, p. 21-23. 3210

Sorensen, Theodore C.
"RFK: a Personal Memoir." Saturday review, June 22, 1968, p. 19. 3211

Look Magazine
"RFK: The Bob Kennedy we Knew." June 1968, entire issue. 3212

Lyons, Louis M.
"America Bereft: RFK" The Massachusetts review 9, Summer 1968, p. 578-580. 3213

Cooke, Terence J.
"Eulogy to Robert F. Kennedy, Delivered at the Funeral, June 8, 1968." Vital speeches 34, July 1, 1968, p. 547-548. 3214

Rogers, Warren & Stanley Tretick
"The Bob Kennedy we Knew." Look, July 9, 1968, p. 31-36. 3215

MacDonald, William W.
"Robert F. Kennedy."
Christian century 85, July 10,
1968, p. 891-894.   3216

Laing, Margaret
"The Kennedy Personality."
Coronet (6: 7), July 1968, p.
10-25.   3217

"Jack Paar Tells What Robert Kennedy was Really Like."
Ladies' home journal
(LXXXV: 8), August 1968,
p. 42-45.   3218

Hamill, Pete
"Why, God, Why? A Friend's Poignant Farewell to Bobby Kennedy." Good housekeeping, September 1968, p. 80-81, 187-188.   3219

"Robert F. Kennedy: A Tribute." See, October 1968,
p. 98-103.   3220

Muggeridge, Malcolm
"The Elevation of Senator Robert F. Kennedy." Esquire 70, November 1968, p. 118.   3221

1969
Reed, Roy
"Mourners Mark the Death of Robert Kennedy." New York times, June 7, 1969, p. 1, 19.   3222

Weaver, Warren
"Kennedy, Apostle of Involvement." New York times, June 7, 1969, p. 19.   3223

Eulogies--Motion Pictures

1968
American Broadcasting Company. Radio News Dept.
Young man with a hope: a remembrance of Robert F. Kennedy; special report.
New York, 1968.   3224

National Broadcasting Company. Television Division.
Robert F. Kennedy, 1925-1968. New York, 1968. 3225

Democratic National Convention Robert Kennedy Memorial. Television broadcast from convention headquarters, Chicago, Ill., August 29, 1968. Narrated by Richard Burton, with introduction by Senator Edward M. Kennedy. Washington? National Democratic Committee? 1968. 3226

Memorials to
Robert F. Kennedy

1968
"Memorial for Kennedy."
Beverly Hills citizen, June 20, 1968, p. 106.
(Robert F. Kennedy Memorial Forest in Israel.)   3227

Robert Francis Kennedy

Photographs of Robert F. Kennedy

Books

1968
American Heritage Magazine
Bobby. New York, Dell,
1968, 58 plus 5p.   3228

In memory of Bobby: dreams--
success--tragedy. New York,
Bee-Line Books, 1968, 65
plus 3p.   3229

Robert F. Kennedy memorial
issue, collector's edition.
New York, MF Enterprises,
1968, 67p.   3230

Robert F. Kennedy: the last
campaign. New York, Award
Books (Universal Pub. &
Dist. Corp.), 1968, un-
paged.   3231

Robert F. Kennedy: victim of
violence. Washington, Metro
Pub., 1968, 60p.   3232

A tribute to Robert Francis
Kennedy. New York, Stanley
Pubs., 1968, 67p.   3233

Motion Pictures

1967
"Discovery '67" (TV program
broadcast on American
Broadcasting Company TV
Network, August 25, 1968).
New York, Jules Powers
Production in cooperation
with the American Broad-
casting Company Dept. of
News and Public Affairs,
1967.
(Discussion on conservation
by Senator Robert F. Ken-
nedy, and scenes showing
the Senator and his family
on trip down the Colorado
River).   3234

Ethel (Skakel) Kennedy

Ethel Skakel was born in Chicago, Illinois on April 11, 1928, the sixth of seven children of George Skakel, a self-made business tycoon, and Ann (Brunnack) Skakel. While Ethel was still a young child, the family moved to Greenwich, Connecticut.

Ethel attended Manhattanville College of the Sacred Heart, where her roommate was Jean Kennedy. She first met Robert F. Kennedy at Mont Tremblant, Quebec, Canada, in 1945, where both the Kennedy and Skakel families were enjoying skiing. Both Ethel and Robert Kennedy were ski enthusiasts, and enjoyed skating and outdoor sports generally.

As a family friend she aided the Kennedy sisters in John F. Kennedy's first campaign for election as a congressman from the eleventh congressional district in Massachusetts, in 1946, and continued to assist in subsequent elections through the 1960 presidential campaign.

Shortly after his graduation from the University of Virginia Law School, Robert F. Kennedy married Ethel Skakel at a ceremony in Greenwich, Connecticut, on June 17, 1950. Their best man was the elder brother of the groom, Congressman John F. Kennedy. On December 12, 1968, a daughter, Rory, was born to Mrs. Ethel Skakel Kennedy. Their family now consists of seven boys and four girls: Douglas (the youngest boy, born in 1967); Joseph P.; Robert F., Jr. (the oldest boy); David A.; Michael L.; Christopher G.; Matthew M.T. (named for General Maxwell Taylor); Kathleen H. (the oldest daughter); Mary C., Mary K., and Rory.

The interest displayed by Ethel Kennedy in the career of her husband was made manifest to President John F. Kennedy. After observing Ethel Kennedy sitting enraptured daily, hour after hour, for almost two years, while her husband was the center of attraction in the hearings of the Senate Select Committee to Investigate Improper Activities in Labor-Management Relations, President (then Senator) Kennedy stated that such an avid interest in politics proved that Ethel was "his kind of sister-in-law." The patriarch, Joseph P. Kennedy, in a similar vein, mentioned that although not born a Kennedy, Ethel acts like one.

Ethel Kennedy has stated that her husband and her children represented to her what matters in her life. Despite the work involved, she regularly drives her children to school, and supervises the preparation of meals, and other household chores. The Kennedys maintain homes in Glen Cove, New York, and at "Hickory Hill" in McLean, Virginia, where they have a Georgian-style home, and where the children have ample room, fresh air, athletic equipment and horses to practice their equestrian ability. Mrs. Kennedy is generally recognized as the perfect hostess, and this outstanding ability was confirmed in 1953 when the Home Fashion League of Washington named her Outstanding Homemaker of the Year. Mrs. Kennedy regularly made public appearances and participated in fund drives for various charities while Senator Kennedy was alive.

Ethel Kennedy accompanied the Senator on his election campaign tours, and his presidential campaign during the spring of 1968 was no exception. At the conclusion of Senator Kennedy's successful campaign for the primary election in the State of Indiana, a front-page photograph, syndicated nationwide, showed Senator and Mrs. Kennedy arm-in-arm, walking slowly down an Indianapolis street, tired but satisfied in their victory.

Ethel Skakel Kennedy has made the acquaintance of tragedy. During the 1950's her parents were killed in an airplane accident, while her brother met the same fate in September of 1966. Ethel Kennedy displayed her bravery on many occasions: when her home was stoned, and threats to her children were made, when their father was serving as a Senate investigator. Her courage, however, was never more apparent than in the early hours of June 5, 1968, when her husband was shot down, following his victory speech in the California primary election, at the Ambassador Hotel in Los Angeles, California. All through the following forty-two hour vigil, prior to the Senator's death, Mrs. Kennedy showed her fortitude. She bore herself with composure on the return airplane trip to New York City, where a mass was said for Robert F. Kennedy on June 8, 1968, and during the train trip to Washington, D.C., where the Senator was buried on that day at Arlington National Cemetery, next to the grave of his brother, President John Fitzgerald Kennedy.

Robert F. Kennedy fought for the under-privileged of the world, as well as for the unfortunate of his fellow citizens. Perhaps one tribute paid by Ethel Kennedy to her late husband, while he was still living, was her participation in the Poor People's March on Washington, in May of 1968.

Articles about Ethel (Skakel) Kennedy

1962
"Ethel on the go." Newsweek 59, March 5, 1962, p. 40. 3235

1963
"Kiss me, Toots, I Love you." Newsweek 61, March 18, 1963, p. 29. 3236

1964
Partido, Corazon R.
"When Mother's Away, Other Kennedys take care of the Brood." Manila, Sunday times magazine, July 26, 1964, p. 60-62. 3237

1968
Hamill, Pete
"The Woman Behind Bobby Kennedy." Good housekeeping 166, April 1968, p. 95-99. 3238

Bergquist, Laura
"Ethel." Look, June 25, 1968, p. 30-37. 3239

Borkan, Lois
"The Tragic Private Life of Ethel Kennedy." The woman (3: 5), August 1968, p. 16-23. 3240

Chamberlin, Anne
'Ethel Kennedy: Profile in American Courage." McCall's (XCV: 11), August 1968, p. 55, 111-113. 3241

The Robert F. Kennedy Family

Articles about

1961
"Bob Kennedy's Family Grows up." Sign 40, July 1961, p. 16-21. 3242

"Ethel Kennedy and her Children." Life 51, November 10, 1961, p. 81-86. 3243

1962
Higgins, Marguerite
"The Private World of Robert and Ethel Kennedy." McCall's 89, February 1962, p. 90-91. 3244

"Private Sphere of a Lively and Loving Family: the Robert F. Kennedys." House & garden 122, July 1962, p. 94-99. 3245

1963
Roper, James E.
'Robert Kennedy Speaks his Mind on Living Outdoors Family Style." Popular gardening & living outdoors 14, May 1963, p. 26-29. 3246

'Kennedy Children and Integrated Schools." U.S. news & world report 54, June 17, 1963, p. 10-11. 3247

"Life Goes to the Christening

of Bobby Kennedy's Son."
Life 55, August 9, 1963, p.
87-89.   3248

1964

Bergquist, Laura
"Hyannis Port Revisited."
Look 28, November 17, 1964,
p. 37-44.   3249

1968

Caplan, Gerald & Vivian Cadden
"Lessons in Bravery." McCall's (XCV: 12), September 1968, p. 85, 151-153, 158.
(Concerning David and Joseph Kennedy III, sons of Senator Robert Kennedy). 3250

1969

"Kennedy of Hickory Hill."
Time 93, April 25, 1969,
p. 46-48.   3251

The Robert F. Kennedy Family

Photographs

1967

Cameron, Gail
"What it Takes to be a Kennedy." Ladies' home journal 84, February 1967, p. 76-77.
                              3252

"Kennedy Children: Photographs." McCall's 94, February 1967, p. 96-100. 3253

Bird, Robert S.
"Robert F. Kennedy: at Home with the Heir Apparent."
Saturday evening post 240, August 26, 1967, p. 28-35.
                              3254

Jean (Kennedy) Smith

Jean Kennedy Smith was born in Brookline, Massachusetts, on February 20, 1928. While her father served as U.S. Ambassador to Great Britain during the years 1937-40, she was a student at the Sacred Heart convent school in Roehampton, England, previously having attended public school in Bronxville, New York, where the family resided in the early 1930's.

In Joseph P. Kennedy's notes concerning his children, there is an often-quoted message received by him from his daughter, Jean, concerning the adolescent John F. Kennedy: "Jack was a very naughty boy when he was home. He kissed Betty Young under the mistletoe down in the front hall. He had a temperature of 102 one night, too, and Miss Cahill couldn't make him mind."

Jean Kennedy attended Maplehurst College of the Sacred Heart, and subsequently was graduated from Manhattanville College of the Sacred Heart, where her roommate was Ethel Skakel, who became Mrs. Robert F. Kennedy in 1950. Interested in public relations as a profession, Jean obtained a position in the Public Relations Division of the Merchandise Mart in Chicago, managed by R. Sargent Shriver, Jr., her brother-in-law. With her sister Eunice Shriver, she traveled to the Middle East in 1951. Eunice represented the Boston *Post* on that trip as its foreign correspondent.

Later in 1951 both Eunice and Jean worked together aiding juvenile delinquents as social workers for the House of the Good Shepherd in Chicago. Following this experience, Jean made the decision to return to her own field of public relations, and became affiliated with the Christophers, the organization established by Father James Keller in New York City, which strives to improve moral and ethical standards in significant activities of twentieth-century life, whether in the fields of labor, education, entertainment, government, etc. In its publishing, radio and television programs, and general informational activities, Jean Kennedy made a significant contribution to the work of the Christophers.

Jean (Kennedy) Smith

In May of 1956 Jean Kennedy and Stephen Edward Smith were married at St. Patrick's Cathedral in New York City by Cardinal Spellman. Both Jean and her husband assisted her brother, John F. Kennedy, in his many election campaigns. Stephen Smith has also utilized his outstanding administrative abilities to aid both Robert F. Kennedy and Edward M. Kennedy in their respective senatorial campaigns. In view of demonstrated ability in management, Stephen E. Smith has risen to the highest administrative-managerial position in the firm of Joseph P. Kennedy Enterprises. Mr. and Mrs. Smith and their children, Stephen, Jr. and William, make their home in New York City.

Stephen Edward Smith

Stephen Edward Smith, husband of Jean (Kennedy) Smith, was born in Bayport, Long Island, N.Y., on September 24, 1927, the grandson of William Cleary, who was a Congressman from New York, and who founded the family business of barge and tugboat shipping. While a student at Polytechnic Preparatory Country Day School in Brooklyn, and later in college, Stephen was a leader in hockey and lacrosse competitions, and during school vacations he was able to remain in good physical condition by working on barges plying New York State waterways.

While a student at Georgetown University (from which institution he was graduated with an A.B. degree in History), he made the acquaintance of Jean Kennedy; this acquaintance was continued while Stephen served in the United States Air Force as an officer during the years 1951-52, for during part of this period, he was stationed at Otis Air Force Base, in Falmouth, Massachusetts, not far from the Kennedy's home in Hyannis Port.

Following graduation from Georgetown, he entered the family business, working his way up from some of the most lowly tasks. When Stephen was only four years of age, his father passed away. His brothers managed the family business until he joined it. In 1956, he and Jean Kennedy were married, and it was in this same year that Cleary Brothers decided to diversify their activities through expansion into the oil industry; Stephen was given the responsibility and went to Texas to learn all he could about oil operations.

In 1957 Joseph P. Kennedy asked Stephen whether he might wish to take charge of the Kennedy investments pertaining to the oil industry. Stephen accepted the offer, and is in charge of the administration of most of the Kennedy investments in all fields of activity. This he accomplished in a quiet, unassuming, efficient and hard-working manner, demonstrating through his performance a genius for administration, with attention not only to overall policy, but also to slight details. The possessor of an extremely keen memory, he has the ability, in addition, to manage personnel very effectively.

Stephen Smith undertook his first job in politics in 1958, when he assisted John F. Kennedy in his campaign for re-election as Senator from Massachusetts. In terms of personnel management, fund-raising and disbursements, he more than proved his managerial and administrative abilities, to the extent that in the 1960 presidential campaign he became John F. Kennedy's right-hand man, traveling with him in 33 states, sizing up local political conditions, scheduling the candidate's speaking dates, handling hotel and transportation accomodations, as well as acting as critic in auditoriums for the candidate prior to the delivery of speeches. The bulk of Stephen Smith's time during the 1960 presidential campaign, however, was devoted to fund-raising work and control of disbursements.

During the senatorial campaign of Edward M. ("Ted") Kennedy, in 1962, Stephen Smith contributed his abilities to the successful outcome of the candidate's efforts, as he subsequently did for Senator Robert F. Kennedy of New York, in the latter's successful 1964 senatorial campaign, and in his campaign (1968) for the presidency.

In 1961, under the administration of President John F. Kennedy, Stephen Smith worked as an unpaid assistant in the State Department, and with the Development Loan Fund. In 1963 the President asked him to work with local Democratic organizations in various states, smoothing out party matters in the interest of party harmony.

Often compared to President Kennedy, Stephen E. Smith is immaculately dressed, has a cool temperament, and a dry brand of humor. Rather than verbalize, he possesses the virtue of being a good listener. Mr. and Mrs. Smith make their home in New York City.

Articles about
Stephen E. Smith

1963

McGrory, Mary
"Don't Look now, but There's Another one." *America* 108, February 2, 1963, p. 161. 3255

Kempton, Murray
"Stephen E. Smith." *New republic* 148, March 9, 1963, p. 15-17. 3256

"People of the Week." *U.S. news & world report* 54, May 13, 1963, p. 20. 3257

Wicker, Tom
"The Name is Smith." *New York times magazine*, July 28, 1963, p. 11. 3258

Otten, Alan L. & C.B. Seib
"The Kennedy Clansman Nobody Knows." *Saturday evening post* 236, September 7, 1963, p. 69-70. 3259

Bergquist, Laura
"The Inscrutable Mr. Smith." *Look* 27, September 24, 1963, p. 29-30. 3260

1967

Reeves, Richard
"The People Around Bobby." *New York times magazine*, February 12, 1967, p. 86.
3261

Edward Moore Kennedy

Edward Moore ("Ted") Kennedy was born February 22, 1932 in Brookline, Massachusetts. While his father served as U.S. Ambassador to the Court of St. James (1937-40), Edward went to schools in England, prior to preparing for Harvard at Milton Academy, Milton, Massachusetts. From 1951-53 he served in the United States Army in France and Germany. Returning to Harvard following military service, he was graduated in 1956 with an A.B. degree, having demonstrated proficiency in history and government, and performing valiantly on the football field.

Subsequent to graduation, Edward studied for one year at the International Law School in the Hague, Holland, and worked as a reporter for International News Service. He subsequently entered the University of Virginia Law School and received his LL.B. degree in 1959. In the same year he married Joan Bennett, of Bronxville, New York. The couple has three children, Kara, Edward M., Jr., and Patrick Joseph.

Aiming for a public service career, Edward aided in the 1958 senatorial campaign of his brother, John F. Kennedy. The native political ability demonstrated in Massachusetts by "Ted" Kennedy in 1958 led to his appointment as Western States campaign manager in his elder brother's 1960 presidential campaign.

Edward's first professional position was as an Assistant District Attorney of Suffolk County, Massachusetts. During the years 1961-62 he traveled in Latin America, Europe, and the Middle East, meeting leaders in all fields and studying economic conditions with respect to their implications for the Commonwealth of Massachusetts. In 1962, at the age of 30, "Ted" announced his intention to seek the Senate seat from Massachusetts formerly held by the President. As the result of a hard-fought, brilliantly-planned and dedicated campaign, he defeated Democratic opponents in the primary, and the Republican candidate in the election in November, by wide margins. During the spring of 1964, while flying with Senator Birch Bayh of Indiana on a campaign tour, he was seriously injured in a plane crash, and was hospitalized for many months. Mrs. Joan Kennedy immediately took over campaigning responsibilities for her husband, who was reelected for his second term as Senator from Massachusetts, in November 1964.

As Senator from Massachusetts, Edward strives to improve the economic situation of his state, especially as regards attracting contracts, and projects of all types. He consistently follows a liberal Democratic policy. He is a member of the Senate Committee on Labor and Public Welfare, the Committee on the Judiciary, the Democratic Policy Committee, the Select Committee on Nutrition and Human Needs, and the Special Committee on Aging. He also serves as a member of the Select Commission on Western Hemisphere Immigration. In January of 1969 Edward Moore Kennedy was elected to the position of Majority Whip in the United States Senate. He thereby automatically assumed the role of Congressional Spokesman for the Democratic Party.

Active in Boston's inter-faith activities, civic welfare programs and in local welfare drives, Edward has worked for the United Fund, Arthritis Foundation, and the Cancer Crusade. He is a trustee of the Children's Hospital Medical Center, Massachusetts General Hospital, the Lahey Clinic, the Museum of Science, and the John F. Kennedy Library, all located in Boston. In addition to acting as President of the Joseph P. Kennedy, Jr. Memorial Foundation (a charitable foundation active in medical research, and named for his older brother who was killed in World War II), he also serves on the Board of Visitors of the Fletcher School of Law and Diplomacy of Tufts University, on the Advisory Board of Emmanuel College, and is a trustee of Boston University, as well as a corporation member of Northeastern University. He is a member of the Trial Lawyers Association, Veterans of Foreign Wars, American Legion, and the Federal Bar Association Club.

In the spring of 1968 Edward Moore Kennedy's book, Decisions for a Decade, was published by Doubleday. Although he had previously written periodical articles, this was Mr. Kennedy's first full-length book, which he sub-titled Policies and Programs for the 1970's. In this considered source-book covering the problems which will inevitably face the American people during the 1970's (and perhaps beyond), Edward Kennedy incisively studies the nature of problems such as the racial crisis, the draft, housing, public health, and education, as well as the matters of gun control, congressional redistricting, and the war in Vietnam. Foreign affairs also are discussed in depth, and he supplies logical suggestions for solving the problems inherent in the American presence in Vietnam, in addition to suggesting viable methods for dealing with domestic matters. It seems to the author that in this work, Senator Edward Moore Kennedy has made a significant contribution to those concerned with directing the policies of the United States government, as well as to the literature of American politics.

On the morning of Saturday, June 8, 1968 Edward Kennedy delivered a eulogy in behalf of his brother, Senator Robert F. Kennedy (who was assassinated in Los Angeles, California, three days previously), at St. Patrick's Cathedral in New York City. In many respects the eulogy contained the qualities of a literary classic.

Books and Speeches by
Edward M. Kennedy

1961
Kennedy, Edward M.
Freedom's destiny; Independence Day ovation. Boston, City of Boston, Administrative Services Dept., 1961, 20p.
(Speech delivered in Boston, July 4, 1961.)   3262

1962
Kennedy, Edward M.
Meet the press: guest, George Cabot Lodge and Edward M. (Ted) Kennedy. Washington, Merkle Press, 1962, 10p.   3263

1964
Kennedy, Edward M.
Meet the press: guest, Senator Edward M. (Ted) Kennedy, Democrat, Massachusetts. Washington, Merkle Press, 1964, 10p.   3264

1966
Kennedy, Edward M.
Meet the press: guest, Senator Edward M. Kennedy, Democrat, Massachusetts. Washington, Merkle Press, 1966, 10p.   3265

1968
Kennedy, Edward M.
Decisions for a decade; policies and programs for the 1970's. Garden City, Doubleday, 1968, 222p.   3266

Kennedy, Edward M.
The eulogy to United States Senator Robert F. Kennedy, by his brother United States Senator Edward M. Kennedy delivered at St. Patrick's Cathedral, New York City, June 8th, 1968. Worcester, A.J. St. Onge, 1968, 27p.   3267

Articles by Edward M. Kennedy

1962
Kennedy, Edward M.
"I Grew up with Politics: Interview." U.S. news & world report 53, July 30, 1962, p. 50-52.　　　　　　3268

1965
Kennedy, Edward M.
"My Boston." Esquire 64, December 1965, p. 174-179.　　　　　　3269

1966
Kennedy, Edward M.
"The Immigration Act of 1965." Annals of the American Academy of Political & Social Science 367, September 1966, p. 137-149.　　　　3270

1967
Kennedy, Edward M.
"Ellis Island." Esquire 67, April 1967, p. 118-121.　3271

1968
Kennedy, Edward M.
"The New Protesters." McCall's (XCV: 8), May 1968, p. 8, 115, 116, 120.　　3272

Kennedy, Edward M.
"Riots and Racial Crisis." Harvard review (4: 3), 1968, p. 49-56.　　　　　　3273

Addresses by Edward M. Kennedy

Articles

1965
Kennedy, Edward M.
"Excerpt from Testimony, February 10, 1965." Congressional digest 44, May 1965, p. 152.　　　　3274

1967
Kennedy, Edward M.
"Address, February 23, 1967 (Excerpt)." Congressional digest 46, May 1967, p. 146.　　　　　　3275

Kennedy, Edward M.
"Address, April 2, 1967 (Excerpt)." Congressional digest 46, August 1967, p. 218-219.　　　　3276

1968
Kennedy, Edward M.
"Man's Relations to Man (Excerpt from Address)." Current 91, January 1968, p. 21-26.　　　　3277

Books about Edward M. Kennedy

1965
Morgan, Thomas B.
Edward Kennedy; Teddy (In his Self-creations: 13 impersonalities. New York, Holt, Rinehart & Winston, 1965, p. 59-77).　3278

1966
Levin, Murray B.
Kennedy campaigning; the

Edward Moore Kennedy

system and the style as practiced by Senator Edward Kennedy. Boston, Beacon Press, 1966, 313p. 3279

Articles about Edward M. Kennedy

1960

"Young Pros." Time 76, July 25, 1960, p. 17. 3280

1961

"Round Four: Kennedy vs. Lodge." Newsweek 58, October 30, 1961, p. 16-18. 3281

1962

"Kennedy Clan: Eddie und Teddy." Hamburg, Der spiegel (16: 38), 1962, p. 68-71.
("Kennedy Clan: Eddie and Teddy.") 3282

Schüler, Alfred
"Teddy, eine Sorge für den Grossen Bruder." Zürich, Weltwoche (30: 1500), 1962, p. 5.
("Teddy: a Worry for the big Brother.") 3283

Page, Joseph A.
"Precocious Ted Kennedy." The nation 194, March 10, 1962, p. 212-214. 3284

Wakefield, Dan & Thomas B. Morgan
"Bobby and Teddy." Esquire (LVII: 4), April 1962, p. 57, 59. 3285

Peters, William
"Teddy Kennedy." Redbook 119, June 1962, p. 36-37. 3286

"Ted Kennedy Builds Massachusetts Senate bid Around Brothers." Wall Street journal 159, June 1, 1962, p. 1. 3287

"Donnybrook Days: Party Nominating Conventions." Newsweek 59, June 11, 1962, p. 26. 3288

"Big Brother's Burden." London, The economist 203, June 16, 1962, p. 1105. 3289

"Kennedy vs. McCormack: Family Ties Stir Row in Primary." Business week, June 16, 1962, p. 35-36. 3290

Saltonstall, John L.
"First Round for Brother Ted." New republic 146, June 18, 1962, p. 7-8. 3291

Cater, Douglass
"How Teddy Beat Eddie." The reporter 27, July 5, 1962, p. 15-18. 3292

"Mr. Edward Kennedy's Test Today." London, Times, September 18, 1962, p. 9. 3293

Alsop, Joseph
"'Dynasty' and all That." Manchester, Manchester guardian, September 24, 1962, p. 16. 3294

"Teddy and Kennedyism." Time 80, September 28, 1962, p. 14-18. 3295

Buckley, William F.
"Why not Teddy?" National review 145, October 9, 1962, p. 254. 3296

Alsop, Stewart
"What Made Teddy Run?" Saturday evening post 235, October 27, 1962, p. 15-21. 3297

McCarthy, Joe
"One Election JFK Can't Win." Look 26, November 6, 1962, p. 23-27. 3298

Phillips, John
"Up in Massachusetts." Commentary 34, November 1962, p. 431-441. 3299

"Defense-Contract Row: Ted Kennedy under Fire." U.S. news & world report 53, December 31, 1962, p. 10. 3300

1963
Steinitz, Hans
"Amerikas Berühmteste Familie. Edward Kennedy, Genannt Teddy." Cologne, Rheinischer merkur (18: 31), 1963, p. 4. ("America's Famous Family. Edward Kennedy, Called 'Teddy'.") 3301

"What a Congressman Does, for U.S., for Folks Back Home." U.S. news & world report 54, January 14, 1963, p. 56. 3302

"Congress Opens, Teddy's at Work." Life 54, January 18, 1963, p. 34-37. 3303

"Family Reunion: First Day on Capitol Hill." Newsweek 61, January 21, 1963, p. 20-21. 3304

1964
"Teddy's Ordeal." Time 83, June 26, 1964, p. 20. (Concerning airplane accident.) 3305

Behr, Edward
"Day of Joy and Sadness." Saturday evening post 237, July 11, 1964, p. 36-37. 3306

1965
Schüler, Alfred
"Senator Edward Moore Kennedy: Benjamin mit Erwartungen." Zürich, Weltwoche (33: 1659), 1965, p. 5. ("Senator Edward Moore Kennedy: Benjamin with Expectations.") 3307

Ajemian, Robert
"In Walks Ted as the 89th gets Under Way." Life 58, January 15, 1965, p. 28-35. 3308

"Senators Kennedy." Newsweek 65, January 18, 1965, p. 21. 3309

Shannon, William V.
"How Ted Kennedy Survived his Ordeal." Good housekeeping 160, April 1965, p. 88-89. 3310

"Teddy's Triumph." Newsweek 65, May 24, 1965, p. 27-28. 3311

Sheehan, Edward R.F.
"Massachusetts: Rogues and Reformers in a State on Trial." Saturday evening

post 238, June 5, 1965, p. 25-32. 3312

Roddy, Jon
"Ted Kennedy on his own: Coming up Strong in the Senate." Look 29, July 13, 1965, p. 29-35. 3313

Shannon, William V.
"The Emergence of Senator Kennedy (D., Mass.)." New York times magazine, August 22, 1965, p. 16-17. 3314

1966
"Two Senators Named Kennedy." Newsweek 67, January 17, 1966, p. 17-20. 3315

Otten, Alan L.
"Politics and People: the Kennedy Boom." Wall Street journal 167, April 7, 1966, p. 18. 3316

Healy, Philip F.
"The Education of Ted Kennedy." Sign 45, June 1966, p. 26-30. 3317

Nolan, Martin F.
"Teddie and Eddie Revisited." The reporter 35, September 8, 1966, p. 33-35. 3318

Levin, Murray B.
"Kennedy Campaigning (Book Review by Donald Young)." Saturday review 49, October 8, 1966, p. 100-101. 3319

Otten, Alan L.
"The Other Kennedy: Partly Eclipsed by Bobby, Ted Makes an Impact of his own." Wall Street journal 168, November 3, 1966, p. 18. 3320

Greenfield, Meg
"Senior Senator Kennedy." The reporter 35, December 15, 1966, p. 19-24. 3321

"Senator Edward Kennedy sees Israel." Jerusalem, Israel digest 9, December 16, 1966, p. 4. 3322

1967
"Kennedy Backs NSF." Science news 92, November 18, 1967, p. 489-490. 3323

1968
"Change of View: Report of Corruption in South Vietnam." Time 91, February 2, 1968, p. 26. 3324

Donovan, Robert J.
"Political Attention Focusing on Last Surviving Brother." Los Angeles times, June 8, 1968, p. 1, 13. 3325

Herbers, John
"Edward Kennedy Against '68 Race." New York times, June 11, 1968, p. 1, 34. 3326

"He's not the Same old Ted." Newsweek, June 24, 1968, p. 28-29. 3327

"Will Edward Kennedy now Move Up?" U.S. news & world report, June 24, 1968, p. 40-42. 3328

"Bombing Halt Urged by Kennedy." Milwaukee sentinel, pt. I, August 22, 1968, p. 3. 3329

1969
"The Ascent of Ted Kennedy."
Time (93: 2), January 10,
1969, p. 12-17.   3330

Honan, William H.
"Yesterday Edward Kennedy
Turned 37; is Teddy, as they
say, Ready?" New York times
magazine, February 23, 1969,
p. 25-27.   3331

Rogers, W.
"Ted Kennedy Talks About
the Past, and his Future."
Look 33, March 4, 1969, p.
38-46.   3332

"Teddy on China." Newsweek
73, March 31, 1969, p. 25-
26.   3333

Mohbat, Joseph E.
"Kennedy Muses: is Time
Right?" Milwaukee journal,
June 8, 1969, p. 1, 11.   3334

Photographs

1962
"Better Ed or Ted? With
Photographs by G. Tames."
New York times magazine,
September 9, 1962, p. 32-
33.   3335

1967
"Edward M. Kennedy: Por-
trait." Montreal, Canadian
business 40, August 1967,
p. 46.   3336

Joan (Bennett) Kennedy

Joan (Bennett) Kennedy was born in New York, N.Y., the daughter of Harry W. Bennett, Jr. and Virginia (Stead) Bennett, on September 2, 1936. She received her B.A. degree from Manhattanville College of the Sacred Heart in the spring of 1958, and on November 29, 1958, was married to Edward M. Kennedy. The couple has three children, Kara, Edward M., Jr., and Patrick Joseph.

Joan has been actively involved in her husband's political campaigns for the Senate, both in 1962 and 1964. During the spring of 1964, after Senator Kennedy suffered extensive injuries in a plane accident while on a Democratic campaign tour, Mrs. Kennedy took over the burden of campaign responsibility. Not only did Senator Kennedy win a stunning election victory, but as a result of her efforts in campaign work for her husband (her compelling beauty is no hindrance in appearances she has made before audiences), she has become a celebrity in her own right.

Senator and Mrs. Kennedy make their home in Washington, D.C., but both are active in the civic activities of Greater Boston. Mrs. Kennedy is on the Board of Advisers of Cardinal Cushing College (Brookline, Massachusetts), and is active in the Joseph P. Kennedy, Jr. Memorial Foundation's work in the field of mental retardation. In Washington she is on the Board of Directors of the National Symphony Orchestra. During the 1964 Democratic National Convention, Joan Kennedy served as a delegate.

Articles about
Mrs. Joan (Bennett) Kennedy

1962
Hoffman, Betty H.
 "What it's Like to Marry a Kennedy." Ladies' home journal 79, October 1962, p. 60-62.   3337

1965
Sadler, Christine
 "The Coming of Age of Joan Kennedy." McCall's 92, February 1965, p. 126-127.
    3338

1966
Nolan, Martin F.
 "The Kennedys at Home

Have a Few Problems." New republic 154, June 25, 1966, p. 10-11.   3339

1967
"Home for Ted." Time 90, December 1, 1967, p. 15.
    3340

Articles about The Edward M. Kennedy Family

1963
"New Mrs. Kennedy in Washington." Look 27, February 26, 1963, p. 21-25.   3341

1965
"EMK's." Vogue 146, July 1965, p. 44-51.   3342

1968
Cheshire, Maxine
"The Ted Kennedys Conquer Fear." Ladies' home journal (LXXXV: 9), September 1968, p. 87, 129-132.   3343

Edward M. Kennedy Family Photographs

1967
"Kennedy Children: Photographs." McCall's 94, February 1967, p. 101.   3344

Index

Abbās, Hāfiz 175
Abel, Elie 1186
Abogadie, Benjamin A. 331
Abosch, H. 1069
Ace, Goodman 2257
Adam, R. 1028
Adams, David K. 1023
Adams, James T. 721
Adenauer, Konrad 1245, 1251, 1263
Adler, Bill 237, 245, 249, 289, 696, 722, 2590, 2960
Agronsky, Martin 162
Ahler, J. 1687
Ajemian, Robert 3047, 3308
Akmentinš, Osvalds 2359
Alberse, J. D. 891, 2100
Albinowski, Stanislaw 1221
Alexander, Holmes Moss 2320, 3095
Al-Hút, Husayn 199
Allan, D. A. 2327
Allarey, Monina 1649, 1699
Alonso Pujos, Guillermo 1951
Alsop, Joseph 780, 1318, 3294
Alsop, Stewart 330, 682, 1344, 1362, 1364, 3141, 3297
Altiery, Mason 2465
Améry, Jean 2998
Anderson, Jack 2720
Andrade, V. 1219, 1660
Antoninus, Brother 1748, 2162
Apollonia, L. d' 422, 1689
Aragón, Leopoldo 728
Araneta-Villasor, Milagros 769
Armour, Richard 2274
Armstrong, Richard 3076
Arroyo, Nimia P. 3035

Artus, O. M. 1181
Ascoli, Max 848, 3128
Auden, Wystan H. 2496
Augstein, Rudolf 971
Austin, Larry 2497

Bachman, Ida 1670, 1857
Bagdikian, Ben H. 946
Bailey, S. K. 2079
Bair, Marjorie 2575
Baker, Dean C. 1563
Baldwin, D. 443
Balough, Thomas 319
Banfield, Edward C. 1152
Banta, Thomas J. 1716
Baptista, Antonio Alçada 243
Bar-David, M. 1691
Barabash, Ernest E. 1183
Barbeau, C. 2101
Barbieri, Frane 1616
Barcella, Ernest 841
Barr, John 3009
Barrow, Lionel C. 375
Barwick, Sir Garfield 1610
Bauman, A. 450
Baxandall, Lee 1725
Bayh, Birch 301
Bealle, Morris A. 1542
Beatty, Jerome 95-6
Becheau, F. 1660
Beecher, William 3004
Behr, Edward 3306
Bekessy, Jean (pseud.) 1543
Bell, Coral 1401
Bell, Jane 2610-2, 2614-6
Ben-Gurion, David 2343
Bender, Marylin 2695
Bendiner, Robert 798
Bennett, Harry W., Jr. p. 309

Bennett, Joan see Kennedy, Joan (Bennett)
Bennett, Virginia (Stead) p. 309
Berendt, John 1831
Berezhkov, V. 1765
Berger, Kurt M. 799, 972, 1222, 2002
Bergquist, Laura 78, 2477, 2668, 2721, 2731, 2741, 3239, 3249, 3260
Berks, R. 2220
Bermeosolo, Francisco 189
Bernières, Luc 1536
Berry, Wendell 2275, 2290
Besson, Waldemar 1187, 1671, 2171
Betancourt, Romulo 1354
Bianciardi, Luciano 150
Bickel, Alexander M. 1936, 1942, 2989
Bilainkin, George 850
Bingham, Worth 935
Bird, Robert S. 3254
Birmingham, S. 2691
Birnbaum, K. E. 1279
Birnbaum, Norman 1029
Birrenbach, K. 973, 1403
Bishop, James A. 708
Bissell, Richard P. 2325, 2484
Blackmore, Colette 849
Blake, E. 452
Blewett, J. 1660
Bloch-Michel, Jean 156
Block, Herbert 2466
Bloom, S. 1863
Blough, Roger M. 994
Blumenthal, Ann 567
Blumenthal, Fred 1008
Blumenthal, Joseph 567
Bonjean, Charles M. 1718
Booker, Simeon 823, 1047, 2141, 2995
Borch, Herbert von 1223, 2080
Borje, Consorcio 881
Borkan, L. 3240
Boussard, Léon 974

Bouvier, Jacqueline Lee See Kennedy, Jacqueline Lee (Bouvier)
Bouvier, Janet (Lee) p. 231
Bouvier, John Vernon p. 231
Bowles, Chester 965, 1216
Boyle, A. 1660
Braden, J. 2656
Bradlee, Benjamin 2360
Braestrup, P. 2807
Brand, Sergiu 1771
Brandon, D. 1379
Brandon, H. 1049, 2179, 2416, 3085, 3129, 3142
Brandt, Willy 1171
Bravo, Francisco 1946
Breig, J. 1658, 1698
Breslin, C. 2690
Breslin, J. 2236
Breslow, Paul 1826
Bridge, John F. 403
Brienberg, Mordecai 1702, 1707
Brissaud, André 697
Britton, A. P. 2415
Brock, T. F. 1322
Brodie, Israel 1952
Brogan, Denis W. 800, 941, 2607
Brooks, Stewart M. 1573
Brooks, W. 135
Brophy, L. 2432
Brothers, Joyce 2692
Brown, N. B. 2747
Brubaker, Herb 2961
Buchanan, Thomas 1544, 1683, 1701, 1724
Buchmueller, A. D. 2726
Buckley, William F. 3045, 3296
Budimac, Budimir 1612, 1980
Bugat, Jean M. 1188
Bundy, McGeorge 1517
Bunzel, Peter 2395
Burke, V. 884
Burnham, W. D. 2063
Burns, James MacG. 348, 789, 866, 892, 920, 922, 1224, 2338

Burton, Richard 3226
Butler, Ewan 1543
Byrd, C.W. 2295

Cabral, Nelson Lustoza
 2309
Cadden, V. 139 3250
Cafiero, L.H. 1808
Calderón, Cicero D. 2077
Câmara, José A. 2003
Cameron, E. 2228
Cameron, Gail 2733, 3252
Cameron, J. 1655
Campion D.R. 1308, 1660
Canãs, José María 152
Canavan, F. 1457
Caplan, Gerald 3250
Cárcano, Miguel A. 2382
Cargas, H. 2102
Carleton, William C. 1030
Carleton, William G.
 1052, 2630
Carlos, Newton 1545
Carney, Frederick S. 1665
Carpenter, L. 2417, 2426
Carpozi, George, 2592
Carr, A. 2103
Carr, Waggoner 1558
Carr, William H.A. 81
Carrion, Arturo Morales
 1037
Carroll, Gladys (Hasty)
 2322
Carter, B. 2827
Carter, M.A. 2289
Carter, Richard 121
Carunungan, C.A.
 1641, 2664, 2667
Carvel, Robert 868
Cassini, I. 2645
Castro, Ruz Fidel
 1108, 1141, 1231, 1312,
 1520, 1537
Cater, Douglass
 317, 343, 942, 2412, 2625
 3292

Cavendish, Kathleen (Kennedy)
 p. 25, 247-8
Cavendish, William
 p. 247-8
Chaçon, Jorge 2361
Chamberlain, John 3064
Chamberlain, Neville
 p. 31, 35
Chamberlin, A.
 2268, 2993, 3241
Chapman, Ann 1851
Chapman, Gil 1851
Chase, Harold W.
 292, 576, 2376
Chatelain, Nicolas
 689, 801, 900-1
Chatterji, Pasupati 210
Cheshire, Maxine 3343
Chiarella, M 2304
Chiari, Remón, Roberto F.
 1335
Childs, Marquis 3010
Chïu - sheng, Li 209
Chriss, N.C. 1812
Christopherson, Edmond
 309
Churchhill, Randolph S.
 1791, 1817
Churchill, Winston
 p. 32, 35
 1077, 1453
Cipes, Robert M 3115
Clark, Albert 407
Cleary, William p. 298
Clemens, C. 1078, 2399
Cleveland, Harlan 709, 1507
Clifford, G. 1922
Clifton, C. 1043
Cline, R.A. 1934, 1938
Coe, Richard L. 1037
Coffin, Tristam
 316, 1290, 3017
Cogley, J. 400, 417, 451,
 869, 1003, 2158
Cohen, J 1812, 1935
Collins, Frederic W.
 314, 2411

Collins, R.S. 1807
Comstock, Jim F. 723
Connally, John B.
 1558, 1835-6
Connelly, Dolly 3069
Converse, P.E. 802
Cook, Fred J. 1945
Cooke, Alistair
 335, 337, 405, 834, 939, 952,
 1007, 1619, 1643, 1761,
 1772, 1784, 1858, 3060
Cooke, Jacob, E. 721
Cooke, Terence J. 3214
Coppinger, E. 2293
Cordaro, Philip 2362
Corry, John 2593
Cort, David 85
Cort, J.O 311
Cosco, Guiliano 200
Costelloe, M.J. 581, 678
Cottrell, John 1546
Coughlan, Robert 115
Cousins, Norman 2046
Coxe, L. 2294
Craig, G.M.
 342, 851, 916, 2081
Crawford, Curtis 1889
Cronan, C. 767
Crossman, R.H.S. 933
Crown, James, T. 691
Cruz, J.V 1709
Cuffaro, H.K. 1731
Cunliffe, Marcus 1816
Cunningham, Kenneth 2579
Curtis, Charlotte 2570
Cushing, Richard, J.
 2040, 2104-5
Cushman, W. 93
Cadden, V. 139, 3250
Cabral, Nelson Lustoza
 2309

Daetwyler, Hans W. 1953
Daguio, Amador T. 2051
Dahlberg, Hans 157, 710
Damburg, Russell 2500

Damore, Leo 2326
Daniel, W.G. 975
Dareff, Hail 2585
Dasuquí, Salah al- 1226-7
Datta, Narayan 174
David, Fernando, S 380
David, Paul T. 300
Davis, T. 326, 2229
De Bedts, R.E. 70
De Carvalho, Leônidas G
 230
De Gaulle, Charles
 1036, 1299, 1301, 1464,
 1523
Deighton, Len 1588
Deindorfer, R.G. 634
De Kooning, E 2226
Delgado, F. 842
Delgado, Luis Humberto
 218
Demaris, Ovid 1856
Deming, A. 59
Denegre Vaught, Livingston
 1547
Dennis, N. 1068
Denson, R.B. 1548
Denzin, N.K. 1751
De Toledano, Ralph 2962
Deuerlein, E. 320
Devlin, Polly 2757
Díaz Casanueva, Humberto
 2004
Di bis, Abd al-Jawwad
 Hamzah 1182
Diefenbaker, John G. 1273
Dies, Martin 1703
Dietz, T. 408
Dikshita, Syama Bihari Lala
 2363
Dillon, Douglas 514, 558
Dineen, Joseph F.
 79, 98, 107
Dirix, B. 1819
Di Salle, Michael V. 729
Dobbins, James J. 2467
Dodd, Thomas 2165

Dodson, J. M. 2005
Dollen, Charles
 2313, 2377
Don, Marido 82
Donald, Aida (Di Pace)
 730
Donaldson, Gordon 3105
Donhoff, Marion (Gräfin)
 1409
Donovan, Robert J.
 2330-1, 3325
Doud, Earle 2734
Dougherty, Richard 3187
Douglass-Home, Alec 1984
Douglas, William O.
 p. 263
Driver, Tom F. 1665
Drummond, Roscoe 1270
Druskovic, Drago 2006
Dudar, Helen 2696
Duff, E. 422, 423
Duggan, M. 824
Duhamel, Marvan 1574
Duhéme, Jacqueline
 2479, 2752
Duino, Michel 2334
Duke, Paul 895
Duncan, Eileen 2680
Duncliffe, William J. 24
Dunning, John L. 1705
Dunson, J. 1673
Durant, Alice 1956
Durant, John 1956
Durniak, J. 2751
Dürrenmatt, Peter
 771, 1410-1

Eban, Abba 1986
Echànove, A. 2106
Eckhardt, William 1533
Eckstein, Günther
 803, 2082
Ecroyd, D. H. 958
Edelman, John W 2314
Edmonds, I. G. 131
Edwards, Robert G. 1412

Einstoss, Ron 3188
Eisendrath, Maurice N. 2083
Eisenhower, Dwight p. 37
 1077, 1192, 1286, 1508
Eleazar 884
Eller, J. 1663
Ellis, W. 1923
Elsnau, Mary 1082
Emmett, Christopher 3196
Epstein, Edward J. 1594,
 1752, 1829, 1888, 1900
Epstein, Julius 1413-4
Erhard, Ludwig 2008
Erskine, Hazel (Gaudet) 1045
Erwen, L. 1230, 1415
Estrada, Nina 2052
Evans, Rowland 2391
Fabian, Rainier 1416
Fairlie, H. 125, 2177
Faith, Samuel J. 2460
Falk, Stanley L. 1508
Falls, Cyril 1231, 1417
Farley, James A. p. 31
Fay, Paul B. 2336
Feiffer, J. 3065
Feldman, J. J.
 305, 376, 1685, 1719
Ferraro, Lance 2468
Ferrer, Aleu J. 2841
Fiedler, Jean 2453
Fine, B 991
Fine, William M. 1565
Fink, L. 138
Fiore, Ilario 2308
Fischer, E. 2067
Fischer, G. 140
Fischer, John 328
Fisher, J. 354
Fitzgerald, Agnes p. 24
Fitzgerald, J. F. ("Honey")
 p. 15, 24, 35
Fitzgerald, Rose See
 Kennedy, Rose (Fitzgerald)
Flammonde, Paris 1595
Flanders, Ralph Edward 2321

Flannery, Harry W. 2978
Flavius, Brother 2456
Fleming, T. 453
Flores, A. O. 2053
Flynn, John T. 34
Fogarty, M. P. 876
Folliard, E. T.
 432, 790, 825, 890, 893, 1073, 1324
Forbes, M. S. 889, 2035
Ford, Gerald R. 1565
Fox, Sylvan 1566, 1756-7
Franco, General Francisco p. 30
Frank, Elke 2388
Frankel, Charles 3194
Freeman, Lucy 1568
Friedel, Frank 1072
Friedman, R. 1628
Friedman, Stanley P. 86
Frisbee, Lucy (Post) 2440
Frolick, S. J. 2441
Fromm, J. 1449
Froncek, T. 1814
Frost, Robert 460, 2270
Fuchs, Lawrence H.
 387, 389, 424, 459
Fuller, E. 2420
Fuller, Helen 698
Furst, H. 177

Gadgil, Pandurang Vasudev 171, 213
Galindo Herrero, Santiago 734
Gallagher, R. 2107
Galledārī, Ādollāh
Gandolfo, Giampaolo 2344
Gannon, T. 2267
Gantman, Vladimir I 295
Gantz, David 2495
Gardiner, John W. 206, 212
Gardner, Gerald C.
 204, 242, 2956
Garduno, Joseph A. 2203

Garrison, Jim
 1595, 1794, 1798-1803, 1805, 1824, 1827, 1828, 1839, 1887
Gass, Oscar 863
Gatbonton, Juan T.
 362, 793, 832
Gauger, Hildegard 568
Gavin, James M. 1523
Gebhart, G. 792
Geer, Candy 2277
Gelb, A. 2418
Gelb, B. 2418
Gellner, J. 1721
Gershenson, Alvin H 711
Gingrich, A. 1797
Glass, Andrew J. 3084
Glikes, Erwin A. 2278
Golden, Harry L. 712, 3070
Goldman, Alex J. 246
Goldman, John J. 3204
Goloy, Gloria G. 2054
Gomes, Abeylard Pereira 2279
Gómez Perez, Fernando 731
Goodfriend, J. 2431
Goodhart, A. L. 1775
Goodman, P. 701
Goodwin, Richard N. 1037
Gordon, Gray 2953
Gordon, W. E. 1674, 1694
Gorman, R. 2108
Gosset, P. 1581
Gosset, R. 1581
Goth, T. 466
Götte, Fritz 1675
Graham, J. 1886
Graves, Charles P. 2449
Gray, Charles H. 381
Gray, R. 2109
Greeley, A. 2187
Green, Joseph 873
Greenberg, Bradley S.
 1567, 1676, 1717
Greenfield, Meg 3321

Greer, Herb 1016
Gregg, R.W. 956
Gresham, M. 804, 1233
Gresman, Hans 2999
Griffiths, B. 2299
Griffiths, E. 1284
Grodin, Joseph 1039
Gromyko, Anatoly 737
Gronouski, John A. 1968, 2201-2202
Gropp, Arthur E. 2312
Grossman, Richard L. 162
Grosvenor, M.B. 2153
Grut, Harald 191
Gun, Nerin E. 1549
Guttenberg, Karl T. zu 1418

Habe, Hans p. 41 1543, 1677
Haddad, William F. 2822
Haereid, Olar 181, 225
Haines, A. 923, 2659
Halberstam, David 2972, 3177
Haldar, M.K 236
Hall, Gordon L. 2577
Hall, Sue G. 2856
Halle, L.J. 896, 1456
Hallén, Sren 193, 223
Hallinan, Hazel (Hunkins) 94
Hamblin, D.J. 2042
Hambro, C.J. 197
Hamill, Pete 3219, 3238
Hamilton, Charles 2260
Hammudah, Ahmad 147
Hamzah, Ahmad 229
Hanff, Helene 2450
Hanley, J. 766, 826, 959, 2110
Hannan, Bishop, P.M. 385, 1516
Hannon, P. 2084
Hansen, B.K. 2224
Hanson, Galen A. 732
Harding, H.F. 371
Harding, Robert T. 2591

Hargrove, Erwin C. 733
Harpprecht, Klaus, 2085
Harriman, W. Averell 2181
Harris, Eleanor 756
Harris, Leon A. 2390
Harris, Patricia (Howard) 2469
Harris, Roy 2501
Harris, Seymour E. 699, 713
Hart, James 3036
Hart, L. 1634, 1695
Hartogs, Renatus 1568
Hatano, Yozô 2843, 2849
Hawley, Earl 2578
Haworth, David 2233
Hayoul, M. 2111
Healy, Philip F. 745, 827, 2975, 2980, 3317
Hearst, William Randolph p. 16
Hebblethwaite, Frank P. 2163
Hechler, Kenneth W. 310
Heckscher, P.H. 2248
Hegyi, Károly 1710
Heikal, H. 1505
Heindl, Gottfried 1209
Heller, David 2567, 2576
Heller, Deane 2567, 2576
Heller, Ernst 434
Henderson, Bruce 1970
Hennessey, Louella R. 110
Hennessey, Maurice N. 1189
Hepburn, James (pseud.) 1592
Herbers, John 3016, 3326
Herman, M. 1746
Hermann, Ingo 2402
Hermann, Kai 1678
Herndon, Booton 233
Herre, F. 1419
Herschensohn, Bruce 2529
Hersey, John 2337
Hessler, William H. 325
Heuiju, Bag 178

Higdon, Hal. 3168
Higgins, Marguerite 75, 3244
Hill, Gladwin 3186
Hill, Lister p. 37
Hill, Richard J. 1718
Hills, Roderick M. 1040
Hilsman, Roger 1194, 3179
Hines, G.F. 760
Hirsch, Phil 89
Hirshberg, A. 2176
Hitler, Adolph p. 31
Hla, Theikpan Soe 180
Hochwalt, F. 2112
Hoffman, Betty H 3337
Holland, J. 2307
Hollis, C. 100, 1989
Holmes, A.L. 2591
Holmes, W.A. 1653
Honan, William H. 3331
Hoogterp, D. 2675
Hoopes, Roy 2435
Hopkins, Thomas A. p.263 2852, 2862
Horowitz, Irving L. 3195
Hosono, Gunji 154
Howard, Anthony 1932, 3172, 3130, 3198
Howard, Mortimer 2603
Howe, Irving 1575
Hoyos, Rubén J. de 853
Hoyt, R 417, 428, 430
Hughes, E.J 1789
Hughes, H.S. 2068
Humphrey, Hubert 3066, 3124
Hurd, Danny 2495
Hutchison, Earl R. 885
Hutlinger, J. 767
Hyman, Sidney 949, 1326
Hymoff, Edward 89

Idris, Soewardi 1550
Inglis, Brian 1420, 1463
Ions, Edmund S. 735

Iorysh, Abram I. 1551
Irons, Evelyn 1796
Izakov, Boris 1654, 1773

Jacobs, Paul 2955
Jacobson, Dan 1927
Jakobsson, Bárður 185
James, Rosemary 1582
Jameson, Conrad 2151
Janssen, Karl-Heinz 1753
Jaszúnski, Grzegorz 2387
Jeffries, Jean 3166
Jellicoe, G.A. 2249
Jenkins, John H. 545
Joaquin, Nick 1650, 2609
Joel, K. 1387
Joesten, Joachim 321, 692, 1754, 1843, 1852-3, 1872, 1901, 2339
John, Pope 1457
Johnson, Claudia A. ("Lady Bird") 2867
Johnson, E.A. 2155
Johnson, Gerald W. 355, 396
Johnson, H. 2014
Johnson, Lyndon B. 1056, 1082, 1192, 1477, 1509, 1647, 1670, 1778, 1949, 2015, 2062, 2087, 2135, 2185, 2672, 3042, 3046, 3050, 3066, 3124, 3130, 3133, 3135, 3138, 3147
Johnson, Marion M. 464
Johnson, Percy E. 2280
Johnson, William O 2958
Jones, B. 2296
Jones, Penn 1795, 1902
Jones, Robert 3026
Joost, Wilhelm 1110
Joyce, James 455
Jung-hi, Bag 179
Just, Ward S. 935

Kahler, Otto 2088-9
Kaiser, Horst 1421

Kalb, Bernard 1220, 2701
Kalb, Marvin 1220, 2701
Kane, J. 2652
Kaplan, H. 1035
Kaplan, John 1806, 1844
Karol, K. S. 1235
Karp, Irwin 1840
Kateb, G. 2183
Katz, E. 305, 376
Kaufmann, W. W. 22
Kavanaugh, J. 1722
Kayser-Eichberg, Ulrich 158
Kazan, Molly (Thacher) 2271
Kazin, Alfred 2400, 2413
Kazuo, Kuroda 565
Keenan, J. 2116
Keinz, Virginia P. 2286
Keller, Father James p. 296
Kempe, Sune 2370, 2476
Kempton, Murray
  944-5, 1679, 1820, 1882-3,
  2422, 2654, 2813, 3027,
  3038, 3054, 3055, 3075,
  3099, 3132, 3256
Kendall, Bruce 1961
Kendall, John 3189
Kenedy, Thomas B. 3201
Kennedy, Caroline p. 38
  Items: 2711-2752
Kennedy, Crawford H. 87
Kennedy, Edward Moore
  ("Ted") p. 25, 30, 264,
  299, 301-3
  Items: 3066, 3226, 3262-3336
  Family: 3341-3344
Kennedy, Ethel (Skakel)
  p. 261, 292-4, 296
  3235-3254 (Items)
Kennedy, Eunice
  See
  Shriver, Eunice (Kennedy)
Kennedy, Jacqueline (Bouvier)
  p. 37, 40, 231-2
  Items: 1138, 1353, 1772,
  1783, 2062, 2265, 2282,
  2396, 2406, 2559-2752, 3119
Kennedy, Jean
  See
  Smith, Jean Kennedy
Kennedy, Joan (Bennett)
  p. 301-2, 309-10
  3337-3344 (Items)
Kennedy, John B. 29
Kennedy, John Fitzgerald
  p. 24-5, 33, 35-42, 231-2,
  250, 261-4, 292-3, 296,
  299, 301
  Items: 130, 142-2558,
  2711, 2716-7, 2722, 2725,
  2729, 2731
  Family: 2734-2752
Kennedy, John Fitzgerald, Jr.
  p. 38
  2711-2752 (Items)
Kennedy, Joseph P.
  p. 15-7, 24-5, 30, 35,
  293, 296, 298
  1-73 (Items)
  Family: 79-129 (Items)
Kennedy, Joseph P., Jr.
  p. 16, 24-5, 30-3, 247,
  261, 130-141
Kennedy, Kathleen
  See
  Cavendish, Kathleen
  (Kennedy)
Kennedy, Mary (Hickey) p. 15
Kennedy, Patricia
  See
  Lawford, Patricia (Kennedy)
Kennedy, Patrick J. p. 15
Kennedy, Robert Francis
  p. 25, 39, 261-264, 292-4,
  297, 299, 303
  Items: 251, 1056, 2152,
  2396, 2752, 2839-3254,
  Family: 3242-3254, 3267
Kennedy, Rose (Fitzgerald)
  p. 15, 24-6, 30, 35
  Items: 74-8, 2558
Kennedy, Rose Marie p. 246

Kennedy, W. 2076
Kerby, Phil 3162
Kerr, H. P. 351
Kessel, J. H. 979
Khatoon, Farida 2851
Khrushchev, Nikita S.
  p. 39-40
  1036, 1091, 1110, 1228,
  1230, 1239, 1257, 1300-1,
  1404, 1533
Kihss, Peter 3183
Kiker, Douglas 3102
Kilpatrick, Carroll
  917, 980
Kim, Gyu-jeong 2850
Kimball, Penn 2967
King, Martin Luther 1955
Kirchwey, Freda 52
Kirk, S. A. 2118
Kirwan, M. J. 426
Kittler, Glenn 2383
Klagsbrun, Francine 3180
Klapthor, Margaret Brown
  2584
Kliman, Gilbert W. 1579
Kluckholm, Frank L.
  693, 702
Klutznick, Philip 1503
Knebel, Fletcher
  393, 872, 878, 954, 2323,
  2672, 2806, 3021
Koch, Thilo
  1070, 1426, 1599
Koenig, Louis W. 720
Kofod-Hansen, Inger 570
Kooy, John 182
Kopkind, Andrew
  1758, 1774, 3078, 3083,
  3133
Korfmacher, W. 2018
Korolovszky, Lajos 1680
Korpi, Kirsti 2581
Kotani, Hidejiro 154
Krafft-Delmari, Fr. 1509
Kraft, J.
  966, 2090, 3024, 3028,
  3051

Krag, J. O. 981
Kramarsky, L. 2019
Kraus, Sidney 306
Krippendorff, Ekkehart
  1031
Kristl, Zvonimir 1539
Krock, Arthur 1001
Kruck V. Paturzyn, M. J
  1239
Kuberzig, Kurt 1178
Kuenster, John 762
Kurnoth, Rudolf 1600
Kuroda, Y. 1529
Kusterer, Hermann 1181
Kyle, K.
  409, 772, 807

Lachelier, B. B. G. 322
Lader, Lawrence 63
La Farge, J. 435
Laing, Margaret 2968, 3217
Lambert, Gilles 2632
Lambert, Tom 3190
Lamm, Hans 194, 226
Land, Emory Scott 26
Land, R. 136
Landis, James M. 7, 690
Landscheidt, Theodor 797
Lane, Mark 1903, 1910
Lane, Thomas A. 714
Langer, E 1656
Lansdown, S. 2620
Larson, David L. 1153
LaSalle, Brother 2091
Lasić, Bozo 2285
Laski, Harold J. 54
Lasky, Melvin J. 2069
Lasky, Victor 2340, 2353
Lauzon, A. 828, 1704, 1867
Lavine, Harold 60
Lawford, Patricia (Kennedy)
  p. 259
  2835-2838
Lawford, Peter p. 259
Lawrence, Lincoln (pseud.)
  736

Lawrence, William H. 1402
Lawson, Don 90
Leach, R. 2149
Lee, Bruce 2442-4
Lee, Janet
　See
　Bouvier, Janet (Lee)
Lehde, Norman B. 715
Lê-Hung-Tâm 155
Leighton, Frances (Spatz) 2572
Lemos, Pinheiro de 2855
Lens, Sidney 2829
Leon, Bernardo de 788, 897, 926, 1300
Lerman, Allen H. 292, 576, 2376
Lerner, Daniel 783
Lerner, Max 1601, 1624
Leuchtenberg, William E 822, 1427
Levin, Bernard 1644
Levin, Murray B. 3279, 3319
Levine, Israel E. 2445
Levy, A. 2693
Levy, Clifford V. 2272
Levy, L. 2663
Lewis, Anthony 3020
Lewis, J. 466
Lewis, Richard W. 1908
Lewis, T. 947, 996
Licuanan, Francisco H. 2020
Lieberson, Goddard 2530
Lifton, David 1777
Lincoln, Abraham
　p.39, 42, 232
　1572, 1723
Lincoln, Anne H. 2594
Lincoln, Evelyn 2378, 2389
Lineberry, William 1715
Lippman, Walter 992
Lisagor, Peter 2617
Locsin, Teodoro M. 1991

Lodge, George Cabot 3263
Lodge, Henry Cabot p.36
Leoning, Grover Cleveland 25
Logan, A. 1832, 2186
Lohmar, Ulrich 2021
Lohr, George 1428
Lomax, Louis E. 940, 3011
Lopez Felix, Francisco 1012
Lorredo, Jorge 2055
Love, Ruth (Leeds) 1764
Lowe, J. 83, 2346, 2749
Lowell, Robert 3202
Lowenthal, Richard 1240
Lowi, Theodore J.
　p.263
　2853-4, 2861
Loxton, Howard 1588
Lubke, Heinrich 1032
Luce, C.B. 1077
Ludwig, J. 1742
Lurie, Diana 128
Luyks, B. 1515
Lynd, S. 1664
Lyons, Louis M. 3213

Maas, P. 105, 3043, 3062
McCarrell, Stuart 2281
McCarthy, Eugene 3163, 3170, 3184
McCarthy, Joseph W. 80, 3298
Mc Conaughy, James L. 748
Mc Connell, Burt M. 2568
McConnell, Jane (Thompkins) 2568
McCormack, John W. 1477, 1947
Mcdonald, D 1904-1929
Mac Donald, William W. 3216
Mc Dowell, J. 2144

Mc Elrath, D. 2159
Mc Geachy, J. B. 962
Mc Ghee, George C. 1346
Mc Grory, Mary
  854, 879, 1781, 1948,
  2070, 2223, 2651, 3008,
  3012, 3058, 3255
Mc Kee, W. 2303
Mac Kenzie, M. 1916
Mc Kitterick, T. E. M. 931
Mc Knight, B. S. 2617
Mc Laughlin, M. 1732
Macleod, Iain 1062
Macleod, Jain 71
Mc Mahan, Ian 1034
Mac Millan, Harold
  1110, 1252, 1257, 1372
Mc Mullen, E. W. 2227
Mac Namara, Robert 1056
Mc Naspy, C. J. 1331, 1681
Mc Naught, K.
  860, 1014, 1217, 2121
Mac Neice, Louis 1466
Mc Nutt, James 315
Mc Reynolds, D. 1937
Mahajani, U. 1526
Mailer, Norman 364, 716, 2641
Malcolm, Donald F. 750
Malkus, Alida (Sims) 2595
Mallan, John P. 743
Manchester, William
  114, 1583, 1176, 1178,
  1782, 1783, 1785, 1788-91,
  1793, 1804, 1807-8, 1810,
  1813, 1816, 1818, 2351,
  2531
Mann, Golo 2092
Mann, Roderick 964
Mansfield, Michael J.
  718, 957, 1947, 1957
Marcus, Raymond 1576
Marder, G. J. 1009
Margolis, H. 339, 369
Markmann, Charles L. 2347
Marks, Stanley J. 1584

Marple, Allen 2618
Marten, Paul 2273
Martin, Dean 3150
Martin, Helen (Hill) 97
Martin, John B. 2981
Martin, Kingsley 809
Martin, Patricia (Miles) 2446
Martin, Ralph G. 298
Martire, D. 969
Marvin, Susan 91
Mary Maureen, Sister 2122
Maslog, Crispin 2138
Mateos, Lopez 1139
Mathoit, Andre 810
Mattias, L. L. 1241
Max, Alfred 1036
Mayes, Stanley 1620
Mayhew, Aubrey 2261
Mayo, John B. 1585
Meagher, Sylvia
  1840, 1905, 1909, 1945
Meares, P. 2679
Meister, Knud 2364
Menard, E. 2301
Mencias, Benito 791
Mendesohn, Harold 1706
Menzies, Sir Robert 1610
Metzger, Hermann 568
Meyer, Karl E.
  346, 905-7, 929, 983,
  1051, 1603-4, 1916, 1920
Meyers, Joan (Simpson) 2403
Meyersohn, Maxwell
  244, 293
Michel, Armaud 1593
Michelson, Edward J. 742
Michener, James A. 302
Miers, Earl S. 2451
Mihovilovic, Ive 1618, 1854
Milic, Zivco
  1613, 1617, 1637
Miller, Helen (Hill) 3108
Miller, J. 1429
Mills, Bert 835
Mina, B. 2292

Minde, Otto 146
Minifie, J.M. 2123, 3101
Minnis, J. 1664
Mironescu, Emil 1769
Misiego, M. 2145
Mitchell, Hugh Burnton 2317
Mitchell, Jonathan 40
Mohbat, Joseph E. 3334
Molénes, Charles M. de 703
Moley, Raymond 871
Mollenhoff, Clark R. 3044
Molz, K. 2124
Mönch, Karl 158, 212
Montagu, Ivor 1921
Montgomery, H. 2266
Montgomery, M. 2266
Montgomery, R. 1745, 2719
Moore, T. 3149
Morgan, Edward P. 1290
Morgan, Thomas B. 3278, 3285
Morgenthau, Hans J. 725, 919, 1026, 1125
Morin, Relman 1586
Morison, Samuel E. 137
Morton, Thurston B. 1666
Moscoso Dávila, Isabel 2282, 2580
Mothner, I. 2815, 2833
Muggeridge, Malcolm 1075, 1767, 3221
Muheim, E. 2329
Mühlen, Norbert 908, 1924, 3079
Muirhead, P. P. 2125
Mullen, James J. 377
Murray, Norbert 1552
Murray, P. 1381, 1645
Myers, Hortense 2954

Nakasone, Yasuhiro 205
Naki, (pseud.) 2365

Narbona González, Francisco 2341, 2352
Nardi, S.S. 1696
Nash, C.K. 1213
Nash, George 1920
Nash, Patricia 2530
Nasser, Gamal Abdel 1110, 1126
Nehru, Jawaharial 1110
Nelson, Harry 3191
Nelson, W.H. 1697
Nenadovic, Aleksandar 1981
Neustadt, Richard E 1024, 1046
Nevins, Allan 148, 158, 222, 226
Newfield, Jack 3112 3158
Newman, James R. 1360
Nicholas, William 2964
Nicolas, Pierre 1191
Niebuhr, Reinhold 1290
Nieburg, H.L. 1518
Nielson, Svend A. 388
Nilson, Ulf 2963
Nixon, Richard M. 299, 301, 303, 357-8, 361, 375-9, 382-3, 592 1087, 1212, 1520, 2505, 3167
Nolan, Martin F. 3318, 3339
Novak, Robert D. 344, 870
Nuri, Khajeh 183

O'Brien, Conor C. 1755, 1880
O'Brien, Lawrence F 1060
O'Broin Leon 1486
O'Connor, J. 2126
Odem, J. 1048
O'Donnell, Kenneth p 264
O'Gara, James 459
O'Grady, R. 746
O'Hara, William T. 248, 291, 2433

Oja, Ratna 211
Okun, A. M 724
O'Lessker, Karl 3173
O'Neill, Paul 129, 3003
Opotowsky, Stan 695
Oppen, Beate R. von 811
Oraze, S 2093
Orren, K 1821
Osborne, John 352, 3171
Osthold, Paul 812-3
Osvald, Frank 1914
Oswald, Lee
  1843, 1847-9, 1851, 1853, 1857-8, 1861-2, 1865, 1867, 1871-7, 1882, 1884-7
Oswald, Marguerite 1878
Oswald, Marina 1852
Otten, Alan L
  3039, 3259, 3316, 3320
Ozbilen, Arif H 169

Pace, Eric D 840
Pachter, Heinz 909, 1211
Pachter, Henry M 1155
Pacis, Vincente A
  365-6, 787, 1667
Paetel, Karl O 1432
Page, Joseph A 3284
Paine, J 1347
Painton, F. C 1449
Palmén, Aili 2581
Palmer, N. D 1242
Palmer, Paul 27, 2315
Paranjoti, Violet 1184
Pardo, Jesús 201
Parker, Edwin B 1567
Parmenter, R 2410
Partido, Corazon R 3237
Passent, Daniel 1080
Pastreich, P 2424
Patacsil, Artemio C 2056
Patten, Thomas H 1021
Paul VI, Pope 1478
Paye, Sister Mary P 116

Payet, G 2146
Pearson, Lester B 1454
Pechel, Peter 1033
Peeters, Paul L 814
Peguy, C 2287
Pellerin, J 883
Penty, George P 691
Percy, Charles H 965
Pereira, Arthur P 2366
Perez Herrera, Carlos 2022
Periodika, Stratiotika 159
Person, Juan Domingo 1096
Persson, Per 2348
Pesenforfer, Franz 1433
Peters, William 3286
Peterson, P 1821, 2571
Peyret, H 1243-4
Phelan, J 1823
Phelps, E 2300
Phillips, Cabel 312, 744
Phillips, Gloria de Cherisey 2844
Phillips, John 3299
Pinchot, Ann 2577
Piñero, Jaime 224
Plaut, Ed 298
Pleyer, Wilhelm 1434
Plimpton, George 2653
Podell, Jack J 2579, 2735
Podhoretz, Norman 1037
Pokorny, Dušan 1554
Polier, S 2073
Poling, Daniel A 406
Polisky, Jerome B 382
Polley, Robert L 220
Pollock, James Kerr 28
Popa, Stefan 1864, 1870
Pope, J. M. 3033
Popkin, Richard H 1848
Possony, S. T 1743
Pottecher, Frédéric 1845-6
Potter, Philip 3046
Pouillon, Jean 2094
Powell, James G 378

Powledge, F. 1827
Poznanska, A. 1712
Prado, Dr. Manuel 1294
Price, Don K. 125
Price, Hugh Douglas 720
Prindiville, Kathleen 2582
Proctor, Kenneth M. 88
Puche, Ignacio 1535
Pyeonjibbu, Habdong Munhwasa 239

Quade, Q. 1660
Quinion, Jean C. 2480
Quinlan, S. 1660
Quirk, Lawrence J. 2969

Rabinowich, Eugene I. 705
Radenkovic, G. 774
Radojčić, Miroslav 1615, 1639
Ragan, L. 2167
Rajski, Raymond B. 1587
Rand, Michael 1588
Rao, Mohini 215
Raskin, A.H. 2816
Rathi, Balder S. 2586
Rauschning, H. 911, 2023
Reed, Roy 3222
Reeves, Richard 3123, 3159, 3216
Reich, Ken 3184
Reichley, A.J. 3155
Reidy, John P. 2457
Reifenberg, Jan 706
Reizner, Lou 2509
Remus, Bernhard 323, 2024
Rendulic, Lothar 1510
Renshaw, P. 410
Reyes Monroy, José L. 1966
Reynaud, Laurence 228
Rhea, Mini 2572
Ribera, Antonio 207
Rider, John R. 379
Ridha, Muhd 2587
Riemer, George 444, 446
Riemer, Neal 1057, 1071

Riesel, Victor 2984
Riesman, David 1266, 2078, 3163
Riess, Curt 2588
Rivers, C. 1918
Rivoire, Mario 227
Robbins, J. 1521
Robert, Peter 1682
Roberts, Charles W 1589
Roberts, David 928
Roberts, Edwin A. 874
Roberts, G. 1887
Roberts, Steven V. 1063, 3097
Robinson, Edgar E. 1192
Robson, W.A. 931
Roche, John P. 725, 960, 1050
Rochette, Edward C. 2262
Rockwell, Norman 2297
Roddy, Jon 108, 1522, 1834, 3313
Rogers, Warren 3164, 3215, 3332
Rojas, Robinson 1555
Romulo, Carlos P. 838, 1061
Romulo, Virginia (Llamas) 2671
Roosevelt, Ekanor p. 35 759
Roosevelt, Franklin D. p. 16, 31, 35-6, 42 1967
Roosevelt, Franklin D., Jr. 1967
Roper, James E. 3246
Röpke, Wilhelm 984
Rosen, Gerald R. 3103
Rosenthal, Jean 190
Ross, Douglas 2970
Ross, Thomas B. 1562
Rossant, M.J. 998
Roucek, Joseph S. 374
Rovere, Richard H 313, 784, 845, 1005, 1310, 1386, 1399, 1471, 3134, 3207

Rowan, Carl T. 1079
Rowen, Hobart 717
Rubin, Berthold 2025
Ruby, Jack 1844, 1855-6, 1859-60, 1863-4, 1868-70, 1879, 1881-3
Rudin, E. 2222
Rudin, Stanislav 961
Ruff, G. H. 817
Rulli, G. 852
Rusk, Dean 1056, 1121, 1315, 2247
Ryan, P. 2173

Sacher, M. M. 2210
Sadler, Christine 2713, 3338
Safran, Claire 2579
Sagnér, Alf 234
Sah, Harin 214
Sahl, Mort 2506
Saint-Jean, Claude 1741
Sakanishi, Shiho 163
Salandria, Vincent J. 1930
Salinger, Pierre E. G. p. 264, 1076, 1958, 2384
Saltonstall, John L. 3291
Saltz, E. 1750
Samhaber, Ernst 1438
Sammis, Edward R 2434
Sanchez Sarto, Manuel 830
Sanghvi, Ramesh 2349
Sassa, Altsuyuki 1720
Saunders, Doris E. 2473
Sauvage, Leo 1683, 1724, 1733, 1849, 1861,1865, 1876-7, 1936
Sawai, Sirimongkon 1556
Saxe, S. 2408
Scanlon, J. 122
Schaap, Dick 2965
Schanpper, M. B. 694
Schappacher, Alfred 1260
Schary, Dore 2316
Scheer, Robert 3120, 3197
Schiller, Lawrence 2531
Schlamm, William S. 700
Schlanders, Ian 113, 120, 948, 2128, 2182, 3019

Schlesinger, Arthur M. 299, 726, 1037, 1049, 1075, 1525, 2072, 3172
Schlette, Heinz R. 2402
Schmidt, Sister M. Bernadette 1959
Schnell, Betty 474, 847
Schoeck, H. 985
Schoemann, Ralph 1925
Schoenthal, Klaus 912
Scholl, Klaus 438
Schonberg, H. C. 2405
Schoor, Gene 2439, 2458, 2486
Schram, S. R. 2095
Schreiber, F. R. 1746
Schrenk, M. 680
Schroers, Rolf 2096
Schubert, John 411
Schüler, Alfred 1605, 3283, 3307
Schutzer, Paul 106
Schwaber, Paul 2278
Schwartz, Milton M. 2495
Schwarz, Urs 2354
Schwelien, Joachim 1684
Schwoebel, J. 1156
Scobey, Alfredda 1926
Scorza, Carlo 2986
Seaborg, Glenn T. 2097
Seeberg, Axel 1439
Seib, C. B. 3259
Sekino, Hideo 529
Seltz, H. A. 308
Semidei, Manuela 1195
Semple, Robert B. 3144
Seter, 'Ido 1157
Settel, T. S. 286, 290
Sevareid, Eric 294
Shaffer, S. 761
Shannon, William V. 1002, 1066, 2066, 2367, 2678, 2684, 2966, 3082, 3104, 3148, 3152, 3310, 3314
Shapp, Charles 2454
Shapp, Martha 2454
Shaw, Mark 2711
Shaw, Maud 2712

Shayon, Robert L. 1943
Shazar, Shneour Zalman 2562
Sheatsley, Paul B. 1685, 1719
Sheehan, Edward R. F. 3312
Sheen, F. 2129
Sheerin, J. B. 401, 414, 768, 1268, 2130
Shepard, Tazewell T. 2335
Sher, Daniel 149, 176
Sherman, Roger N. 383
Sherwin, Mark 2347
Shikhare, Damodar Nahar 2368
Shimojima, Muraji 187, 198
Shriver, Eunice (Kennedy) p. 16, 249-51, 296 2753-2757
Shriver, Robert Sargent p. 249-50, 252-53, 296 2758-2834
Sicat, A. C. 475
Sidey, Hugh 61, 2379, 2409
Siegler, Heinrich 2355
Sigel, R. S. 445
Sigless, Thomas 2350
Silesius (pseud.) 775, 1261
Silva Herzog, Jesús 1313
Silva, Reil R. da 192
Silver, Lily (Jay) 2957
Silverman, Al 2474
Sinclair, Andrew 1067
Singh, Ram 236
Sip, Emil 1314
Sirhan, Sirhan B. 3183, 3186, 3188, 3193, 3195, 3200
Skakel, Ann (Brunnack) p. 292
Skakel, Ethel See Kennedy, Ethel (Skakel)
Skakel, George p. 292
Skipworth, J. T. 2174
Skrede, Haŵar 153
Sloane, L. 2490
Smith, Alfred E. p. 38
Smith, Howard K. 2509

Smith, Jean E. 1532, 1534
Smith, Jean (Kennedy) p. 292, 296-9
Smith, M. 995, 1006, 1479, 1800, 2655
Smith, Norman 2670
Smith, R. H. 1786
Smith, Stephen Edward p. 297-9
Smith, Terry 3068
Smith, W. D. 458
Smith, William R. 1578, 1912
Snell, David 1304
Snider, A. J. 1787
Snyder, L. 1875
Solar, Tony 1157
Soloveytckik, G. 119
Sommer, Theo 324, 1140
Sorensen, Theodore C. 1056, 1074, 1158-9, 2162, 2184, 2380, 3211
Sosa-Rodriguez, C. 2061
Sottile, Antoine 987
Sover, Z. 2045
Spaan, J. B. T. 2356
Sparrow, John H. A. 1840, 1873, 1911
Speaight, R. 867
Speel, Charles J. 986
Spellman, Cardinal Francis p. 297
Spence, Brent 2318
Spina, Tony 2475
Spitzer, S. P. 1751, 1737
Spivak, Jonathan 2817
Squirru, Rafael 2288, 2291
Stafford, Jean 1878
Stain, Walter 1441
Stanislaus, Sister 2305
Stark, J. T. 2640
Steamer, Robert J. 1000
Stearn, J. 60
Stebbins, Richard P. 1160, 1179
Steinem, Gloria 2682
Steiner, Paul 2369
Steinitz, Hans 776, 818, 1442, 3301

Steinmetz, Eigel 2370, 2476
Sterling, Claire 427
Stern, James 1041
Stern, R. 1855
Stevenson, Adlai, E. 242, 1130, 1143, 1161, 1960, 2061
Stewart, C. 1749, 2150
Stewart, Charles J. 1961
Stiles, John R. 1565
Stolley, Richard B. 2677
Stolley, Robert B. 2814
Stone, I. F. 1700
Strasser, Rudolf 777
Stravinskii, Igor F. 2498-9
Strousse, Flora 2447
Stuart, Roger W. 707
Studer, Hans K. 2193
Studnitz, H. G. von 112
Sufrin, Mark 132
Sukia, Narasimha Rama 2371
Sullivan, Donald F. 1065
Sulzberger, Cyrus L. 74
Summerlin, Sam 1970
Sundermann, Helmut 1263
Sutherland, J. P. 875
Sweezey, Paul M. 2131
Syer, W. B. 2156
Sypher, Alden 3139
Szasz, Frank V. 251
Szu, Wang Yang 184

Takita, K. 1264
Tames, George 2745, 2751
Tamney, J. 1687
Tanner, Werner 2028
Tanzer, Lester 84
Tebbel, J. 2148
Thant, U. 1180, 2061
Thayer, Mary (Van Rensselaer) 2569
Therese, Sister 2306
Thimmesch, Nick 2958
Thomas, Harford 1762
Thomas, Helen 2610-2, 2614-6, 2676, 2728-9
Thomas, J. 1686

Thomas, P. J. 173
Thompson, Josiah 1590, 1835, 1838, 1945
Thompson, Robert E. 2954
Thomson, George C. 1890
Thonnessen, W. 988
Thornley, Kerry W. 1847
Tingson, Gregorio 882
Tito, Joseph Broz 1110
Tobin, R. L. 1531, 1659
Toch, Joseph 194
Tomalin, Nicholas 1818
Towne, Anthony 1939
Townsend, Dorothy 3185
Townshend, William 997
Travell, Janet (Graeme) 880
Tregaskis, Richard W. 2332, 2436-7
Tretick, Stanley 3215
Trevor-Roper, Hugh 1766, 1928
Truett, Randle (Bond) 2589
Truman, Harry S. 1192, 1508
Tschäppät, R. 2030
Tse-tung, Mao 1036, 1110
Tugwell, Rexford G. 1081
Tuohy, William 2255
Tupa, Stefan 1866
Turnbull, John W. 425
Turner, Russell 754
Turner, William W. 1839
Twain, Mark 2399
Twomey, L. J. 476
Ty, Leon O. 373

Ulloa, Alberto 989
Ushkov, G. 1711
Uyse, Stanley 3080

Valente, Vasco Pulido 243
Van Camp, John 763
Van Der Karr, Richard K. 1571
Van Gelder, Lawrence 1591
Vanier, G. P. 1974
Vanocur, Sandor 1958
Varga, Eugene 943

Vargas MacDonald, Antonio 1137
Veiga, Veiriz M. 1444
Velie, Lester 3002
Venkateswarrao, Potluri 1560
Verrier, A. 1513
Vidal, Gore 126, 3018
Vigil, Manuel 2342
Vile, Maurice J. C. 932
Vilnis, Aija 2283
Vinterhalter, Vilko 2243
Vinton, Iris 2455
Volek, Jindrich 2381
Vorspan, Albert 2098
Vrhovec, J. 1978, 1982
Vuilleumier, John F. 1572

Waas, Johannes B. 2284
Wagman, Frederick H. 2031
Wagner, J. 456
Wakefield, Dan 3285
Waldron, James R. 2324
Walker, G. 2327
Walsh, L. 2683
Walsh, William G. 2373
Walter, Frederica 123
Walter, V. 2430
Waltz, Jon R. 1844
Wardlaw, Jack D. 1582
Warnecke, J. C. 2238
Warner, Dale G. 1561
Warner, R. 794
Warren, E. G. 1635
Warren, Earl 1947
Warren, Sidney 719, 2374
Watanabe, Tsuneo 205
Waters, Bob 2959
Watson, Richard L. 1185
Weaver, Warren 3071, 3087, 3223
Webb, Robert N. 2448, 2805
Weber, Heinz 1181
Wechsler, James A. 1019, 2132, 3072
Weil, Otto 2385
Weil, Ursula 2385
Weintal, Edward 3126

Weisberg, Harold 1898-9, 1907
Wells, W. 1660
Welsh, David 1777
Wendell, F. 2133
Werner, Richard 1445
Werther, Maurice 2386
Wesley, David 1350
West, A. P. 353, 925, 1295
Westin, Alan F. 720
Wetzig, Mina 2486
Whalen, Richard J. 23, 68, 69
Whelan, C. M. 858
Whipple, Chandler 2333
White, Nancy (Bean) 2452
White, Ralph K. 1533
White, Stephen
White, Theodore M. 304, 2157
White, William S. 582, 831, 864, 924
Whitney, David 3180
Whitney, Doris 688
Wicker, Tom 738, 936, 2375, 3258
Wickey, J. 1750
Wieck, Paul R. 3176
Wild, H. 2172
Wilde, R. de 820
Wilkins, Frances 2438
Will, Marion 2579
Willing, Foy 2521
Wills, Gary 1779, 1792, 1804, 1856, 3131
Wilson, Edith (Bolling) Galt 2319
Wilson, G. C. 2427
Winter, A. 3146
Wise, David 1562, 1841, 3174
Witcover, Jules 2973, 3106, 3117
Wiznitzer, L. 1760
Wolfarth, D. L.
Wolfenstein, Martha 1579
Wolff, Perry S. 2574
Wollenberg, Otto 2099
Wood, Playstead 2401

Woodruff, D. 124
Wortman, Eugene 2464
Wright, Esmond 1366
Wszelaki, Jan 1174
Wyden, Peter 761
Wyndham, Francis 1782

Xājenuri, Ebrāhim 186

Yajnik, Amritlal B 172
Yeğinobali, Nihal 188
Yoakum, R. D. 308, 3170
Yôichi, Yokobori 2843
Young, A. A. 2600, 2991
Younger, J. 2559

Zabludowsky, Jacobo 124
Zehrer, Hans 1280
Zeiger, Henry A. 2971
Zimmerman, A. H. 2147
Zumel, Antonio 1997